John J Brown

The American angler's guide

Complete fisher's manual, for the United States

John J Brown

The American angler's guide
Complete fisher's manual, for the United States

ISBN/EAN: 9783337374594

Printed in Europe, USA, Canada, Australia, Japan

Cover: Foto ©Lupo / pixelio.de

More available books at **www.hansebooks.com**

THE
AMERICAN ANGLER'S GUIDE;

OR,

COMPLETE FISHER'S MANUAL,

FOR

THE UNITED STATES:

CONTAINING

THE OPINIONS AND PRACTICES OF EXPERIENCED ANGLERS OF BOTH HEMISPHERES;

WITH THE VARIOUS MODES ADOPTED IN OCEAN, RIVER, LAKE, AND POND FISHING; THE USUAL TACKLE AND BAITS REQUIRED; INSTRUCTIONS IN THE ART OF MAKING ARTIFICIAL FLIES; METHODS OF MAKING FISH-PONDS, TRANSPORTATION OF FISH, ETC., ETC.

FIFTH EDITION,

REVISED AND GREATLY ENLARGED AND IMPROVED, WITH THE ADDITION OF A

THIRD PART,

CONTAINING A MORE PARTICULAR DESCRIPTION OF SOUTHERN AND WESTERN FISHES, AND OTHER MATTER OF INTEREST TO THE ANGLER, TOGETHER WITH A COPIOUS INDEX.

HANDSOMELY ILLUSTRATED

WITH TWENTY-FIVE ENGRAVINGS OF THE PRINCIPAL ANGLE-FISH OF AMERICA, AND EMBELLISHED WITH NUMEROUS ENGRAVINGS ON STEEL, STONE, AND WOOD.

BY

JOHN J. BROWN.

NEW YORK:
D. APPLETON AND COMPANY.
549 AND 551 BROADWAY.
1876.

ENTERED, according to Act of Congress, in the year 1849,
BY JOHN J. BROWN,
In the Clerk's Office of the District Court for the Southern District of New York.

ENTERED, according to Act of Congress, in the year 1876,
BY JOHN J. BROWN,
In the Office of the Librarian of Congress, at Washington.

CENTENNIAL EDITION.

ADVERTISEMENT TO THE FIFTH EDITION.

I TAKE much pleasure in presenting to the fraternity of Anglers, and the people of the United States, a Fifth Edition of this work, greatly enlarged and improved, with the addition of a Third Part, more particularly enumerating and describing many kinds of Western and Southern Fishes, and their location, together with the latest improvements in implements for taking all descriptions of the finny race. The great success attending the sale of the previous editions, and the high encomiums passed upon them by the press and the angling community, not only as a book of information and reference, but also as "the most *complete* and *practical* fisher's manual ever issued," have induced me to keep up its former reputation by making it attractive and valuable to *all* who go a-fishing. Of the many thousands who use the rod-and-line, not one-tenth part of them become scientific and accomplished anglers—mostly for the need of the requisite time to perfect themselves in the "gentle art;" hence, in preparing this edition for the press, it has been considered necessary not only to inform and instruct in regard to game-fishes, but also to describe all the inhabitants of the waters that give pleasure to the angler. Hoping that I have reached that aim, and that this edition as now completed will be a true "Angler's Guide" to those who, for recreation or pleasure, use the implements of the art, I remain a true friend to all who delight in fish or fishing.

THE AUTHOR.

LIST OF
ILLUSTRATIONS AND EMBELLISHMENTS.
Part I.

	PAGE
FRONTISPIECE (STEEL ENGRAVING), TROUTING.	
A FRESH WATER MESS	x
BAITING NEEDLE AND DISGORGER	xii
PRIMITIVE HOOK, USED BY THE NATIVES OF THE SANDWICH ISLANDS	12
BASSE BASKET, WITH GAFF HOOK, ROD, REEL, &C.	19
LIMERICK AND GRISWOLD SPRING SNAP HOOKS. PLATE 1	26
BLACK FISH, VIRGINIA, SPRING SNAP HOOKS, &C. PLATE 2	28
ARTIFICIAL MINNOW	45
BAIT, OR LANDING NET	51
THE SALMON	52
ARTIFICIAL SALMON FLY	63
THE LAKE TROUT	64
THE HOLLOW WOODEN FLOAT	65
THE BROOK TROUT	66
TROUT FISHING IN SULLIVAN COUNTY	74
THE PICKEREL, PIKE, OR JACK	115
TROUT BASKET	130
THE STRIPED BASSE, OR ROCK FISH	159
THE WEAK FISH, OR SQUETEAGUE	170
THE KING FISH, OR BARB	174
SWIVEL SINKER	177
THE BLACK FISH, OR TAUTOG	178
THE DRUM	187
THE BLACK BASSE	189
MULTIPLYING BALANCE HANDLE REEL	194
THE SALT WATER SHEEPSHEAD	195
CLEARING RING	202
THE COD	203
THE FLOUNDER	207
EEL SPEAR	209
THE BLUE FISH	210
CORK FLOAT FOR TROUT AND PERCH ANGLING	213
THE SEA BASSE	214
LANDING HOOKS, OR GAFFS	215
THE PORGEE	216
THE PERCH, CHUB, AND EEL	219
FOLDING NET RING	224

LIST OF
ILLUSTRATIONS AND EMBELLISHMENTS.
Part II.

	PAGE
ENGRAVED TITLE PAGE (ON STONE)	225
THE RED FISH, OR SPOTTED BASSE	235
SPOON BAIT	236
NATURAL SQUID	239
MACKINAW TROUT	240
TROUT CAUGHT	244
O'SHAUGHNESSY TROUT HOOK	246
THE SMELT	247
ARTIFICIAL GREY DRAKE TROUT FLY	249
O'SHAUGHNESSY SALMON HOOK	251
RED HACKLE TROUT FLY	256
BAIT KETTLE	257
KNOTS, LOOPS, &C. (FIVE ILLUSTRATIONS)	259, 260
NATURAL SALT WATER SHRIMP	261
ARTIFICIAL GRASSHOPPER BAIT	263
A WHITE PERCH	269
SCENE ON HARLEM RIVER, N. Y.	271
TROUT COOKED	273
A CANADIAN FISHING SCENE	283
AN EEL IN A FIX	287
ARTIFICIAL TIN SQUID FOR BLUE FISH AND SEA TROLLING	291
THE SPEARING	297
MAJOR JACK THOMAS, OR CHESTERTOWN HOOK	308
BAIT BOX FOR WORMS, GRASSHOPPERS, &C.	310
THE MACKEREL	311
THE LUCKY FISHERMAN'S RETURN	312
A HAND LINE FOR THE FISHING BANKS	314
THE KILL DEVIL	318
ARTIFICIAL FROG BAIT	323
A FAMILY OF ANGLERS	331

CONTENTS TO PART I.

	PAGE
PREFACE	
INTRODUCTION	9
INTRODUCTORY REMARKS ON ANGLING	13
CHAPTER I—On the Materials used in Angling	20
CHAPTER II—On Baits used in Angling	34
CHAPTER III—Observations on the Practice of Angling	46
CHAPTER IV—The Salmon	52
CHAPTER V—Of the Salmon Trout, Lake Trout, or Lake Salmon	64
CHAPTER VI—Of the Trout	66
CHAPTER VII—Of the Pike, Jack, or Muscalinga	115
CHAPTER VIII—Of the Perch	140
Sun-Fish	149
CHAPTER IX—Of the Carp or Tench	151
CHAPTER X—Of the Striped Basse, or Rock-Fish	159
CHAPTER XI—Of the Weak-Fish, Wheat-Fish, or Squeteague	170
CHAPTER XII—Of the King-Fish, or Barb	174
CHAPTER XIII—Of the Black-Fish, or Tautog	178
CHAPTER XIV—Of the Drum	186
CHAPTER XV—Of the Black, or Oswego Basse	189
CHAPTER XVI—Of the Sheepshead	195

CONTENTS.

	PAGE.
Chapter XVII—Of the Cod and Tom-Cod	203
Chapter XVIII—Of the Flounder	207
Chapter XIX—Of the Blue-Fish	210
Chapter XX—Of the Sea-Basse, Porgee, &c.	214
Chapter XXI—Of some of the other Inhabitants of the Waters	217
The Eel	217
The Chub	218
The Bull-Head, Sucker; Bream, Roach, Dace, Bleak, Gudgeon and Herring	219
The White-Fish and Cat-Fish	220
Chapter XXII—Concluding Remarks	221

PREFACE TO PART I.

THE author of the following pages having been situated for a number of years where the necessity of some general information on the subject of the art of Angling was daily seen, at first conceived the idea of publishing an American edition of Walton's Complete Angler; but on a later and more careful perusal of its pages, and that of other writers, it was found that but little, comparatively, real practical knowledge could be given of the large variety of the fishes of our own country; he therefore concluded to publish, in a small form, the opinions and practice of the various English authors, with remarks, thereon, and such information as could be gathered from American books and American sportsmen. Of the former, very few could be obtained: magazines and philosophical works were searched with but little success; the sportsmen were consulted, and much valuable information obtained; still there was a general lack of proper knowledge of the nature and habits of the great body of our northern and western fishes, and it was found a much more difficult matter than was at first imagined; yet the necessity of the case seemed to invite a continuation of the task. With the object in view of a small pocket edition, of 150 pages, the work was commenced and prosecuted under many difficulties; but it was found that the field was vast and almost unlimited; that compared with England, a work to embrace all the varieties of the subject in the United States, would require the labor of many years, and almost countless pages. The work therefore has been restricted to the description of fishes most generally angled for in the United States. The writer has endeavored to give in plain language, and as far as could be ascertained, the modes adopted by the anglers and experienced authors of both hemispheres, leaving the amateur, in many cases, a selection of all, according to his own views, as occasion may require.

To the friends who have assisted him, and to the authors consulted, he considers himself under many obligations for the favors bestowed and the benefits derived. To those into whose hands the work may fall, he submits it as an humble attempt to impart practical information on an interesting subject.

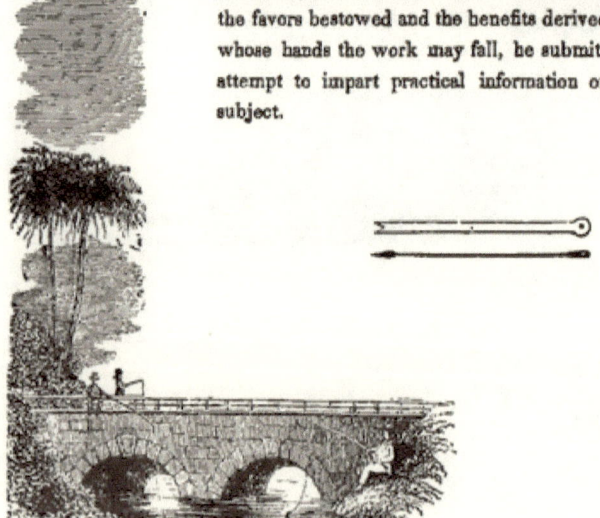

INTRODUCTION.

In every library of any magnitude, there are well written histories of the tenants of the air, from the smallest insect to the "feathered King" that sits on the rocky tops of our majestic hills, and emblems our glory to the world: and of that class, also, which walk the earth, from those that minister to or oppose our comfort and happiness, to the "gigantic unknown," whose ante-deluvian origin appears almost fabulous. Man has analyzed man; and it has been supposed that the intricate machinery of the greatest work of the Maker, was well understood, yet every day seems to give new and convincing proofs that our knowledge is yet but limited.

The sciences of Phrenology, Electricity, Magnetism, and, more latterly, Mesmerism, are daily opening new fields to the learned and curious; and regions which have formerly been considered as explored to their utmost depths, now prove mines of inexhaustible inquiry. Europe has furnished a GOLDSMITH, a BUFFON, a LINNÆUS, and a CUVIER, and our own country has not been backward in scientific researches.

INTRODUCTION.

Mr. AUDUBON, so well known to every American, has explored the air, and opened to the world an enlarged and faithful picture of the feathered songsters of the Western Hemisphere. His History of Quadrupeds, also, promises for him a fame equal to that accorded any who have preceded him in this department.

But amidst all these researches, but little, comparatively speaking, has been done in the Natural History of Fishes. The boundless ocean, with its vast waters, and numberless tributaries, remains unexplored: and the fact, that scientific inquirers of all ages, have neglected to penetrate so far into the philosophy of this branch of Nature's productions as into many other departments of her wonderful and deep-hidden mysteries, is certainly a source both of surprise and regret.

The objects that continually present themselves in our every day relations, naturally invite the attention and awaken an interest for the wonderful creations of Nature. Hence we have a history of Birds, Beasts, Insects; works on Botany, Geology, and Astronomy; but as yet no standard treatise on Ichthyology. The dangers attending navigation, are by the aid of steam power becoming daily less formidable; and where but few could formerly be tempted, thousands now are induced to view the sublimity of Nature on the great deep, and will consequently be led to study the natural history of its inhabitants.

Linnæus has defined nearly 400 species of fishes in the Old World, while our own country, possessing as it does great advantages over any other, cannot boast of a single treatise on a subject so fraught with interest to the admirer of Nature.

The late Dr. Mitchell, of New-York, together with Governor De Witt Clinton, have furnished to the Literary and Philosophical Society of this city, a great amount of valuable scientific information on the natural history of the Fishes of the State of New-York. Dr. Smith, of Massachusetts, has written a very able work on the Fishes of his own State. But of the history of the fishes of our boundless western rivers and lakes, but little is known. The celebrated Buffon has said, "that in America animated nature is weaker, less active, and more circumscribed in the variety of its productions, than in the old world: that there is some combination of elements, and other physical causes, something that opposes its amplification; that there are obstacles to their development, and perhaps to the formation of large germs; and that even those which, from the kindly influences of another climate, have acquired their complete form and expansion, shrink and diminish under a niggardly air and unprolific land"!! How absurd and foolish a remark from a person whom knowledge, and that too of a great general character, should have taught better! One is almost tempted to believe that it is tinged with envy. It is true, that at the time it was uttered, our resources were comparatively small, our institutions weak and enfeebled, and in fact our country itself but little known abroad; yet the reproach, even were the facts as stated, was ill-timed, and not in taste: its falsity is too plain to need comment.

The plan adopted by many of our State Legislatures, of ordering geological surveys, bringing to its aid some of the best talent of the country, is well calculated to advance this science. As our country gradually progresses in wealth and prosperity, let us also advance in the culture of the sciences and arts; and although its age as a nation, will not admit of as great perfection in literary or scientific attainments as those of the old world, let there be no obstacles to the full development of its prolific power; and we may then hope that that day is not far distant, when the Natural History of America shall be as thoroughly explored as that of the mother country, giving valuable and important scientific information to the inquirer after knowledge as well as to the lover of aquatic sports.

INTRODUCTORY REMARKS ON ANGLING.

ANGLING, from the earliest periods of the world, has been considered a source both of amusement and profit. Walton, or old Izak, as he is more familiarly called, in his remarks on the Antiquity of Angling, goes back as far as the days of the sons of Adam, and the Book of Job, in which latter he proves the first mention of fish-hooks. The earliest authentic information, however, *we* have of Angling as an amusement, can be dated as far back as the days of the Romans. Trajan, the Roman Emperor, is mentioned as one who loved Angling, and also, if we may credit history, of eating the result of his days' sport in epicurean style. Plutarch also speaks of Mark Antony and Cleopatra as using angling as a principal recreation! We know little, however, of any perfection in the art, until the year 1486, when a treatise on the subject was published by a lady, celebrated at that time for her beauty and accomplishments, entitled "The Treatyse of Fyssynge with an Angle, by Dame Julyana Berners, Prioress of the Nunnery near St. Albans." The book would at the present day be considered a curiosity, if we may judge from the following quaint extract, in which she shows the superiority of fishing over fowling:

"The Angler atte the leest, hath his holsom walke, and mery at his ease, a swete ayre of the swete sauoure of the mede floures, that makyth him hungry; he hereth the melo-

dyous armony of fowles; he seeth the yonge swannes, heerons, duckes, cotes, and many other fowles, wyth theyr brodes; whyche me semyth better than alle the noyse of houndys, the blastes of hornys, and the scrye of foulis, that hunters, fawkeners, and fowlers can make. And if the angler take fysshe; surely, thenne, is there noo man merier than he is in his spyryte."

Walton also makes mention of a Dr. Nowell, Dean of the Cathedral of St. Paul's, and author of the present Church Catechism, who lived in the reign of Henry the Eighth. He is represented as a good man, a constant practiser of angling, and as employing the tenth part of his time in that sport. In an ancient picture, (which would, by the way, be rather more curious than the book above-mentioned) he is represented as leaning with one hand on a desk, holding a Bible, whilst at his side lie his lines, book, and other tackle, with several kinds of rods; underneath is written "that he died in 1601, at the age of 95 years; that age had neither dimmed his eyes nor weakened his memory; and that Angling and Temperance were the causes of these blessings." Sir Henry Wotton, who lived about the same period says, "'twas an employment for his idle time, which was not then idly spent; for Angling was after tedious study a rest to his mind; a cheerer of his spirits; a diverter of sadness; a calmer of unquiet thoughts; a moderator of passions; a procurer of contentedness."

Joe Davors,* who wrote about the same time, runs prettily off in this style:

"Let me live harmlessly; and near the brink
Of Trent or Avon have a dwelling place;
Where I may see my quill or cork down sink,
With eager bite of perch, or roach, or dace:
And on the world and my Creator think;
Whilst some men strive ill gotten goods t' embrace,

* John Dennys, Esq., author of " Secrets of Angling." A. D. 1613.

And others spend their time in base excess
Of wine, or worse, in war and wantonness.

" Let them that list, these pastimes still pursue,
    And in such pleasing fancies feed their fill;
So I the fields and meadows green may view,
    And daily by fresh rivers walk at will,
Among the daisies and the violets blue,
    Red hyacinth, and yellow daffodil,
Purple narcissus like the morning rays,
Pale gander-grass, and azure culver-keys.

I count it higher pleasure to behold
    The stately compass of the lofty sky,
And in the mist thereof, like burning gold,
    The flaming chariot of the world's great eye;
The watery clouds that in the air up-roll'd,
    With sundry kinds of painted colors fly;
And fair Aurore, lifting up her head,
Still blushing, rise from old Tithonus' bed.

' The hills and mountains raised from the plains,
    The plains extended level with the ground;
The grounds divided into sundry veins,
    The veins enclosed with rivers running round;
The rivers making way through nature's chains
    With headlong course into the sea profound;
The raging sea, beneath the valleys low,
Where lakes, and rills, and rivulets do flow.

" The lofty woods, the forests wide and long,
    Adorn'd with leaves and branches fresh and green,
In whose cold bowers the birds with many a song,
    Do welcome with their choir the Summer's queen
The meadows fair, where Flora's gifts among
    Are intermix'd with verdant grass between;
The silver scaled fish that softly swim
Within the sweet brook's chrystal, watery stream.

" All these, and many more of His creation
    That made the heavens, the Angler oft doth see

> Taking therein no little delectation,
>   To think how strange, how wonderful they be;
> Framing thereof an inward contemplation
>   To set his heart from other fancies free :
> And whilst he looks on these with joyful eye,
>   His mind is wrapt above the starry sky."

If Angling can give birth to such pleasant and wholesome thoughts as these, who will deny that it is an employment both profitable and amusing?

WALTON further says, that " it is the contemplative man's recreation; for it is eminently calculated to still the stormy passions of the breast, and lead to the calm and tranquil pleasures arising from frequent meditation of the beauties of nature." What more powerful argument can the Angler have in justification of this amusement? Volumes could not have said more.

Sir HUMPHREY DAVY remarks: " For my health, I may thank my ancestors, after my God: and I have not squandered what was so bountifully given: and though I do not expect, like our Arch-Patriarch Walton, to number ninety years and upwards, yet I hope as long as I can enjoy a vernal day, the warmth and light of the sunbeams, still to haunt the streams, following the example of our late venerable friend, the President of the Royal Academy,* with whom I have thrown the fly, caught trout, and enjoyed a delightful day of angling and social amusement, by the bright clear streams of the Wandle."

The celebrated Dr. Paley said, in reply to a person anxious about the completion of one of his great philosophical works, that " it would be finished as soon as the fly-fishing season was over;" evidently considering this diversion of equal importance with those mental efforts that have rendered his name almost immortal.

* Benjamin West.

GAY, THOMPSON, JOHN TOBIN, S. T. COLERIDGE, Professor WILSON, Sir WALTER SCOTT, and Sir FRANCIS CHANTRY, were all ardent disciples of Walton; and Admiral Lord NELSON was so passionately fond of the sport, that he fished with his left hand a long time after he had lost his right.

BENJAMIN WEST, who enjoyed many a day's sport with Sir Humphrey Davy, was an American Painter; and to come down to our own day, HY. INMAN, one of the best American Painters living, now on a visit to Europe, divides his time partly in painting the portraits of the nobles of England, and partly in the noble sport of trout and salmon fishing, in the beautiful lakes and rivers of Scotland.

DANIEL WEBSTER finds relief, after a tedious winter's session of Congress, in angling for salmon in the Kennebec, and for trout in the various streams of Massachusetts. It is said, moreover, that this distinguished statesman is quite as much at home in preparing a kettle of chowder, as he is in the halls of legislation at Washington; and MARTIN VAN BUREN is acknowledged to be equally successful in angling for pickerell as in the cultivation of his beautiful farm.

Many other names of distinguished men, who

> Oft have tried with baited hook
> To tempt the tenant of the brook,

could be added to this list, to prove that angling is held in high regard by all classes of people, but it is unnecessary. The observant reader will draw his own conclusions.

When, however, we take into consideration the extent of our country, its many beautiful streams and quiet lakes, where the finny tribe abound, we will find that the number of anglers, when compared with that of England, is astonishingly small. But the fact is, (and a deplorable one it is, too,) that the majority of the American people are so much engaged in "getting rich," that they scarcely ever think of enjoying the

solid pleasures of this life, until, by the fatigues and perplexities of business, they are better fitted for the grave, than for any proper and healthy recreation.

An eminent divine and sound philosopher of this city, in a discourse a short time since, remarking on the habits of the people of this country, said: "that they always seemed to be in a state of perpetual excitement—one continual hurry and bustle; and that it would not be surprising to him to see half of the population of New-York fall down in its streets in epileptic fits; and that chronic diseases, in most cases caused by excessive mental excitement, close application, and want of air and proper exercise, were fearfully on the increase."

WALTON says, "And for you, that have heard many grave and serious men pity anglers, let me tell you sir, there be many men that are by others taken to be serious and grave men, which we contemn and pity. Men that are taken to be grave because nature hath made them of a sour complexion—money-getting men—men that spend all their time *first* in getting, and *next* in anxious care to keep it—men that are condemned to be rich, and then always busy or discontented: for these poor rich men, we anglers pity them perfectly, and stand in no need to borrow their thoughts to think ourselves so happy." No, troth, we should be very sorry to borrow *anything* from persons of this stamp, much less their thoughts, the poorest things probably by far in their possession. Good Isaac, verily *thou* didst know human nature!

It is true, as WALTON has remarked, that many have ridiculed this noble science and pitied its followers; but let those whose extreme and somewhat morbid sensibilities have rendered them blind to the beauties of nature, remember that he "who went about doing good," chose a number of his apostles from among fishermen, and considered *them* worthy objects of his confidence and love.

It seems, in fine, a work of supererogation to attempt to

justify this agreeable pastime, after the expressed opinions of so many learned and distinguished men of every age; and let us ask the reader if there is any recreation at once so harmless, and with which so many happy associations are blended —which combines so many rational inducements to health and true enjoyment, as Angling.

> " Adieu! ye sports of Noise and Toil
> That Crowds in seoseless strife embroil;
> The Jockey's Mirth, the Huntsman's Train,
> Debauch of Health, and waste of Gain,
> More mild Delight my Life employ,
> The ANGLER'S unexpensive Joy.
> Here I can sweeten Fortune's Frowns,
> Nor envy Kings the Bliss of Crowns."
>
> BROOKES ON ANGLING, 1766.

CHAPTER I.
ON THE MATERIALS USED IN ANGLING.

> " My rod and my line, my float and my lead,
>   My hook and my plummet, my whetstone and knife,
>   My basket, my baits, both living and dead,
>   My net, and my meat, for that is my chief,
> Then I must have thread, and hairs green and small,
>   With mine ' Angling Purse '—and so you have all."
> WALTON.

> ' You must have all these, and twice as many more, with which, if you mean to be a fisher, you must store yourself."—IDEM.

IT is necessary, in order to become a successful Angler, to have a complete assortment of tackle ; and as many Anglers pefer making and arranging their own materials, it will not be improper to give here a list of the articles which constitute a well arranged Angler's establishment. Therefore, let the sportsman provide himself with the following articles :

Salmon and Trout Rods for both bait and fly-fishing ; rods for bass and pickerel ; and also for bridge fishing and trolling ; spare tops of different sizes.

Lines of silk, silk and hair, twisted and platted, silk-worm gut, India grass ; and hemp, or flax lines for trolling or sea fishing.

Reels or Winches, small and large, for light or heavy fishing.

Hooks of various patterns, from No. 0 to 12, on silk-worm gut, hair, gimp or wire, snap-hooks for trolling, hooks on hemp lines, &c., loose hooks of all sizes.

Floats of quill, cork, or wood, of various sizes.

Sinkers, plain, swivel and hollow, for sea, middle or bottom fishing, split shot, and swivels for fly-fishing.

Leaders of hair, gut or grass, of various lengths, loose gut for making or repairing leaders or tying on hooks, and gimp or wire for pickerel tackle.

Squids of pearl, ivory, bone, tin or lead, for sea or river trolling, artificial flies, minnows, grasshoppers, frogs, mice, shrimp, &c.

Disgorgers of various sizes, bait needles, clearing rings, bait and landing nets, bait box, and baskets.

A Book containing a full assortment of artificial flies; a box containing a variety of feathers, worsted, silks of all colors, gold thread, shoemakers' wax, &c.; also, a book for general tackle.

A pair of plyers, a pair of scissors, a penknife, hand vice, and a file for sharpening the points and barbs of hooks.

RODS.

There is probably no article of tackle upon which the Angler looks with so much pride and pleasure, as a good Rod; like the fowler's gun, or the jockey's horse—next to his wife, they are always the best. They are made of various kinds of woods, and of various lengths, for the different species of Angling. The best rods were formerly imported from England, and made of hazel or hickory, but they were little adapted to our modes of fishing, and have consequently grown into disuse. American rod makers have introduced great improvements in the article within the last ten years, and can now turn out rods which, for workmanship and beauty of finish, cannot be surpassed. They are made to suit the tastes

of all Anglers, from the single ferruled rod for the novice, at the cost of from $2 to $5, to the more expensive one of the scientific Angler, varying from $5 to $50. Those now in general use are made either from ash, bamboo, Calcutta reed, or lance wood. The three former woods are preferred by good Anglers; the latter wood is objected to on account of its weight, and as it is the main object of the sportsman to have his tackle as light as strength and durability will permit, this description is seldom used. There are three requisites for all good rods, viz. strength, lightness and pliability; and it is absolutely necessary that the wood should be of such a nature as to admit of a uniform flexibility from butt to top.

Rods for salmon are usually from 18 to 20 feet in length, the butt made of well seasoned maple, the second and third joints of ash, and the fourth joint, or top, of lance wood; and if for fly-fishing, the top should be in three pieces, neatly spliced, say in equal proportions of lance wood, bamboo, and whalebone.

For striped, or black bass, and pickerel, a rod from 12 to 15 feet in length is used; the butt of ash, the second and third joints of ash or bamboo, (this latter wood is preferred by many Anglers on account of its lightness and toughness, and if it can be procured, is quite as good as the best ash,) the last joint, or top, of lance wood. The Calcutta reed also makes a very good rod, when it can be had of a regular taper, and free from worm-holes, or other imperfections, and is used mounted with rings, in its natural state, or cut up into joints, and ferruled. Some country Anglers prefer these rods in their rough state, and will send many miles to procure them. Those of the city sportsmen, also, who have their regular fishing grounds, provide an extra rod of this description, which they generally leave at the tavern where they stop. They cost but little, and if kept in a proper manner, will save

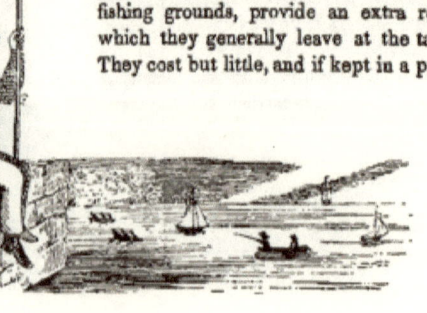

the Angler much trouble; as, in case of accident, his rod is always at the place of destination.

The rods used for Trout are from 12 to 16 feet in length; the butt of maple, the second and third joints of ash or lance wood, and the last joint, or top, of lance wood, for bait; if for fly-fishing, of spliced lance wood, bamboo, and whale-bone. similar to the salmon rod: in fact, a trout rod may be called a small salmon rod, and is very often used for the same purpose.

The general rod is very useful in travelling where the Angler expects a variety of sport. It is composed of various kinds of woods, with a hollow butt, commonly of maple, and is made to contain several spare tops, of different sizes, by which it can be altered to suit any kind of fishing.

The walking-cane rod, if well made, is also a very useful article for travelling, or where the Angler does not wish his business or profession known. Each joint is made to slide into another, and the whole is contained in a hollow butt, similar to the walking-cane. This rod suits very well for trout, perch, or any light fishing, but will not answer for heavy fishing, as it cannot be made sufficiently large to be strong. Heavy rods have been made to slide into metal cases, but they are large, and more inconvenient to carry than the ordinary jointed rod.

The true Angler should if possible have a separate rod for each kind of fishing. All the varieties of rods above mentioned are for sale at the principal tackle stores in the Union, put up in compact form, in linen, woollen, and canvas bags, or neat leather cases.

The Angler will therefore bear in mind, that in choosing a rod of any description, it is necessary to observe that it is perfectly straight, tight in the joints, without shaking, a gradual tapering from butt to end, and that it springs equally in all its parts.

REELS.

Many old-fashioned Anglers think that this is a superfluous article in the equipment of a sportsman; but to any one who has used it, it is almost as indispensable as the rod itself. The main object of the reel is to give the fish a sufficient quantity of line to tire itself, and consequently affords more sport than could be obtained by the rod alone. By means also of this valuable accessory, fish of almost incredible weight, may be captured where the rod would prove utterly useless.

They are generally made of brass or German silver, and are of two kinds, simple and compound, or plain and multiplying. Those used for trout, perch, or any kind of light fishing, are mostly imported from England, and hold from 20 to 50 yards of line. The majority of good Anglers prefer a multiplying reel, because they can wind up much faster, and consequently enjoy more sport in the same length of time; some prefer the plain reel on account of its simplicity, and object to the multiplier on opposite grounds, and also reason that with a heavy fish, the wheels of the multiplier are apt to be clogged by friction, or bent by pressure. This may apply to the cheap imported reels, but not to those of American manufacture, which have almost entirely superseded the foreign; in fact, with the exception of artificial baits, all articles of tackle made in this country are equal, if not superior, to those of England; and if the Angler can procure the American, he should patriotically avoid any thing else.

The reels used in bass or salmon fishing, are manufactured altogether in this country, and are calculated to hold from 50 to 200 yards of line each. They are made of the best hammered brass, or German silver, with balance handles, without stops, and with plain or steel bushings. They run with little friction, and the least possible noise, and when in perfect order are the pride of the scientific Angler.

LINES.

Lines are made of silk, silk and hair, gut, India grass, flax, hemp, and cotton. They vary in size and length—coming from the size of a hair to that of a quarter of an inch, and in some cases even thicker, and being from 12 to 200 yards long.

A line for trout, should be either of silk, silk and hair, India grass, or fine flax; the most common one in use, however, for this fish, is the India grass, which is to be had in lengths of from 12 to 20 yards, and of various sizes. The silk plaitted line has an extensive reputation in England for this species of angling, as also that of twisted silk and hair. They are expensive, but considered by far the best for trout and salmon fishing.

For salmon, lake pickerel, black or striped bass, the lines in general use are made of flax, hemp, grass, silk, or hair, all of which can be obtained in lengths of from 50 to 200 yards.

The cotton and hemp lines (50 to 100 yards long) are used in *trolling* for blue fish, bass, pickerel, or any kind of sea fish.

The size and length of a line should always vary in proportion to the sport anticipated. For instance, you cannot have too light a line in clear trout streams, provided it is strong enough to take your fish; and the same rule may also apply to striped bass, salmon, and other timid fish. On the subject of lines generally, much must be left to the discretion and judgment of the sportsman.

HOOKS.

There is no article of tackle of so much importance to the Angler, and concerning which such a variety of opinion exists, as the *Hook*.

The most common Hook in use in this country is the "*Kirby,*" which the reader will perceive is not included in either of the plates, for the reason, that until a few years since, it has been the only kind in use, and consequently its shape and construction are well known to every sportsman. The sizes and numbers are similar to the "Limerick," so that a person wishing to procure a Kirby Hook, can do so by giving the number of the Limerick pattern. These hooks derive their name from one Kirby, who first made them, according to instructions given him by Prince Rupert, a member of the Royal Society of London. They vary materially in shape, being more or less *kirb'd** or bent; high or low in the point; with long or short shanks, some marked, and others flatted. Those with flatted shanks are used in taking salt water fish *only*—such as black-fish, porgies, eels, flounders, &c., where a hemp line is attached. Those with marked or indented shanks are tied to gut, hair, or other light materials, and are used in all kinds of fresh water fishing. There are many cheap hooks of the Kirby description, imported and sold in this country.† Within a few years, an inferior quality, made in Germany, has been sold at cheap rates and in large quantities to the country trade. Hooks of this latter quality may always be tested (as in fact may any hook) by merely sticking the barb into a pine board and pulling moderately; it will be found as brittle as glass. It may not be improper to state here, that one of the reasons why the Kirby hook has gone into comparative disuse, is because the Limerick, for *fine fishing*, is far superior, and has consequently superseded them; although the former,

* A phrase denoting the peculiarity in all Kirby hooks, derived from the name of the inventor.

† There are many goods imported, and labelled "*manufactured expressly for the American market*," which are absolutely unfit for any market.

PLATE I.

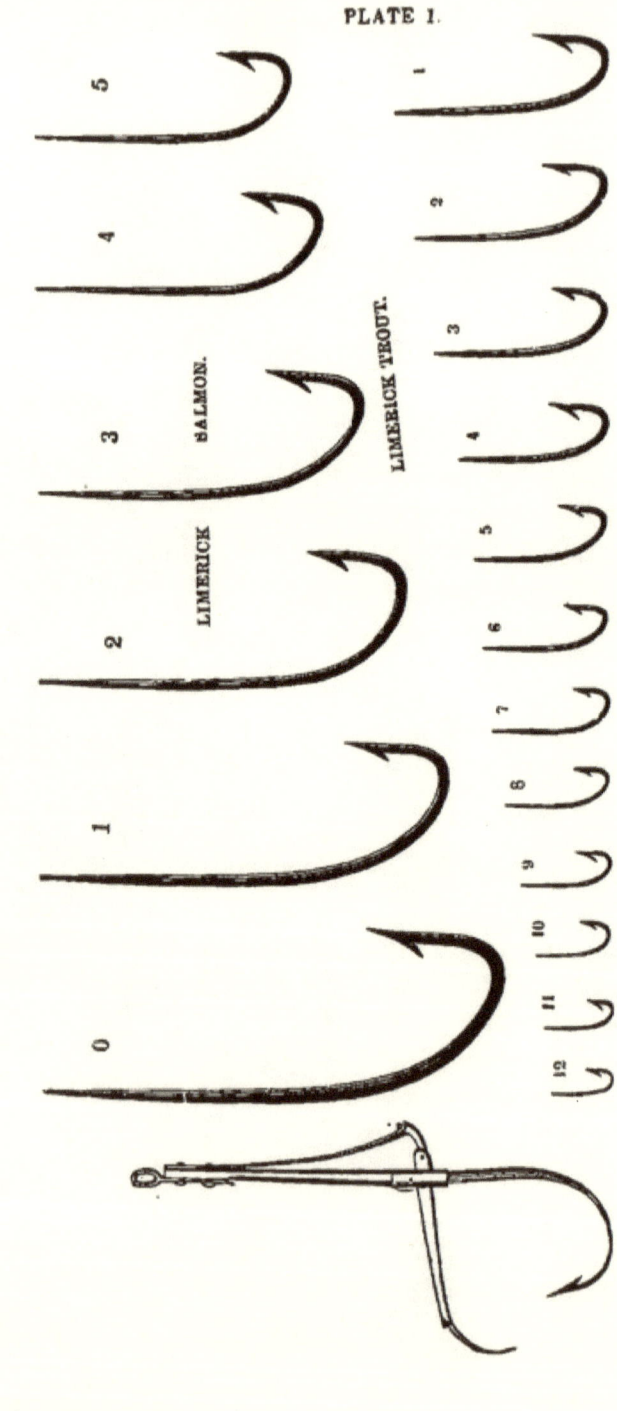

when of fine quality, are still preferred by many scientific Anglers.

Plate No. 1, represents the best pattern of *Limerick* hook now in use. They are, as the reader will perceive, perfectly straight, without the slightest* kirb or bend, the point and barb delicately finished, and the hook neatly japanned black, to prevent corrosion. Its great superiority, over any other hook, consists in its perfect adaptation to artificial fly-fishing; in fact, it is rarely the case that any other hook is used for that purpose. They were originally invented and made by one O'Shaughnessy, of Limerick. Sir HUMPHREY DAVY, in his " *Salmonia,*" says : " I never use any hooks for salmon fishing, except those I am sure have been made by O'Shaughnessy, of Limerick."† He also gives the following method of tempering hooks: " It is requisite that the iron be pure and malleable, such as is procured from old horse-shoe nails, which we believe to be generally made from Swedish iron. This should be cemented with charcoal into good soft steel, and that into wires of different sizes." The original O'Shaughnessy hook thus highly spoken of, is not made of wire like the ordinary hook, but is forged and hammered into shape from the rough steel, which gives an opportunity of varying the form, and of throwing proper strength into those parts of the hook which most require it. This latter advantage, it will be remembered, cannot be attained in the ordinary *wire* hooks. Their general superiority, as Anglers say, consists in their excellence of temper, perfection of the barb, shape of the bend, and position of strength. The price of the

* Some Anglers prefer the Limerick slightly kirb'd, which can be easily done by subjecting them to a moderate heat in the flame of a candle, and bending them with a pair of plyers.

† Professor Rennie objects to Davy's opinion, and says that inferior hooks were made at that time, but good hooks could be had both at London and Birmingham.

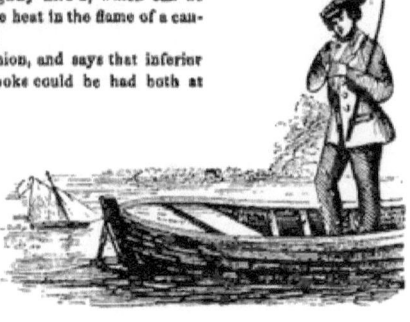

O'Shaughnessy hooks in Limerick, vary from one-and-six-pence to four shillings sterling per dozen, and when the cost of importation is added thereto, it will be found that they are rather expensive. The style and shape of the best Limerick hook described in Plate No. 1, when well made, and properly tempered, however, give satisfaction to the majority of Anglers.

Those marked " *Limerick Trout* " are in general use for trout or perch; and

Those marked " *Limerick Salmon*." for pickerell, bass, weak-fish, salmon, or salmon trout.

The hooks designated in Plate No. 2, as numbers 1 and 2, are the kinds used for black-fish, eels, and flounders. Number 1 represents the *ordinary* round bent black-fish hook, and number 2 the *Virginia* hook. This latter was originally made to suit the fishing south of the Delaware, and is highly esteemed in that region of country, where it finds a large and ready sale. The numbers are the same as those of the Limerick pattern.

No. 3 represents the " *Aberdeen* " pattern, which is made of small blued steel wire, with a perfectly round bend, low point and long shank. It is used by some Anglers for weak-fish, trout, salmon, and salmon trout.

Nos. 4 and 5 are correct drawings of the " *Pickerell Spring Snap Hook*," which the reader will notice consists of three hooks. The small hook, used for the bait, is placed at the top, whilst the two larger ones, made of spring steel, are lower down, and slide in a groove. No. 5 *shows the hook at rest*. The exertions used by the fish, when finding himself caught, will naturally cause him to run, (if it may be so called,) and in so doing he pulls the hooks down, and thus springs them, securing him more safely than could be done with a common hook. No. 4 *presents the hook in a state of action*, and one too, it would appear, rather uncomfortable to

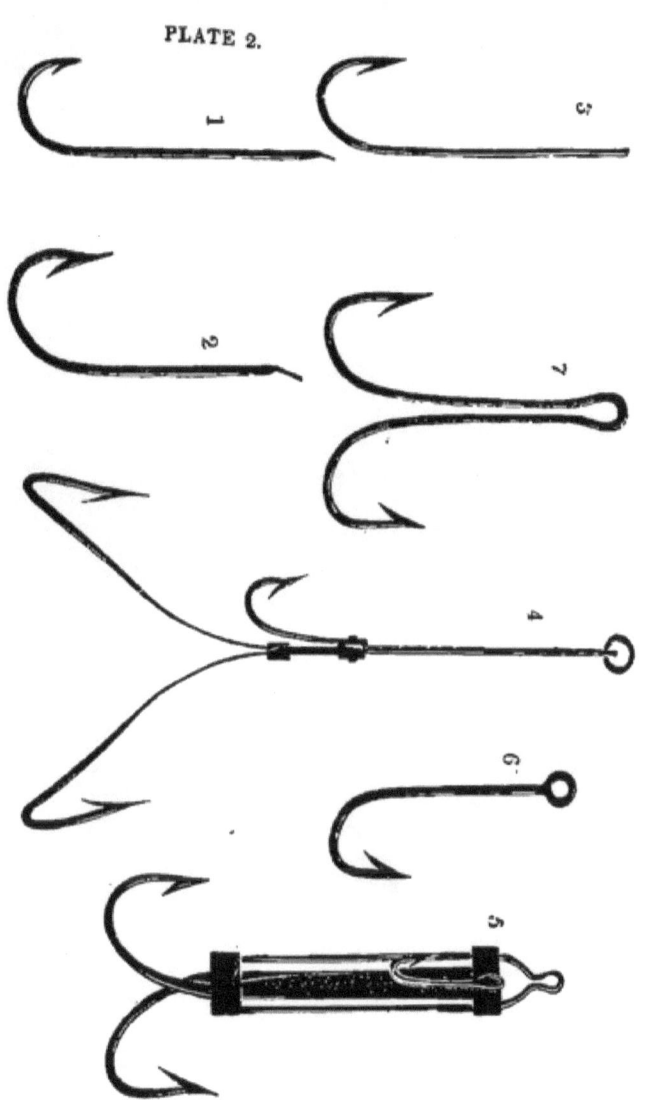

the member of the "finny family." This hook is much used in Europe, and produces good sport.

The *single* pickerell hook is numbered 6, on Plate 2, and is a stout hook, either bent or straight.

The *double* pickerell hook is numbered 7 on the same plate, and is made of a single piece of wire, similar to the last. It has been found necessary, from the great voracity of this fish, to attach twisted brass wire, or gimp, instead of gut or line, to the hook used in angling for them.

The weak trout hook, which is a superior quality of Kirby, made of slim wire, with a long shank, similar to the Aberdeen, will be found an excellent hook for trout, salmon, or bass.

Since the establishment of a manufactory of hooks in this country, the Angler can gratify his own taste in selection, but he must bear in mind that a great portion of his success depends upon the quality of these small articles of his equipment, and he should therefore take particular care to choose those that are well tempered. Let him test every hook before attaching it to his line, and see that the barb and point are perfect and sharp. A small file will be found convenient for this latter purpose.

SINKERS, DIPSIES, OR LEADS, AND SWIVELS, &c

These articles of tackle are believed to be peculiar to this country—no mention of them being made in English works on Angling, split shot and bullets being used in their stead.

There are three kinds in use, the *Plain, Slide,* and *Swivel Sinkers.*

The first of these, the *Plain* Sinker, is made of lead, with brass wire loops at each end, and of various sizes, from a quarter of an ounce in weight, for trout or perch fishing, to that of one or two pounds for sea angling.

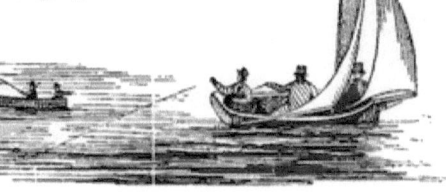

The *Slide* Sinker, is nothing more or less than a thick lead tube, slightly rounded at each end. It is used principally in bottom fishing; the object of the tube being to allow the line to pass through at the least motion of the fish, which is thus immediately felt. It is considered much better than the old plan, where the fish moves the weight of the sinker, before the Angler has notice of his luck.

The *Swivel* Sinker is decidedly the best in use for any kind of fishing, and is made similar to the Plain, with the exception of the swivels at each end, instead of the plain stationary loops. This arrangement gives the double advantage, both of " *spinning* " the bait in trolling, and of preventing the line from twisting, and consequent entanglement of the leaders, hooks, &c.

Split Shot are used almost universally for trout fishing. They should be quite small, and where greater weight is necessary, should be used in larger numbers rather than of large size, as these latter make much noise when the line is thrown, and are apt to frighten the fish.

Swivels are used for " spinning " bait, and for preventing entanglement of the line. They are placed in various parts of the tackle, but usually on the gut-length, or leader, and should be a necessary appendage to the equipment.

Should this chapter prove rather *heavy* for the patience of the reader, it is to be hoped that the buoyancy of the next may enable him to recover his equilibrium.

FLOATS.

Floats are made of quills, cork, and red cedar, of various sizes, adapted to the current of water, or the peculiar description of angling, and are of two shapes, egg and oblong.

The float used for trout is generally made of quills or cork, and cannot be too light for fishing in clear streams:

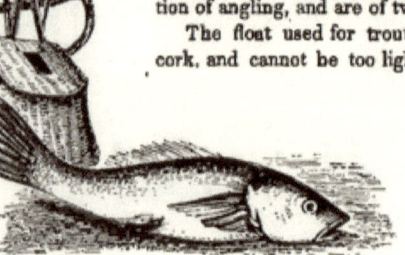

where the current is strong or water muddy, a larger float may be used without inconvenience.

For bass, pickerell, or salmon, there are two kinds of floats employed, the cork, and that made of hollow red cedar, which are made of different sizes, varying from three to eight inches in length, and of neat proportions. Those of red cedar are very light, and much preferred in angling for bass and weak-fish, in the vicinity of New-York.

SILK-WORM GUT, LEADERS, &c.

This extraordinary substance is comparatively little known, except among dealers and scientific anglers. It is manufactured in large quantities in Spain, and sent thence to London, Edinburgh, and the United States.* It is a source of much surprise, and by many viewed as incredible, that this gut is taken from the silk-worm, at the time when it is about to spin. The size of the gut varies according to the capacity of the worm, some strands being as small as a fine hair, while others are as thick as the 1-32 part of an inch. It is a beautiful, semi-transparent substance, and is in strands of from twelve to twenty inches in length, but usually not exceeding fifteen inches. When used by the Angler, it becomes quite soft and pliable, but at the same time extremely strong and durable. It is almost imperceptible in the water, and if of

---

* Inferior qualities of this article are manufactured in China and Italy but the best is imported from Alicant, in Spain. No mention is made of its ever having been successfully manufactured in any other country Mr. Durand, of Jersey-City, opposite New-York, succeeded in making some a few years ago, but the strands were entirely too short to be useful to the Angler. Latterly, however, an enterprising American in the same neighborhood, has had still better success, and produced some almost equal to the Spanish. He is still experimenting, and will no doubt succeed to his entire satisfaction.

good quality, and carefully used, will outlast anything of the kind which can be procured.

It is used singly, twisted, and plaitted for lines, leaders or snells, for hooks. The smallest sizes are used for trout, and the larger, when of superior quality, are highly esteemed and in great demand for salmon or bass.

Leaders are made from the above-mentioned article, twisted horse-hair, and India grass, and should always be as light as possible.

LANDING AND BAIT-NETS, GAFF-HOOKS, AND CLEARING-RINGS.

In the pleasure of anticipation, the enthusiastic fisherman is very apt to forget many little things which are very important items in the success of his day's sport; among these are the articles enumerated above.

The *Landing-Net* in ordinary use is made of linen twine, or fish-line, sixteen inches in diameter, and about two feet in depth, with a mesh of three-eighths of an inch, and is attached to a stout wire ring, of iron or brass. The latter material is better adapted to the purpose, for the reason that it does not corrode the net, whereas with almost every precaution, the former cannot be prevented from acting on the twine. The handle should be made of stout hickory or ash, and not less than five feet in longth. A very convenient form of this net is now made, and which occupies about half the space of the ordinary net. The ring or hoop is composed of three joints or hinges, by which it is folded into a very portable shape. The handle to this contrivance, in order to carry out the principles of its space-economizing inventor, is made of three joints, which slide into each other like a telescope, or, as *Blaine*, in his " Rural Sports," calls it, " *a swallowed-uv handle.*"

The *Bait-Net* is made in a similar manner to the Landing, but of small size, for shrimp, minnows, spearing, or like fish. It should be about twelve inches in diameter by eighteen inches deep, with a quarter inch mesh.

The *Gaff-Hook* is found to be very important in securing large fish after their strength is expended, and where the landing-net cannot be used. The hook is usually about four inches in length, with or without a barb; but as the latter is the more safe hook of the two, it is preferred. The handle should be of hickory or ash, and from five to six feet in length

The *Clearing-Ring* is a useful article to the *Angler in difficulty*, (for he is not wholly infallible, and will occasionally have some trouble,) and as Walton says the fisher should be patient and not swear, his disciples, to prevent any thing of the kind, should avail themselves of this valuable implement The most simple and useful is made of iron, or stout lead, and is in the form of a ring of from four to six ounces in weight, and about three inches in diameter, with a joint or hinge similar to that in the net bow before described. It is attached to a stout line, about twelve or fifteen yards in length, and when needed is opened, placed around the line, and sent down as a messenger. The reader can probably infer from the name, the use to which this ring is applied; it is found very serviceable in removing any obstructions which the Angler may encounter in the enjoyment of his sport. It may be well to observe here that in *many cases* this little apparatus should only be used with the oil of " patience," so highly spoken of by Walton.

This brings us to the last item of the materials of the Angler's equipment, which however necessarily tedious in the minutiæ of explanation, will, we trust, be relieved by other more interesting, or at least amusing, parts of the Angler's instructions

CHAPTER II.

ON BAITS USED IN ANGLING.

THE most common Bait used in this country for ensnaring almost all varieties of the finny tribe that inhabit fresh water, is the common earth-worm, or, as it is called, dew-worm, dug-worm, and the angle-worm; which latter, from its universal use in angling, would be the most proper name. It can generally be obtained by digging a foot or two in the ground, except in sandy soils, which produce clear streams, and where the fly will be found the better bait. Another method, recommended by Blaine, is " to walk cautiously over close cut lawns, or clean fed meadows, with a candle or lantern, during the night. If the weather be moist, and the search be conducted with a very light tread, almost any quantity may be procured; for as they are blind, it is not the light but the motion which disturbs them." When they are not wanted for immediate use, a good plan is, to wet some straw, or hay, and lay it on the ground for a few days, by which means they will be brought to the top, and can be easily gathered. Another, and a more expeditious plan, practised by Walton, and others, is to take the green leaves of the walnut-tree, and squeeze the juice into fresh or salt water, and pour it on the ground, which will make them rise in a very short time.

The common *White Grub-Worm*, is also a very good bait, and will often take trout when all others have failed. They can be procured in the Spring of the year, underneath decayed trees, foliage, stumps, &c., and sometimes in fresh ploughed ground.

The *Grasshopper* is an excellent bait for trout, when in season, and is approved by all Anglers.

The *Minnow*, that beautiful little fish so highly esteemed among all English sportsmen, is found in many of our streams, under a variety of names, and makes a good trout, pickerell, or salmon bait.

The trout or salmon *Spawn*, however, takes the lead as the best trout bait in the world; so much so, that many Anglers in Europe deem it unworthy a sportsman to use it.

Wasps, Beetles, Flies, Caterpillars, Locusts,* and many other insects, also make very good trout baits.

The *Frog*, used whole or in parts, is one of the best baits for pickerell. The hind legs, when skinned, which operation leaves them perfectly white, is preferred.

The *Shiner* or *Mullet*, the *Gold-Fish*, and in fact any small fish, is acceptable to this all-devouring subject of the Angler's toil.

For salt water angling, the *Shrimp*, like the worm in fresh water, takes its place as the best bait, and is a great favorite with all anglers for striped bass or weak-fish.

The *Shedder-Crab*, when it can be procured, is a dainty morsel and a most killing bait for striped bass—many of the largest fish being taken with it.

The *Soft-Shell Clam*, when cut up into small pieces, makes a very good bait for black-fish, flounders, or any kind of sea fish.

These are the only kinds of baits in general use; many others are occasionally used, but are not worthy of special

---

* In the summer of 1843, Locusts were used as a bait for weak-fish, in the Hudson river, opposite Hoboken, with great success.

notice. The Angler, to insure success, should always take a variety of baits: as the fish, like the fisher, in his tastes is often hard to please.

In addition to the abovementioned baits, the following, taken from "Hofland's Angler's Manual," and used with much success in England, may be found useful to the Angler.

The *Marsh-Worm*, is smaller than the dew-worm, and of a paler color, with a broad flat tail. It is an excellent bait for trout, when well scoured, and two of them may be used on a hook.

The *Brandling*, is streaked from head to tail in round ringlets, alternately red and yellow, and is found in old dung-hills, but chiefly where various kinds of dung are mixed together, and in decayed tanners' bark. It is considered a fine bait for trout, perch, or eels.

The *Little Gilt-Tail*, or *Tag-Worm*, is of a pale yellow towards the tail, and knotted like the dung-hill red-worm, and found in old horse-dung.

The *Red-Worm*. This worm is small, and of a bright red. It is found in old manure heaps, in decayed tanners' bark, and on the borders of old drains, and is highly spoken of for almost every kind of fresh water fish.

The *Peacock-Red*, or *Black-Headed Red-Worm*, is found under cow or horse-dung, three parts dried in the fields, but chiefly under cow-dung. He is also found under stones in the beds of rivers, and is a good trout worm.

The *Gentle*, or *Maggot*, is a universal bait, and will take any kind of fresh water fish, save salmon and pike. It is a very killing bait for trout.

The *Cadis*, or *Cad-Bait*, and *Straw-Worm*, are found in the shallow, sandy parts of rivers, small brooks, and even ditches. The first is a yellowish grub, with a reddish head, and is covered with a case or husk of straw, bark, bits of

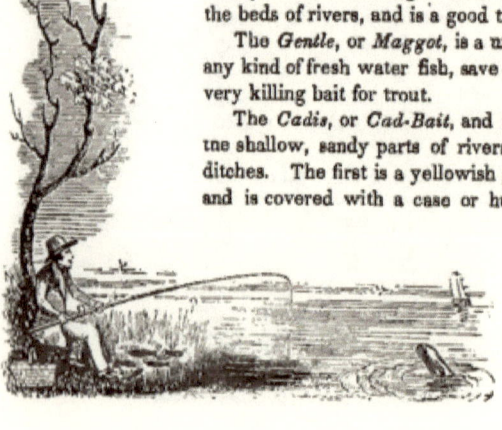

rushes, particles of gravel, &c., and with this covering to shelter it, is enabled, by protruding its head, to creep on the bottom of the stream where it is found. There is another similar kind, of several varieties, called the straw-worm, which produce different sorts of flies. They are all excellent bait for trout.

The *Cow-Dung, Bob, or Clap-Bait*, is found in the fields, and old pastures, under cow-dung, from April to September. It is something larger than the gentle, has a reddish head, and is a capital bait for trout. They may be preserved in a tin box, with a little of the earth from which they were taken

The *Dock Grub*, is a large white grub, a reddish head, and is found in the root of the common water-dock from April to June. A killing bait for trout, by dropping into a gentle stream, or a still deep hole.

The *Oak Grub* is a small green caterpillar, and may be procured in the months of June, July, and August, by shaking the branches of an oak tree over a sheet or table-cloth. They should be preserved in a large tin box, with a few of the oak leaves in it. A most successful bait for trout.

Bobs. These are found by following the plough in Spring and Autumn; they are twice the size of a gentle, and have red heads—are good bait for trout.

The *Ash Grub*, is found under the oak, ash, and beach. when filled, and when they have lain a long time on the ground; also in the hollow of those trees when rotten. They are very tender, require careful handling, and are excellent for trout.

The majority of these baits without doubt can be found in similar locations in this country; perhaps not in the same months as in England, but in as great perfection and numbers, and possibly as tempting baits for fish of the same description.

How to scour and preserve worms.—The practice of

scouring and preserving worms, is little practised in this country among Anglers' generally; but as the method is very simple, it should be followed by all sportsmen, on account of the increased activity, brightness, and toughness it gives to this favorite bait. A variety of modes are recommended by different writers. The best method is to take a quantity of moss, which can readily be procured in any part of the country, wash it well, and squeeze it till nearly dry, after which place it in an earthern pot together with your worms. A few days will be sufficient to make them thoroughly scoured, and fit for use. They can be preserved in the same manner for a number of weeks, by changing and washing the moss every three or four days. Should any of them be found sickly or dead, they should be immediately removed, or they will eventually destroy the others.

The mode of baiting hooks with worms.—" To bait with single worm, enter the point of the hook a little below the head, threading it carefully, without breaking or bruising it, to within a quarter of an inch of the tail; the shank of the hook must be well covered with the worm."

" To bait with two worms on a hook, enter your hook at the head of the first worm, and bring it out at the middle, and then draw it over the arming* of your hook on the line, then enter the hook at the middle of the second worm, and bring it up to within one quarter of an inch of the head; draw down the first worm till it meet the second, and your bait will then travel freely on the bottom."

Another mode of baiting with a single worm, is to enter the point of the hook at the head, and bring it carefully down to within a quarter of an inch of the tail; and if the worm be

* The place where the hook is tied or whipped on

very large, part of it may be drawn above the arming of the hook on to the line.—*Hofland.*

"*To bait with a brandling.* The point of your hook is to be put in at the very tag of his tail, and run up his body quite over all the arming, and still stripped on an inch at least upon the gut, the head and remaining part hanging downward.

"*The Grubs are to be baited thus:* It will be necessary to wrap on a piece of stiff hair or gut, with your arming, leaving it standing out about a straw's breadth at the end of your hook. The hook is to be put in under the head or chaps of the bait, and guided down the middle of the belly, without suffering it to peep out of the way, (for then the ash-grub, especially, will issue out water and milk till nothing but the skin shall remain, and the bend of the hook shall appear black through it,) till the point of your hook come so low that the head of your bait may rest, and stick upon the hair or gut that stand out to hold it, by which means it can neither slip of it self, neither will the force of the stream, nor quick pulling out upon any mistake, strip it off.

"The *Cadis* may be put on to the hook two or three together, and is sometimes (to very great effect) joined to a worm, and sometimes to an artificial fly, to cover the point of the hook, but is always to be angled with, (when by itself especially,) with the finest tackle, and is the most holding bait for trout."—*Cotton.*

OF PASTES FOR BAIT.

Pastes are considered of much importance in England, in taking carp, chub, dace, perch, and trout. Some of them have been tried with success in many of our own brooks and ponds. The following will tax the Angler's ingenuity, and a trial in many cases more than compensate him for his trouble.

Salmon Roe. Barker, author of a work on angling, was the first to discover this most tempting bait. In a letter to a "noble lord," he says: "I have an experience of late which you may angle with, and take great store of this kind of fish. First, it is the best bait that I have seen in all my time; and will take great store. and not fail, if they be there. Secondly, it is a special bait for dace, or dare, good for chub, or bottlin, or grayling. The bait is the roe of a salmon or trout;" if it be a large trout, that the spawns be any thing great, you must angle for the trout with this as you angle with the brandling, taking a pair of scissors, and cut as much as a large hazel nut, and bait your hook, so fall to your sport; there is no doubt of pleasure. If I had known it but twenty years ago, I would have gained a huudred pounds only with that bait. I am bound in duty to divulge it to your honor, and not carry it to my grave with me. I do desire that men of quality should have it that delight in that pleasure. The greedy Angler will murmur at me, but for that I care not."

Blaine gives the following most approved method of preserving this spawn.

"A pound of spawn is immersed in water, as hot as the hands can bear it, and is then picked from membranous films, &c. It is now to be rinsed with cold water, and hung up to drain for 24 hours; after which, put to it two ounces of rock or bay salt, and a quarter of an ounce of salt-petre, and again hang it up for 24 hours more. Now spread it on a dish, and gently dry it before the fire or in the sun, and when it becomes stiff, pot it down. We should, however, recommend that the potting be not in one mass, but that it be divided in small pots, pouring over each some melted suet, by which method a part can be opened when wanted, instead of dis

---

* A late writer in the " Spirit of the Times," says he has used the bait for trout, in the vicinity of the White Mountains, New-Hampshire, and found it a most killing bait.

turbing the general store. It forms an additional security to cover each over with a moistened skin or bladder. To bait, first put on the hook (which should be sized according to the fish intended to be tried for) a mass which shall fill up the hollow of the bend and hide the steel. On the point, put two or more firm large grains, both to conceal the snare and tempt the fish."

Shrimp Paste is used by some Anglers for perch, and is prepared and used in a similar manner to the salmon roe paste.

Cheese Paste is a favorite with some Anglers. It is made of either old or new cheese, grated, and worked into a paste with a little butter and saffron, and also with stale bread if the cheese be new, and new bread if the cheese be stale.

Sweet Paste, is made by mixing a proportion of bread and honey together, until they become thoroughly incorporated, and of sufficient tenacity to remain well on the hook. When honey cannot be procured, white sugar, made into a syrup, or molasses, will be found equally good.

Bread Paste. The following simple method is recommended by Hofland. Take the inside of a French roll, or a piece of fine white bread, nearly new, soak it a few seconds in water, then squeeze from it with *very clean hands*, knead it, and work it patiently till it becomes a perfect, smooth, and compact paste.

Pastes are sometimes colored, to give them the appearance of fish spawn. For this purpose, to give a yellow color, use saffron or turmeric, and for a reddish, vermillion or red lead.

Wheat, Rye, Barley, and other grains, and *Malt*, are also used for taking small fish of various kinds, in still water. They should be soaked in water, or boiled in milk, until soft. The Angler will find them useful in taking minnows, shiners, spearing, and other small fry for bait.

Graves or *Tallow-Chandlers' Scratchings.* The lates

English writers on angling highly approve of this bait for barbel, roach, dace, chub, and eels. As it can be easily procured, and may prove a good bait for some varieties of our own fish, we conclude our Chapter on Baits, by giving Blaine and Hofland's manner of preparing it. Blaine says: "To prepare them, break a sufficient quantity, over which first pour some cold water, and let it stand by all night: in the next morning, pour off the cold, and in lieu of it pour some warm, but not very hot water; after this has stood an hour or two, the parts of the greaves will separate, from which choose as baits the largest, whitest, and most connected pieces, which cover with leaves, or wrap in a moist cloth for use. When fishing, hang one, two, or three of the whitest pieces on the hook, concealing the point." Hofland says: "They must be chopped into small pieces, placed in an earthen pan, and boiling water poured on them till covered, when in one hour, the slimy particles will have softened and separated, and become fit for use: when mixed with clay and bran, they form an excellent ground bait. Graves should be newly scalded for every day's fishing, for if stale, they do more harm than good."

The following beautiful lines by Cotton, the celebrated Angler, and friend of Walton, may serve to remind their disciples of many requisites for success, which put in plain prose might possibly be forgotten.

> Away to the brook,
> All your tackle out-look,
> Here's a day that is worth a year's wishing,
> See that all things be right,
> For 'twould be a spite
> To want tools when a man goes a-fishing.

Your rod with tops two,
For the same will not do,
If your manner of angling you vary;
And full well may you think,
If you troll with a pink,
One too weak may be apt to miscarry.

Then basket, neat made
By a master in's trade,
In a belt at your shoulders must dangle;
For none e'er was so vain
To wear this to disdain
Who a true brother was of the angle.

Next pouch must not fail,
Stuff'd as full as a mail,
With wax, crewels, silks, hairs, furs, and feathers,
To make several flies,
For the several skies,
That shall kill in despite of all weathers.

The boxes and books
For your lines and your hooks;
And, though not for strict need notwithstanding,
Your scissors and hone
To adjust your points on,
With a net to be sure of your landing.

All these being on,
'Tis high time we were gone,
Down and upward, that all may have pleasure,
Till, here meeting at night,
We shall have the delight
To discourse of our fortunes at leisure.

The day 's not too bright,
And the wind hits us right
And all nature does seem to invite us;
We have all things at will
For to second our skill,
As they all did conspire to delight us.

IMPROVEMENTS IN ANGLING INSTRUMENTS.

MANY improvements have of late years been made in the materials used in angling, both in this country and in Europe.

RODS.

This important article of the angler's pleasure is made adapted to every variety of sport, and indepeudently by itself, although the general rod, for salt and fresh water bassefishing, is still used and found serviceable. The best and lightest trout-rods are made either of split bamboo or greenheart, and do not weigh over 9 or 10 ounces, while many scientific anglers prefer a 7-ounce rod, "a graceful wand," that can be bent from tip to butt, and with which a cast can be made of from 60 to 90 feet. Salmon-rods are made equally as fine and pliable in proportion, of the same materials. These rods are made with metal ferrules or splices, many sportsmen preferring the latter style. Heavy trolling-rods will be found at all the outfitting establishments, especially adapted to trolling or casting in the surf.

REELS.

Click-reels, for trout and salmon fishing, are made to suit the taste of those who tread the banks of the stream or roam o'er rocks and rushing river. Fine bronzed reels are imported from London and find sale, and checks or drags in reels for heavy work are adopted as important. Reels of hard rubber, instead of brass or German silver, find favor with some, and others consider a style composed of metal and rubber as much superior. A little experience will enable the beginner to select with care and judgment from an honorable dealer, and "they are all honorable, because they are all faithful anglers."

ARTIFICIAL BAITS

Are made to imitate Nature so closely, that it is sometimes difficult to distinguish between the imitation and the natural. The trolling minnow is made of plated metal and silver, so as to imitate the original, and can be used, as are the spoon and other trolling devices, with scarlet feathers or worsted; and, with every variety of flies, can be had of quality to please the most fastidious fish or fisher.

The ponderating or adjustable sinker, made in several parts to screw together, is an improvement, angler to change the weight of his lead without detaching it from his line, is an improvement worthy of notice.

HOOKS.

These little indispensable articles of the angler's outfit have been introduced by the manufacturers of this country and Europe in a variety of new styles. A form called the Sproat-bend, imported from England, finds much favor with some; while the Kinsey or Pennsylvania hook is preferred by others. They are both excellent in shape, and approach nearly in form and style the original O'Shaughnessy hook, which if drawn out with the hammer and properly tempered, as described on page 27, may be considered the *ne plus ultra*. For fine fishing, for salmon or trout, the expense of this little article of equipment should be a secondary consideration —the best is the cheapest; the form, such as fancy or experience may dictate.

CHAPTER III.

OBSERVATIONS ON THE PRACTICE OF ANGLING.

> "For Angling may be said to be like the Mathematics, that it can never be fully learned; at least not so fully but that there will be still more experimenting left for the trial of other men." WALTON.

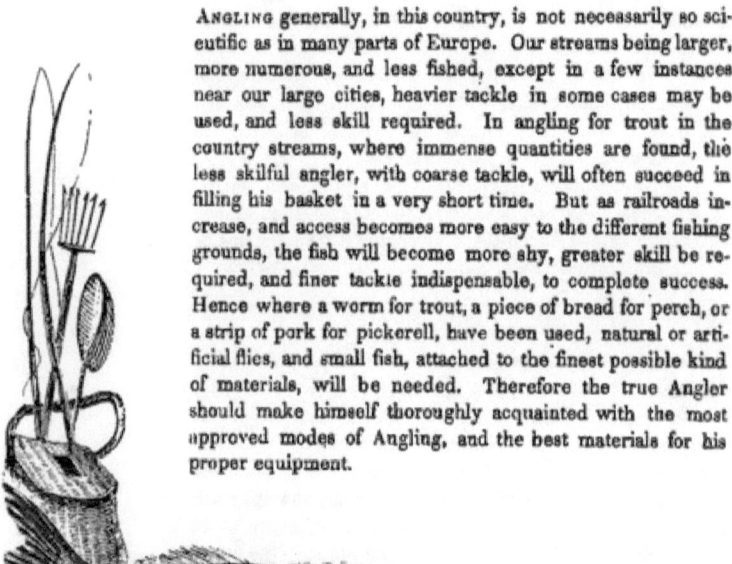

ANGLING generally, in this country, is not necessarily so scientific as in many parts of Europe. Our streams being larger, more numerous, and less fished, except in a few instances near our large cities, heavier tackle in some cases may be used, and less skill required. In angling for trout in the country streams, where immense quantities are found, the less skilful angler, with coarse tackle, will often succeed in filling his basket in a very short time. But as railroads increase, and access becomes more easy to the different fishing grounds, the fish will become more shy, greater skill be required, and finer tackle indispensable, to complete success. Hence where a worm for trout, a piece of bread for perch, or a strip of pork for pickerell, have been used, natural or artificial flies, and small fish, attached to the finest possible kind of materials, will be needed. Therefore the true Angler should make himself thoroughly acquainted with the most approved modes of Angling, and the best materials for his proper equipment.

ON THE PRACTICE OF ANGLING. 47

The *Artificial Fly*, so much used in England, finds but little favor in this country, not because it is not as good a bait, but because more skill is required in using it; consequently many of our Anglers only fish in the spring months, when the water is thick and turbid, and the worm can be used, while the more experienced sportsman from foreign parts,* will astonish the native by his dexterity in throwing the fly and killing an almost incredible number of fish, where the unbeliever regarded the fly as a useless article of tackle. There are some that attain to greater proficiency in fly-fishing than others, as is the case with almost any kind of sport. But the skill necessary to success in this branch of our subject, is not so great as the novice imagines: certainly it is the more genteel, as well as the most pleasant mode, as those who have successfully tried it can testify. It is therefore to be hoped it will be more generally adopted by

> All who seek the lake or brook,
> With rod and line, and float and hook.

Great improvements have been made within a few years in the manufacture of artificial baits. Every variety of fish and insect has been most successfully imitated, defying *almost* the scrutiny of the Angler, and *certainly* the object of his sport. These improvements every brother of the angle should adopt, and thereby remove the objections of the few who oppose the art on Bacon and Byronic grounds.†

As the enjoyment of angling naturally makes the sportsman a keen observer, he should pay particular attention to the winds, those

---

* Parties are often made up in England for fishing in the Canadas and the United States.

† Byron and Bacon both objected to angling on account of the necessity which then existed of using various live animals on the hook as baits

> "Unseen currents of the air,"

as Bryant has it. Walton says: "You are to take notice, that of the winds, the south wind is said to be the best. One observes, that

> ———When the wind is in the south,
> It blows the bait in the fish's mouth.'

Next to that, the west wind is believed to be the best; and having told you that the east wind is the worst, I need not tell which wind is the worst in the third degree: and yet (as Solomon observes) 'that he that considers the wind shall never sow,' so he that busies his head too much about them, if the weather be not made extreme cold by an east wind, shall be a little superstitious; for as it is observed by some that there is no good horse of a bad color, so I have observed that if it be a cloudy day, and not extreme cold, let the wind set in what quarter it will, and do its worst, I heed it not, and yet take this for a rule, that I would willingly fish standing on the lee shore; and you are to take notice that the fish lies or swims nearer the bottom, and in deeper water than in summer; and also nearer the bottom in a cold day, and then gets nearest the lee side of the water.

Sir Humphrey Davy says: "For fly-fishing,

> A day with not too bright a beam,
> A warm but not a scorching sun.

Also, "never fish with your back to the sun, as your shadow is thrown on the water, and the fish are frightened at your movements." These are important instructions to the Angler, and the high source from whence they come should be considered by him as law. It would be well to notice here, also, that after protracted rains or severe storms, the Angler should fish at the bottom if he expect sport, and that it is useless to angle after a long drought in summer, or in the autumn or spring, when the high east, or cold north winds blow.

In fresh water angling the best time is early in the morning, or at the close of the day. The proper time for salt water angling depends upon the tide. The best time is at the last of the ebb or the first of the flood, whether at morning, at mid-day, or at night.

In all kinds of angling it is necessary to be very cautious, but particularly in taking the wily trout. Many novices in the art wander up and down streams, and wade creeks, with little or no success, from the want of this—a proper requisite of every good angler. The more skilful, also, sometimes fail from the same fault.

A story is told, which serves well to show the necessity of caution. An Angler, who had risen with the sun, and fished till near noon-day without success, was outdone by a knowing one, who, with proper precaution, passed his rod and line between the legs of the Angler (which like his line were pretty well stretched) into a hole underneath the bank. He soon had a bite, and succeeded in taking a two pound trout, almost before the astonished tyro was aware of his presence.

Some are of opinion that trout, and similar fish, can hear* the tread on the ground. It is certain that it will start at the least noise, when nothing can be seen. Salter, in his "Angler's Guide," says: "Keep as far from the water as you can, and go quietly and slily to work, for fish have so many enemies that they are suspicious of every thing they see, feel, or hear; even the shaking the bank of a river (un-

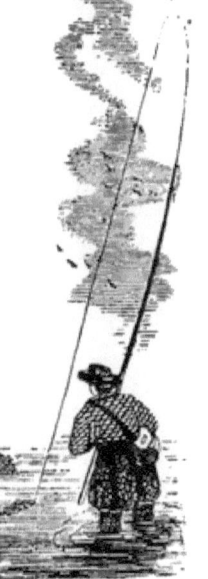

---

* Smith, in his "History of the Fishes of Massachusetts," says that the acoustic apparatus is boxed up in the solid bones of the skull, so that sound propagated through the water, gives a vibratory motion or tremor to the whole body, and which, agitating the auditory nerve, produces hearing.

der which they frequently lie) will alarm them, and spoil the Angler's sport, &c.; and also, when two or three anglers are fishing near each other; therefore avoid agitating the water by trampling on the bank unnecessarily; drop your baited hook in the water gently, and you will kill more fish than three Anglers who act differently."

Blaine also says: "*Avoid every thing that may attract the attention of the fish:* stand so far from the water's edge as you can, and never let your shadow fall on the water. If possible, take the advantage of a bush, tree, &c., completely to conceal the person. When an Angler fishes near home, an artificial screen of rushes, twigs, &c., may be employed for that purpose. In dropping or dipping with the natural fly, the greatest caution is necessary to keep completely out of view of the fish; not only the shadow of the person, but that of the rod also, should be kept from falling on the water."

The dress of the Angler is of great importance in trout angling. If it be true, as before stated, that this timid inhabitant of the brook is disturbed by the least motion, certainly the best means should be taken to render any motion imperceptible. There are two colors of dress for angling, desirable on different occasions. If your sport be in the summer, and lie mid the brilliant green foliage of the trees, bushes, and meadows, your dress should undoubtedly be green throughout. On the contrary, should you be pleased to enjoy yourself in autumn, when nature has changed the scene, and draped herself in sober brown, the most proper uniform is a drab from top to toe. A disciple of Walton, who angles on Long-Island, and takes more trout than any ten sportsmen who visit that delightful resort, is represented as standing as still as a ghost, his rod extended in his hand, without any apparent motion, equipped in drab pantaloons, drab vest, drab coat, and drab hat; and so quiet is he in his movements, that he will take a mess of trout, when a person but a few yards distant would hardly be aware that he moved a muscle. How different from many who profess to understand the art, and who go whipping and splashing the water for miles around.

As health is of great importance, the lover of this sport should adopt the physician's prescription, and "keep the head cool and the feet warm." To this end he should provide himself with a pair of water-proof boots, to be ready should he wish to wade the stream, or cross a marsh. He should also pay strict attention to all laws regarding angling, and all rules laid down for bridge, boat, or brook fishing, and on no account transgress the laws of the different States with respect to spawning time, and the size of the fish to be taken.

It is much to be regretted, that there are many who call themselves anglers, who set all laws at defiance, by taking many kinds of fish out of season; such conduct is unworthy a sportsman, and should meet with rebuke from every member of the angling community.

Finally, let the disciple of the rod

"Use all gently,"

and when he has made up his mind to pass a few days, or even hours, in this delightful amusement, let him be fully prepared with *everything necessary, and everything in order*

CHAPTER IV.

THE SALMON.

This noble fish was known to the world as early as the days of the Romans. Pliny speaks of them as being in the rivers of Aquitaine. They are found at the present day in the waters of France, England, Ireland and Scotland, and on this continent as far north as Greenland. They are found in the greatest abundance in Ireland and Scotland. In some of the rivers of the latter country, large rents are paid for these fisheries. In England and Wales, at certain seasons, they have been taken by thousands in a day, and on some occasions in such abundance that they have been fed to the swine. "In Scotland, they have been so plenty, that the farmer's servants have stipulated to have them but twice a week for food!"

Smith, in his "History of the Fishes of Massachusetts," relates the following: "Captain Charles Kendall, a respectable and intelligent navigator of Boston, assured us, that when on the northwest coast of America, within a few years, he stood in a small stream that came leaping down the crags of a mountain, in which these delightful fishes were urging their way in such astonishing crowds, with hardly water enough to cover their backs, that he stood with an axe and killed hundreds of them as they passed between his feet. He saw birds of prey dive down from the long branches of trees

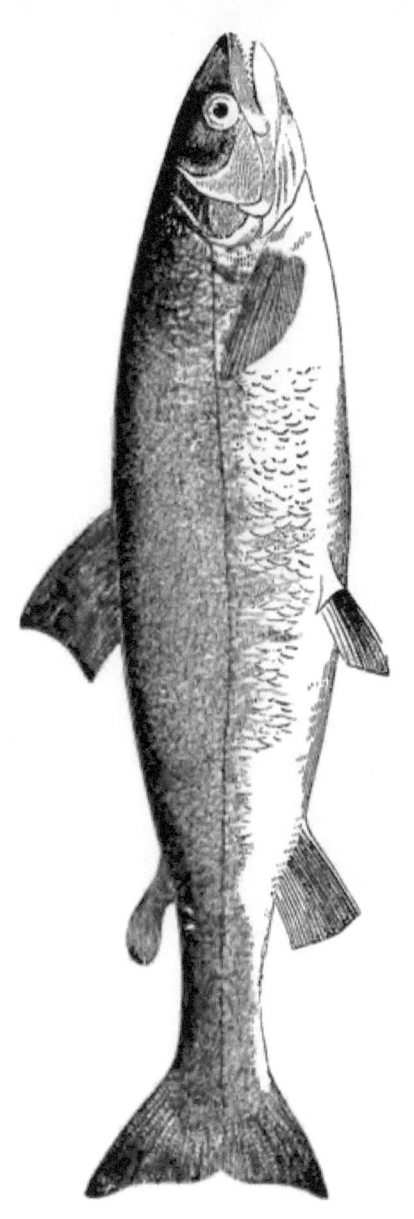

that waved over the falls, and pick out the eyes of several at a time, before they flew back to their resting-places."

The Salmon formerly frequented the Hudson* and Connecticut, but the steamboat navigation on these beautiful rivers, have interfered with their passage, and by increasing interruption, they have been driven farther north, and like the aboriginal inhabitants of our land, seem destined to find a resting-place far beyond the home of their fathers. The Kennebec, the St. Lawrence, the waters of California and Oregon, and many of our western lakes, now furnish large quantities, equal in beauty and flavor to those of any part of the world. They leap up the falls of many of these rivers with astonishing and almost incredible velocity, surmounting obstacles of great magnitude by the extraordinary muscular power of their tail. Michael Drayton, an English writer, speaks of their summersault, or leap, in the following lines:

" As when the salmon seeks a fresher stream to find,
(Which hither from the sea comes yearly by his kind,)
As he towards season grows; and stems the watery tract
Where Tivy, falling down, makes a high cataract,
Forced by the rising rocks that there her course oppose,
As though within her bounds they meant her to enclose;
Here, when the laboring fish does at the foot arrive,
And finds that by his strength he does but vainly strive,
His tail takes in his mouth, and bending like a bow
That's to full compass drawn, aloft himself doth throw,
Then springing at his height, as doth a little wand,
That bended end to end, and started from man's hand
Far off itself doth cast; so does the salmon vault;
And if at first he fail, his second summersault
He instantly essays, and from his nimble ring
Still yerking, never leaves until himself he fling
Above the opposing stream."

* A number were taken in netts, in the Bay of New-York, in the month of June, 1844.

Like the trout, they are very timid; and if, at the time of their advent, they are suddenly frightened by any noise, or splashing of the water, will turn and swim in a contrary direction at a surprising rate of velocity. It has been ascertained by calculation, that they can move at the rate of 30 miles an hour. They run up the rivers from the sea, to deposit their spawn, from April to July, and are at this time in fine condition for the table; after which they return again to the sea. They are much troubled with what fishermen call the salmon-louse, and are known in some instances to return to the fresh water in the months of September and October, to rid themselves of these annoying insects. Smith says: "The young are about two inches in length when they visit the sea for the first time. After the parent fish have passed up the rivers, the spring following, the young ones follow at a respectable distance, having grown about six inches. At the end of two years, they weigh five, six, and seven pounds; at the end of six years, they have attained their ordinary dimensions."

An English writer, called the "North Country Angler," says: "The roe of the salmon becomes salmon fry in March and April, and they very soon find their way to the sea, where they grow with amazing rapidity; as on their return to their native streams in June or July of the same year, they weigh six or seven pounds. They are usually called grilse until they weigh about nine pounds, after which they are called salmon."

The following account of late experiments on salmon in Scotland, taken from the "Kelso Mail," a Scotch paper, rather contradicts the opinions of former writers on the rapid increase in size of this species of fish. "In the month of April, 1843, Mr. James Keras, a game-keeper at Bowhill, Selkirkshire, took from the Ettrick, and marked from six to seven dozen of the salmon fry going down to the sea, by inserting a piece of wire through the tail of each, and twisting

it at both ends. In the last week of July last, (1844,) a grilse of from five to six pounds weight, was caught at the shore-side fishery near Berwick, by James M'Queen, fisherman, and in the tail was a piece of wire twisted at both ends, as described. M'Queen did not preserve the wire, but is satisfied in his own mind that it was brass, and of the description inserted in the fry by Mr. Keras. There can therefore scarcely be a doubt that it was one of the fry marked by the latter, and proves to a demonstration, that the fry occupy a much longer period in arriving at a state of maturity than has been generally supposed."

This extraordinary fish grows to a very large size. Hofland says, the largest ever heard of in England was sold in the London market, and weighed 83 pounds. He also tells a story of a Scotch Highlander, who, whilst fishing in the river Awe, struck a salmon, which he played with great skill and patience until night came, when the fish *sulked* at the bottom. The persevering fisher, not to be subdued, took the line in his mouth and lay down for a snooze, when *he sulked* until three o'clock in the morning, when his angling friends aroused him, and the fish, after a further run, was brought to land, and weighed 73 pounds. Sir J. Hawkins says that the largest salmon ever taken in England was caught in April, 1789 ; " it measured upwards of four feet in length, three feet around the body, and weighed nearly seventy pounds." There may be some in this country of like size and weight among our undiscovered waters and virgin streams where yet the angler's line is to be thrown. The largest on record at present remembered weighed about forty pounds.

The common length of the salmon is from two to three and a half feet, except when of the extraordinary English weight mentioned, when they would probably measure five or six feet. They are of a beautiful silver gray color, running into white on the belly and blue on the back, and are marked with numerous irregular dark and copper colored spots. The male is gener

ally of a larger and more slender shape than the female, with a slight difference in the shape and color of the spots. The upper jaw is larger than the lower, and in the males the under jaw is curved upward. Considered as a whole, he may be called the most extraordinary and most beautiful fish in the world; and whether we admire him as leaping the cataract, fresh floured from his native element on the green carpet of the meadow, or in smoking anticipation as a viand on the table, he well deserves the appellation of king of the watery course, or, as Willis in his quaint way would probably call him, the prince of *fish-dom*.

The sport in taking him is of the most exciting kind, requiring the utmost skill of the truly scientific Angler. Sir Walter Scott says: " Salmon fishing is to all other kinds of angling, as buck shooting to shooting of any meaner description. The salmon is in this particular the king of fish. It requires a dexterous hand and an accurate eye to raise and strike him; and when this is achieved, the sport is only begun where, even in trout angling, unless in case of an unusually lively and strong fish, it is at once commenced and ended. Indeed the most sprightly trout that ever was hooked, shows more child's play in comparison to a fresh run-salmon. There is all the difference which exists between coursing the hare and running the fox. The pleasure and suspense are of twenty times the duration—the address and strength required infinitely greater—the prize when attained, not only more honorable but more valuable. The hazards of failure are also an hundred-fold multiplied; the instinct of the salmon leads to the most singular efforts to escape, which must be met and foiled by equal promptitude on the part of the angler "

They love to haunt the rapid rivers or large lakes, with sandy or pebbly bottoms, that run into the sea, and are usually, when on the feed, found in the roughest and boldest parts. They will best take the bait early in the morning or late in the afternoon, when there is a light breeze on the water. When not on feed they retreat to deep water, and also under banks, bushes, &c. The best time for angling for them is from May until August. In July and August they will often take the fly freely; for the months of May and June, worms, shrimp, or small fish, will be found the best baits.

Bait-fishing for Salmon is generally practised with a rod of from sixteen to eighteen feet in length, with a hollow butt and spare tops, either for worm or minnow fishing. Some sportsmen prefer a lighter top for worm fishing than for spinning the minnow; the hollow butt allows him to use his taste, and also the advantage of extra tops against breakage. There are two ways of rigging the rod for the line—the old-fashioned plan of rings, whipped on with thread, is preferred by some, and the patent guide, a solid stationary ring, (a new invention) by others. Attached to the rod should be a multiplying reel, capable of holding from three to six hundred feet of line; to insure success with large game, the largest sized reel, with six hundred feet of line, should be used. The line adapted to the reel should be either of silk, hair, silk and hair, or grass. The two former descriptions are most in use, but the latter is now preferred by many on account of its strength, durability, and lightness. Affixed to the line should be a swivel sinker, and a leader, either of single or twisted gut, of from three to six feet in length, according to the depth of water. For middle fishing, use a large size float of cork or red cedar. The proper size of hook should be No. 0, 1, 2, 3, of the Kirby or Limerick pattern, attached to single or twisted gut. A very few Anglers use gimp instead of gut, but the show it makes in the water, both from its size and color, preclude the idea of much success. From the timid nature of the object of your sport, your tackle should combine strength with imperceptibility.

For *Fly-Fishing for Salmon*, the customary rod used is

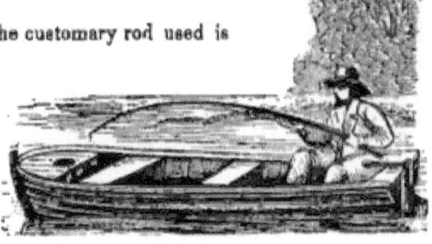

from sixteen to twenty feet long, with a gradual taper, and uniform from the end of the first or butt joint to the end of the top, which latter should be of the most elastic substance, and brought almost to a point: in fact the proper form of a fly rod, is a perfectly *whip taper*. The rings should be of the lightest kind, and wound on with thread or silk, and the whole apparatus as light as the necessary strength will allow. In some instances they are provided with a spike or spear, which screws into the butt, and which is found very useful to the Angler on many occasions, for sticking the rod in an upright position, for the purpose of altering or arranging the line or other tackle. The same arrangement of tackle is required for the fly rod as for the bait rod, with the exception of substituting a swivel, instead of a swivel sinker.

Worm fishing for Salmon. For worm bait, use a Salmon Limerick hook, from No. 0 to 4, as the size of the game may indicate. Attach the worms according to the method described in Chapter II.; throw them gently in the current; let them flow easily down a few yards; then draw them back; then to the right and left; keeping up a continual motion of the bait. By this method, if you are cautious, and keep out of sight—*and if there be fish*, as Walton would say —you will be sure to have your share of good luck. In bright clear weather, a hook of either No. 3, 4, or 5, will be large enough. It will also be necessary, if the stream be clear, on some occasions to use only one large worm.

When the bait is taken, the premonitory symptoms are a distended line, and sometimes a sudden jerk. *In either case keep a tight line:* the former admonition generally promises success, and when it is well understood, will give the most pleasure. After allowing a short time for gorging, you should give a sharp strike, and if done with precision, and not too

violent, you will rarely fail to hook your fish. On the contrary, the sudden jerk is seldom more or 'ess than a nibble; you should therefore give a moderate pull, which will rather excite your game, and induce him to *call again for worms!*

The following practical information, taken from "Fisher's Angler's Souvenir," will give the reader some idea of the manner of taking a large fish, after he is hooked; for as it is one thing to catch a fish and another to cook it, so it is one thing to hook a fish and another thing to *take him* after you get him on. "Judging from his pull, you estimate his weight at 30 pounds, the largest and strongest, you verily believe, you ever have hooked. With that headlong plunge, as if he meant to bury his head in the gravelly bottom, he has hooked himself. Your hook, which will hold 30 pounds dead weight, is buried in his jaws to the bend, and now that he feels the barb, he shoots up the stream with the swiftness of an arrow, and fifty yards of your line are run off before you dare venture to check him. Now his speed is somewhat diminished, hold on a little, and as the river side is clear of trees, follow up after him, for it is bad policy to let out line to an unmanageable length, when you can follow your fish. There are some awkward rocks towards the head of the pool, which may cut your line; turn him, therefore, as soon as you can. Now is the time to show your tact, in putting your tackle to test, without having it snapped by a sudden spring. Hold gently—ease off a little—now hold again—how beautifully the rod bends, true from top to butt, in one uniform curve! He has a mouth, though bitted for the first time! Bravo! his nose is down the water! Lead him along—gently, he grows restive, and is about again. Though his course is still up the stream, he seems inclined to tack. Now he shoots from bank to bank, like a Berwick smack turning up Sea Reach in a gale of wind. Watch him well in stays, lest he shoot suddenly ahead, and carry all away. He is nearing the rocks—give him the butt and turn him again. He comes round—he cannot bear that steady pull—what excellent tackle! lead him downwards—he follows reluctantly, but he is beginning to fag. Keep winding up your line as you lead him along. He is inclined to take a rest at the bottom, but as you hope to land him, do not grant him a moment. Throw in a large stone at him, but have both your eyes open—one on your rod, and the other on the place where the fish lies— lest he make a rush when you are stooping for a stone, and break loose. Great, at this moment, is the advantage of the angler who has a 'cast' in his eye! That stone has startled the fish—no rest for salmo—and now he darts to the surface. ' Up wi taily!' what a leap! it is well you humored him by dipping the top of your rod, or he would have gone free. Again and again! these are the last efforts of despair, and they have exhausted him. He is seized with stupor, like a stout gentleman who has suddenly exerted himself after dinner, or a boxer who has just received a swinging blow on the jugular. Draw him towards the shore, he can scarcely move a fin. Quick, the gaff is in his gills, and now you have him out; and as he lies stretched on the pebbles, with his silver sides glancing in the sun, you think that you never caught a handsomer fish in your life, though you perceive that you have been wrong in your estimate of his weight— thirty pounds—for it is evident that he does not weigh more than thirteen. It was exactly half-past seven when you hooked him, and when you look at your watch after landing him, you perceive that it wants a quarter to nine, so that he has kept you in exercise exactly an hour and a quarter."

Artificial Flies for Salmon Fishing. The flies used in this country for taking salmon, do not differ materially from those used in England, Ireland, or Scotland. In the fly season, those of the most gaudy description are generally used.

The most approved are made of the choice feathers of the peacock, pheasant, parrot, partridge woodcock, ostrich, macaw, turkey, guinea-hen, &c., with bright colored bodies, and gold twist. They can be procured ready made, and of all descriptions, at the general tackle stores. The following list, used in Ireland, Scotland, and Wales, and to some extent in the United States, may be found useful to the Angler.

No. 1. Body of the fly half dark blue and half orange mohair, ribbed with silver twist and red tip; legs of black hackle, wings of the grey mottled feather of the wing of the mallard.

No. 2. The body half blue and half light green, or greenish yellow, with a gold rib and red twist, black hackle legs, and wings from the heron's wing.

No. 3. Body, light green mohair, ribbed with gold twist; tips, orange mohair and turkey's wing; legs black hackle; wings of the black and white tail feathers of the turkey.

No. 4. Body of orange colored silk or worsted, with gold twist; dun hackle legs; wings dark brown mottled feather of the bittern.

No. 5. Wings of the speckled feather of the mallard's wing; body of blue mohair, with silver twist, with a dark blue hackle for legs.

No. 6. Body, claret and orange colored mohair, with green tip and gold twist; wings of the turkey feather, with white tips; legs black and red hackle.

No. 7. Body of yellow silk or mohair, with gold twist; wings of the brown mottled feather of the turkey; dark red hackle for legs.

No. 8. Wings of the woodcock or partridge, body purple mohair, legs coch-a-bonddu hackle.

No 9 Wings light speckled feather of the wing of the mallard; body yellow silk with fine gold twist; tail three strands of red hackle, and legs of the same.

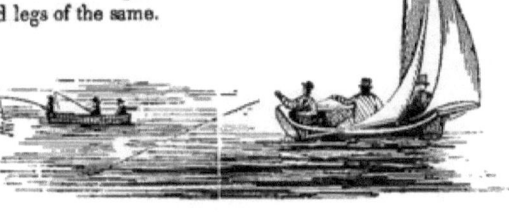

No. 10. Body black ostrich ——, with silver twist; wings from the mallard's wing, and black hackle for legs.

There are other varieties of flies, both of English and American manufacture, used in the United States and Canada, which can generally be procured at the tackle stores in the city of New-York.

Salmon Spearing. This is a mode of taking fish not approved of by the regular sportsman. It is practised to a great extent on many of our western lakes and rivers, usually by persons who take fish for a livelihood, and where they are found in such immense quantities, that there can be no objection to the plan, as it is an active and invigorating pastime, almost equal to that of hunting. It is generally practised at night, with torches, and gives many an hour of evening sport, after a day's business, to the inhabitants in the vicinity of the lakes where they are found. The Indians, who in their rude manner surpass many of their more civilized brethren in water or land sports, are very fond of this amusement, and in the season can be seen traversing the lakes in their canoes, with varied and brilliant pine lights, presenting a most beautiful and picturesque appearance.

There is a law of the State of New-York, prohibiting the taking of salmon by net, hook, or spear, " or any other device whatsoever," in the months of October and November, but which, like many of our State laws, is better known by its breach than its observance.

How to cook a Salmon. The following method of cooking and crimping a salmon, given by Sir Humphrey Davy, will be found useful *after he has been taken;* and as the reader has been led through the instructions of taking the game, concluding that the fish *is taken*, directions for cooking will be here in place.

"He seems fairly tired, I shall bring him into shore. Now gaff him; strike as near the tail as you can. He is safe; we must prepare him for the pot. Give him a stunning blow on the head, to deprive him of sensation; and then give him a transverse cut, just below the gills and crimp him, by cutting, so as almost to divide him into slices, and hold him by the tail that he may bleed. There is a small spring I see, close under that bank, which I dare say has the mean temperature of the atmosphere in this climate, and is much under fifty degrees; place him there, and let him remain ten minutes, and then carry him to the pot and let the water and salt boil furiously, before you put in a slice; and give time for the water to recover its heat before you put in another; leave the head out, and throw in the thickest pieces first"

CHAPTER V.

OF THE LAKE TROUT.

(SALMO CONFINIS.)

THIS species of Trout is entirely distinct from that known as the Mackinaw Trout or Mackinaw Salmon; he is not so much of a game fish, neither is he so tasteful to the palate as the former description. The following, taken from Dr. Dekay's New York Fauna, will enable our friends to make the proper distinction between the two:—

"CHARACTERISTICS:—Blackish, with numerous gray spots. Body robust, comparatively short in proportion to its depth. Caudal fin, with a sinuous margin. Length two to four feet.

"It occurs in most of the northern lakes of this state;* and I have noticed it in Silver Lake, Pennsylvania, adjacent to Broome county, which is, as far as I know, its southernmost limits. The average weight is from eight to ten pounds, but I have heard fishermen speak of its weighing thirty pounds, and even more. Some idea of their abundance may be formed from the fact that a single fisherman has been known to capture, on Paskungameh or Long Lake, five hundred weight in the course of one week."

They are taken with stout lines and tackle similar to that used for the Mackinaw Trout; the deepest holes in the deepest

* New York.

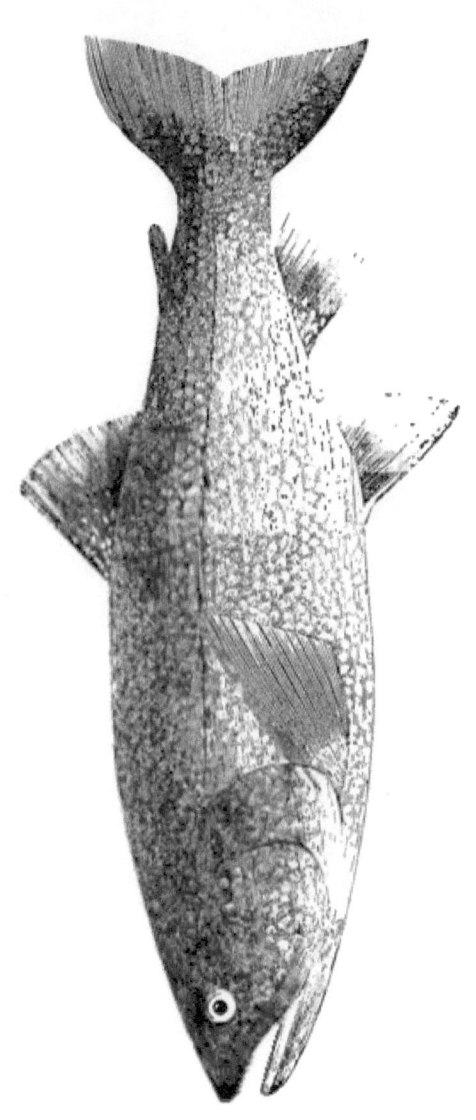

parts of the lakes are their haunts. The best bait for taking them is the shiner, although they are not very particular as to feed, and can be captured with almost any kind of small fish that populate the brooks that run into the lakes. Although not so valuable as an article of diet or sport, still they should be preserved from certain and inevitable extinction by a protective law during their spawning season. They have the misfortune to spawn in the month of October; a pleasant time for active out-door exercise, and for the favorite practice with many of the foolish inhabitants near the lakes, of spearing this fish when they go into shallow water to spawn. It is said that legislative enactments against this wholesale murder would be useless. It might be so; but were our angling friends on the lakes to take the subject in hand, have proper laws passed, and see that they were put in execution against every offender, this member of the finny family might be preserved as long as waters run and fish swim.

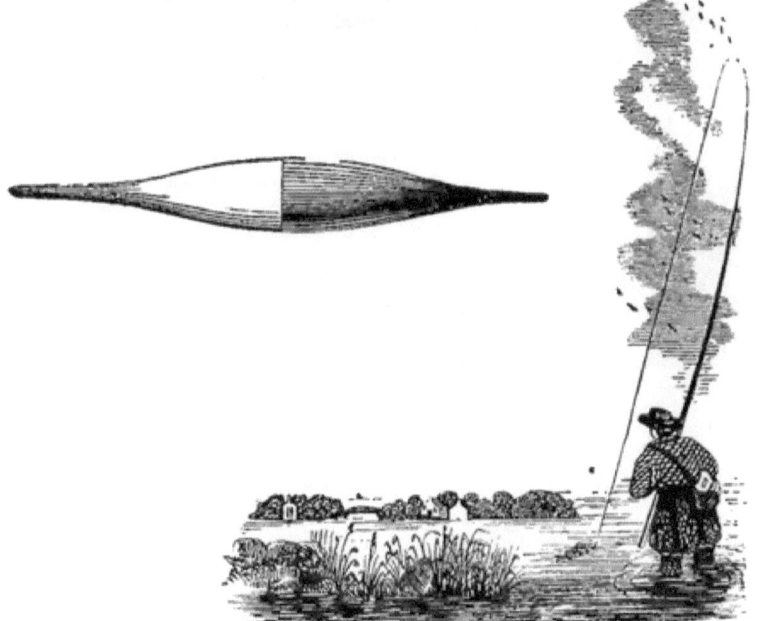

CHAPTER VI.
OF THE TROUT.

This beautiful and well known fish inhabits the waters of almost all countries on the globe. In England, Ireland, Scotland, Germany, and Prussia, it is sought for by the angler and the epicure as the height of their admiration. Our own country, with its countless streams and lakes, furnishes quantities equal to all the rest combined; and although they have been much sought after within a few years back, still there are many streams where the line never floated, or the trout ever had the *satisfaction* of being tempted by the angler's scientific art They vary greatly in size, color and description, according to the climate, the nature of the water, or the quality of their feed. They go under the different names of common or silver trout, black trout, sea trout, and bass.

The Silver Trout, or common trout, is found in almost all of our clear swift running northern streams, and weigh from one to 15 pounds. A splendid specimen of this species of trout is taken in Bashe's Kill, Sullivan County, New-York, said to surpass any thing of the kind in the world. This stream winds along the western side of Shawangunk mountain, through the beautiful and well cultivated valley of Memekating, has a smooth gravelly bottom, and so remarkably clear and transparent is it, that the smallest insect is perceptible on its bed.

TROUT-FISHING IN SULLIVAN COUNTY.

"We break from the tree-groups, a glade deep with grass;
The white clover's breath loads the sense as we pass.
A sparkle—a streak—a broad glitter is seen,
The bright Callikoon, through its thickets of green!
We rush to the banks—its sweet music we hear;
Its gush, dash, and gurgle, all blent to the ear.
No shadows are drawn by the cloud-covered sun,
We plunge in the crystal, our sport is begun.
Our line, where that ripple shoots onward we throw,
It sweeps to the foam-spangled eddy below,
A tremor—a pull—the trout upward is thrown,
He swings to our basket—the prize is our own!"—STREET.

THE TROUT. 67

Common Trout,* (*Salmo Fontinalus—Mitchill*,) " with yellow and red spots on both sides of the lateral line, concave tail, and sides of the belly orange red ; back mottled pale and brown, sides dark brown with yellow and red spots, the yellow larger than the red surrounding them ; the latter appear like scarlet dots ; lateral line straight, the yellow spots and red dots both above and below that line ; lowest part of the abdomen whitish with a smutty tinge ; first rays of the pectoral ventral and anal fins white, the second black, the rest purplish red; dorsal fin mottled of a yellowish and black ; tail is rather concave, but not amounting to a fork, and of a reddish purple, with blackish spots above and below ; eyes large and pale, mouth wide, teeth sharp, tongue distinct, skin scaleless. Is reckoned a most dainty fish. He lives in running waters only,† and not in stagnant ponds; and therefore the lively streams, descending north and south from their sources on Long Island, exactly suit the constitution of this fish. The heaviest Long Island trout that I have heard of weighed four pounds and a half."

"The common trout of Massachusetts‡ is from 8 to 12 inches long, dotted on the back with brownish spots, shaded by a paler circle. On the gill-covers is a broad spot; the under jaw is the longest; the soft rayed fins tinged with yellow, and on the sides of the body are red spots."

The *Black Trout* is usually found in muddy sluggish streams or large ponds, with clay bottoms, in the roughest and wildest parts of our country. They are not considered as

---

* The trout of Long Island.

† This is not always the case. They are taken in great quantities at Stump Pond, Long Island, of a large size, but not of as fine a flavor and color as in swift running waters. They are also found in various other ponds throughout the country, and are often transferred to artificial ponds supplied from springs.

‡ Smith.

game a fish as the ordinary trout, neither do they possess as fine a flavor for the table. They are supposed to take their color from the quality and color of the water, which has generally a dark smoky appearance, occasioned by the decayed leaves and timber which there abound. Many of the streams in the western and mountainous parts of Pennsylvania, contain this species. They are found also in great abundance, in the wild and uninhabited parts of Hamilton county, New-York, and in some parts of New-Hampshire and Vermont.

Of the *Sea Trout*, the writer is enabled to give a better and more satisfactory description than his own. Smith says: "They are found, as may be inferred from the name, in the salt and brackish waters of tide rivers, inland bays in various parts of this* and the adjoining states. When taken from the salt water early in the spring, they are in high perfection, and nothing can exceed their piscatory symmetry. The general appearance of the skin is of a silvery brightness; the back being of a greenish and mackerel complexion, the spots of a vermilion color, mixed with others of a faint yellow, and sometimes slightly tinged with purple, extend the whole length on each side of the lateral line; the fins are light in color and firm in texture, and together with the tail are rather shorter and more rounded than the common trout. They have a firm compactness of form from head to tail, which accounts for the superior sprightliness of their motion; the head and mouth are very small, and the latter never black inside like the common, or fresh water trout; the flesh is even redder, or rather we would say, more pink colored than the salmon, to which, by many, they are preferred as a delicacy, having, like the salmon, much of what is called the curd or fat between the flakes.

"A fish of a pound weight measures about 11 inches in length. Their average size is considerably larger than the fresh water, or brook trout—having been taken in the waters to

* Massachusetts.

which we refer* of nearly five pounds weight; such instances, however, are rare, three pounds being considered a very large fish. We do not remember ever seeing a poor fish of this kind taken; they are invariably in good condition, let the size be what it will; their principal food is the minnow and shrimp, particularly the latter, with which early in the season their stomachs are found to be filled; they feed upon the minnow rather later in the season, when the increasing warmth of the water invites it to leave the warmer springs of fresh water, where it has passed the winter, and venture into the shallows round the margin of the bay, it then becomes an easy prey to the voracious trout, which pursues it with desperate boldness to the very feet of the angler as he stands in the water, obliging it in shoals, to leap from the surface, and sometimes even to be cast on shore in its attempts to escape its hungry jaws. Though they are, on the whole, the best bait; the shrimp on the contrary, living as they do among the eel-grass in the bay, which also affords shelter to the trout, being more within reach, may consequently be said to supply their principal food, at least through the winter months. As it is necessary in the pursuit of all game to be governed by a knowledge of its particular food, so it may be said of the sea trout; their motions while in the salt water being regulated by those of the minute fish on which they live. Both minnows and shrimp are more or less affected by the action of the tide, particularly the latter, which in its reflux sweeps the *passive* shrimp in shoals across a sandy eddy of the bay, into the very mouths of the expectant trout, who there collect and lie in wait to feast upon them."

The last mentioned species, (*Lepomis Salmonea*,) is peculiar to our southern rivers, and with many southerners go under the name of *Trout Bass*, or *Brown Bass*. They grow to a much larger size than the northern trout, varying in

* Waquoit Bay, upon Cape Cod, and Fire Place, L. I.

length from 6 to 24 inches; they are of a darker color, and do not possess that beauty of appearance when out of the water, or that delicious flavor when upon the table; neither do they contribute as much to the Angler's sport, as those of more northern latitudes.

Another species of trout, mentioned by Smith, is the *Hucho Trout*, (*Salmo Hucho*,) resembling very much the sea trout; it is found, on careful inspection, to be more slender, and to have a greater number of red spots; the back is dusky; the ventral fin has a yellowish tinge; all the others are of a palish purple; the tail is forked, and the fish measures sometimes four feet through; ordinarily they are only about two, and caught by the hook. This trout certainly exists in the large rivers and ponds in the interior, but deteriorate in size They are brought from New-Hampshire in the winter, frozen for the markets, and from the northern parts of Maine, where specimens have been taken, large as any produced in the great rivers of Europe.

There is no fish that varies so much in size, shape, color and flavor, as the trout. They are found in different varieties in the same stream, and vary so much in external appearance and flavor in some parts of the Union, as to lead to different appellations from experienced and scientific men.

They usually spawn in the months of September and October. The best time for taking them is from April until August; but if the weather is mild and pleasant, they are often taken in fine condition and of large size, in the month of March. They are not, however, considered in perfection until the months of May and June, until which time, owing to the coldness of our climate, they do not obtain sufficient quantity of the proper food to make them active and healthy. They are also more difficult to take, and will give the sportsman more pleasure than in the months of March and April, when they bite more freely, but not with that zest and vigor.

Of the nature and habits of the trout, Walton says: "And you are to note that he continues many months out of season; for it may be observed of the trout, that he is like the buck or the ox, that will not be fat in many months, though he go in the very same pastures that horses do, which will be fat in one month. And so you may observe, that most other fishes recover strength and grow sooner fat and in season than the trout doth.

"And next you are to note, that till the sun gets to such a height as to warm the earth and water, the trout is sick and lean, and lousy, and unwholesome; for you shall in winter find him to have a big head, and then to be lank and thin, and lean; at which time many of them having sticking to them sugs, or trout-lice; which is a kind of worm, in shape like a clove, or pin with a big head, and sticks close to him and sucks his moisture; those I think the trout breeds himself; and never thrives till he frees himself from them, which is when warm weather comes; and then as he grows stronger, he gets from the dead still water into the sharp stream and the gravel, and there rubs off these worms or lice; and then as he grows stronger, so he gets him into swifter and swifter streams, and there lies at the watch for any fly or minnow that comes near him."

The North Country Angler, an English writer, says: "The burn (or common) trout, grows fast if it has plenty of food and good water; several experiments have been made in fish-ponds; some fed by river water, some by clear fluent springs, into which the young have been put about five or six months old—that is, in September or October, reckoning from April, when they come out of their spawning beds, at which time they will be six or seven inches long; and though there has been but little difference in their age and size when put into the pond, yet in 18 months after there will be a surprising change. I have seen a pond drained ten months after

the fish were put into it, which was in July, when they were about 15 months old, at which time they were 15 or 16 inches, others not above 12. But when the pond was drained ten months after, in March, when they were almost two years old, some were 21 or 22 inches, and weighed three pounds or more; others were about 16 inches; and a fourth part not above 12. I do not know to what we can attribute this difference; it could not be either in the food or the water, or the weather, they faring all alike in these. But if I may be allowed my opinion, perhaps some of the fry may have been the spawn of those that were only 17 months old, which is the soonest that any of them spawn; others of parents 29 months, or two years and a half old; and others a year older. This difference in the age of the parent trout may, I believe, occasion the difference in the size of their breed; otherwise I cannot account for it. Trout, in a good pond, will grow much faster than in some rivers, because they do not range so much in feeding. How long they live cannot be determined in any other way so well as by observation on those in ponds, which observation I never had an opportunity of making myself, and therefore shall only mention what a gentleman told me. He assured me that at four or five years old they were at their full growth, which was, in some, at about 30 inches, and in many much less; that they continued about three years pretty nearly the same in size and goodness; two years after they grow big headed and smaller bodied, and died in the winter after that change; but he thought the head did not grow larger, but only seemed to be so, because the body decayed; so that, according to this gentleman's computation, nine or ten years is the term of their life; and yet I think they may live longer in some rivers, and grow to a much greater size, when they have liberty to go into the tide-way and salt water."

The evidence of other writers goes to show that they live

to a much greater age, an instance being known in England where a trout remained in a well upwards of sixty years, being visited by the neighboring country as a remarkable curiosity. Another one, for 28 years was an inhabitant of a well at Dumbarton Castle, Scotland. It had never increased in size from the time it was placed there, when it weighed about a pound, and became so tame that it would receive its food from the hands of the soldiers.

When in prime condition the trout is short and thick, having a small head and broad tail; the spots on the sides are red tinged with purple, and the belly of a beautiful bright silver color.

This fish, from its extreme beauty, delicacy of flavor and extraordinary activity as a game fish, has attracted the attention of all classes of people, from the boy with a pin-hook, to those that have swayed the destiny of empire. The divine, the philosopher, the poet, the artist, and the statesman, from the earliest dates, have enjoyed many days of recreation in his pursuit, sang songs to his praise, or written pages of instruction of their own experience in taking him from his native element. Under such circumstances, it would be superfluous, at this late day, to attempt to give any new instructions to the young Angler, or the seeker after piscatorial information. And as the opinions and practice of well known advisers will no doubt be preferred, they are here given, with such comments as may be found necessary.

There are three different methods pursued in the capture of the trout:—angling at the top, with a natural or artificial fly, grasshopper, or other small insect; at the middle, with a minnow, shrimp, or similar small fish; and at the bottom, with a worm, or different kinds of pastes.

Of Fly Fishing. Of all the various modes adopted and contrived by the ingenuity of man for pulling out the " cun-

ning trout," this at once recommends itself as the perfection of the art; but as it is considered by a majority of our brethren more difficult than worm fishing, it has many objectors. But the difficulties are more in the imagination than the practice, and when once understood, it gives the highest pleasure of the art. Others think they will not take the fly at all in this country, and having fished with a worm all their life, they cannot be persuaded that with a simple fly made of feathers, they can take as many fish, and often times more. Tell them that Isaac Walton, Sir Humphrey Davy, and some of the greatest Anglers the world ever saw, adopted this mode altogether, and that all writers on Angling have devoted pages of their works to explanatory drawings, &c., in reference to it; that it is the most gentlemanly, the most elegant, the least trouble; that you can take your rod enclosed in a small bag a couple of feet long, and about half a pound in weight, or in the more portable form of a walking stick, and your flies in your pocket-book; that you can traverse the stream, and enjoy its beautiful scenery for miles and miles with the least possible trouble; and they will still adhere to their *only* method of worm fishing.

From the fact of there being *comparatively* few who practice with the fly, some English writers are of the opinion that there are *no fly-fishers in America*, and many of our own countrymen think there are *very* few; but this is a great mistake. There are hundreds of good fly anglers, and many that can throw a fly with the most experienced of Europe.

In the Spring, when the streams are muddy, the worm, of course, is preferred, as it is the only method that can be practised, owing to the state of the water, and also from the fact that the trout lie deep, and in the holes under the banks. It is also sometimes better towards the close of the day in summer; the worm will then tempt the trout when nothing else will. But as a general rule, in clear streams, no matter

in what part of the country, in the summer months, the artificial fly can be used with success.

Fly-fishing is usually practised with a short one-handed rod, from ten to twelve feet in length, or a two-handed rod, from fifteen to eighteen feet in length. The first mentioned is the most common in use, and is calculated for the majority of our streams, which are small, and require but little length of rod or line. Attached to the rod should be a reel, containing from thirty to fifty yards of hair, grass, silk, or silk and hair line—the latter description should be used if it can be procured, tapering from the tenth of an inch almost to a point; to this should be attached a leader of from one to two yards in length ; and finally your fly, on a light length of gut ; if you wish to use two or three flies, place them on your leader with short gut, about 24 inches apart.

The latter description of rod is used in larger streams, where it is necessary to throw a great distance; for this purpose, the reel should be large enough to contain 100 yards of line, with the other tackle precisely the same as with the smaller rod. It should be recollected that the trout rods should be made similar to the salmon rods, and of the lightest woods, as formerly described.

The above descriptions are generally used in this country, but the following information from Hofland, one of the latest and best English writers, may be preferred:

"A slight rod, 12 feet long, or, if wanted for a narrow or wooded stream, one of 10 or 12 feet only would be more convenient, a reel containing 30 yards of line, a book of artificial flies, and a landing-net, and you are fully equipped for the sport. * * * I have already said that a one-handed rod should be 10 or 12 feet long, and a two-handed rod from 16 to 18 feet; to either of which must be attached a reel containing 30 yards of twisted silk and hair line, tapering from a moderate thickness up to a few hairs, at the end of

which you are by a loop to attach your bottom tackle. This should be made of round, even gut, and three yards long: some persons prefer four yards; but I think too great a length of gut increases the difficulty in casting the line. These lines should also taper gradually, the gut being much stronger at the end which is to be attached to the line on the reel, than at the end to which the stretcher fly is to be fixed. When you fish with only two flies, the second (or drop fly) should be at a distance of 36 or 40 inches from the bottom or stretcher fly; but if you use three flies, the first drop should be only 34 inches from the stretcher, and the second 30 inches from the first. These drop flies are attached to the line by loops, and should not be more than three inches long; and by having the gut rather stronger than for the end fly, they will stand nearly at a right angle from the line. I recommend the beginner to commence with one fly only; but at most he must not use more than two; and, as for his mode of casting or throwing his fly, now his tackle is prepared, I fear little useful instruction can be given, as skill and dexterity, in this point, must depend upon practice. I may, however, advise him not to attempt to cast a long line at first, but to try his strength and gain facility by degrees. He must make up his mind to hear many a crack, like a coachman's whip, and find the consequent loss of his flies before he can direct his stretcher to a given point, and let it fall on the water as light as a gossamer."

Cotton says: "For the length of your rod, you are always to be governed by the breadth of the river you shall choose to angle at; and for a trout river one of five or six yards is commonly enough; and longer, though never so neatly and artificially made, it ought not to be, if you intend to fish at ease; and if otherwise, where lies the sport? The length of your line, to a man that knows how to handle his rod and to cast it, is no matter of encumbrance, except in woody places.

and in landing of a fish, which every one that can afford to angle for pleasure has somebody to do for him.* And the length of line is a mighty advantage to the fishing at a distance; and to fish fine and far off, is the first and principal rule for trout angling. Your line in this case should never be less than one, nor ever exceed two hairs, next to the hook; for one (though some, I know, will pretend to more art than their fellows) is indeed too few, the least accident, with the finest hand, being sufficient to break it; but he that cannot kill a trout of twenty inches long with two, in a river clear of wood and weeds, deserves not the name of a true angler.

"Now, to have your line† as it ought to be, two of the finest lengths nearest the hook should be of two hairs a-piece; the next three lengths above them of three; the next three above them of four; and so of five, and six, and seven, to the very top; by which means your rod and tackle will in a manner taper from your very hand to your hook; your line will fall much better and straighter, and cast your fly to any certain place to which the hand and eye shall direct it, with less weight and violence, than would otherwise circle the water and fright away the fish.

"In casting your line, do it always before you, and so that your fly may first fall upon the water, and as little of your line with it as possible; though if the wind be stiff, you will of necessity be compelled to drown a good part of your line to keep your fly under water. And in casting your fly you must aim at the farther or nearer bank, as the wind serves

* This is the method of fishing without a reel, and with very fine hair lines, mostly practised in Cotton's day. We hardly think that every body in Republican America, that can afford to fish for pleasure, has an attendant to land his fish for him.

† This mode is given for the benefit of those who live in the country, are obliged to make their own lines, and find it necessary to fish without a reel.

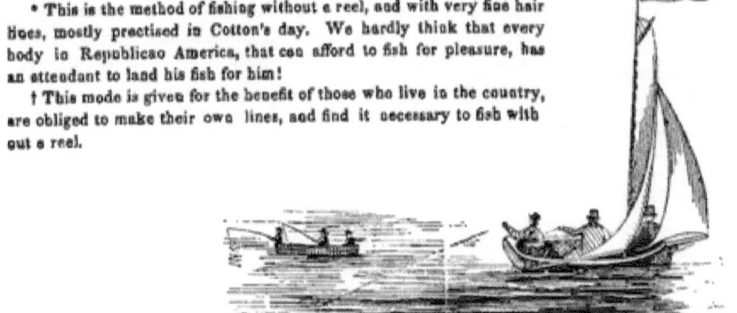

your turn, which also will be with and against you on the same side, several times in an hour, as the river winds in its course, and you will be forced to angle up and down by turns accordingly, but are to endeavor, as much as you can, to have the wind evermore on your back. And always be sure to stand as far off the bank as the length will give you leave, when you throw on the contrary side; though when the wind will not permit you so to do, and that you are constrained to angle on the same side whereon you stand, you must then stand on the very brink of the river, and cast your fly at the utmost length of your rod and line, up or down the river, as the gale serves."

Management of the Line, when Fishing either with one Fly, or two or more Flies. The following minute and easy method of the management of the line, and throwing the fly from Taylor's "Art of Angling," will be found to be excellent advice to the young beginner.

"When you have fixed your rod properly, with your winch thereon, and brought your line from it through the rings of your rod, loop on to it by the strongest end your foot length,* which should be about three yards and a half long, made of good strong silk-worm gut, well tied, and the knots neatly whipped, running (very little) finer towards the bottom end, at which place there must be a neatly whipped loop; then take your end fly, or stretcher, which should be made of one or two lengths of good level gut, full as fine, or a little finer, than the bottom link of your foot length, tied and whipped neatly together, and looped nicely at the end; loop this to the end of your gut length; and then, your drop fly, just above a knot, where whipped, about a yard from the end fly, to hang from the line not more than two or three

* Called in this country a leader, as described on page 32.

inches. If you choose to fish with more, keep them all at the same distance. And observe, that if your droppers be larger than, or even as large as, your stretcher, you will not be able to throw a good line: but a beginner should never use more than one fly.

"When thus prepared, let out the line *about half as long again as the rod;* and holding the line properly in one hand, and the line, just above the fly, in the other, give your rod a motion from right to left, and as you move the rod backwards, in order to throw out the line, dismiss the line from your hand at the same time; and try several throws at this length. Then let out more line and try that; still using more and more till you can manage any length needful; but about nine yards is quite sufficient for a learner to practice with. And observe, that in raising your line in order to throw it again, you should wave the rod a little round your head, and not bring it directly backwards; nor must you return the line too soon, nor until it has streamed its full length behind you, or you will certainly whip off your end fly. There is great art in making your line fall light on the water, and showing the flies well to the fish. The best way that I can direct is, that when you have thrown out your line, contriving to let it fall lightly and naturally, you should raise your rod gently and by degrees; sometimes with a kind of tremulant flourish, which will bring the flies in a little towards you; still letting them go down with the stream, but never drawing them against it, for it is unnatural; and before the line comes too near you throw it again. When you see a fish rise at a natural fly, throw out about a yard above him, but not directly over his head; and let your fly or flies move gently towards him, which will show it to him in a more natural form, and tempt him the more to take it. Experience and observation alone, however, can make a man a complete adept in the art, so as to enable him to throw his fly behind bushes and trees, into holes, under banks, and other places mentioned as the 'trout haunts,' and where the best fish are to be found."

There is much diversity of opinion about the manner of fishing, whether up or down the stream; the great majority of Anglers, both in Europe and this country, favor the latter method, and a very few the former. Hofland remarks on this: "Some persons recommend fishing up the stream, and throwing the fly before them. For my own part, (after much experience,) whenever I can do so with convenience, I cast my fly above me, and across the stream, drawing it gently towards me. If the wind should be against you, you will be constrained to stand close to the water's edge, and make your cast close to the bank on which you stand, either up or down the stream, as the wind may serve. Avoid, if possible, fishing with the sun behind you, as the moving shadow of yourself and rod will alarm the fish. The finer the tackle (particularly the bottom tackle) and the lighter the fly falls on the water, the greater will be your sport; indeed some Anglers use only a single hair for their bottom tackle; but when the water you fish is weedy, or much wooded, a single hair is difficult to manage; but in ponds or streams, free from impediments, it may be used by a skilful hand to a great advantage."

Of Bush-Fishing, sometimes called Dibbing, Dabbing, or Daping. This is a cunning mode of fishing on the part of the Angler, quite equal to any of the curious manœuvres of the trout himself. It is practised in the summer months, when the water is low, and the bushes are in leaf, thereby giving the Angler a biding place; and when it is almost impossible to take him by any other method; and although it requires extreme care, and all the ingenuity of the fisher, it will

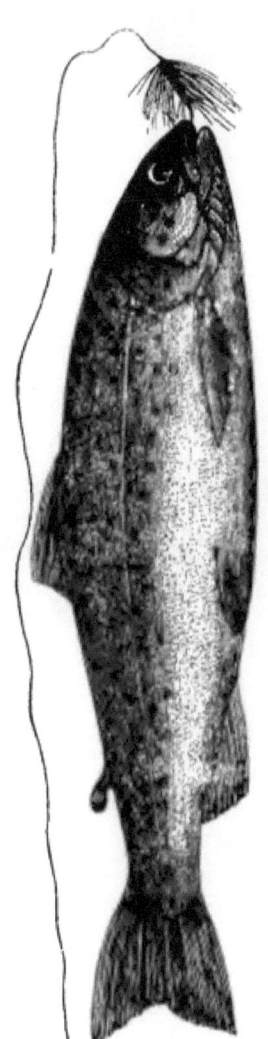

amply repay him, by the size and quality of the game, the largest, oldest, most wary of the tribe, being often taken by this process. Hofland gives the following instructions:

" The Angler must be provided with a 14 feet rod, with a stiff top, and strong running tackle; he will seldom have to use more than a yard of line, the bottom of which should be of strong silk worm gut. I recommend strong tackle, because in confined situations, overhung with wood, you will not have room to play your fish, but must hold him tight and depend on the strength of your tackle.

" The size of your hook must depend upon the size of the fly, from No. 7 to 9 for small flies and grubs, and for beetles No. 4 or 5. For bush-fishing, you should be provided with well scoured brandlings and red worms, cad-baits,* clock-baits, earth-grubs, beetles, grasshoppers, and a horn of flies; or at least as many of the above as you can procure.

" Great caution is necessary in using your rod and line, for if there are few bushes or brambles to conceal you, the water must be approached warily, as the large trout often lie near the surface, and if you are once seen they will fly from you. If the water should be deep, dark, and overhung with thick foliage, so that you can scarcely find an open space for your bait, your line must be shortened to half a yard, and sometimes less.

" If your flies are small, use two of them at once, as they frequently fall in the water in couples. When daping with the fly, if you see your fish, drop the fly gently on the water about a foot before him, and if you are not seen, he will eagerly take it. When your fish is struck, do not allow him to get his head down, for fear of roots and weeds, but keep him to the top of the water, when his fins and strength will

* Cad-baits and clock-baits are not known amongst Anglers in this country; the others will be found useful if they can be procured.

be of little use to him; and in this situation, with good tackle, you may soon exhaust h'm, and make him your own by a landing-net, the handle of which should be two yards long; or he may be landed by a hook or gaff, with a long handle, and thus in some situations, amidst close thorny brambles, will be found more useful than the landing-net, which is liable to be caught in the bushes. When you use the worm, caddis or any other grub, you will require a single shot, No. 6,* to sink your bait, for it cannot sink too slowly, or cause too little disturbance in the water."

The North Country Angler says: "There are some observations I have made, which the Angler may find the benefit of; one is, that although the shade of trees and bushes, is much longer and greater on the south or sun side of the river, than on the north; yet I always find the most and largest trout on that side. I suppose the sun's being more intense and warm on the north side, may occasion more flies, erucas, and insects, to creep upon those bushes, and consequently the more fish will frequent them.

"When the trees or bushes are very close, I advise the bush Angler to take a hedge-bill or hatchet, and cut off two or three branches here and there, at proper places and distances, and so make little convenient openings, at which he may easily put in his rod and line; but this is to be done some time before you come there to fish.

"If you come to a woody place, where you have no such conveniences, and where perhaps there is a long pool, and no angling with a fly, or throwing the rod, there you may be sure of many large fish. For that very reason, I have chosen such places, though very troublesome, when I have been

* It has not been thought necessary to remark upon the sizes of hooks, shot, or sinkers, in speaking generally, as they should vary materially in the various waters where the different sizes of fish are found, and where streams run more or less rapid.

forced to creep under trees and bushes, dragging my rod after me, with the very top of it in my hand, to get near the water; and I have been well paid for my trouble. Whilst you are getting in your rod, throw a brandling, or grub, or what you fish with, into the water, which will make the fish take your bait the more boldly.

"There are some pools that have no bushes at all, but only hollow banks, in some places under which the great fish will lie in the day time. I have gone softly to such places, and have dropped in a suitable bait, close by the bank, and have presently had a good fish. When I use cork, shamois, or buff, instead of natural baits, I always drop them in strong scented oil, in shade-fishing, because the fish comes slowly to the bait, and if he does not smell something like the natural bait, he will not take it, though well imitated."

Cotton gives the following, with which we conclude our remarks on Daping or Dibbing. "These are to be angled with a short line, not much more than half the length of your rod, if the air be still, or with a longer, very near or all out as long as your rod, if you have any wind to carry it from you. And this way of fishing we call Daping, Dabbing, or Dibbing, wherein you are always to have your line flying before you, up or down the river, as the wind serves, and to angle as near as you can to the bank of the same side whereon you stand, though where you see a fish near, you may guide your fly quick over him, whether in the middle or on the contrary side; and if you are pretty well out of sight, either by kneeling, or the interposition of a bank or bush, you may be almost sure to raise and take him too, if it be presently done; the fish will otherwise peradventure be removed to some other place, if it he in still deeps, where he is always on the motion, and roving up and down to look out for prey, though in a stream you may always, almost, especially if there be a good store, find him in the same place.

Your line ought, in this case, to be three good hairs next the hook; both by reason you are in this kind of angling to expect the biggest fish, and also that, wanting length to give him line after he has struck, you must be forced to tug for it; to which I will add, that not an inch of your line being to be suffered to touch the water in Dibbing, it may be allowed to be the stronger."

Having given two of the methods of taking the trout, it will be well to introduce the reader to his hiding-places. On this subject, Hofland gives the best and most minute information. "He is fond of swift, clear streams, running over chalk, limestone, or gravelly bottoms; but he is more frequently in the eddies by the side of the stream, than in the midst of it. A mill-tail is a favorite haunt of the trout; for he finds protection under the apron, which is generally hollow, and has the advantage of being in the eddy, by the side of the mill-race, awaiting his food. He delights also in cascades, tumbling bays, or wiers. The larger trout generally have their hold under roots of overhanging trees, and beneath hollow banks in the deepest parts of the river. The junction of little rapids, formed by water passing round an obstruction in the midst of the general current, is a likely point at which to raise a trout; also at the roots of trees, or in other places where the froth of the stream collects. All such places are favorable for sport, as insects follow the same course as the bubbles, and are there sought by the fish. After sunset, in summer, the large fish leave their haunts, and may be found in the sewers, and at the tails of streams; and during this time, so long as the Angler can see his fly on the water, he may expect sport."

Of Fishing in the Middle, with a Minnow, or any Small Fish. The rod used in this kind of angling, is from 12 to 16 feet in length, with a stiffer top than that used for fly-fishing, and goes under the name of a bait-rod. The smaller, say 12 feet, for *small wading streams*, and the longer for wider and deeper waters. Attached should be an American* reel, holding from 30 to 50 yards of *American laid*† grass, or silk line, with from two to three yards of silk-worm gut, terminating with a Limerick hook, from No. 2 to 5, according to the size of your bait, fastened by a loop as before described. For baiting the minnow, pass your hook in at the mouth and out at the gills, then in again at the commencement of the dorsal fin and out again just beyond, tying the hook at each end with a piece of thin silk or thread. By this method you can, if you use a live minnow, and are *very careful*, keep your bait animated for a great length of time.

The North Country Angler gives a very good mode of baiting with the minnow, as follows: " I have a gilse-hook (No. 3 or 4) at the end of the line, but wrapped no further on the end of the shank than to make it secure, and leave more room to bait. An inch, or very little more, from the shank end of the gilse-hook, I wrap on a strong hook, about half the size of the other. I put the point of the large hook in at the mouth of the minnow, and out at the tail, on the right side of the minnow, binding it half round as I put it in; then I put the other hook in, below the under chap, which keeps the minnow's mouth quite close.

"When I am in no hurry, I tie the tail and hook together, with a very small white thread; before I enter the little hook, I draw up the minnow to its full length, and make it fit the bending of the great hook, to make it twirl round

* The imported reels are used to a great extent, but those of American manufacture are much superior, and should be preferred.

† This description of line has of late years become much used. The grass is imported from Canton and laid here, or taken in a finished state, untwisted, and relaid, which makes it much stronger and firmer than when first imported.

when it is drawn in the water. When all is in order, I take the line in my left hand, a little above the bait, and throw it under-hand, lifting up my right and the rod, that the bait may fall gently on the water.

" I stand at the very top of the stream, as far off as my tackle will permit, and let the bait drop in a yard from the middle of it; I draw the minnow by gentle pulls, of about a yard at a time, across the stream, turning my rod up the water, within half a yard of its surface, keeping my eye fixed on the minnow. When a fish takes it, he generally hooks himself; however, I give him a smart stroke, and, if he does not get off then, I am pretty sure of him. In this manner I throw in three or four times, at the upper part of a stream, but never twice in the same place, but a yard lower every cast. I always throw quite over the stream, but let the bait cross it in a round, like a semicircle, about a foot below the surface, which two of No. 3 or 4 shot, which I always have upon my line, nine or ten inches from the hooks, will sink it to. When I am drawing the bait across the stream, I keep the top of the rod within less than a yard from the water, and draw it downwards, that the bait may be at a greater distance from me, and the first thing that the fish will see. Sometimes I can see the fish before he takes the bait, and then I give in the rod a little, that the minnow may, as it were, meet him half-way; but if I think he is shy, I pull it away, and do not throw it in again till he has got to his feeding place.

" The twirling of the minnow is the beauty of this kind of angling, the fish seeing it a greater distance, and fancying it is making all the haste it can to escape from them; and they make the same haste to catch it."

Hofland has the following: " The minnow rod should be of bamboo cane, at least 16 feet long, with a tolerable stiff top; and 20 or 25 yards of line, something stronger than

your fly-line, will be sufficient. Some Anglers use a rod 20 feet long. To enable them to fish a wide stream, this length of rod is necessary, as the line, in spinning the minnow, is somewhat short of the rod; if you wade the stream, a rod of 12 feet will be long enough.

"*For Baiting with the Minnow.* In the first place, procure a piece of brass wire, about three inches long; one end of which must be hammered into a small loop, and the other end flattened with a hammer, and sharpened in the shape of a spear-head. This must be drawn through a tapering piece of lead,* cast for the purpose. Wires of this description may be kept by you, of different lengths, to suit the size of the bait-fish used.

"Enter the spear end of the leaded wire at the mouth of the minnow, and bring it out at the fork of the tail. Then take a triangular hook, formed by tying together three No. 8 or 9 hooks on a piece of strong gut, one inch and a quarter long, with a small loop on the end. Now, with a baiting-needle, enter the point under the back fin of the bait, when one of the triangular hooks will enter the bait under the back fin, the other two will lie by its sides, and the loop of the gut will be even with the brass loop in the minnow's mouth.

"You must now prepare a minnow-trace, of three yards of gut, at one end of which tie on a Limerick hook No. 9; 12 inches above this, place a fine swivel, and 24 inches higher up another swivel, and your trace is ready. Next, enter the hook at the end of your trace, at the back of the bait's head, and pass it through the two loops now in its mouth, and bring it out under the lips, when the bait's mouth will be closed. Then, bend gently the spear of brass wire, so as to gently curve the tail of the minnow, and then tie the tail fast to the wire with white thread, and you are ready for the stream."

* These articles can be purchased at the tackle stores, of different sizes and descriptions.

The following is from Walton, who by many writers was considered the best minnow Angler in England: "And of these minnows, first you are to know, that the biggest size is not the best, and next, that the middle size and the whitest are the best; and then you are to know, that your minnow must be put on your hook, that it must turn round when it is drawn against the stream; and that it may turn nimbly, you must put on a big sized hook, as I shall now direct you, which is this: put your hook in at his mouth and out at his gill; then having drawn your hook two or three inches beyond or through his gill, put it again through his mouth, and the point or beard out at his tail; and then tie the hook and his tail about very neatly, with a white thread, which will make it apter to turn quick in the water; that done, pull back that part of your line which was slack when you did put your hook into the minnow the second time; I say, pull that part of your line back so that it shall fasten the head, so that the body of the minnow shall be almost straight* on your hook; this done, try how it will turn by drawing it across the water, against a stream; and if it do not turn nimbly, then turn the tail a little to the right or left hand, and try again till it turn quick; for if not, you are in danger to catch nothing; for know, that it is impossible for a minnow to turn too quick."

The Minnow is beautifully and faithfully imitated in England, and imported into this country, and will be found a valuable addition to the Angler's stock of artificial baits.†

Although in this and the following methods, the float is not mentioned as an article of tackle, it is much used by

* Rennie, in his notes on Walton, says: "I have never been able to cause a minnow to swim well in trolling, unless the tail was bent nearly to a semicircle."

† Smearing the artificial baits with fish-slime is recommended by Rennie.

Anglers generally. It should be of small size, and made of light cork, or quills, suited to the weight of your shot and the current of the stream.

Of Bottom or Worm-Fishing. This is, and has been from the earliest periods, the standard mode of trout angling. It is practised principally at the opening and closing of the season by Anglers generally; but by some of our piscatorial friends, who adjure fly-fishing, from the time the trees bud, until autumn scatters their leaves upon the ground.

The rod generally used is from 12 to 15 feet in length, for small streams, and from 15 to 20 feet (according to circumstances) for the larger. The reel, and other appurtenances, should be similar to that described for minnow-fishing.

Hofland says: "For worm-fishing, your rod should be of bamboo cane, and from 16 to 20 feet long, and the line generally something shorter than the rod; but it may be shortened or lengthened, according to circumstances, by your reel. The best worms for a large trout are the lob-worm and the marsh-worm, but with many Anglers the brandling is a great favorite.

"The method of casting your line will depend upon the nature of the water; but as a general rule I may say, keep the point of your rod, as nearly as possible, perpendicular to your bait, steadily following it, as the bait drags along the bottom, with the point of your rod, and when you feel a bite, let the fish turn before you strike. Unless the stream be rapid or deep, a single shot (No. 4) will be sufficient to sink your worm; but in a deep heavy current, two or three more of the same size will be required. In fishing across a stream with a single hair, and a small red-worm, run, from your reel, line to the length of the rod, and, taking hold of the line about 12 inches above the bait, with your left hand draw it towards you till the line tightens, and the top of the rod bends. Holding the rod firmly in the right hand, let go the line, and with a little practice you will find the bait drop lightly into the water at the extremity of the rod and line; and then, either draw your line gently across the water, or carry your bait down the stream, as above directed. The eddy by the side of a mill-tail, or flood-gate, or water-fall, is a good place to try the lob-worm. The deep holes near overhanging trees and old stumps, and those parts of the river where the stream has undermined the banks, are also the haunts of the largest trout.

"When the water is discolored by rain, your tackle may be strong, and you will not easily be seen by the fish; but if the water be clear, and the day bright, your only chance for taking trout with the worm, will be by using fine tackle, and keeping completely out of sight.

"The lob-worm is also used, without any shot on the line, after sunset in summer, by drawing it on the top of the water, across a sharp mill-stream, when the trout will rise and take the bait at the top of the water, as they would the fly; and in this manner very large trout are frequently taken.

"The gentle, or maggot, is a good bait for a trout, during the months of June, July, and August, and may be used, with a small float, carrying one or two shot-corns, in mill-dams, ponds, and other still waters, allowing your bait to nearly touch the ground.

"I shall now describe a method of bottom-fishing, with a bait which I have found, in certain situations and seasons, more successful than any other. The same tackle may be used as before described for the gentle, *i. e.* a fine gut bottom, with hook No. 10, and a small quill float, carrying one or two small shot-corns.

"Procure a wide-necked bottle, and fill it with blue bottle-flies, or the flies caught on newly scattered cow or horse-dung, and with two of these flies bait your hook, and

let it nearly touch the ground In this manner I have caught many fine trout in mill-dams, ponds, and deep quiet waters, during July and August, when not a single fish would rise at any kind of artificial fly which could be offered. I have never seen the method described by any author on the subject, but I can with confidence recommend it to my brothers of the angle, at those times when the usual baits fail to procure a dish of fish.

" When you have struck a good fish, keep him as near the top of the water as possible, and carry him down the stream above the weeds, and, if you succeed in getting him into clear water, with a little care he is your own."

Cotton gives the following method of angling by the hand with a ground bait: " And by much the best of all other, is with a line full as long, or a yard longer than your rod; with no more than one hair* next the hook, and for two or three lengths above it; and no more than one small pellet of shot for your plumb ; your hook little; your worms of the smaller brandlings, very well scoured; and only one upon your hook at a time, which is thus to be baited: The point of your hook is to be put in at the very tag of his tail, and run up his body quite over all the arming, and still stripped on an inch at least upon the hair; the head remaining part hanging downward. And with this line and hook, thus baited, you are evermore to angle in the streams, always in a clear rather than a troubled water, and always up the river, still casting out your worm before you with a light one-handed rod, like an artificial fly, where it will be taken, sometimes at the top, or within a very little of the superficies of the water, and almost always before that light plumb can sink it to the bottom; both by reason of the stream, and also that you must always keep your worm in motion by drawing still back

* If the American Angler prefer any of Walton's or Cotton's instructions, he should in all cases use fine gut, instead of hair as described.

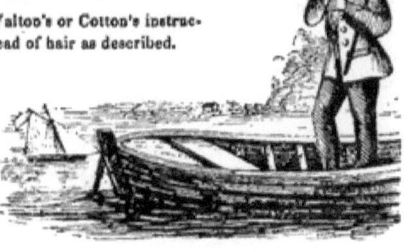

towards you, as if you were angling with a fly. And believe me, whoever will try, shall find this the best way of all others to angle with a worm, in a bright water especially; but then his rod must be very light and pliant, and very true and finely made, which, with a skilful hand will do wonders, and in a clear stream is undoubtedly the best way of angling for a trout or grayling, with a worm, by many degrees, that any man can make choice of, and of most ease and delight to the Angler. To which let me add, that if the Angler be of a constitution that will suffer him to wade, and will slip into the tail of a stream, to the calf of the leg or the knee, and so keep off the bank, he shall almost take what fish he pleases."

The following pertinent remarks for clear weather, from Blaine, should have place in the memory of every lover of trout angling:

"Trout are to be taken in clear weather, when they will not touch either minnow or fly; and there is certainly more art and sportsmanship in fishing with the worm at that time, than some people imagine or acknowledge. When to the advantage of bright weather are added those of clear and shallow streams, much artifice must be employed. Your tackle very fine. your hook small, (No. 5, 6, or 7,) and your baits well scoured and lively. A wheel will enable you to vary the length of your line as occasion dictates; and though in general it must be as long or longer than your rod, yet where there is wood, &c. &c., you may by shortening it, get at the holes, and still contrive to *keep out of sight*, for completely so to be must never be forgotten—kneel, stoop or stand—out of sight you must be; and then if you can lightly and neatly drop in a lively brandling, near the likely holds or haunts in a strong stream, especially near the top of it, let the sun shine ever so bright, be the wind rough or calm, and the water ever so clear, you will kill fish when they are not to be taken by any other mode."

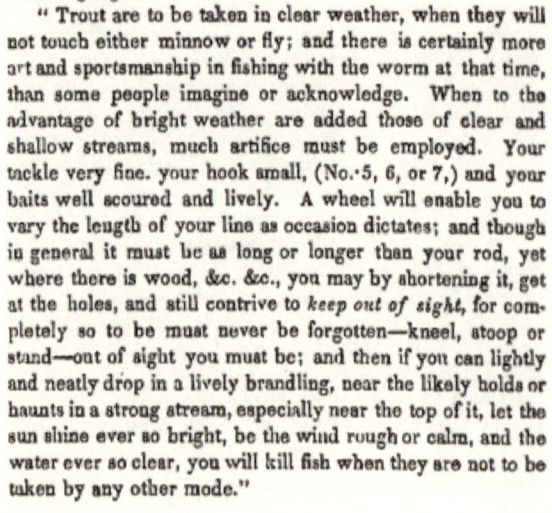

Franks gives the following pleasant mode of killing a trout which is well worthy of repetition:

"And now, Theophilus, I must reprove your precipitancy, because a great error in young Anglers; be mindful, therefore, to observe directions in handling and managing your rod and line, and cautiously keeping out of sight; all of which precautions are requisite accomplishments, which of necessity ought to be understood by every ingenious Angler; and so is that secret of striking, which should never be used with violence, because by a moderate touch, and a slender proportion of strength, the artist for the most part hath best success. Another caution you must take along with you; I mean when you observe game to make out, that is, when he bolts, or when he launcheth himself to the utmost extent of your rod and line, which a well-fed fish at all times, frequently attempts, upon the least advantage he gains of the Angler; be mindful, therefore, to throw him line enough if, provided, you purpose to see his destruction; yet with this caution, that you be not too liberal. On the other hand, too straight a line brings equal hazard, so that to poise your fish and your foresight together, as by keeping one eye at the point of your rod, and the other be sure you direct on your game, which comes nearest the mediums of art, and the rules and rudiments of your precedent directions. But this great round may be easily solved, for if when you discover your fish fag his fins, you may rationally conclude he then struggles with death, and then is your time to triffle him on shore on some smooth shelf of sand, where you may boldly land him, before his scales encumber the soil.

"Lest precipitancy spoil sport, I'll preponder my rudiments and prognosticate, here's a fish, or something like it, a fair hansel for a foolish fisher. This capering, for aught I know, may cost him his life, for I resolve to hold his nose to the grindstone: dance on and die, that is the way to your

silent sepulchre, for upon that silty, gravelly, shelf of sand I resolve to land him, or lose all I have. And now I fancy him weary of life, as aged people that are weary of infirmities, yet I want courage to encounter him, lest fearing to lose him, which if I do I impair my reputation. However, here is nobody but trees to reprove me, except these rocks, and they tell no tales. Well, then, as he wants no agility to evade me, I'll endeavor with activity to approach him, so that the difference between us will be only this, that he covets acquaintance with but one element, and I would compel him to examine another. Now he runs to divert me or himself, but I must invite him nearer home, for I fancy none such distance.

"Though his fins fag, and his tail wriggles, his strength declines, his gills look languid, and his mettle declineth—all of which interpret tokens of submission—still, the best news I bring him is summons of death. Yet, let not my rashness pre-eugage me to the loss of my game, for, to neglect my rudiments is to ruin my design, which in plain terms, is the ruin of this resolute fish, who, seemingly, now measures and mingles his proportion with more than one element, and, doomed to a trance, he prostrates himself on the surface of the calms, dead to my apprehension, save only I want credit to believe him dead, when, calling to mind my former precipitancy, that invited me to a loss, and so this adventure may prove, if I look not well about me, to land and strand him on that shelf of sand, where I resolve with my rod to survey his dimensions Welcome on shore, my languishing combatant, if only to entertain my friend Arnoldus."

The following beautiful lines from the poet and fisherman Gay, "*run*" directly from the "*reel*" of his imagination, and from the crystal "*waters*" of the fount of inspiration; every "*line*" "*plumb'd*" to the nicety of a "*hair*," the "*point*" needs but the aid of the "*fly*" press of the printer and the "*cast*" of the founder, to stereotype on, or cause it to "*worm*" itself into, the "*gentle*" affections of every true piscatorial sportsman, and make it ever "*float*" around the "*net*"-work of his memory, giving him "*buoyancy*" of spirit, a "*full length*" of courage, and a "*mess*" of patience, sufficient to make him master of his "*rod*."

> "He lifts his silver gills above the flood,
> And greedily sucks in th' unfaithful food,
> Then downward plunges with the fraudful prey,
> And bears with joy the little spoil away;
> Soon, in smart pain, he feels the dire mistake,
> Lashes the wave, and beats the foamy lake
> With sudden rage he now aloft appears,
> And in his eye convulsive anguish hears;
> And now again, impatient of the wound,
> He rolls, and writhes his straining body round,
> Then headlong shoots beneath the dashing tide,
> The trembling fins the boiling wave divide:
> Now hope exalts the fisher's beating heart,
> Now, he turns pale, and fears his dubious art;
> He views the trembling fish with longing eyes,
> While the line stretches with the unwieldly prize;
> Each motion humors with his steady hands,
> And one slight hair the mighty bulk commands;
> Till tired at last, despoil'd of all his strength,
> The game athwart the stream unfolds his length;
> He now, with pleasure, views the gasping prize
> Gnash his sharp teeth, and roll his blood-shot eyes;
> Then draws him to the shore, with artful care,
> And lifts his nostrils in the sickening air;
> Upon the burden'd stream he floating lies,
> Stretches his quivering fins, and gasping dies."

How to Cook a Trout. As the sportsman, after a few hours diversion and toil, often needs a little refreshment, and as a meal of his own providing is generally ate with more zest and satisfaction, he should be possessed of the proper information, either to prepare, or direct the preparation, of his re past. Barker, before spoken of, gives the following approved methods, which will be found sufficiently epicurean to tickle the palate of the most dainty, or to bring into requisition the talent of a most finished Parisian cook.

" We must have one dish of broyled trouts; when the entrails are taken out, you must cut them across the side; being washed clean, you must take some sweet herbs, thyme, sweet marjoram, and parsley, chopped small, the trouts being cut somewhat thick, and fill the cuts full with the chopped herbs; then make your gridiron fit to put them on, being well cooled with rough-suet; then lay the trouts on a charcoal fire, and baste them with fresh butter until you think they are well broyled. The sauce must be butter and vinegar, and the yolk of an egg beaten; then beat it altogether, and put it on the fish for the service.

" The best dish of stewed fish that ever I heard commended of the English, was dressed in this way: first, they were broyled on a charcoal fire, being cut on the sides as fried trouts; then the stew-pan was taken, and set on a chafing-dish of coles; there was put into the stew-pan half a pound of sweet butter, one pennyworth of beaten cinnamon, a little vinegar; when all was melted, the fish was put into the pan, and covered with a covering-plate, so kept stewing half an hour; being turned, then taken out of the stew-pan and dished; be sure to beat your sauce before you put it on your fish; then squeeze a lemon on your fish: it was the best dish of fish that ever I heard commended by noblemen and gentlemen. This is our English fashion. The Italian, he stews upon a chafing-dish of coles, with white wine, cloves, and mace, nutmegs sliced, and a little ginger; you must understand, when this fish is stewed, the same liquor the fish is stewed in must be beaten with some sweet butter and the juice of a lemon before it is dished for the service.

" The French doth add to this a slice or two of bacon.

Though I have been no traveller, I may speak of it, for I have been admitted into the most ambassadors' kitchens that have come into England this forty years, and do wait on them still, at the Lord Protector's charge, and I am duly paid for it; sometimes I see slovenly scullions abuse good fish most grossly.

"We must have a trout-pie to eat hot, and another to eat cold: the first thing you must gain must be a peck of the best wheaten flour, two pounds of butter, two quarts of milk, new from the cow, half a dozen of eggs to make the paste. Where I was born there is not a girl of ten years of age, but can make a pie. For one pie, the trouts shall be opened, and the guts taken out, and cleaned, and washed; seasoned with pepper and salt, then laid in the pie; half a pound of currants put among the fish, with a pound of sweet butter cut in pieces and set on the fish, so close it up; when it is baked and come out of the oven, pour into the pie three or four spoonsfull of claret wine, so dish it up and send it to the table. These trouts shall cut close and moist.

"For the other pie, the trouts shall be boyled a little; it will make the fish rise, and eat more crisp; season them with pepper and salt, and lay them in the pie; you must put more butter in this pie than the other, for this will keep, and must be filled up with butter when it cometh forth of the oven."

A common mode of cooking the trout, is by cutting them, as before directed by Barker, seasoning them well with salt and pepper, dredging them with oat meal or wheat flour, and frying them in butter.

Another method is to cut them in two, sprinkle with a small quantity of Cayenne pepper, a due proportion of salt, and broil them.

Of the Artificial Fly. The idea of having flies for every

month in the year, is long since exploded, and although some authors in England still arrange them according to the months, it is found that they cannot be depended upon as a certainty. Walton, one of the first authors who arranged them in this manner, in his preface has these remarks: "That whereas it is said by many, that in fly-fishing for trout, the Angler must observe his twelve several flies for the twelve months of the year; I say, he that follows that rule shall be as sure to catch fish, and be as wise as he that makes hay by the fair days in an almanac, and no surer; for those very flies that used to appear about and on the water in one month of the year, may, the following year, come almost a month sooner or later, as the same year proves colder or hotter; but for the generality, three or four flies, neatly and rightly made, and not too big, serve for a trout in most rivers all the summer; and for winter, fly-fishing is as useful as an almanac out of date."

Barker gives his instructions in his favorite vein, thus:

"A brother of the angle must always be sped
With three black Palmers, and also three red;
And all made with heckles. In a cloudy day
Or in windy weather, angle you may.

"But morning and evening, if the day be bright;
And the chief point of all is to keep out of sight.
'In the month of May, none but the May-fly,
For every month one.' is a pitiful lie.

"The hawthorn-fly must be very small;
And the sandy hog's-hair is, sure, best of all
(For the mallard-wing May-fly, and peacock's train,
Will look like the flesh-fly) to kill trout amain.

"The oak-fly* is good if it have a brown wing,
So is the grasshopper, that in July doth sing;

* The oak-fly is also known in England by the names of the ash-fly, the woodcock fly, and the cannon, or dowuhill-fly.

With a green body make him, on a middle sized hook,
But when you have catch'd fish, then play the good cook.

" Once more, my good brother, I'll speak in thy ear;
Hog's, red cow's, and bear's wool to float best appear;
And so doth your fur, if it rightly fall;
But always remember, make two, and make all."

It would be equally absurd to name any precise description of fly for any particular month in this country, and perhaps more so, as our weather is more changeable than that of any part of Europe.

There are many kinds of flies used both here and in England, but two descriptions have the preference, and accompany all Anglers as the universal fly, and are consequently necessary requisites to a well arranged Fly-Angler's establishment. The *Red Hackle*, or *Soldier Palmer*, and the *Black Hackle*, or *Black Palmer*, are " *the Flies.*" They are both made in a variety of ways, with different colored bodies, but with the same kind of hackle or legs. The most killing kind of the red hackle is made with a red worsted or mohair body, wound around with gold twist. The black hackle is used more particularly in very bright days, when the sun shines unobscured by clouds. It is made with black worsted body, and a black cock's hackle for legs; the body is sometimes wound with silver twist, which in many streams, at certain times, offers additional attractions to the dainty subject of our discourse. They are both made in various ways and of various sizes, and are known under different names. The body of the red hackle is sometimes made with crimson, black, yellow, green, and various other hues of worsted, for bodies; the black, also, with red, white, green, and other colors intermingled. They are also made under different names with and without wings.

The *White Hackle*, or *Miller*, is a good fly in dark, lowering days. It is made with a white worsted body, and

white dog's hair for legs, and is sometimes varied with a dark colored or gold twist; also, sometimes with wings and sometimes without. The *Green Drake* is also considered a good fly in some streams. It is made with a yellow floss silk or worsted body, wound with a red or ginger hackle for legs, and dark yellow or light green parrot feather for wings.

As there are no particular names given to the different varieties of flies with us, the following list from Hofland, will be of assistance to the American fly-fisher, in making up his book of flies.

The Chantrey. It takes its name from being a favorite of Sir Francis Chantrey, the celebrated sculptor. Body, copper-colored peacock's herl, ribbed with gold twist; legs, a black hackle; wings, partridge or brown hen's feather, or pheasant's tail. Hook No. 9 or 10.

Hofland's Fancy. Body, reddish, dark brown silk; legs, red hackle; wings, woodcock's wing; tail, two or three strands of red hackle. Hook No. 10.

March Brown, also called the *Dun Drake.* Body, fur of the hare's ear, ribbed with olive silk; legs, partridge hackle; wings, tail feather of the partridge; tail, two or three strands of the partridge hackle Hook No. 8 or 9.

Blue Dun. Body, dubbed with water-rat's fur, and ribbed with yellow silk; legs, a dun hen's hackle; wings from the feather of the starling's wing; tail, two strands of a grizzle cock's hackle. Hook No. 10.

Carshalton. Body, black silk, ribbed with silver twist, legs, a dark grizzle hackle; wings, the dark feather of the starling's wing, made spare and short. Hook No. 10.

Carshalton Cocktail. A dun fly. Body, light blue fur; legs, dark dun hackle; wings, the inside feather of a teal's wing; tail, two fibres of a white cock's hackle. Hook No. 9 or 10.

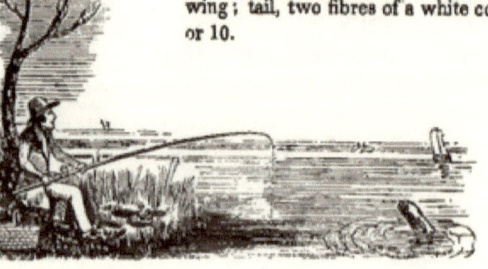

The Pale Yellow Dun. A very killing fly. Body, yellow mohair, or martin's pale yellow fur, tied with yellow silk; wings, the lightest part of a feather from a young starling's wing. Hook No. 12.

The Orange Dun. Body, red squirrel's fur, ribbed with gold thread; legs, red hackle; wings from the starling's wing; tail, two fibres of red cock's hackle. Hook No. 9.

The Coachman. Body, copper-colored peacock's herl; legs, red hackle; wings, from landrail. Hook No. 8.

Cow-Dung Fly. Useful chiefly in dark, windy weather. Body, dull lemon colored mohair; legs, red hackle wings, from feathers of the landrail or starling's wing. Hook No. 8 or 9.

The Hare's Ear Dun. Body, the fur of the hare's ear; wings, the feather from a starling's wing; tail, two fibres of the brown feather of a starling's wing. Hook No. 10, sometimes dressed without the wisk or tail.

Edmonson's Welsh Fly. Body, dull orange mohair; legs, the back feather of a partridge; wings, the feathers from a woodcock's wing, or the tail of a hen grouse. Hook No. 8.

The Kingdom or Kindon. Body, pale yellow silk, ribbed with crimson silk; legs, black hackle; wings, the feather of a woodcock's wing. Hook No. 9.

Brown Shiner. This is a hackle fly. Body, peacock's aerl, twisted spare, with a grouse hackle over it.

Gravel or Spider-fly. Body, water-rat's fur; legs, black hackle; wings, the feather from the rump of a partridge. Also made with a dark dun hackle. Hook No. 10 or 11.

The Iron Blue Body, the fur of the water-rat; legs, a light dun hackle; wings, the tail feather of a tom-tit, or of an American robin.

The Great Red Spinner, may be used as an evening fly during the whole summer season. Body, hog's wool, red

and brown, mixed with gold twist; legs, bright red cock's hackle; wings, the light feather of the starling's wing; tail, three strands of a red cock's hackle. Hook No. 7.

Black Gnat. Body, black hackle, or ostrich herl, tied with black silk; wings, the feather from a starling's wing. Hook No. 13.

Wren Tail. An excellent killer in small bright streams, is always dressed as a hackle fly. Body, dark orange silk, with wings and legs of a wren's tail. Although the feathers of a wren's tail cannot be properly called hackles, they are here used as such, and this remark will apply to other feathers similarly employed. Hook No. 12.

The Bracken Clock. A kind of beetle. Body, peacock's herl, dressed full, and tied with purple silk; wings, feather of a pheasant's breast. Hook No. 9 or 10.

Red Ant, in imitation of the small red ant. Body, peacock's herl, made full at the tail, and spare toward the head; legs, red or ginger cock's hackle; wings, from the light feather of the starling's wing. Hook No. 9 or 10. By substituting ostrich herl for peacock's herl, and a black hackle instead of a red one, the black ant may be imitated.

The Sand Fly. Body, the fur from a hare's neck twisted round silk of the same color; legs, a ginger hen's hackle; wings, the feather from the landrail's wing. Hook No. 9.

The Stone Fly. One of the larger kind of flies used in windy weather. Body, fur of the hare's ear, mixed with brown and yellow mohair, and ribbed with yellow silk, the yellow color towards the tail; legs, a brownish red hackle; wings, the dark feather of the mallard's wing; tail, two or three fibres of the mottled feather of the partridge. Hook No. 6.

Alder Fly. Body, peacock's herl, tied with dark brown silk; legs, coch-a-bonddu hackle; wings, the brown speckled feather of a mallard's back. Hook No. 8. Sometimes dress-

ed on a No. 6 or 7 hook, and winged with the red rump feather of a pheasant, when it is found excellent as a lake fly.

Green Drake. Body, yellow floss silk, ribbed with brown silk, the extreme head and tail coppery peacock's herl; legs, a red or ginger hackle; wings, the mottled wing of the mallard, stained olive; tail or whisk, three hairs from a rabbit's whiskers. Hook No. 6. The natural fly appears in May and June, in such vast numbers that the trout become glutted with them, and grow fat upon their good living. Sometimes preferred dressed on a No. 4 or 5 hook.

Grey Drake. Body, white floss silk, ribbed with dark brown or mulberry colored silk; head, and top of the tail, peacock's herl; legs, a grizzle cock's hackle; wings, a mallard's mottled feather, made to stand upright; tail, three whiskers of a rabbit.

The Black Palmer. This is a standard fly, and its merits are too well known to need a description. It is a valuable drop-fly in dark, rainy, or windy weather, and in full water. Body, ostrich's herl, ribbed with silver twist, and a black cock's hackle over all.

The Soldier Palmer. This fly, and its varieties, may be considered the most general fly on the list, and many Anglers never fit up a fly-book without having a red hackle of some kind for a drop-fly. The one given as a specimen may be used with success for large trout, and a strong water; but for a bright stream a smaller hook must be adopted, and the fly must be more spare of hackle; and, should the water be very clear, the gold twist had better be omitted, and a spare hackle be tied with red twist; another variety, is the using a black hackle for the head of the fly, body red mohair, or squirrel's fur, ribbed with gold twist, and red cock's hackle over all.

The Governor. Body, coppery colored peacock's herl, ribbed with gold twist, tipped with scarlet twist; legs, red

or ginger hackle; wings, the light part of a pheasant's wing. Hook No. 9.

Coch-a-bonddu. This fly is a well known favorite throughout the United Kingdom, though not always under the same name. The cock that furnishes the peculiarly mixed deep and red black feather, necessary to make this fly, is in great estimation. Body, peacock's herl; legs and wings, red and black, or coch-a-bonddu hackle. Hook No. 8 or 9. For clear streams it is dressed on a No. 12 hook.

The Yellow Sally. Body, pale yellow fur, or mohair, ribbed with fawn colored silk; legs, a ginger hackle; wings, a white hackle, died yellow. Hook No. 9.

Ginger Hackle. Body, short and spare, of yellow silk; legs and wings, a ginger hackle. Hook No. 8.

Grouse Hackle. Body, varied to the water and season, such as peacock's herl, orange silk, &c.; legs and wings, a grouse hackle. Hook from No. 8 to 12.

The Dotteril Hackle. Body made of yellow silk; legs and wings from the feather of a dotteril. Hook from No. 6 to 12. This is an excellent fly, and in the north parts of England considered superior even to the red hackle.

The Water Cricket. Body, orange floss silk, tied on with black silk; legs, are made best with peacock's topping: if this cannot be easily procured, a black cock's hackle will answer the purpose. Either of these must be wound all down the body, and the fibres then snapped off.

The Blue-Bottle Fly. Body, dark blue floss silk, tied with brown silk; legs, a cock's black hackle; wings, feather of the starling's wing. Hook No. 9 to 12.*

Common House-Fly. Body, ostrich herl, rather full; legs, a black hackle; wings, the feather of the starling's wing.

---

* The sizes of hooks used by Hofland are entirely too small for the majority of our streams. Where a hook No. 9 or 10 is recommended, No. 4 or 5 should be used. Those spoken of by Blaine are more suitable.

The following night, and other flies, are from Blaine:

The Mealy White Moth. Upper wings, the dappled light feather of the mallard, or any very light clear colored feather; under wings, the soft mealy feather of a white owl, or in default, any soft white feather; body, white rabbit's fur or white ostrich herl, dressed full, and exhibiting a brown head; legs, a white cock's hackle, carried two or three turns only behind the wings. Hook No. 3, 4 or 5.

The Mealy Brown Moth. Upper wings, the dappled feather of a mallard, dyed a reddish brown; under wings, the soft feather of a brown owl, or a soft reddish feather or two from the landrail; body, any soft brown fur, as of the hare, brown hog's down, bear's fur, and the nearest the shade is to tan the better, to be dressed moderately full and long; legs, a brown cock's hackle, carried one turn beyond that of the preceding fly. Hook No. 3, 4 or 5.

The Mealy Cream Moth. Upper wings, the cream colored feather of the gray owl; under wings, the soft feathers of the same a shade lighter; body, any dubbing or fur of a cream color; legs, a ginger hackle, wrapped three times. Hook No 4, 5, or 6.

The Evening White-Winged Harl Fly. Wings, of a white fowl's feather; body, peacock's herl, dressed full and short; legs, a very minute portion of red hackle. Hook No. 5, 6, 7, or 8.

The Humble Bee. Wings, of the cock black-bird, to lie flat; body, fore part dubbed with black glossy mohair or fur; hinder part of a deep orange; legs, dress two-thirds of the body with a brown hackle. Hook No. 3 or 4.

The Large Blow, or *Flesh-Fly.* Wings, any transparent looking feather, to be dressed flat; body, dubbed with black bear's fur, and a very small portion of glossy purple mohair with it, tied with silk of the same. Dress the body full, and pick out the dubbing to make it look rough; legs, a very dark

brown or black hackle, dressed two turns only behind the wings.

The Hazle Fly, or Lady Bird, crustaceous wings. A small stumpy portion of the red feather of a partridge's tail or landrail's wing, to be dressed extended; under wing, transparent looking feather of a hen black-bird, rather longer than the former, to be dressed thin, and rather less extended; body, dubbed thick and round with dark purple mohair, and a small quantity of brown fur intermingled, which, when picked out, form the legs. Hook No. 7 or 8.

The Orl Fly. Wings, a brown hen's or a landrail's ruddy feather, to be dressed long and close to the back; body, ribbed alternately with dark brown and orange dubbing, adding antennæ, or horns; legs, a grizzle cock's hackle. Hook No. 6 or 7.

Cinnamon Fly, or Fetid Light Brown. Wings of a ruddy cream color, from the feather of the landrail, or any other of a flame color, to be dressed long, large, and flat; body, seal's fur of the natural hue; legs, a reddish brown hackle. Hook No. 6.

There are many other flies not enumerated in the foregoing lists, which the trout will occasionally fancy. On this subject, Blaine says:

"The number of artificial flies required for the practice of fly-fishing, is very differently estimated by different writers. The angling patriarch Walton, gives a list of twelve 'reasonable flies,' which his friend Cotton judiciously doubled. The experience of a century and a half has since greatly increased the list, as more extended observation proved the universality of appetite in fish for the insect race. It appears, therefore, strangely extraordinary to find a writer of such credit as Salter, contracting the required numbers into the confined limits of Red and Black Palmers, Red and Black Hackles, Ant-flies, the May-fly, Stone-fly, Gnats, a Red

Spinner, and a Moth! A fly-hook so furnished, might secure a medley of roach, dace, chub, and a few unhappy trout, which had strayed out of bounds; but the exhibition of both bait and fish would not be very creditable to the professed fly-fisher. We have no doubt that many of the flies which the books of some excellent Anglers contain, are seldom called into action; but as they are when collected not very cumbrous in carriage, eat and drink nothing, and may now and then suit the 'lucky occasion,' we see no disadvantage, but approve the judgment of those Anglers in being furnished with them. In our own fishing practice, we have met with numerous gratifying proofs of the benefit of an ample store; but infinitely more have we felt the benefit arising from our ability to increase our stock from our own resources, whenever we found occasion so to do.

Many of the flies mentioned will be found useful to the Angler in this country. They may be had at the regular tackle stores, can be made to order, or procured from England. Some difficulty may arise should the sportsman wish to make his own flies, in procuring the exact feathers and materials as described, but similar feathers can be taken from many of our birds, or can be dyed the same colors, which will answer every purpose.

Although flies of every description can be procured in the principal cities, there are many in distant parts of the country who will not be able to procure them at all. Besides, the most skilful fisher may have the misfortune to lose his best flies at the beginning of a day's sport, and it would be well, therefore, for every brother of this branch of angling to be always ready with his materials and his knowledge for making the artificial fly. In fact, it is the practice of many Anglers, always to examine the waters and shake the boughs of the trees, to procure the latest insect that will most probably

fall a prey to the voracious trout, and imitate nature's handiwork on the spot.

Gay, the celebrated poet, who was a great proficient in fly-fishing, in his "Rural Sports," gives the following beautiful description of fly-making:

> "He shakes the boughs that on the margin grow,
> Which o'er the stream a waving forest throw,
> When, if an insect fall, (his certain guide,)
> He gently takes him from the whirling tide,
> Examines well his form with curious eyes,
> His gaudy vest, his wings, his horns, his size;
> Then round the hook the chosen fur he winds,
> And on the back a speckled feather binds;
> So just the colors shine in every part,
> That nature seems to live again in art."

And also—

> "To frame the little animal provide
> All the gay hues that wait on female pride:
> Let nature guide thee; sometimes golden wire
> The shining bellies of the fly require;
> The peacock's plumes thy tackle must not fail,
> Nor the dear purchase of the sable's tail;
> Each gaudy bird some slender tribute brings,
> And lends the glowing insect proper wings;
> Silks of all colors must their aid impart,
> And every fur promote the fisher's art:
> So the gay lady, with expensive care,
> Borrows the pride of land, of sea, of air;
> Furs, pearls, and plumes, the glittering thing displays,
> Dazzles our eyes, and easy hearts betrays."

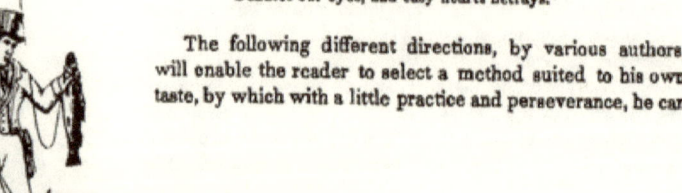

The following different directions, by various authors, will enable the reader to select a method suited to his own taste, by which with a little practice and perseverance, he can succeed in forming flies suitable for his different fishing-grounds, with very little trouble.

How to make the Artificial Winged Fly.—(Hofland.)—
" There are several modes adopted in making the artificial fly; one is to tie the wings on the hook, in the natural position, in the first instance; another method is, to place the feathers for the wings in a reverse position, in the first instance, and naturally afterwards; and the third and last way, is to tie the wings on the hook, after the body is made, instead of beginning the fly with them.

" The most expeditious way of completing a number of flies, is to have every necessary material arranged immediately under your eye, and every article separate and distinct; all the hooks, gut, or hair, wings, hackle, dubbing, silk, and wax, ready assorted and prepared for instant use. The hooks require to be sized for your different flies; the gut requires the most careful examination and adjustment; the hackles have to be stripped, and the dubbing to be well mixed; the silk assorted, and to be of the finest texture; and the wings to be tied the length of the hook they are to be fastened to, in order that the fibres of the feather may be all brought into the small compass of the hook. This previous trouble not only saves time, but insures a degree of neatness that is otherwise almost unattainable.

" The tying of the wings is thus performed: a piece of well waxed silk is laid in a noose on the fore-finger of the left hand, the wings or feathers are put on the under part of the noose, and at the distance of the length of the wing required; the thumb is then applied closely to the feather, and with one end of the noose in the mouth and the other in the right hand, the noose is drawn quite tight, and the silk is then cut within an inch of the knot, to leave a handle by which to hold the wing. If the thumb is not closely pressed, the feathers will be pulled away.

"*First Method—How to make the Fly with the Wings in the natural position in the first instance.* Hold the hook by the bend, with the point downwards, between the fore-finger and thumb of the left hand; with your waxed silk in your right hand, give one or two turns round the bare hook, about midway; lay the end of the gut along the upper side of the hook, (if tied on the under side, the fly will not swim true, but continually revolve,) wrap the silk firmly until you get within a few turns of the top; you then take the wings, lay them along the shank with the right hand, and hold them firmly in their place to the hook with the left hand. Next, tie the feather tightly at the point of contact, with two or three turns; cut off the superfluous ends of the feather, and tying the head of the fly very firmly, you carry the silk around the gut beyond the head, that the end of the hook may not chafe, or cut away the gut; then retrace the silk, until you come to the tying on of the wings. Divide the wings equally, and carry the silk through the division alternately, two or three times, to keep the wings distinct from each other. Now prepare the hackle, by drawing back the fibres, and by having two or three less on the butt, on the side of the feather that comes next the hook, that it may revolve without twisting away. Tie the butt-end of the hackle close to the wings, having its upper or dark side to the head of the fly. The Scotch reverse this, and tie the hackle with its under side to the head; and likewise strip the fibres entirely off that side which touches the hook. Take the dubbing between the fore-finger and the thumb of the right hand, twist it very thinly about your silk, and carry it around the hook as far as you intend the hackle or legs to be carried, and hold it between the fore-finger and thumb of the left hand, or fasten it. Then, with your plyers, carry the hackle around your hook, close under the wings, and down to where you have brought your silk and dubbing, then continue to finish your body, by carrying over the end of the hackle; and when you have made the body of sufficient length, fasten off by bringing the silk twice or thrice loosely around the hook, and passing the end through the coils, to make all tight.

"Some finish the body of this fly thus:—when the hackle is fastened, after it has made the legs of the fly, the bare silk is carried to the end of the intended body; dubbing is then carried up to the legs and there fastened.

"*Second Method.* This manner of proceeding differs from the first in fixing on of the wings. When you have fastened the gut and hook together, to the point where the wings are to be tied, apply the wings to the hook, with the butt of the feather lying uppermost; when the wings are well fastened, pull them back into their natural position; and when the head of the fly is finished, pass the silk alternately through the wings; and, having your silk well tied to the roots of the wings, (and not over the roots,) the fly is to be completed, as in the first method, having cut off the roots of the feather."

How to make the Hackle or Palmer Fly.—(Rennie.)— "Hold your hook in a horizontal position, with the shank downwards, and the bent of it between the fore-finger and thumb of your left hand; and having a fine bristle, or strand of silk-worm gut, and other materials, lying by you, take half a yard of red marking silk, well waxed, and with your right hand give it four or five turns about the shank of the hook, inclining the turns to the right hand; when you are near the shank, turn it into such a loop as you are hereafter directed to make for fastening off, and draw it tight, leaving the ends of the silk to hang down at each end of the hook. Having singed the end of your bristle, lay the same along the inside of the shank of the hook, as low as the bent, and whip four or five times round; then singing the other end of the bristle to a fit length, turn it over to the back of the shank, and.

pinching it into a proper form, whip down and fasten off as before directed, which will bring both ends of the silk into the bent. After you have waxed your silk again, take three or four strands of ostrich feather, and holding them and the bent of your hook as at first directed, the feathers to your left hand and the roots in the bent of your hook, with that end of the silk which you have just now waxed, whip them three or four times round and fasten off; then turning the feathers to the right, and twisting them and the silk with your forefinger and thumb, wind them round the shank of the hook, still supplying the short strands with new ones, as they fail, till you come to the end and fasten off. When you have so done, clip off the ends of the feathers and trim the body of the palmer small at the extremity, and full in the middle, and wax both ends of your silk, which are now divided, and lie at either end of the hook.

" Lay your work by you; and taking a strong bold hackle, with fibres about half an inch long, straighten the stem carefully, and holding the small end between the fore-finger and thumb of your left hand, with those of the right stroke the fibres the contrary way to that which they naturally lie; and taking the hook, and holding it as before, lay the hackle into the bent of the hook, with the hollow (which is the palest) side upwards, and whip it very fast to its place; in doing whereof, be careful not to tie in many of the fibres: or if you should chance to do so, pick them out with the point of a very large needle.

" When the hackle is thus made fast, the utmost care and nicety is necessary in winding it on; for if you fail in this, your fly is spoiled, and you must begin all again: to prevent which, keeping the hollow or pale side to your left hand, and as much as possible the side of the stem down on the dubbing, wind the hackle twice round; and holding fast what you have so wound, pick out the loose fibres which you may have

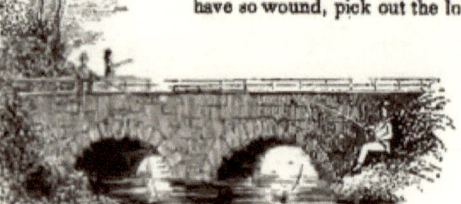

taken in, and make another turn; then lay hold of the hackle with the third and fourth fingers of your left hand, with which you may extend it while you disengage the loose fibres as before.

"In this manner proceed till you come within an eighth of an inch of the end of the shank, where you will find an end of silk hanging, and by which time you will find the fibres at the great end of the hackle something discomposed; clip these off close to the stem, and with the end of your middle finger press the stem close to the hook, while with the fore-finger of your right hand, you turn the silk into a loop; which when you have twice put over the end of the shank of the hook, loop and all, your work is safe.

"Then wax that end of the silk which you now used, and turn it over as before, till you have taken up nearly all that remained of the hook, observing to lay the turns neatly side by side; and lastly clip off the ends of the silk."

On making the Palmer or Hackle-Fly, with the cock's or hen's feathers, Hofland remarks, "is simply as described in the fore-named methods, (pages 110 and 111,) by twisting on the legs and body, taking care that the hackle has fibres as long as, or rather longer than, the hook it is to be twisted upon.

"But in making hackle-flies with birds' feathers, such as those of the snipe, dotteril, &c., the feather is prepared by stripping off the superfluous parts at the butt-end, then drawing back a sufficient quantity of fibre to make the fly; take the feather by the root and point, with both hands, (having its outside uppermost,) and put the whole of the fibres into your mouth, and wet them, that they adhere together back to back. When the gut is fastened to the hook, you must tie on the feather near to the head of the hook, and the feather may be tied either at the butt-end or point; then twist the feather twice or thrice round the hook, and fasten it by one

or more loops; the fibres of the feather will then lie the reverse way, cut off the superfluous part of the feather, that remains after tying, and twist on the body of the required length; fasten by two loops, draw down the fibres of the feather to the bend, and the fly is finished.

" If tinsel, or gold and silver twist be required for the body of the fly, it must be tied on after the hackle, but carried round the body before the hackle makes the legs. If the tinsel be required only at the tail of the fly, it must be tied on immediately after the gut and hook are put together; the hackle next, and then the body, &c.

" The choice of your fly must depend much upon the nature of the water you fish in, and the state of the weather, if the water be full, and somewhat colored, your flies may be of the larger and darker kind; if, on the contrary, the water should be low and clear, and the day bright, your fly should be dressed accordingly, *i. e.*, it should be pale in color and spare in the dressing."

Of the different Feathers spoken of. A very good imitation of the starling's wing, which is a plain pale grey, can be taken from the wing of a duck, and also from the wing and tail of the black-bird. The mallard's wing, which is a light grey feather, with black specks, can be nearly imitated by the feather taken from the wing and shoulder of the common drake, and also by some of the light colored feathers of the game-hen. A similar to the landrail, which is a palish brown, can be supplied from the woodcock or pheasant. The cocha-bonddu feather is neither more nor less than the black and red feather of the cock.

CHAPTER VII.

OF THE PIKE JACK, PICKEREL OR MUSCALINGA.

This, with the Trout, may be considered the universal fish of the world. It appears to inhabit the inland waters of all northern countries. We read of them as far back as the days of ancient Rome; and they have been known in Germany and Poland from time immemorial. A late writer on Natural History in England, says that they were introduced into that country in the year 1537, and that they were sold for double the price of a lamb; but the lady writer on angling, Dame Julianna Berners, who lived and wrote some time before the abovementioned year, (1496,) gives the following instructions for taking him, which rather tends to a different conclusion as to the period in which they were brought to that country. " Take a codlynge hoke; and take a roche, or a fresshe heeryng; and a wyre with an hole in the ende, and put it in at the mouth and out at the taylle, down by the ridge of the fresshe heeryng; and thenne put the line of your hoke in after, and draw the hoke into the cheke of the fresshe heer yng; then put a plumbe of lede upon your line a yerde longe from your hoke, and a flote in mid way betweene; and cast it in a pytte where the pyke usyth; and this is the beste and moost surest crafte of takynge the pyke." In all probability they are natives of England as well as other parts of Europe

He is certainly one of the *oldest inhabitants* of our own country, as he was well known to the natives, and in some parts is still called by the Indian name of Muscalinga. At all events, he does not need such restrictions for his preservation as were a short time since proposed in the Legislature of the State of New-York, for the protection of carp in the Hudson river. On a debate for the passage of a law to protect some newly imported fish of the carp species, a Mr. Bloss said: " that he was in favor of a term of *naturalization*, not over five years, and so he would protect the fishy foreigner, at least for that space of time." This well-timed joke caused so much merriment and good feeling amongst the members of the House, that the law of protection passed with but little opposition.

The pike is also called the Tyrant of the Waters, the Wolf-Fish, and the Fresh Water Shark; and certainly, from his ravenous disposition, he well deserves all these names; and although not quite so voracious as that very peculiar bird, that devoured the boards, shavings, and even the jack-planes and hand-saws of the carpenter employed to fit up its cage, still his masticatory apparatus must be very powerful, and his digestive machinery equally strong, if all that is said of him be true.

> " A thousand foes the finny people chase:
> Nor are they safe from their own kindred race:
> The PIKE, fell tyrant of the liquid plain,
> With rav'nous waste devours his fellow train."

It is said that in Germany a mule, while drinking from a pond, was seized at the mouth by a large pike, and nearly

drowned, but by the aid of an attendant, the mule succeeded in getting his head above water, and brought the pike on shore, still clinging to his mouth. They have also been known to devour young goslings, rats, and mice, and when placed in ponds with other fish, have sometimes devoured them all.

Smith relates the following story, which serves to show the "ruling passion strong in death:" " A gentleman was once angling for pike, and succeeded in taking a very large one, at which time he was encountered by a shepherd and his dog. He made the man a present of his fish, and while engaged in clearing his tackle, he saw the dog, who had for some time been expressing his satisfaction by the most unequivocal signs, seat himself unsuspectingly, with his tail at a tempting proximity to the jaws of the pike, which suddenly caught at it. It would be impossible to express the terror of the dog, on finding such an appendage *entailed* upon him; he ran in every direction to free himself, but in vain, and at last plunged into the stream as a last resource—but this was equally fruitless. The hair had become so entangled in the fish's teeth, that it could not release its hold; accordingly, he struggled over to the opposite side, now above and now below the surface. Having landed, the dog made for his master's cottage with all haste, where he was at length freed from his unwilling persecutor; yet, notwithstanding the fatigue the latter had endured, he actually seized and sunk his teeth into a stick which was used to force open his jaws."

They are known to live to a very great age. A Russian with an unpronounceable name,* makes mention of a pike that lived to the age of ninety years; and Gesner says, one was taken in a lake in Suabia, Germany, in 1479, having a

---

* As some of our readers may want our authority, and may be willing to run the risk of breaking their jaws, we give the name, RZACZNSKI.

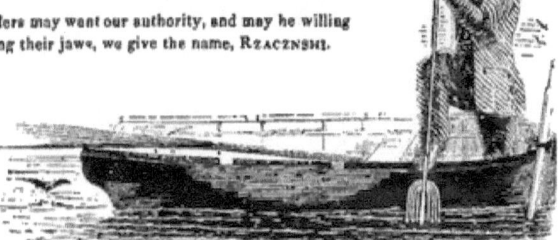

ring attached, stating that it had been placed there in the year 1280, making its age 249 years. It weighed 350 pounds. The identical ring is still preserved at Manheim. On drawing a pool near Newport, (Eng.) one was taken weighing 170 pounds. They are said also to grow to a very large size, and to live to a very great age in Persia.

"In 1801." says Blaine, "a hook, baited with a roach, was set in the manor pond at Toddington, Bedfordshire; the next morning a large pike was caught, which with difficulty was got out. It appeared that a pike of three and a half pounds weight was first caught, which was afterwards swallowed by another weighing thirteen pounds and a half, and both were taken.

"From the size of the fish which have occasionally been taken from within them, there appears to be hardly any limit to their voracity. One caught in the Iris was found to contain a barbel of six pounds, and a chub of more than three: these nine pounds of food formed nearly a third of his own proper bulk, which was 31 1-2 pounds. The circumstance of two fish of such dimensions being within the animal at one time, is a proof that the calls of appetite in this tribe are of a peculiar kind; they are most imperative but not incessant. The desire to fill the stomach is such that no offal is refused; animal substances of every kind, living and dead, are equally well received, and sometimes other matter; for the clay plummet of the Angler, the clay and bran balls for ground-baiting, when he is in one of his gormandizing moods, are not refused, of which many instances have occurred; and it is at such times that he dashes at large flies on the water, prompted to it probably by his habits of receiving there many savory morsels, in the shape of rats, mice, and frogs, as well as the young of ducks, geese, swans, and other aquatic birds, which he is known to prey on as readily as fish."

They are found in our streams, ponds, and lakes, from one

extremity of the Union to the other, and do not materially differ from the same species in other countries, and, as the Yankee would say, will live as long, eat as much, and grow as large, as in any other place on airth. The largest within recollection was taken in one of our western lakes, and weighed 46 pounds.

They increase in size faster than any other fish known. Block, a German author, says, that " in the first year they grow from eight to ten inches, in the second from twelve to fourteen, and in the third from eighteen to twenty."

They are observed by Walton to be "a solitary, melancholy, and bold fish; melancholy because he always swims or rests himself alone, and never swims in shoals or with company, as the roach and dace and most other fish do, and bold because he fears not a shadow, or to see and be seen, as the trout and chub, and all other fish do." Rather sorry company for any kind of fish would be the pike, according to Rennie, who says that a pike placed in a pond with an abundance of fish, in one year devoured all but one, which was a carp weighing nine pounds, and he had taken a piece out of him. Poor satisfaction would it be for any of the finny tribe to promenade down the stream with this voracious animal, and to have the peculiar satisfaction of being devoured at once without sauce, or perhaps gradually consumed by a piece out of the back or tail at intervals. No amusement, as the song goes,

' Like the trout and the salmon,
  Sitting down playing a nice decent, agreeable, pleasant, sociable
  game of backgammon.'

No wonder they have no company, or are not sociable; they should stay by themselves and prefer the Angler's hook, by all means, and keep away from *evil associates*, that they may " come smoking," according to Barker's rules, " as a viand

for the well set appetite of man, instead of the sharpened teeth and unsatiable desires of one of their own species."

They generally spawn in the months of March and April, and sometimes, in some parts of the country, as early as February. Their colors, when in good water and under favorable circumstances, are exceedingly beautiful. Smith remarks that "during the height of the season, their colors are extremely brilliant, being green, diversified with bright yellow spots; at the close of the season the green fades to a grayish hue; and the yellow spots become faint and indistinct."

They are fond of still, shady spots, under and near the weed called pickerel-weed, and appear to grow better and larger in ponds and lakes than in swift running streams. In the extreme heat of summer, they are often found near the surface, where they are sometimes taken with a wire noose, attached to a long pole. They are so bold that they will often take a bait after breaking their hold a few minutes previous, and they have been taken in several instances with a number of hooks imbedded in the flesh in the inside of their mouths.

In winter, they retreat to the deep holes, and under rocky projections, stumps of trees, roots, &c., from which places by making a hole in the ice, they are readily taken by spearing, or with a drop-line with a small live fish for bait. At this season of the year their appearance is somewhat changed, their colors being less brilliant, and their spots of a darker hue.

Blaine remarks: "The abstinence of the pike and jack is no less singular than their voracity; during the summer months their digestive functions are somewhat torpid, which appears a remarkable peculiarity in the pike economy, seeing it must be in inverse ratio to the wants of the fish, for they must be at this time in a state of emaciation from the effects of spawning; and the circumstance is fortunate, for were the appetite as usual, few young fry could escape; but during

the summer they are listless, and affect the surface of the water, where in warm sunny weather they seem to bask in a sleepy state for hours together, and at these times frequently get ensnared by the wire halter of the poacher. It is not a little remarkable, also, that smaller fish appear to be aware when this abstinent state of their foe is on him; for they who at other times are evidently impressed with an instinctive dread at his presence, are now seen swimming around him with total unconcern. At these periods, no baits, however tempting, can allure him; but on the contrary, he retreats from every thing of the kind. Windy weather is alone capable of exciting the dormant powers; and then, if a cool sharp breeze spring up, he may sometimes be tempted to *run*; but even then he will rather play with the bait, and may be seen even sailing about with it across his mouth; after doing which he commonly ejects it. This inaptitude to receive food with the usual keenness, continues from the time they spawn, until the time of their recovery from the effects of it; and thus pike and jack fishing are not productive of much sport between March and October, unless an occasional breeze should blow a hungry fit on them; and it is thus also that when they are attempted between these periods, the experienced fisher often at once commences his practice by snap-tackle.

"We are disposed to think that the decreased voracity of these fish during the heats of summer, is in some measure likewise influenced by the increase of temperature. This animal thrives best in frigid climes, and the further we proceed within certain limits, the larger is his growth; thus, in the Canadian lakes he exists in vast numbers, and grows to the length of four or five feet; and he does the same in the cold waters of Lapland, also disappearing, according to Walhenburg, in geographical distribution with the spruce fir. It is no wonder, therefore, that only a slight approximation to the equator should unnerve his powers, particularly during the summer heats."

In this country, generally speaking, except in the more southern parts, the habits of the pike, although very similar, are not quite so indolent as they are in England. In the northern parts of the States of New-York and Pennsylvania, and the more northern states, where the climate is colder than that mentioned by Blaine, they are frequently taken in fine condition, and with the usual quantity of sport, in the months of August and September. Generally speaking, the months of September and October are found to be the best months, and in many parts of the country, afford the Angler as much true enjoyment and diversion, as any other of the numerous modes of piscatorial amusement.

The streams and ponds containing them are abundant, and furnish immense quantities. There is perhaps more angling for the pike than for any other of the finny tribe, insomuch that it is almost impossible to mention a section of the country, except within some of our more southern states, which do not furnish fine grounds for the pike, from the moderate size contained in the ponds, to the essex or muscalinga of our western lakes.

The most common mode of taking them in the ponds and lakes, is with a stiff rod of ash or bamboo, about 12 feet long, accompanied with a reel containing from 50 to 100 yards of strong flax or grass line, with a small fish, or the leg or hinder part of a frog for bait. The hook, which should be a Limerick or Kirby salmon, from No. 0 to 5, according to the size of your game, is attached to strong gimp or wire, from 12 to 24 inches long, for spring and autumn fishing, and for summer fishing, if the pike are shy, strong twisted gut is preferable. In stream fishing, the addition of a swivel sinker and a cork or hollow float, will be found necessary.

Of the Rod, Blaine remarks : " Mr. Nobbs, with more

truth than good taste, has observed, that if your hook and line be good, you may make shift with an indifferent rod; and he seems to ridicule 'those precise craftsmen who spend their time in admiring their instruments;' for he adds, that he has 'often put a ring on his walking-stick, and with his line thus mounted, has killed his pike;' and no one doubts him. We have also heard a boy discourse sweet music on a jew's-harp; and yet, somehow, jews'-harps have not superseded the use of the violin, which is passing strange!

"We shall not, however, have much difficulty in persuading the true Angler that an appropriate rod will not only add to the success of his practice, but will render that practice more convenient and agreeable than otherwise. It will certainly be more professionally characteristic. In the rod or rods used for jack fishing, the method to be employed, the nature of the water, and the probable size of the fish, are all matters necessary to be taken into account. In live-bait fishing, and in trolling, a rod of nearly similar length and dimensions is required; but in snap-fishing, one of greater strength but diminished length is generally employed. In a very wide water, considerable length of rod is necessary for the purpose of reaching the probable haunts of the fish, and making a cast over the reeds or sedges which frequently skirt the banks and edges of some waters. Without a rod of considerable length, the bait often falls short, and not only misses its object, but gets torn by falling within, instead of without the reeds; and an opening between weed-beds, (so likely a situation for jack,) either in rivers or lakes, can seldom be reached without a length rod. A proper rod, however, for the intended sport, not only adds to the pleasure of the practice, but likewise to the success of it. Notwithstanding all which, it must be conceded, that in pike and jack fishing, it is more the method of the Angler than the merits of his rod, that is essentially requisite to his sport."

As pike angling has become a favorite practice with many sportsmen, both in this country and Europe, the particular directions, practice, and instructions of the best, will be selected for the benefit of those not initiated. The following, from the last mentioned writer, the reader can adapt to his peculiar situation, compared with the localities mentioned.

"The rod or rods, for both live-bait fishing and trolling in the rivers of the southern parts of the kingdom, may be made throughout of bamboo; but a rod so made must be composed of the very best possible materials; in which case, in good hands, it will be fully equal to land any pike that does not exceed eight or ten pounds in weight. But where pike may probably be met with of heavier weight, the butt and top at least, should be of some solid wood; the former may be of willow,* for lightness, and the latter of any tough, condensed wood, at the discretion of a good rod maker, surmounted with one-third whalebone.

"For the lochs of Scotland, the lakes and meres of English counties, known to contain pike from 15 to 20 pounds, or more, in weight, the rod must wholly be formed of solid wood.† But even here we recommend that the butts be bored, both to lighten, and also to contain one or two spare tops, which it may very well do without weakening it. Every trolling rod should be fitted up with at least one spare top, but it may with still more propriety have two. One should be made shorter and stronger than

---

* The butts of rods sold at the fishing-tackle stores, are usually made of maple, and the tops of lance-wood, which is a good arrangement of woods, the former being perfectly strong and solid, and the latter tough and pliable; add the bamboo joints, as above described, of a proper taper, and you have a rod that cannot be surpassed for lightness, strength, and durability. See Article on Rods, page 22.

† Well seasoned ash, with a maple butt and lance-wood top, is the best description that can be used, and is suitable for lake fishing.

the other, to vary the fishing according to circumstances, and likewise to enable the Angler at a distance from his stores, to have recourse to snap-fishing, if he find the jack dainty; this purpose may, however, be still more effectually answered by a second top, made wholly of whalebone, and less than half the length of the other. Where the angling mania has possession of a traveller, as it had of ourselves, it is of much importance that an article should be capable of being converted into many purposes. By such a rod as we have just described, he may troll in every water in the kingdom; nay, he may extend his fishings to the enormous pike of the Canadian lakes, mailed over with rhomboidal scales, and yet he may not return without a successful run.

"Captain Williamson says, that 'the spare top of an ordinary bottom-rod, which is occasionally employed for jack trolling, should be firm, and not too pliant, so that it will bear a weight of four pounds hung to the hook without breaking.' Mr. Salter on this head, says: 'I have two tops to my trolling rod, which I always carry with me, in case of breaking one, &c.; one is made very flexible of wood, and a whalebone top, about two feet long; to this, for strength and security, I have a ring in the wood part, as well as the large one at the whalebone top; this top I always use when trolling with the gorge-bait, or when fishing with live bait; the other top is made wholly of stout whalebone, about one foot long; this I use only when snap-fishing, for which it is well adapted by its superior strength and stiffness.'

"The length of the rod for live-bait fishing and trolling, may vary from 15 to 17 feet, according to circumstances; if its wood and workmanship can be depended upon, 16 feet is in no case too much; and where extensive streams are fished over, one of 16 or 18 feet is convenient."

The Rings or Guides for the Line, 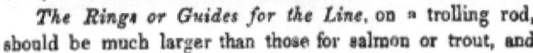 on a trolling rod, should be much larger than those for salmon or trout, and

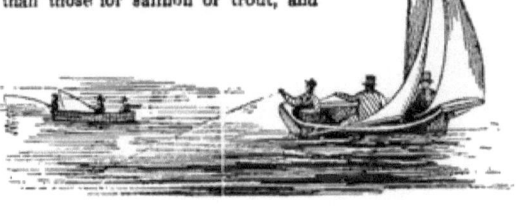

wider apart, say from two to three feet from each other. The solid rings, or patent guides, as they are called, and the patent tip or end, should be preferred.

The manner of baiting, where a single hook is used, for live or dead bait-fishing, is the same as that before described for trout.

The Bottom-Tackle is sometimes fitted up with swivel-traces, which Blaine thus describes: " The *single*, is thus made: to about 10 or 12 inches of gimp, add a hook-swivel at one end, and a loop at the other; the hook of the swivel will receive the loop also of the gimp-hook, and the gut loop will receive the reel line by a draw bow-knot, which it will be prudent occasionally to examine, when the reel line used is one either of hair, or silk and hair, as such knots made in them sometimes loosen, but in the plaited silk this never happens. It will be necessary to add three or four swan shots to the trace, or otherwise a dip-lead,* either of which should be fixed just above the swivel. Note here, that it is necessary to add some weight to all the fish-bait beyond their own: the intention of which is, that the increased resistance to the water, made by this means, occasions an increase in the velocity of their spinning, by way of counteraction.

" *The Double Swivel-Trace*, is made by uniting two 10 inch lengths of gimp by a box-swivel: to one end of this trace, add another swivel of the hook kind, loop the remaining end, and finish by adding to the trace by way of ballast, either swan-shot or a dip-lead. Note, that in the application of these traces, it may be sometimes more convenient, instead of making a loop for receiving the hook-loop, to whip the hook at once to the trace, and this may be more particu-

* A sinker, with swivels attached to each end, dispensing with the swivel described, is generally preferred by American Anglers; and also in the double swivel-trace, one of the swivels is often omitted, and a swivel sinker used instead.

larly proper when the water is shallow. On this subject, Salter says: ' In the summer months, when the water gets low and bright, from a continuance of dry weather, I have found, when I used traces made of the choicest twisted gut, instead of gimp, and hooks also tied to twisted gut, that I have killed more jack and pike, either when trolling with the gorge, or live-bait fishing, than I could if I used gimp. This, you are to observe, is only during the summer, when jack and pike are not much on the feed, and the water is very bright—they seem shy of coarse tackle; but not so in winter and spring, for they are then well on the feed and the water is generally somewhat discolored, at which time and seasons I believe jack and pike would take a baited hook if it was tied to a clothes' line or rope."

Another mode of taking the pike is by baiting with a small fish on the *gorge-hook*, which Hofland says is " either a double or single hook, fixed on a twisted brass wire, and loaded on the shank with lead, to which is attached a piece of gimp, eight or ten inches long, at the end of which is a small loop. To bait this hook you must have a brass needle, about seven inches long; put the loop of the gimp in the eye or small curve of the needle; then put the point of the needle in at the mouth of the fish, and bring it out at his tail; bring the gimp and wire along with it, the lead being fixed in the belly of the bait fish, and the hook or hooks lying close to the outside of the mouth; then turn the points of the hooks towards his eyes, if a double hook, but if a single one, directly in a line with his belly; next tie the fish's tail to the arming wire very neatly with a strong thread. To the line on your reel you must attach a gimp trace 24 inches long, having a swivel at each end, and one in the middle. The spring-swivel at the end of your line, is to be hooked on the loop of your baited trace, and you are ready for sport.

" When you are thus prepared, drop in your bait lightly

before you, then cast it on each side, and let the third throw be across the river, or as far as you can reach; still letting the bait fall lightly on the water. In each cast let your bait fall nearly to the bottom; then draw it up gently towards you, and again let it sink and rise till you draw it out of the water for another cast.

"The further you throw your bait if the water be broad, (provided always that it fall lightly,) the greater your chance of success, so that you are not interrupted by weeds, roots of trees, &c.; and if the water should be very weedy, you will be compelled to drop your bait into deep clear openings.

"When you feel a run, let your line be perfectly free, and allow the fish to make for his haunt without check; and when he stops, give out a little slack line; by your watch give him ten minutes to pouch the bait before you strike, which you may then do, by first gently drawing in your slack line, and then striking gently; but should your fish move soon after he has been to his haunt, give him line, and he will stop again; but, after this, if he move a second time before the ten minutes are expired, strike, and you will most likely secure him; but if he has only been playing with the bait, you will have lost him. When I have been so served once or twice, I generally resort to my snap-tackle.

"If you have fairly hooked your fish, he cannot easily break away; and as your tackle is strong, unless he is very large, you need not give out much line, but hold him fast and clear of the weeds, giving him but a short struggle for his life. The gaff is better than a net for landing a large pike, for he is dangerous to handle, and his bite is much to be dreaded.

"When you are without either gaff or landing-net, seize the fish by putting your finger and thumb into his eyes."

The pike is sometimes angled for with worms, when the water is clear, and the game runs small. Blaine says:

"Worm-fishing for jack is a species of live-bait angling,

that we and others have sometimes practised with success, particularly where small jack are numerous, in ditches and dykes, in marshes, &c. In our worm-fishing for jack, we have found the brandling the most successful of all the varieties, and our practice has usually been to employ two at a time on a No. 3 or 4 hook; we however did not use the common wire hook, but the barbed or stronger kind, by which means the strength was increased, though the appearance was not rendered more formidable. And note, that this kind of hook may be prudently used in all the various methods to be detailed, when single hooks of small size are required. Use a float correspondent to the nature of the water; and if that be moderately deep and at all ruffled, let the float be a small sized cork one; but when the surface is not disturbed, use a porcupine's quill, for the finer the tackle, the greater the chance of success. Retire as far as possible from the banks, and strike tolerably quick, at least after the second tug is felt, by which time the jack has usually got the worm within the throat."

Live-Bait and Snap-Angling. These are favorite modes of sport with many Anglers, but objected to by others on account of the spice of inhumanity with which the practice is tinctured, by attaching the live bait to the hook, in anticipation of a bite from the all-devouring jack. It is usually practised in the summer months, when the water is low and clear, and the game requires particular attention. The following methods of baiting, from Blaine, are sufficiently compassionate for the most fastidious member of the Humane or Peace Societies.

" One of the most simple and least painful, is to pass the hook under the back fin, just even with the roots of its rays, including a small portion of its skin only, by which means the fish will not be materially injured, and will continue to swim strong, and show itself. In this method it has been found that the struggles of the fish, or even the violence of the striking

of a jack, has often forced the bait from the hook; to prevent which, a thread has been carried round the point of the hook on one side, and being passed under the belly, has been fastened to the shank of the other side; but this deforms the fish, and injures its vitality, it is therefore not an eligible practice: its object may be obtained in a more effectual manner, thus: instead of one, make use of two strong but small hooks, No. 3, 4 or 5, according to the size of the bait; hang each of these to a small piece of strong gut, of three inches in length, and loop each end. Introduce each of these hooks a very little removed from each other, under the dorsal fin, one on one side, and the other on the other side; this done, if they are critically placed, these two loops will meet so exactly as to be received into the loop of the trace-lines, without dragging one side more than the other. This method, we can venture to promise, will prevent the escape of the bait, and is, as we believe, much more effective in taking the prey also.

"*The Snap-Bait variety* is seldom chosen in pike-fishing by preference, but is rather forced on the fisher, in the spring and summer months, when the pike and jack are not much on the alert in taking baits. On the contrary, if one of them does seize a bait at these times, he is apt to pouch or gorge it, but after roving about with it in his mouth for some time, he ejects, or *blows* it out, as Anglers term it. Snap-fishing, we may add, intermixes itself with live-bait fishing, and with trolling also; or rather, on some occasions we add a snap mode of striking the pike to the other methods; we have therefore a live-snap and a dead-snap, and now and then snap-hooks are likewise added to a gorge-hook in trolling, and that with perfect success. In all cases, therefore, if the bait-hooks are such as can be depended on, and the rod be sufficiently strong, the methods already described, and such as are to follow, may be made snap-fishing, by simply striking

the fish at once, instead of allowing him to take the bait away to his hold; the principal, and indeed the only difference being, that when we go out with the intent of snap-angling, our hooks are large, and ought to be strong also, and our rod is strong and short.

"*Directions for making a Live Snap-Bait.* Take two strong hooks, of size No. 3 or 4, according to the strength of their make, as well as the size of the bait: tie each to about an inch and a quarter of fine twisted wire, and again tie these two wires together, including in the tie a hook* No. 8 or 9, and also eight or ten inches of gimp, which loop at the other end: but in the tying, place the large hooks, contrariwise, so that one may point towards the head, and the other towards the tail of the bait-fish, which will greatly increase the chance of success when using it. To apply this, enter the small hook under the back fin, and allow one of the two large hooks to apply itself close to one side of the bait, and the other to be similarly placed on the other, but with the direction of their points reversed. We have often, even when the spring-snap has been in our book, made use of this more simple plan in preference, particularly where our only baits were gudgeons. A good sized roach or dace can conceal the snap, but it is hardly applicable in any way to a small fish.

"*Dead-Bait Spring-Snap.* This machine can be applied either to the dead or living bait; it is, however, we think, more applicable to the former, as it requires a sufficient hold on the bait to offer a resistance equal to the springing snap, or the benefit is lost: such a hold is injurious to the live bait, and soon destroys it. No bait answers so well for the placing of the spring-snap, as either a 'roach, bream,† or perch, on

---

* These hooks should be tied near the top, in a similar position to that on the spring snap-hook, described on plate of hooks.

† Any of the small fish that inhabit the stream with the pike, will answer the purpose, and be equally acceptable.

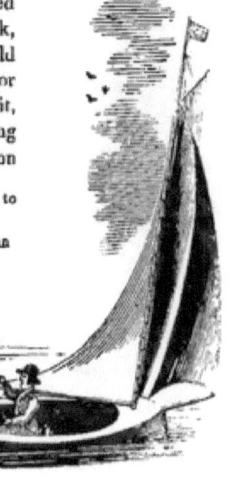

account of the breadth of their figures; but to either of these, and to the roach particularly, it can be readily and conveniently attached. Choose a fresh dead roach, of from three to five ounces; insert the small hook of the spring as above directed for the common snap, but a little deeper, so as to take a firmer and deeper hold, than when applied to the living one. If the apparatus, from its size, must project beyond the line of the fish form, let it be above; but by no means allow the bend of the hooks to appear under the ventral surface. The figures Nos. 4 and 5 on Plate No. 2, exhibiting the snap sprung and unsprung, furnish a sufficient exemplification of its mode of action; in seizing of the bait, the pike or jack draw the hooks out of the detaining frame, and in consequence they immediately expand and fix themselves into the jaws of the fish which has seized it.

"*Of the Hooks in Snap-Fishing.* We must again say, it is of great consequence that those to strike the pike be so placed as to easily clear themselves; if, therefore, it is expected of these hooks that they shall support and play the fish, and yet be ready at a moment to disengage themselves from this attachment, then too much is expected of them; and when they ought to be *free*, to strike at once into the mouth of the pike, they are apt to be *buried deep* in the body of the bait. It was purposely to relieve this strain on the bait that we added to the traces a small hook, which then left the large hooks at liberty to disengage themselves: for on the small hooks the stress of the action of playing the fish, was then altogether placed. It is on this principle that the snap-baits in general should be formed, and where they have not some sustaining hooks, independent of the snap-hooks, then they ought never to pass through the centre of the body of the bait-fish, but superficially under the skin only, so that when the pike strikes, the skin of the bait may readily tear away by the united forces of the stroke of the Angler and his prey, the consequence of which is, that the hook or hooks immediately disengage themselves from the bait, and penetrating the mouth of the pike they retain him.

The Bait being properly fixed, cast it lightly into the water, with the line drawn out to two-thirds the length of the rod, observing to make the first cast *in shore*, but be as much concealed as possible from view. If success does not follow this, extend the throw further into the water, and to do that with effect, give the impulsive swing of the bait with the same length of line as before, but have in addition a yard or two of loose line in the left hand, which as the bait flies forward, loosen quickly from the hand, and as it arrives at its destination, drop the point of the rod, which will ease the bait into the water without injury to itself, or alarm to the pike. The attempts of the live bait to make for the weeds or the shore, must be counteracted by drawing it back or giving it a new direction, and as it flags in liveliness, *stimulate* it by shaking the rod a little, which often *stimulates* the jack also to strike the bait. In drawing up the bait to remove it to a new situation, observe to do it gently, and at the same time watch the water, for it is not at all uncommon for a jack to follow on its attempted removal. If any thing of this kind is perceived, by no means remove the bait, but lower it again into the water, and begin moving it quickly at a few inches below the surface, backwards and forwards. In all cases, keep the float in sight, but avoid showing yourself if possible, particularly in the summer months, and when the weather and water are both bright. At such a time, to increase your small chance of sport, try to get the sun before you, and the wind behind; the former you might well dispense with altogether, the other will prove your best friend; but if there be sun, you must at least take care that it do not reflect either your own shadow or that of your rod on the water. In the months of February, October and November, this may be of

little consequence, but it is otherwise in the spring and summer months.

"*Be careful not to mistake the motions of the bait* for those which are made by the pike or jack when seizing it. With the experienced Angler there is no danger in this, but one less initiated might be apt to fall into the error, particularly as the mere sight of the jack will sometimes make the bait throw himself out of water to avoid his dreaded foe. The proficient at such a time will do nothing more than gently move his bait as though it were going to leave the spot, which alone will sometimes occasion the jack to seize it at once. The seizure of the bait by the pike is marked by the float, which is not thrown up, but on the contrary is drawn violently down, and the water is likewise observed to undulate, unless the bait be seized at a considerable depth. Be prepared for this with a free line as regards the reel; it is also a good plan to have in the left hand a yard or two of loose line to give out as the pike runs, which is infinitely preferable to allowing it to be pulled by the fish himself from the reel; which alone, with a pike not well on the feed, will cause him to reject it. Whatever line, therefore, is required in the progress of the fish to his hold or haunt, veer it out by the hand, and such hold is seldom far off, and he will when there, stop to gorge the bait.

"*In striking, let not impatience tempt you:* wait until you are certain that the pike has actually gorged the bait; otherwise your slight hold on your bait and prey will tear away, and you will lose both at the same effort. The pouching time is by no means definite, but is regulated by circumstances: thus, having satisfied yourself by the previous stillness of the pike or jack, that he is gorging, and by his again moving out from his retreat (which signal you must look for) that he has actually done so, give your line a smart hand stroke, which will fix the barbs into the maw beyond the power of ejection."

Trolling for Pike. This method, the last given, is perhaps the best of the series of the different contrivances for taking this species of game. It is generally practised in two ways, by roving or drawing the line from the shore, or by trolling the line gently from a small sail-boat or skiff, with an attendant, to be guided by your directions. With a stiff rod, reel, and other tackle, without a float, as before described, the latter method, with a good ground and large game, is decidedly at the *top* of pike-angling. Whether on shore or in a boat, the manner of proceeding should be the same.

Of Bank-Trolling, Blaine, the best authority, has the following: " The method of *holding the rod* differs in the practice of different Anglers, some grasp it firmly in the right hand, and depend on the strength of their arm for delivering the bait out to its extent; but we apprehend that much the better method is that of resting the butt against the hip, thigh, or stomach, or wherever convenient support can be obtained, (we always use our hip for the purpose,) by which much exertion is saved, the bait can be cast much wider, and when the Angler is accustomed to the habit, he may, by this means, direct it within a few inches of the spot he aims at. The rod placed, and the bait swinging on such a length of line as can be managed, retain within the left hand a yard of it loose, which as the bait is cast gradually run off the hand, directing it rather slantingly; by such means it will shoot diagonally forward, with a natural appearance impelled by the weight of the lead." When delivered, begin to move it after the manner of the motion, about mid-water, observing always to avoid removing it quickly from the water for another throw, for

* This is where the leaded gorge-hook is used, the method of baiting most adopted in trolling.

both pike and jack often follow the bait, and seize it at the moment it rises towards the surface, fearful it is going to throw itself out of the water to avoid the pursuit.

"*When you have a run*, or in other words, when a pike or jack has seized your bait, lower the point of the rod towards the water, and at the same time draw the line gradually from the reel with the left hand, so that nothing may impede or check the progress of the fish in carrying the bait to its hold in order to pouch it; do not strike until he has had possession of the bait about seven minutes, or till the line shakes or moves in the water, then wind up the slack line, and turn the rod, so that the reel may be uppermost instead of underneath, then strike, but not with violence."

Taylor offers an excellent practical remark on striking, when he says: "The pike will as soon as he has seized a bait, run to his hold to pouch or swallow it; allow him therefore five minutes to do so, (unless the line slackens before that time, which is a signal that he has already done it,) and then strike. But if after he has run off with the bait, he makes scarcely any stay with it at his hold, but goes off with it again, you should not strike till after he has rested a second time allowing him still about five minutes; but if he should run off a third time before the five minutes are expired, draw a tight line, and strike him instantly."

Captain Williamson observes, that "when you see a great number of very small bubbles rising from the spot where you know, by the direction of your line, the jack is lying, you should forbear from striking, it being a certain sign that he has not pouched your bait."*

"*The pike being struck*," the first directions continue,

---

* There is much difference of opinion about the time to be given for pouching the bait, some giving in some cases fifteen or twenty minutes, and one writer recommends thirty minutes! The most experienced, in particular instances, give ten, and even fifteen minutes; but thirty, or

" if it should be a large fish, and the place open, give more line, and do not pull hard at any time, unless your tackle should be in danger of entangling among weeds or bushes, and when this is the case, the utmost caution is necessary lest the rod, line, hook, or hold, should break. When completely exhausted, and brought to the side, take it up with a net, or fix a landing-hook in it, either through the upper lip or under jaw; or, if in want of either of these, put your thumb and finger into its eyes, which is the most safe hold with the hand."

It is also most judiciously remarked by Mr. Salter: " When you have hooked a jack or pike, and played him till he is quite exhausted, and you are drawing him ashore, make it a rule to float him on his side, and keep the head a little raised above the surface of the water, that the nose or gills may not hang to or catch hold of weeds, &c., while you are thus engaged bringing your prize to the shore; for sometimes you cannot avoid drawing it over or among the weeds; and I have seen a pike touch and get entangled in this way, and before it could be disentangled, it recovered from its exhaustion or stupor, and occasioned much trouble and hazard before it could again be subdued.

" *When a pike has been brought to land*, the inexperienced should be warned to be careful of his jaws, and to observe that after he appears wholly exhausted, he can yet bite severely. He can also, if he be not immediately stunned, make his way again to the water most artfully, by repeated jumps, of which we witnessed a most ludicrous instance. The pike being stunned, it becomes necessary to recover the gorge-hook from the maw. To do this, turn him on his side, and set the hollow of your foot behind his gills; then with your spud wrench open his mouth, and introduce your dis-

even twenty minutes, would tire the patience of the most ardent of the followers of Isaac Walton.

gorger. If the books are in the maw, as they usually are under the gorging system, open the fish's stomach about the middle, and you will be opposite to or rather under the points, so that your gimp will be safe. Cut away the parts that are hooked, and unslipping the knot that holds the gimp to the reel line, draw your bait, hooks, and gimp, all through the aperture made in the stomach. This will disfigure the fish less than cutting down the jaws, until the hook can be got out through the mouth. It is a good plan in trolling to be provided with two or three sticks of various lengths; one of these will assist to prop open a jack's mouth, while the Angler is attempting the extraction of the hook, but by no means trust your fingers in his mouth unless he be gagged."

In addition to the common pike, jack, or pickerel, the following notice of different species, by Flint, in his History of the Mississippi Valley, may be interesting to the reader.

"*Pike Essex*. We have noted many species of pike in the Ohio and Mississippi, and their waters. They are called pike, pickerel, and jack-fish, and perfectly resemble the fish of the same name in the Atlantic waters. The Indians of the Wabash and Illinois call them *piccanau*. They are of all sizes, from a half to twenty pounds.

"*Essex Vittatus*, jack-fish, white pickerel. Length sometimes five feet."

The latter appears to be a distinct species. They are very good for the table, and further as to his angling qualities we are not informed.

Having given the pike a *long run* through many pages and over what may appear to the uninitiated the *rocks* and *weeds* of instruction, it is to be hoped, notwithstanding, that the subject is sufficiently clear to introduce him to the pot, which shall be done through Mr. Nobbs, an English author, quoted by Hofland.

"*How to Cook the Pike.* Take your pike and open him;

rub him within with salt and claret wine; save the melt, and a little of the bloody fat; cut him in two or three pieces, and put him in when the water boils; put in with him sweet marjoram, savory, thyme or fennel, with a good handful of salt; let them boil nearly half an hour. For the sauce, take sweet butter, anchovies, horse-radish, claret wine, of each a good quantity; a little of the blood, shalot, or garlic, and some lemon sliced; beat them well together, and serve him up."

CHAPTER VIII.

OF THE PERCH.

This, like the last described, is a bold and voracious fish, and with the pickerel and trout, has his place in the numerous ponds and lakes throughout our country. There are many varieties, the most common of which may be described under the general heads of Common, Yellow, White, and Black Perch.

The Common Perch—(Perca Fluviatillis—Smith.) "A beautiful fish this, having an olive brown tinge, mingled with a golden hue, together with dark bands transversely coursing the sides. The first dorsal fin is somewhat larger than the second, and marked posteriorly by a particular dark spot. All the fins are tinged with a lively red, when first brought out of the water; the same color is also observed on the under edge of the gill membrane."

The Yellow Perch—(Bodianus Flavescens—Mitchill.) "A beautiful fresh water fish of a foot or more in length, and three inches in depth. Head rather small, and tapering towards the snout. Both jaws roughened with very small teeth.

Eyes large and yellowish. Body deep and thick, but becoming slender towards the tail. Scales rather rough and hard. Lateral line almost straight. Tail rather concave. First ventral ray spinous; as are also the two first and anal rays, all the rays of the foremost dorsal fin, and the first of the second dorsal. Colors, brown or olive on the back, turning yellow on the sides, and white on the belly. Faint brown zones, to the number of four, or more, diversifying the sides from the back to belly. Dorsal and pectoral fins brown. Ventral and anal scarlet.

"In the year 1790, I transported about two dozen of these yellow perch from Rockankama Pond, in Suffolk County, to Success Pond, in Queens. The distance is about 40 miles. Since that time there have been as many of them as could subsist. My assistant in the undertaking, was my uncle Uriah Mitchill, Esq., High Sheriff of Queens County. We filled a large churn with the waters of Rockankama Pond. We put so few perch into it, that there was no necessity for changing it on the road. We were in a wagon, and came the whole distance on a walk, without stopping to refresh either man or horse. The project of transporting the fish to Success Pond was completely answered; and in this way was the yellow perch carried to Hempstead waters."

The first-mentioned pond furnishes immense quantities of the finest kind of yellow perch, and is the resort of parties of pleasure, and those who are fond of light sport, during the summer season. It is situated in the northwest part of the town of Islip, Long-Island, is a beautiful and picturesque sheet of water, almost large enough to deserve the name of a lake; its shape is nearly circular, the water perfectly clear, and of great depth—so deep in some places that no bottom has been found. The water is said to rise and fall once in seven years.

Smith remarks: "Under favorable circumstances, for in

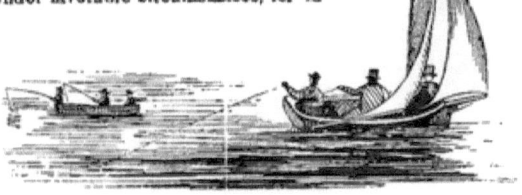

stance, in a deep large pond, shaded by a thrifty growth of brushwood on the margin, the yellow perch attains to a large size, and becomes elegant in its proportions."

It is the opinion of a late writer on Natural History, that this fish, and that called the silver perch, is one and the same thing. He says: "In our humble view, the yellow fins of the silver perch, entitle it to the name and rank of the one before us, (the yellow perch,) and further we believe, they are one and the same thing—the trifling difference in color depending on circumstances. The love and ambition of subdivision—the longing to be the creator of new genera and new species—has introduced more confusion into works of natural history, than can be expurgated in fifty years of common sense to come."

White Perch—(Bodianus Pallidus—Mitchill.) "With soft and connected dorsal fins, pale back, and white sides. Length eight inches, depth two and a half. Color whitish, with a dark hue, according to the angle of reflected light. Back, pale; tail even; lateral line extending through it. Small teeth in the lips. Patches of them in the throat. Eyes large and pale. Nostrils double."

Smith gives a similar description, and also has the following: "*Pond Perch* is another common name for the same fish: we cannot discover any kind of difference whatever."

Black or Red Perch—(Bodianus Rufus—Smith.) "This is a little larger than the silver perch, and though denominated *red*, is really nearly black, after it has done spawning. Operculum serrated, the tail slightly forked, and the jaws and swallow set with fine sharp teeth. Usually the three first rays in the anal are stiff. Very common wherever the others are found."

Flint also mentions a species of this perch peculiar to western waters, and a fine table fish, which he calls Brown Bass. It is called Brown Bass (Lepomis Fluxuolaris) or Black Perch, and grows from one to two feet in length.

There are many other varieties in the ponds and brooks spread over the length and breadth of the country; and although they do not give as much sport to the Angler in their capture, as the trout and similar descriptions, still they are much sought after, and considered a fine table fish. They generally spawn in the month of March; and although they may be taken at almost any time, either in winter or summer, they may be had in the largest quantities and in the finest condition, from May to July. The time of day in which the fisher will be most successful in taking them, is from seven until ten in the morning, or from four until dusk in the evening. They are very slow in their growth, though sometimes attaining a very large size, and multiply very fast.

Smith remarks: " Perhaps there is not another fish, with the exception of the eel, so universally spread over the globe, as the fresh water perch. It is delicate food, and therefore exceedingly valued. From the largest rivers above the influence of tides, to the smallest rills which trickle down the sides of the lofty mountain, the perch is always to be found. They swim swiftly, keeping near the surface, feeding on flies and minute insects. In the lake of Geneva, a female was caught, from which 992,000 ova were taken. This fact shows very clearly that it is marvellously prolific, yet not ten in a hundred of the ova arrive at maturity, being the food of others. To the Greeks and Romans, this fish was perfectly familiar."

Of English authority, Blaine says: " The perch is considered slow in its growth; but its increase depends much on the nature of its habitation: in ponds, and other small and perfectly stagnant waters, it grows slowly, and seldom arrives at last to any great size or weight; but in rivers, in estuaries, and particularly in such waters as are subject to the rising tide, and as are slightly impregnated with brackish particles, although without current, they grow fast, and become very fat. Of the *notitiæ* of large perch, we have before observed on one taken in the Serpentine River, in Hyde Park, which weighed nine pounds, and another of eight pounds. taken in Dagenham Breach, by a Mr. Curtis. In 'The Angler's Sure Guide,' mention is made of the portrait of one caught near Oxford, which was twenty-nine inches long, and of a proportionate depth; and supposing such measure to have been correct, the weight must have been very great.

" The perch is gregarious, in the strictest sense of the word: a number herd together by a sort of compact, which confines them to situation, to size, and to habit as well as manner; all are alike; the same hole contains them, and the same swim maintains them; and if one should be taken, it is the Angler's own fault if the whole do not share the same fate. This circumstance is remarkable in a fish of prey, since predatory fish in most instances are solitary; and it is even more singular in one so voracious as to swallow its own eye, as heretofore stated.*

The common mode of angling for perch in ponds, is with a light stiff rod, similar to that used in worm-angling for trout,

* The following is the circumstance alluded to: " Some time ago, two young gentlemen of Dumfries, while fishing at Dalswinton Loch, having expended their stock of worms, &c., had recourse to the expedient of picking out the eyes of the dead perch they had taken, and attaching them to their hooks—a bait which this fish is known to take as readily as any other. One of the perch caught in this manner struggled so much when taken out of the water, that the hook had no sooner been loosened from its mouth than it came in contact with one of its own eyes, and actually tore it out. In the struggle, the fish slipped through the holder's fingers, and again escaped to its native element. The disappointed fisher, still retaining the eye of the aquatic fugitive, adjusted it on the hook, and again committed his line to the waters. After a very short interval, on pulling up the line, he was astonished to find the identical perch that had eluded his grasp a few minutes before, and which literally perished in swallowing its own eye."

with a short line, about the length of the rod, a light float, and a small sinker, with a trout hook No. 2. This is not, however, the safest mode; for although the Angler expects small game, he should be prepared for large; and as the pickerel is a common inhabitant of ponds with the perch, he should always have attached to his rod a reel, to contain from 20 to 50 yards of line, unless, like the negro who was sent by his master to catch eels, he mean to take perch, and nothing else. The colored gentleman spoken of was sent by his master to catch a mess of eels for his breakfast. After sitting a long time, and taking only a few of his favorite fish, he had a severe tug at his line, and with his strong tackle he immediately pulled out a fine three pound bass, but to the astonishment of the bystanders, unhooked him, and threw him overboard, saying, "*Massa tell me cotch eels.*"

The usual bait for the perch, in pond-fishing, is the common ground-worm, which they will take generally if they take any thing. The brandling, and other worms, are sometimes used, as also cheese and bread pastes. For stream-fishing, for large game, in addition to the worm, the minnow, or any similar small fish that delight in the same water; also, the parts of frogs, as in pickerel-fishing; and, when the stream runs into or near salt water, and they can be procured, the shrimp will be found an excellent bait. They are used in the same manner, and with the same kind of tackle, as in trout and pike-fishing, as before described.

For Minnow-Fishing for Perch, Hofland gives the following: "The minnow may be used by fixing a No. 9 hook under the back fin, or by passing it through his lips, with a cork float, carrying shot according to the depth of the water. You should fish within a few inches of the bottom, and when a fish bites, a little time should be given before you strike, as the perch is tender mouthed, and if not well hooked, is apt to break his hold.

"Some Anglers prefer roving for perch, in the following manner: Use a reel on your rod, and have bottom tackle of three yards of gut, a hook No. 8 or 9, one or two shot-corns to sink the bait, which should be one or two well scoured red worms; and you must then cast your line across the stream, letting it sink, and drawing it towards you alternately, until you feel a bite, then allow a few seconds before you strike. You may also drop this bait into a deep still hole, as in trout-fishing; indeed a practical Angler (especially an old trout-fisher, will prefer this mode of worm-fishing to the use of the float."

Taylor directs: "If the Angler roves with a minnow, let it be alive, and the hook stuck in under the back fin, or through the upper lip; let the minnow swim in mid-water, or rather lower; use a cork float, of a size that he cannot sink it under the water, with a few shot, about nine inches from the hook, to keep him down, or when tired he will rise to the surface. When using the frog, put the hook through the skin of its back, and it will swim easier than if the hook was thrust through the skin of its hind legs; recollect to keep the bait as far from the shore as possible, for he will constantly be making to it; always give line enough at a bite to let the perch gorge. Where pike are suspected to haunt, the hook should be attached to gimp, as in this way of fishing they will take the bait as well as the perch."

For taking the perch, some Anglers affix the bait by two hooks, one inserted at the root of the back fin, and the other attached to either the gill, lip, or nostril. We think this by no means a bad plan; but on the contrary, that it increases the chance of fixing the fish, when he only makes a snatching bite, as is common with the perch when not well on the feed.

The former pages of this work having passed through the press, the following description of the perch of Western New York, his haunts, and mode of preparing for food, by an ardent

and enthusiastic follower of Walton, taken from the Buffalo Commercial Advertiser, will, though rather out of order in this place, be fully appreciated by the perch angler.

"*The Yellow Perch.* This beautiful and active fish is almost omnipresent in the fresh waters of the Northern States. There are probably two distinct but similar species in our country, blended together under this common name. The perch of New England differs from ours principally in the shape of the head. In the Saratoga Lake, Owasco Lake, Cayuga Outlet, the Flats of Lake Huron, and many other localities, the perch is larger than with us, frequently weighing three pounds. Among the perch of our streams and river, a half pounder is a very portly citizen—though on a few particular bars they are sometimes taken in considerable numbers, averaging nearly a pound each. It is almost always to be had, from earliest Spring to the commencement of Winter; and when poor Piscator has had all his lobsters taken by the sheepshead, and utterly despairs of bass, he can, at any time, and almost any where, in our river, bait with the minnow and the worm, and retrieve somewhat from frowning fortune, by catching a mess of perch.

"In the Spring, as soon as the ice has left the streams, the perch begins running up our creeks to spawn. He is then caught in them in great plenty. About the middle of May, however, he seems to prefer the Niagara's clear current, and almost entirely deserts the Tonawanda, and other amber waters. You then find him in the eddies, on the edge of swift ripples, and often in the swift waters, watching for the minnow. As the water weeds increase in height, he ensconces himself among them, and, in mid-summer, comes out to seek his prey only in the morning and towards night. He seems to delight especially in a grassy bottom, and when the black frost has cut down the tall water-weeds, and the more delicate herbage that never attains the surface is withered, he

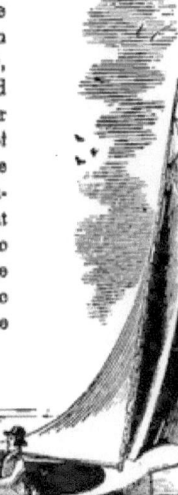

disappears until spring,—probably secluding himself in the depths of the river.

"The back fin of the perch is large, and armed with strong spines. He is bold and ravenous. He will not give way to the pike or to the black bass; and though he may sometimes be eaten by them, his comrades will retaliate upon the young of his destroyers.

"The proper bait for the perch is the minnow. He will take that all seasons. In mid-summer, however, he prefers the worm, at which he generally bites freely. He is often taken with the grub, or with small pieces of fish of any kind.

"He is a capital fish at all times for the table. His flesh is hard and savory. He should be fried with salt pork rather than butter, and thoroughly done. He makes good chowder, though inferior for that purpose to the black bass or the yellow pike.

"A difference of opinion exists among our most tasteful icthyophagists, as to whether this fish should be scaled or skinned. Let me tell you how to skin him. Take a sharp pointed knife, and rip up the skin along the back, from the posterior extremity of the back fin, on one or both sides of it along its whole length—then take the fish firmly by the head with the left hand, and with the right take hold of the skin of the back near the head, first on one side and then on the other, and peel it down over the tail. This being done, all the fins are thereby removed except those of the back and belly, which are easily drawn out by a gentle pulling towards the head. Cut off the head, and you have a skinless, finless lump of pure white flesh. Some say this is the only way a perch should be prepared for the cook's art—others say it impairs the flavor, and should never be pursued. As for me, I say, '*in medio tutissimus ibis*,'—neither of the disputants is infallible. Much, very much of the sweetness of the perch and indeed almost all fishes, resides in the skin, which should never be parted with except for some special reason, therefore as a general thing, I scale my perch. But, in summer, the skin of the perch is apt to acquire a slight bitter taste, or a smack of the mud—therefore, in summer I skin my perch."

"*Of the Gastronomic Properties of the Perch*," says Blaine, " whoever has heard of the broiled perch *flitches*, and *water souchy*, of Sir Bamber Gascoyne's cooking, would not hold us blameless were we to be totally silent. This fish has indeed stood the test of time, and has been as little subjected to the mutations of fashion, perhaps as any one of the finny tribe: it was highly esteemed by the Romans, as we are informed by Aristotle, and its praises were sung by Ausonius:

" ' Nec te delicias mensarum, perca silebo
Amnigenos inter pisces dignande marinis ! ' "

How to cook the Perch. The pan, in proper hands, will do justice to this fish : many epicures, however, prefer broiling. Either method, according to former directions for others of the race, will give satisfaction to the Angler, particularly if very tired, and *on the feed.*

Of the Water Souchy, Hofland gives the following method: " Scale, gut, and wash your perch; put salt in your water; when it boils, put in the fish with an onion cut in slices, and separate it into rings; a handful of parsley, picked and washed clean; put in as much as will turn the water white ; when your fish are done enough, put them in a soup-dish, and pour a little water over them, with the parsley and the onions; then serve them up with parsley and butter in a boat."

Large perch may be crimped and boiled in the same way.

THE SUN-FISH.

This is a small fish, that generally tenants the same pond

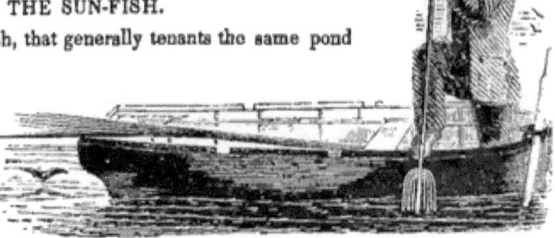

with the perch. They vary in size, shape, and color, in different parts of the country, and are taken readily with perch tackle. Their general size is from three to eight inches in length, except a species found in the Ohio, Kentucky, and other western rivers, where they are frequently taken twelve inches long.

Angling for sun-fish, when found in ponds, with small perch, is a favorite amusement of lady Anglers, who often make the best part of pic-nic fishing parties, and, as Walton says, "angle for men and fish at fish, at the same time." Determined old bachelors should be as wary in making up such parties, as they would be in taking a trout, or they will be caught in their own net; and when beguiled by one of the fair sex, he might break out into a *stream* of rhyme like the following, by Dr. Donne:

" Come live with me, and be my love,
And we will some new pleasures prove,
Of golden sands and chrystal brooks,
With silken lines and silver hooks.

* * * * * *

" Let coarse, bold hands, from slimy nest,
The bedded fish in banks outwrest;
Let curious traitors sleave silk flies,
To witch poor wandering fishes' eyes:

" For thee, thou need'st no such deceit,
For thou thyself art thine own bait;
That fish that is not catch'd thereby,
Is wiser far, alas, than I."

CHAPTER IX.

OF THE CARP OR TENCH.

This beautiful fish is not a native of our own country; but as they have been imported from England by a number of persons in many parts of the United States, for the purpose of stocking their ponds, and protection having been given them by the laws of the State of New-York, they will undoubtedly become an object of the Angler's pleasure, it will be well to give some information of their habits, and the modes of taking them in other countries.

"The family of carps," says Smith, " is distinguished by not possessing an adipose fin; by a small mouth, and weak jaws, destitute of teeth. The brancial rays are few; the body scaly; the intestines short and without cæcums. They have a swimming bladder, divided into two sacks, somewhat like an hour-glass, and live in fresh water, being harmless, inoffensive, and quiet inhabitants.

"In the United States we have not yet discovered the true carp of Europe, which is so extensively bred in pleasure grounds. Usually it grows to a length of 12 or 18 inches, but in the stagnant waters of Persia, still larger. It is gene-

rally supposed to have been carried to England about 1514.*
The quantity of roes exhuded by the female far exceeds the
weight of her body.

"Though denominated the *wise* on account of its sagacity,
yet in the spawning season it will allow the Angler to tickle
its sides, and is thus easily captured."

In warm climates they are said to grow to a very large size,
and often weigh thirty to forty pounds, and measure in length
three or four feet. They are known generally in England,
Germany, Russia, France, Italy, and Prussia, in which latter
country they grow to the enormous size mentioned. They
are said to live to a great age, instances being found where
they have been supposed to be 100 years old.

There are from twenty to thirty different species of the
carp, most of which give sport to the Angler. Of the common
carp of England, Blaine remarks: "Its general color is
a yellowish olive, much deeper and browner on the back,
and accompanied with a slightly gilded tinge on the sides;
the scales are large, rounded, and very distinct; the head is
large, and the mouth furnished on each side with a moderately
long cirrus or beard, and above the nostrils is a much
smaller and shorter pair; the lateral line is slightly curved,
and marked by a row of blackish specks; the fins are violet
brown, except the anal, which has a reddish tinge; the dorsal
fin is broad, or continued to some distance from the middle
of the back towards the tail, which is slightly forked,
with rounded lobes."

* There is an old distich in reference to their introduction into England
in 1514, which says—

"Hops and turkies, carp and beer,
Came into England all in a year;

which is entirely disproved by the authoress of 1486, who says he is a
"deyntous fysshe," and gives directions for the "harnays" or tackle for
taking him.

The carp generally feeds on worms and water insects, and are very tenacious of life, having been known to live a great length of time out of water. As an instance of this, it is related that they have in Holland a way of fattening them, by hanging them up in a net in a damp cellar, and feeding them with bread and milk. They are then placed in wet moss, and moistened twice a day; and by which method they grow very large, and increase in flavor.

Hofland gives the following instance of their tenacity of life, through a Mr. Hilditch, who painted the full length portraits of a carp and tench. "He kept these fish in a tub for a week, taking them out alternately in the morning at ten o'clock, to paint from, and putting them into water again at four, during six days; and I may add, that his amiable sister pleaded so well for the lives of these two fish, who had seen so much land service, that Mr. Hilditch took them down from Ludgate-Hill to Black-Friar's-Bridge, when, to use his own words, 'they swam away fresh and lively.'"

They are said to spawn several times in the course of a year, but their time or times of spawning depends much on the state of the weather and the temperature of the water. The time when they are known to spawn, is in the months of May or June.

They are found near the bottom of muddy streams and ponds, and choose to lie under and near the weeds, plants, and water lilies. When old, they are like the trout, shy and crafty, and sometimes, where they are scarce, require all the skill of the most finished Angler in taking them. In large ponds, however, where they are found in abundance, they are often very tame, and are known in some instances in Germany, to be called to feed by the ringing of a bell.

Hofland says: "Even large carp become very tame in ponds where they are regularly fed; for Mr. Jesse says of

some carp or tench* retained by him in a stew, that 'they were soon reconciled to their situation, and ate boiled potatoes in considerable quantities; and the former seemed to have lost their original shyness, eating in my presence without any scruple;' and Sir John Hawkins says he was assured by a friend of his, that he saw a carp come to the edge of a pond, from being whistled to by a person who daily fed it; and I have, myself, seen carp come to the edge of the water, to be fed with bread† by the visitors to Roche Abbey."

The time for angling for them is from March till September, with worms of various kinds, caterpillars, grasshoppers, beetles, wasps, and pastes. They are generally taken at or near the bottom, with a worm attached to a small strong hook, say No. 9 or 10 trout.

The time of day for taking the carp is thus given by one of England's poets:—

> "At early dawn, or rather, when the air
> Glimmering with fading light, and shadowy eve
> Is busiest to confer and to bereave;
> Then, pensive votary! let thy feet repair
> To silent lakes, or gentle river fair."

Mr. Salter recommends a red worm on the hook, with a gentle on the point of it. They are also taken with fruit and vegetables of different kinds. Salter says they may be taken with marrow-fat peas. Taylor and Walton prescribe

* The tench is a species of the carp, differing considerably in appearance from what is called the common carp. It is of a dark olive color, with quite small scales and nearly even. The mode of angling for him is the same adopted for the subject of our present chapter.

† It may not be generally known that the gold-fish and silver-fish, which are seen about in glass globes, and small artificial ponds, and eat bread from the hand, are a species of the golden carp. They are natives of China, where they are bred and sold in great quantities.

fruits and vegetables. In the use of peas, Taylor's plan is to hang one on the hook, about a foot from the ground, and throwing in a few now and then by way of a lure. In order to insure success at any time in taking the carp, ground-bait should be used in all cases, and in the evening previous to your expected sport, if possible.

Of the requisite Tackle, and Manner of Taking the Carp, Hofland gives the following: " Notwithstanding the instances of familiarity, it is by no means easy to make a large carp familiar with your bait: to do this, the greatest nicety and caution must be observed; but if the young Angler, who has been often foiled in his attempts, will patiently and implicitly follow my instructions, he will become a match for this cunning fish.

" Use a strong rod with running tackle, and have a bottom of three yards of fineish gut, and a hook No 9 or 10; use a very light quill float, that will carry two small shot, and bait with a well scoured red worm.

" Now plumb the depth with the greatest nicety, and let your bait just touch, or all but touch the bottom; but you are not yet prepared; for a forked stick must be fixed in the bank, on which you must let your rod rest, so that your float shall exactly cover the spot you have just plumbed. Now throw in a sufficient quantity of ground-bait, of bread and bran, worked into a paste, and made into little balls; or in want of these, throw in the garbage of chickens or ducks; and all this is to be done the evening of the day before you intend to fish.

" The next morning, if in summer, be at the pond side where you have baited and plumbed your depth, by four o'clock, at latest, and taking your rod and line, which is already fixed to the exact depth, bait with a small, bright red worm; then approach the water cautiously, keeping out of sight as much as possible, and drop your bait exactly over the spot you plumbed over night; then rest part of your rod in the forked stick, and the bottom of it on the ground.

"You must now retire a few paces, keeping entirely out of sight; but still, near enough to observe your float; when you perceive a bite, give a little time; indeed it is better to wait till you see the float begin to move off before you strike, which you may then do smartly; and as the carp is a leather-mouthed fish, if you manage him well, there is no fear of losing him, unless the pond is very weedy. Be careful to have your line free, that, if a large fish, he may run out some of your line before you attempt to turn him; as he is a very strong fish, and your tackle rather slight, you must give him careful play before you land him.

"The extreme shyness of the large carp, makes all this somewhat tedious process necessary to insure success; but I can safely assert that I scarcely ever took this trouble in vain. Various baits are recommended for carp; such as green peas parboiled, pastry of all descriptions, gentles and caterpillars, &c.; but I have found the red worm the best, and next to this, the gentle, and plain bread paste. Those who prefer a sweet paste, may dip the bread in honey. Pastes and gentles will answer better in autumn than in spring. April and May are, in my opinion, the best months for carp fishing, and very early in the morning, or late in the evening, is the best time for pursuing your sport."

Walton remarks: "The carp bites either at worms or pastes; and of worms, I think the blueish marsh or meadow-worm is best; but possibly another worm, not too big, may do as well, and so may a green gentle; and as for pastes, there are almost as many sorts as there are medicines for the tooth-ache; but doubtless sweet pastes are best; I mean pastes made with honey or with sugar, which that you may the better beguile this crafty fish, should be thrown into the pond or place in which you fish for him, some hours or

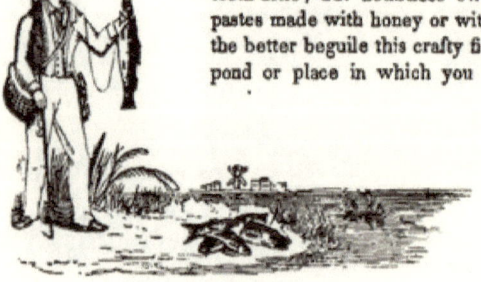

longer, before you undertake your trial of skill with the angle-rod; and doubtless, if it be thrown into the water a day or two before, at several times, in small pellets, you are the likeliest, when you fish for carp, to attain your desired sport.

"And if you fish for carp with gentles, then put upon your hook a small piece of scarlet, the sixth of an inch square, it being soaked in, or anointed with oil of petre, called by some, oil of the rock; and if your gentles be put, two or three days before, into a box anointed with honey, and so put upon your hook as to preserve them to be living, you are as like to kill this crafty fish this way as any other; but still as you are fishing, chew a little white or brown bread in your mouth, and cast it into the pond about the place where your float swims. Other baits there be; but these, with diligence and patient watchfulness, will do it better than any that I ever practised or heard of."

Blaine has the following: "When the angling commences, if possible, keep entirely out sight of the fish; make no noise; let the bait slide silently into the water; and try their fancy for taking it at various depths, beginning with the lowest. If rain falls lightly, the angler would do well to pursue his practise during the whole day. Sometimes, also, success will attend him through the whole of a gloomy day without rain, but in general cases, during the hot months, it is not possible to fish too early or too late for carp. In a starlight or moonlight night of July, they have been taken after the 'witching time' even.

"*When the angler perceives a bite*, he must strike according to the nature of his bait. If, for instance, in fishing with a lob-worm, he were to strike the moment he felt the float move, he would pull the worm out of the mouth of the carp, who sucks in after the manner of a barbel. On the contrary, if paste be employed, it is prudent to strike it on the slightest warning, otherwise the wary animal will suck away all

the paste; but with a small hook, and a very slight wris stroke, the nibbling fish may be probably struck; or if he i not effectually hooked, the fineness of the stroke will not alarm him, and he will return to the charge. Again, when fishing for carp in rivers, it will be found that the habit of meeting the insects which pass down the stream, makes the fish more on the alert to prevent their escape; they take the bait quicker in rivers for this reason, and they should therefore be struck much quicker."

Walton prepares and dishes up this dainty fish in the following sufficiently luxurious style, to make the Angler or reader smack his lips in anticipation.

"But first, I will tell you how to make this carp, that is so curious to be caught, so curious a dish of meat as shall make him worth all your labor and patience. And though it is not without some trouble and charges, yet it will recompense both. Take a carp, (alive if possible); scour him, and rub him clean with water and salt, but scale him not; then open him, and put him with his blood and liver, which you must save when you open him, into a small pot, or kettle; then take sweet marjoram, thyme, or parsley, of each a handful; a sprig of rosemary, and mother-of-savory; bind them into two or three small bundles, and put them to your carp, with four or five whole onions, twenty pickled oysters, and three anchovies. Then pour upon your carp as much claret wine as will only cover him; and season your claret well with salt, cloves and mace, and the rind of oranges and lemons. That done, cover your pot and set it on a quick fire, till it be sufficiently boiled. Then take out the carp and lay it with the broth into the dish, and pour upon it a quarter of a pound of the best fresh butter, melted and beaten with a half a dozen spoonsful of the broth, the yolks of two or three eggs, and some of the herbs shred; garnish your dish with lemons, and so serve it up, and much good do you."

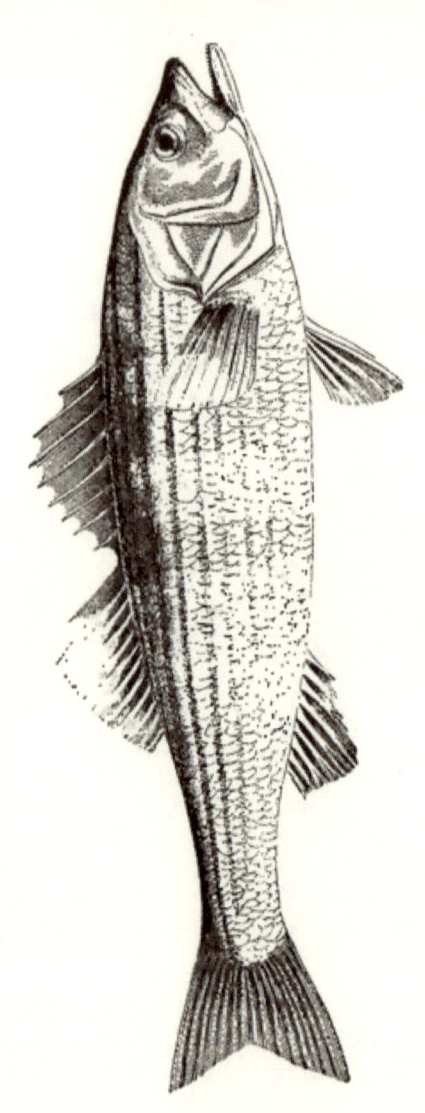

CHAPTER X.

OF THE STRIPED BASSE, OR ROCK-FISH.

This noble and highly prized fish is peculiar to our own country, and to particular parts of it. As an object of sport, for perfect symmetry and beauty of appearance, and as a dish for the table, it is considered second only to the salmon. They are found in the rivers, bays, and inlets, from the Capes of the Delaware to Massachusetts Bay, and also in the rivers and bays of Florida. They appear in the greatest abundance in the Chesapeake Bay,* and in the rivers, bays, inlets and creeks in the vicinity of New-York, and are taken in large quantities, from the size of a common trout to the weight of upwards of a hundred pounds.

In addition to the above described names, they are sometimes called Perch. The late learned and distinguished Governor De Witt Clinton, who was a member of the Philoso-

---

* A friend who angles in Chesapeake Bay, below Baltimore, says that he has seen them as long as a crow-bar! This is not quite so bad as being as big as a lump of chalk, as the crow-bar was in sight at the time, and measured about five feet six inches.

phical Society of the city of New York, says that Basse is a Dutch word, signifying perch. As there is a difference of opinion among the few American authors, in respect to this fish, we give their own words.

Smith of Massachusetts, defines this species as the *Striped Basse, Rock Basse*—Perca Labrax—(Lin. Sciæna Bloch.) " On the sides are parallel lines, like narrow ribbons, eight in number, which give it the name of the striped basse; the scales are large, of a metallic lustre; in the opperculum, the middle plate is serrated; the last portion of the third plate the gill cover, constituted of three pieces, has two nearly concealed spines. In the brancial membrane are seven rays; pectoral, sixteen; ventral, six; dorsal, eight in the first, fourteen in the second; anal fifteen, and in the caudal 17; some of them in each fin, according to the size, it would appear, of the individual, are stiff or spinous.

" Three or four of the stripes reach the tail,—the number not always being constant; and the remainder gradually disappear at different points on the abdominal walls; the eyes are white, the head strikes one as being long, and the under jaw, as in the pike, juts beyond its fellow. Next to the mackerel, this is decidedly the handsomest of native fishes.

" Striped Bass, are a sea fish, and principally subsist near the mouths of rivers, up which they run as high as they can conveniently go. During the approach of winter, instead of striking out into the deep water of the open ocean, like most other anadromous species, the basse finds a residence in ponds, coves, rivers, and still arms of the sea, where undisturbed and comfortable, it remains till the following spring. The principal rivers in the state of Maine, as the Penobscot, &c., are the places where they are now* taken in the greatest abundance, and of the finest flavor and size. In all the rivers, too, of Massachusetts, they are also found, at the in-

* 1833.

clement season of winter, but the fishery is not so productive as in Maine, whence the best in the Boston market are annually brought."

The following is from the Transactions of the Literary and Philosophical Society, by Dr. Mitchill.

"*Mitchill's Perch, Striped Basse or Rock-Fish*, (Perca Mitchilli), with eight parallel lines from head to tail. One of the largest and most excellent of the New York fishes: may be found from the weight of an ounce to that of seventy pounds and upwards. The position of the ventral fins rather behind the pectoral, made me once incline to place him in the abdominales. His second gill plate is finely serrated. That circumstance, if he remained among the thoracic, would rank him among the percæ, and when I decided in favor of changing his order, I was obliged to constitute a new genus for him, which I called roccus. But having since found that there are fishes whose ventral fins are further back on the abdomen than this, that are nevertheless considered as thoracic, I have, on reconsideration, persuaded myself it will be most correct to place him among his compeers of the perch family."

After a similar description to that given by Smith, our naturalist continues: "But one of the most obvious and distinguishing features of this fish, is the striped appearance of his body. From head to tail his back is marked by longitudinal lines. The ground color is pale, brown, whitish and silvery. On this are delineated the aforesaid lines in parallel rows. These rows, at some seasons, appear black, and make a strong contrast. At other times they are more faint, and seem to be faded into a reddish brown. When the brown thus predominates, dark specks or spots can be traced at regular distances along the stripes, particularly toward the back.

"The number of these stripes is usually eight; and four of them most commonly reach the tail. The rest are fre

quently shorter; vanishing unequally in their progress. Belly a fine mixture of silver and white. Scales adhere firmly.

"This fish is very highly prized by the New-Yorkers. He is savory and excellent beyond the generality of fishes. His common abode is the salt water; but he migrates to the fresh streams and recesses to breed during the spring, and for shelter in winter.

"He takes the hook, especially when baited with soft crab, Small ones are catched by the boys, from the wharves and boats every where near the city.

"Their greatest run is late in the fall. Instead of going away on the approach of winter, the striped bass seeks refuge in bays, ponds, and recesses where he may remain warm and quiet. Here the fishermen find him, and make great hauls during the coldest season, when very great numbers are brought to market in a frozen state. At this time it is usual to take some very large and heavy ones. Yet I have seen a dozen at a time, of the weight of fifty pounds each, in October, while the weather was very mild.

"He is also taken in seines during the summer, and in autumn. Indeed, there is no fish that stays more steadily with us all the year round, than the rock; and he is found of all sizes, to suit all sorts of palates."

The basse has been believed, as stated at the commencement of this article, to be a native of this country, and was supposed first to have been noticed by Mitchill; but the following from Smith, would lead to a different conclusion.

"By what authority Dr. Mitchill gave his own name to the striped bass, ' *Perca Mitchilli*,' we cannot divine: he might with equal propriety have tacked his name to the white shark, or to the bones of the mastodon, and the last would have savored less of vanity, than affixing his cognomen to a common table fish, known from time immemorial all over Europe."

If the above assertion of Smith's is correct, it is very strange that so important an angle fish has not been known to the angling community of Europe; for out of upwards of an hundred books on the subject of angling, in Europe, only one or two makes mention of any kind of basse whatever, and they are a species of trout, differing entirely from the striped basse of our waters. However, to us Anglers, (although we should like to see the learned Doctors agree,) it matters not " whether we have the name so long as we have the game."

As an object of sport, they are sought after with great avidity, by the sportsmen of the parts of New York and New-Jersey, bordering on the Hudson river, and have been taken of quite a large size as far up as Albany* and Troy. They are also made very profitable to market fishermen, at some seasons being taken in great numbers, with very little trouble. In the early part of January of the present year, 25,000 pounds were taken in Point Judith Ponds, the majority of a large size, that netted the proprietors $5,000.

They are generally angled for with a strong, pliable rod, 12 to 15 feet in length, made of ash, with a lance-wood top. For boat fishing, a rod about 12 feet in length is considered long enough, but for bridge or bank fishing, 14 to 18 feet have the preference. They may be had in every variety of style at the tackle stores in the city of New-York, where no pains or expense is spared in adapting them to the peculiar tastes of the Angler. Attached to the rod should be a reel, sufficiently large to contain from 300 to 600 feet of flax, grass, or silk line; to your line a swivel sinker, and float, according to the current of your fishing ground, and a leader, from three to six feet in length, double for fall fishing, and single for the spring run. Some of the best Anglers, however, prefer using

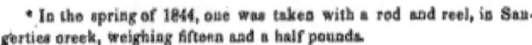

* In the spring of 1844, one was taken with a rod and reel, in Saugerties creek, weighing fifteen and a half pounds.

angle gut throughout the season, and if it can be procured of a large size, round and even throughout, in experienced hands it will be apt to take the most and largest fish. To your leader should be a Limerick or Kirby hook, from No. 0 to 3, according to the season and size of the game.

In no species of angling is it so necessary to have superior quality of tackle, as in the one under consideration. The beginner should therefore provide himself with such descriptions as will meet any emergency; for in salt water, in the bays and large rivers, the fisher will often be crossed by fishes of great magnitude, and by taking the proper precaution to have every thing strong and durable, he will often prevent loss of tackle and loss of patience, two very important items of a successful Angler's stock.

An experienced Angler and mechanic, who has made many a rod, gives the following description of a proper one for basse fishing. "Your rod should be about 12 or 13 feet in length, not too stiff nor yet too limber, for by being too stiff you are apt to break your tackle, or lose your fish by being struck too hard, and by being too light you are apt to break it, and thus spoil your sport. Besides, a rod of medium size is lighter, more convenient to handle, and much more likely to give you satisfaction after a tedious day's angling, if any such should be your lot, than if it were stiff—a fault which many new beginners are apt to acquire. For general basse angling, the one I should prefer (and it is the one most in use with good sportsmen) would be about seven-eighths of an inch in diameter at the butt ferrule, and a true taper to the point, which should not exceed three-sixteenths of an inch in diameter, making your butt sufficiently large for the grasp of your hand, say an inch and a quarter in diameter, which is about as large as will well fill your hand; larger is inconvenient—smaller will be likely to cramp your fingers.

"Your hooks should be about No. 2 of Kirby, or No. 1 of

Limerick, firmly lashed to one or two strands of gut, according to the run of your fish. If you fish with one strand of extra strong gut next your hook, you will be safe enough, and be as likely to take as good fish as with stronger tackle; but be sure that your leader, where your sinker is put on, and where the heaviest strain generally comes, be stronger than your hook length, and of two strands of strong gut, or three strands of medium size; for by that means, if you should be so unfortunate as to get fouled on the bottom, you will escape with the loss of your hook only, whereas if your tackle be of an uniform strength, you will most likely lose the whole, *line, sinker, hooks, and all*, which may probably make you *swear;* and this, according to Walton, is a bad practice; for as the old adage goes, ' He who swears takes no fish.'

" You are to remember that in boat fishing, if you do not fish with a float, or with a running or sliding sinker on the bottom, your sinker should be light enough to float off with the tide, and be able to feel the bottom at all times, so that if your sinker be 20 feet off, you can still feel it strike the bottom, and lift it up, when you can let out more line. I prefer this mode of fishing, both for basse and weak-fish, to any other; and you will be likely to get better fish, and more of them.

" You are to consider, also, the times of tide, the baits in season, the quietness of the spot selected for your fishing, (for the basse, like the trout, will avoid all places where there is an unusual noise,) and the full or neap tides, which latter are allowed by all salt water Anglers to be the best time for taking fish, and which I know to be the fact from experience. This time of tide, when it happens early in the morning, or towards sun-down, with the wind off shore, and a gentle ripple on the water, is the time when basse are most upon the feed, and the sportsman's efforts are generally crowned with success.

"You are to fish as near bottom as possible, either with float or without; if the tide be too strong, the float should be dispensed with; but a little experience will give proper judgment as to the time of using either, or both."

The following, from an old and experienced amateur, who has angled for many years in the vicinity of New-York, will be found excellent information for those who think that

"No angling can surpass
The taking of the basse."

"The Striped Basse is one of the finest fish of our waters. By sportsmen it is considered a game fish of the salt water tribe, affording capital amusement to the angler, by his great strength and activity. There are many places in the vicinity of New-York city, where these fish are frequently found in great plenty. They commence taking the hook generally in April. The first fishing ground in the neighborhood, in the spring, is in the creeks at Kingsbridge—next at Macomb's Dam, Newtown creek, and Jersey flats. At this early season, shrimp is far the best bait, especially where the water is salt, though in the Passaic, at Belleville, anglers are very successful in the use of shad-roe as a bait. This bait is rather difficult to manage by a novice. The experienced angler makes use of tow, or wool, cutting his bait with as much of the skin as possible, and winding a few strands of the tow or wool around it on the hook, which prevents the current from washing it off, which it would soon do without this precaution On the reefs of the Passaic and Hackensack rivers, many of these noble fish are taken early in April. The shad-roe has been tried repeatedly at Macomb's Dam and in Newtown creek, without success; the reason is obvious to the writer. The shad run up the fresh water streams to spawn, and are never known to spawn at either of the places just mentioned, and I have never had much success with this boat, excepting in fresh water streams. The shrimp is a much pleasanter and cleaner bait, and is very generally found to be successful in the early spring fishing, and continues so until crabs commence shedding their coats freely. In the latter part of June, the bass prefer the soft or shedder crab, though the shrimp continues to be used with success, until near the first of August, when the crab is decidedly the best of all baits that can be used. The mode of angling consequently varies at this time. While using the shrimp, the angler is generally most successful, by using the float, and suspending his hook from mid-water to within a foot of the bottom, excepting where the water is quite shallow, when it should hang just so as to clear the bottom, as in water of little depth the fish look for their prey near the bottom. But when crab bait is used, the best mode of fishing is for the bait to lie on the bottom; a sliding sinker is then the best, always as light as the tide or current will allow. The largest fish are generally taken by thus fishing at the bottom, without a float; and the reason for dispensing with the float is obvious, if we will look at the habits of the fish. In angling with shrimp, the bait should be suspended as above stated, because the shrimp, by the action of the current, are frequently swept from the edges of the channel, or driven out by eels, or other enemies, and the bass look for them accordingly; when feeding on the crab, however, these fish search along the bottom to find the crab in his helpless and defenceless state, and swim with their bodies at an angle, with the head downward, examining the bottom, where experience teaches them to find their prey; thus a crab bait suspended by a float at midwater would usually escape their observation, and the angler unacquainted with these facts would mourn over his want of success without being able to account for it. In the latter part of September, the shrimp again begin to come into use, and in October, these, with the

common kill fish, or, as it is usually called, killey fish, and the spearing in October, are decidedly the best baits, especially in running waters, such as the streams at Macomb's Dam, Pelham Bridge, &c.; while in some of our fresh water fishing grounds, such as Hackensack river and English Neighborhood creek, the white opened soft-clam is found by far the best bait in October and November, especially for large fish.

"Another mode of fishing for striped bass is practiced by fishermen and amateurs, by which very large fish are often taken. It is by trolling with a strong hand line, with a real squid for bait, or an artificial bait made in various ways: sometimes of the white leg bone of a sheep, or of bright metal, such as block tin, pewter, &c.: these can be had at the fishing tackle shops. The boat is gently rowed along by a skilful oarsman, who rests on his oars the moment a fish is struck, giving the angler full opportunity to play his fish with skill and care, both of which are highly requisite, for the fish thus taken are sometimes very large. Those weighing 20, 30, and even 40 pounds have often been taken in the East river, in the neighborhood of Hellgate, and in Harlem river, little Hellgate, which is the arm of the stream which passes between Ward's and Randall's islands, and in Morrisania creek. This is all fine trolling ground, but as the best success is usually met with at night, this precludes any but the most robust from enjoying this kind of sport—though frequently fine fish are taken during the day.

"The fishermen who supply our market with these fine fish, have lately been very successful in the use of set lines late in the fall. In the neighborhood of Piermont, on the Hudson, this mode has been employed to great advantage: a strong line is extended from one stake or anchor to another at given distances, and to this cord are attached short lines with strong hooks, baited with a small tomcod or other live fish: at the proper time of tide the fishermen raise one end

of the line and proceed to take the fish from the hooks. In one night several hundred weight of these excellent fish have been taken from two or three of these set lines, to be seen alive on the stands in Washington market late in December Some of the finest the writer has ever eaten were bought at the stand of Mr. Hiscox in that market."

On the subject of the different baits for the basse, it is proper to remark that, like the trout, the rock is very particular about the quality of his food: in some places at some seasons he will jump readily at clam bait, and at other places he will take nothing but shrimp or crab. At Macomb's Dam, Harlem river, at particular periods, the best bait is a small, beautiful fish called the spearing, which sometimes he will take and nothing else, and other times nothing but shedder crabs will satisfy his dainty palate. At many places in the Hudson river, and in the bay, the clam bait is sufficient to hook him in large quantities. At the former place he is rather epicurean, and as long as Astor House fare is offered him by the peculiarity of the ground, he will not be content to take small dishes, and rejects everything for his favorite fancy at the time.

In the striking and running of the basse, equally as much pleasure is given as with the trout and salmon, and is to be treated in the same manner as directed for those fishes.' Care should always be taken, after having hooked him, to keep him well up from the bottom, with the line well stretched; and if the angler be not so fortunate as to have a cast in his eyes, as so elegantly described on former pages, from the "Angler's Souvenir," let him be watchful of every movement, have *faith in his tackle*, (which should always be examined for that purpose previous to wetting his line,) courage, patience and perseverance, and there will be no difficulty in taking the largest run of fish with little trouble.

CHAPTER XI.

OF THE WEAK-FISH, WHEAT-FISH, OR SQUETEAGUE.

This is another native fish, as far as known, and is found chiefly in the vicinity of New-York and Massachusetts. It takes the various names, of weak-fish, wheat-fish, and squeteauge from different ascribed causes; the first from the weakness of its mouth. The second name has its origin from the fact of its having made its appearance always at harvest time, which is not now the fact, as they begin to run during the month of May, and are taken in small quantities in the month of April. The latter bold and elegant name is given by the native inhabitants of the island of New-York, who once were free to roam where the more refined now find a home.

There are two species, as described by Mitchill, as follows:

"The *Weak-Fish*—(Labrus Squeteague)—with even tail, speckled back and sides, one or more sharp, long front teeth in the upper jaw, and yellowish ventral and anal fins. One of the most numerous and useful of New-York fishes, particularly during the season when the cold is not consider-

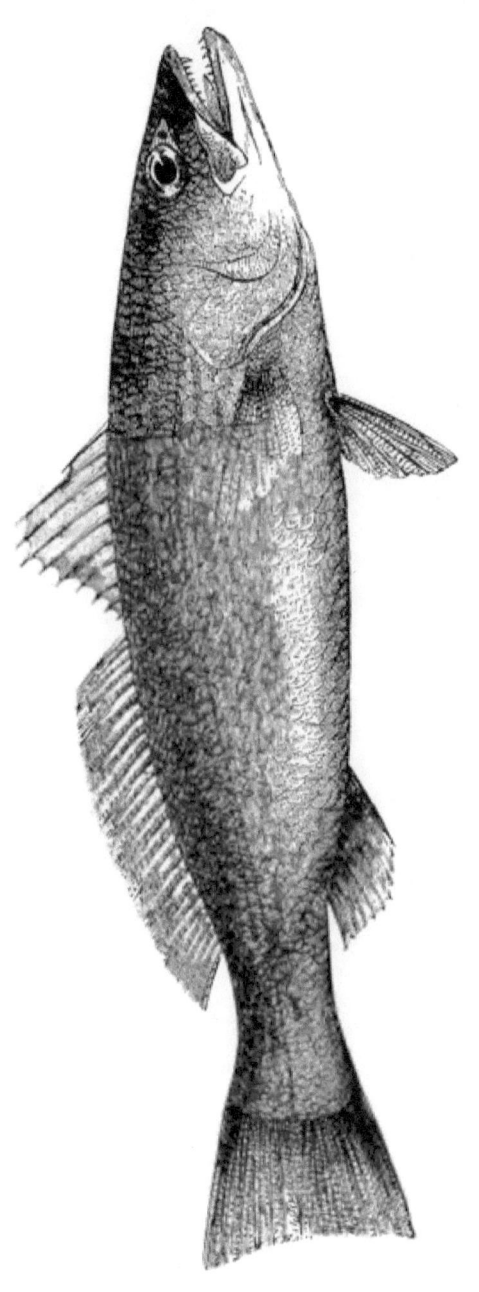

able. Size commonly from a foot to fifteen inches; but often grows larger. I weighed one, for example, that measured 27 inches in length, by seven in depth, and found him heavier than six pounds. He never goes into fresh streams, or ponds, but within the limits of the salt water is taken in almost all the places where the rock-fish is caught. The weak-fish is so much the companion of the basse, that I once gave him the specific name of *Comes*. He resembles the rock in the following particulars: 1. A wide mouth, with small teeth in the lips and jaws; 2. Patches of teeth at the bottom of a capacious throat; 3. Two dorsal fins, the foremost of which has eight rays; 4. A lateral line passing into the caudal fin; 5. A nearly corresponding number of sixteen rays in the pectoral, and seventeen in the caudal fins; 6. Double nostrils, and an elongated lower jaw; 7. A projecting head; and, 8. Large pale yellow eyes on its sides. But there are no tangible serræ on the gill cover, the divisions at the edge are visible only. They are not long, but yield to the slightest touch. Also the gill cover is not fairly triparite; but consists of no more than two plain divisions. * * * * The weak-fish cannot, therefore, be deemed a *perca*. I have been obliged to separate him from his companion, the rock, notwithstanding their numerous points of similitude. I have, upon the whole, associated him with the great family of labrus; a connexion he seems to be qualified for, by his smooth and scaly gill covers, his sharp and strong teeth, and the softness of his dorsal rays. I have given him the specific name by which the Narraganset natives distinguish him—squeteague. It would have been as easy to have assigned the Mohegan appellation, Checouts. Head and back of the weak-fish, brown, with frequently a tinge of greenish. The spaces towards the sides, faintly silvery, with dusky specks. These gradually disappear on the sides, until on descending to the belly a clear white pervades from the chin to the tail. The swimming bladder is convertible to good glue. I have eaten as fine *blanc-mange* from it as from the isinglass of the sturgeon. He is a fish of goodly appearance; and is wholesome and well-tasted, though rather soft: is brought to market in great abundance during the summer months. He is taken by the line and the seine. He is called weak-fish, as some say, because he does not pull very much after he is hooked;* or as others allege, because the laboring men who are fed upon him are weak by reason of the deficient nourishment in that kind of food. Certain peculiar noises under water, of a low rumbling or drumming kind, are ascribed by the fishermen to the squeteague. Whether the sounds come from these fishes or not, it is certain that during their season, they may be heard coming from the bottom of the water; and in places frequented by weak-fish, and not in other places; and when the weak-fish depart, the sounds are no more heard.

"A beautiful variety of this fish is sometimes seen, with the following characters, to wit:

"*Spotted Squeteague*—(Lab. Sq. maculatus).—There are black, well defined spots among the specks over the back and sides, and checkering the caudal and second dorsal fins. The pectoral fins are rather small: ventral and anal fins not yellow but brownish. The parts thus variegated with spots have a pretty appearance."

They bite freely at the shrimp and shedder crab, and will often take clam bait as readily. In the vicinity of New-York they are found in the greatest abundance in the bay off Communipaw, Oyster Islands, Buckwheat Island, below Elizabethtown Point, at Buttermilk Channel, the Owl's Head, Gowanus Bay, and Manhattanville; and although they ac-

---

* This is a great mistake; the squeteague, considering the weakness or softness of the inner part of his mouth, is a fair pulling fish; and when they are hooked of a good size, are known to give nearly as much sport as the more favored rock.

company the basse in salt water, they generally swim deeper, more in the eddies, and farther off from the shore. The experienced angler will often after angling for basse without success, change his ground, drop his bait a little deeper in the water, and return satisfied with his quota of weak-fish if not his expected sport in basse.

Although they are not as active when hooked, and do not compare as a game fish with the basse. the same description of tackle is requisite; and the angler who occasionally *lays off* with a slack line, has to *suffer some* from the larger and more nimble rock, who will often be off with hooks, line, float and sinker, without particular notice.

Some of those who make the squeteague a favorite object of their pursuit, prefer a light, round, bent hook called the Aberdeen, and others a light Kirby size No. 1, which they think increases their chance of success. A large hook, say No. 1, or even No. 0, on the whole, should be used, although the Limerick* is a good and sure hook. The Kirby, baited with a good sized shrimp, will be found for this weak mouthed animal a more sufficient guaranty for the faithful landing of any size that swims.

A friend who pursues this sport during the season, with much success, says—"I once saw one taken by a friend of mine, that weighed eight pounds and a half. which is the largest I ever saw." You frequently take from 10 to 40 pounds of this fish in a day, when they are in abundance. The afternoon tides are always the best, about two hours before sundown, and as long after that as they keep from croaking, when you had better leave off, as you will take no more of them.

* Some prefer the Limerick, slightly curbed, both for rock and squeteague.

CHAPTER XII.

OF THE KING-FISH, OR BARB.

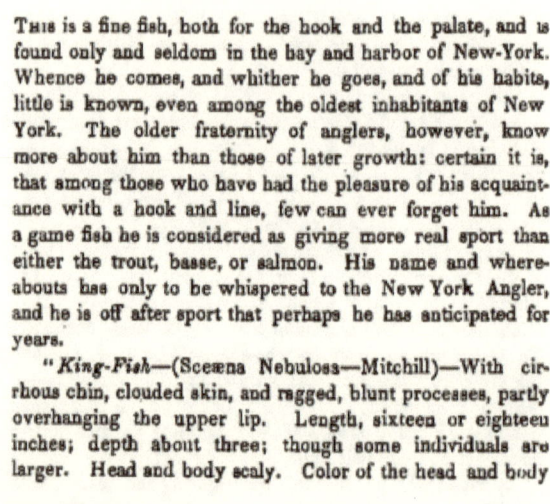

This is a fine fish, both for the hook and the palate, and is found only and seldom in the bay and harbor of New-York. Whence he comes, and whither he goes, and of his habits, little is known, even among the oldest inhabitants of New York. The older fraternity of anglers, however, know more about him than those of later growth: certain it is, that among those who have had the pleasure of his acquaintance with a hook and line, few can ever forget him. As a game fish he is considered as giving more real sport than either the trout, basse, or salmon. His name and whereabouts has only to be whispered to the New York Angler, and he is off after sport that perhaps he has anticipated for years.

"*King-Fish*—(Scæna Nebulosa—Mitchill)—With cirrhous chin, clouded skin, and ragged, blunt processes, partly overhanging the upper lip. Length, sixteen or eighteen inches; depth about three; though some individuals are larger. Head and body scaly. Color of the head and body

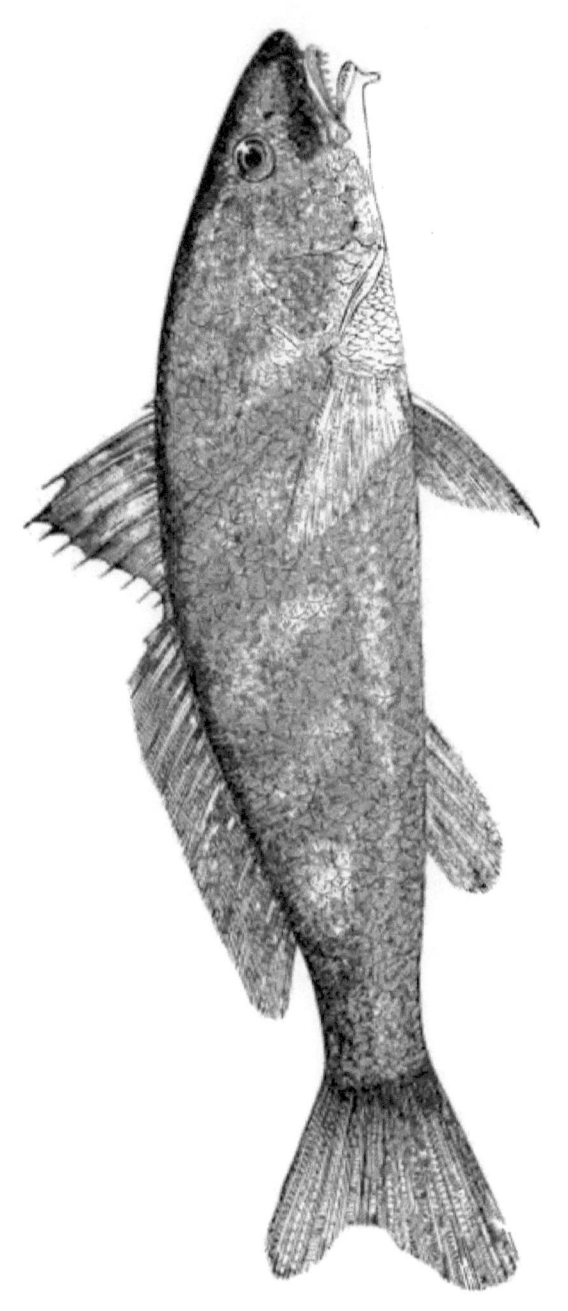

a light brown, glossed with silvery and blue, and interspersed with spots and blotches of a darker hue. Some of these clouds slant obliquely forward from the dorsal fin; some run obliquely backward from the nape of the neck; and some pass midway from the sides to the tail. There is here and there an insulated dark patch, with dirty discolorations towards the white belly. He grows rapidly thick and stout towards the thorax, and then gently and gradually slopes away towards the tail."

He is taken by the angler for basse and weak fish with their ordinary tackle, with the exception of the hook, which should be rather smaller, say No. 4, Limerick or Kirby salmon, to accommodate the mouth of the barb, which is rather small.

The following description of his grounds, and manner of taking him, by a friend who has had much experience, will close our article on the king-fish to the gratification of all who have or ever expect to *bite* or get a bite from this interesting fish:

"This is one of the finest fish for the table, procured from the salt water. They are not plenty in the neighborhood of this city, though occasionally a season occurs when they are taken in considerable numbers. I have often taken 20 or 30 in a tide, in the neighborhood of Communipaw, that delightful little Dutch town, rendered famous in history by the renowned Knickerbocker.

"A little below this village there is a piece of hard bottom on the extensive flat which is spread out from Jersey City down nearly to Bergen Point. A single rock is bare at low water on this hard ground, called Black Tom. The best ground, in my experience, is found thus: Row your boat from Black Tom directly for the Jersey shore, sounding with an oar until the bottom becomes soft and the water a little deeper than on the hard. You are then at the edge of what is called Caving Channel—a channel running north from Caving Point. Back your boat about ten feet on the hard, and anchor at low water: as the young flood comes in, if there are any of these fish in the harbor you will most probably find them here. I have taken from ten to thirty on this ground, together with basse and weak-fish, in a tide.

"The best bait for king-fish is shedder crab: the hook should be smaller than for basse, as they have not a large mouth. They are fine fish for the rod, being very powerful and active, running deeper than basse or weak fish, and in a way peculiar themselves, so that an experienced angler can always distinguish them on their first run. The largest I have ever taken in this harbor I have found on this ground, weighing up to one and a half pounds. They are sometimes taken of larger size in the south bays of Long Island, but rarely if ever over two pounds. There are many other spots on the extensive oyster beds on these flats, particularly along in front of Communipaw, and along the fyke fences between Jersey City and Ellis' Island. In Jamaica bay I have had many a fine day's sport with these capital fish.

"The following communication, giving an account of my excursions in that bay, was written by me at the time, and published in the Commercial Advertiser of 6th July, 1827. This I admit was an extraordinary performance, but I have many times taken over one hundred in a tide: but of late years these fish have become scarce in those waters, it being supposed that their enemy the blue-fish, by preying on their young, have caused the scarcity. Poor Bannister, the guide spoken of, has long since slept with his fathers. A pleasanter guide, and a more honest man, could not easily be found. Mrs. Hicks is still "at home" to her friends, and as kind and accommodating as ever.

"'*Great Fishing*.—On Friday last, a gentleman of this city went out from Rockaway, into Jamaica bay, with his son, a lad of twelve years of age. They commenced fishing at half past seven in the morning, spent half an hour in dining at noon, and quit fishing at half past one; having taken with their rods in the six hours, *four hundred and seventy-two* king-fish. Their guide was Joseph Bannister. None of these fish were taken by him, as he was diligently employed during the whole time in preparing bait. That it may not be said that this was a wanton waste of one of the finest kinds of fish produced in our waters, it is deemed right to add, that a large number of families in the neighborhood were supplied gratuitously with them, and none of this lot of noble fish were wasted. Mr. Bannister will be found on inquiry at Mrs. Phebe Hicks' boarding house, where the parties were staying. This house is most cheerfully recommended for its delightful situation, great cleanliness, excellent fare and kind and obliging family, as well as for the highly respectable company usually frequenting it.

"N. B. Mr. Bannister provides a boat and bait, and is the oarsman for the day. His charge is $1.25."

The friend who so well describes the king-fish, and his particular grounds, is among the few who have enjoyed the pleasant sport of taking this rare and active game, informs me that since the period alluded to, they have visited the harbo. of New-York but seldom and in small quantities. As there is a time for everything, there will no doubt be times when the barb will condescend to call on the angling community of the goodly city of Gotham, when the foregoing instructions will be sufficient to make them "Non semper non paratus."

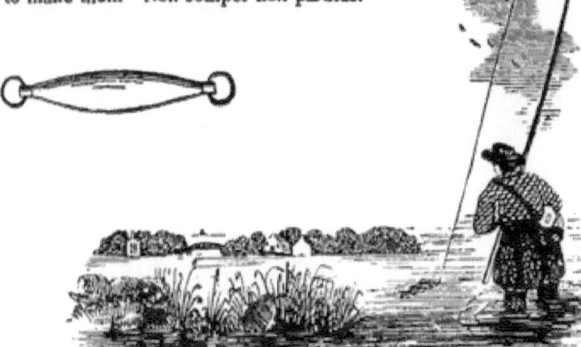

CHAPTER XIII.

OF THE BLACK-FISH, OR TAUTOG.

This is another of our native fishes, found only in the waters of New-York, Massachusetts, Rhode-Island and vicinity They are not so much an object of sport as the two last named, but as they come early, and sometimes in great abundance, and when taken and fresh cooked are a fine table fish, they deserve a particular place in our extended catalogue of angle fishes.

Black-Fish of New-York, Tautog of the Mohegans—Tide Black-Fish, or Runners—(Mitchill)—"The name of this fish is derived from the color of its back and sides, being of a bluish or crow black.

"The black fish abounds in the vicinity of Long Island, and is a stationary inhabitant of the salt water. He never visits the rivers, like salmon or sturgeon; nor, on the other hand, deserts his dwelling place as they do. He is fond of rocks, reefs and rough bottoms. He is taken through the whole course of Long Island Sound, Fisher's Island Sound, and in the neighborhood of Rhode-Island. The tautog was

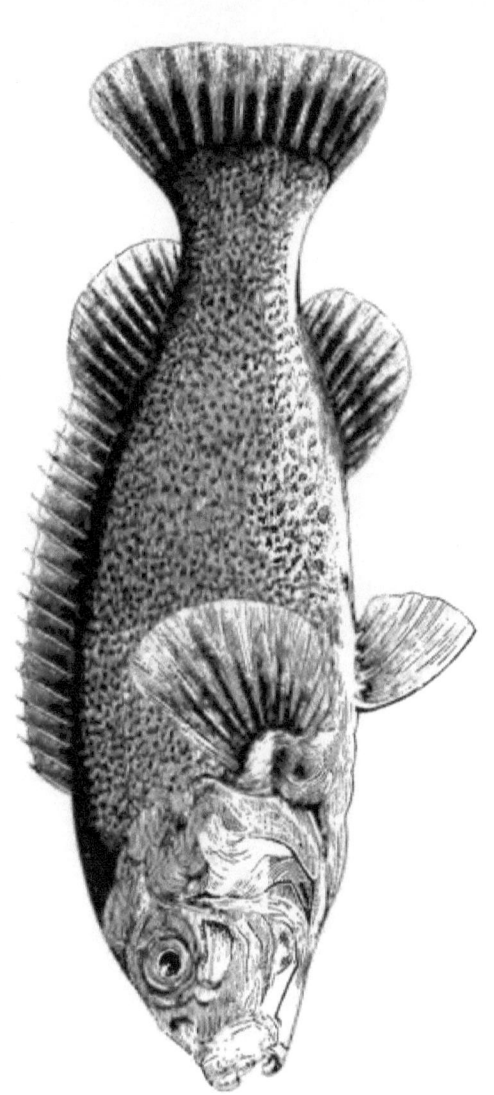

not originally known in Massachusetts bay; but within a few years he has been carried beyond Cape Cod, and has multiplied so abundantly that the Boston market has now a full supply, without the necessity of importing from Newport and Providence. Black-fish, however, does not confine himself to rough bottoms; for he is also caught in the southern bays of Long Island, and on the banks of the ocean off Sandy Hook. He is considered, by the New-Yorkers, as a very fine fish for the table. He grows to the weight of ten or twelve pounds, and even more; but it is a fish of a good size, that equals two or three.

"He may be kept for a long time in ponds or cars; and fed, and even fatted there. When the cold of winter benumbs him he refuses to eat any more, and a membrane is observed to form over the vent, and close it. He begins to regain appetite with the return of warmth in the spring. The blossoming of the dogwood, (cornus florida,) early in April, is understood to denote the time of baiting black-fish. As soon as these flowers unfold, the fishermen proceed with their hooks and lines to the favorite places. If there is no dogwood, a judgment is derived from the vegetation of the chestnut tree (castanea vesca). The season of baiting is reckoned very favorable until the increasing warmth of the season brings food enough to fill their stomachs, and they thereupon afford less pastime to the sportsman and less profit to the professor. The people express this sentiment in these coarse rhymes:

"'When chestnut leaves are as big as thumb nail,
Then bite black-fish without fail;
But when chestnut leaves are as long as a span,
Then catch black-fish if you can.'"

"The common bait for black-fish is the soft clam, or pisser, (mya.) The soldier crab, or fiddler, (ocypoda,) will frequently tempt him when he refuses to taste the other. And he snaps very readily at the large finny worm of the salt water beaches, (nereis,) when used on a hook for him.

"Some persons, who live contiguous to the shores where are situated the rocks frequented by tautog, invite the fish there by baiting. By this is meant the throwing overboard broken clams or crabs, to induce the black-fish to renew their visits, and fine sport is procured.

"Rocky shores and bottoms are the haunts of black-fish. Long experience is required to find all these places of resort Nice observations on the land-marks, in different directions, are requisite to enable a fishing party to anchor on the proper spot. When, for example, a certain rock and tree range one way, with a barn window appearing over a headland the other way, the boat being at the point where two such lines intersect each other, is exactly over some famous rendezvous. To insure success on such expectation, it is proper to have a pilot along, well versed in all the local and minute knowledge. According to the number and distance of the rocks and reefs visited, will be the time consumed, from the duration of a few hours to a long summer's day. An opinion prevails, that the black-fish can hear very well; and, for fear of scaring them away, the greatest stillness is observed. He is a strong fish, and pulls well for one of his weight and size.

"At some places black-fish bite best upon the flood: in others, they are voracious during the ebb. Thunder accompanying a shower, is an indication that no more of them can be caught. The appearance of a porpoise infallibly puts an end to sport. Curious stories are told of fish in the wells and ponds, floating in their native element, having been found dead, after sharp and repeated flashes of lightning. Dull weather, with an easterly wind, is generally the omen of ill luck. The exploits performed in fishing for tautog, are recounted occasionally, with remarkable glee, and they afford a never-failing theme of entertainment to those who are engaged in this sort of adventure. Though the hand line is generally used, the rod is sometimes employed to great advantage. The black-fish is remarkable for retaining life a long time after he is taken out of water. He sometimes swims over even ground, and is caught in seines."

An observant New-York amateur, who delights in black-fish angling, gives us the following:

"The black-fish, or, as he is called in the eastern states, the tantog, is a very fine fish for the table, well known to all epicures, and affords fine amusement to the angler. He is taken on reefs or around detached rocks, where the food in which he delights is found. The usual baits employed in taking black-fish are the hard and soft shelled clam, the rock crab and soldier crab or fiddler, shrimp and shedder lobster or crab: these two last are decidedly the best that can be used, though in many situations the shrimp and the two small kinds of crab above named are sometimes to be preferred. As a general bait for these fish, the shedder lobster is my favorite, and I have long been a successful angler for these fish. There is a very great difference observable in the black-fish, even those feeding together at the same rock. Those taken close to the rock, especially if it has shelving sides, are shorter, much darker colored, and thicker than those which are found playing in the edge of the tide as it sweeps past the rock—these are the long fish, with larger heads than the others, and of much lighter color, especially about the head and snout, the latter frequently being nearly white, whence they are called white-noses and tide-runners. They seem to delight in the eddies at the very edge of the swift water, where they watch for the shrimp, or small crabs, which are borne along by the tide. By casting the line a little above the rock, and letting the bait float with the current past it, holding the rod with an even and ready hand you present the bait to his expecting eye in the most natural way—and this should always be the study of the angler who wishes to succeed. His bite is much more powerful than that of the rock-fish, though both are bold biting fish, and to the experienced angler, with good tackle, rarely missed.

"The rock-fish lie under the overhanging rock-weed, on the watch for live bait, shrimp, or crabs, dart out and seize their prey, and retire to their harbor, drawing the line from the perpendicular to a slanting position, and that without the angler feeling him; and I have taken many a dark-sided fellow, merely from watching the slant of the line. Both kinds are very powerful, and although they rarely run far from the rock when hooked, their extraordinary vigor, and stubborn resistance, make them a capital subject for the rod. The largest I have ever taken with the rod, weighed five and a half pounds. This was at Oyster-Pond Point, at the Sound end of Long Island. This is one of the best places which I know, of easy access from New-York, for taking these fine fish. An excellent temperance hotel is kept by Mr. Latham, and good boats and guides are to be had.

"The best mode of arranging rod tackle for black-fish is this: Attach two plaited gut snells, one of twelve inches and one of eight, to a small brass ring, the size of those used on the second joint of the rod from the hand; put a slide sinker on the line, and tie to the ring, and all is ready. The slide sinker is by far the best, as it is frequently desirable to throw from your boat to a sunken rock, and as the sinker lies on the bottom, the smallest action of the fish at the bait is readily felt.

"For hand-line fishing I prefer the same mode of arranging the hooks to any other: the usual way is to have a loop at the end of the line; attach the loop to the eye of the sinker, and fasten the snells on the line just above the latter, so that they will hang about twelve and eight inches below."

The rod proper for taking black-fish, should be similar to that described for trolling, say about twelve feet long, and quite stiff; the line stout, and of strong flax or hemp; and although not absolutely necessary for black-fish alone, should be attached to a good running reel; by this arrangement, the sportsman will be prepared, which is often the case, to meet a drum or large basse, which are sometimes found on the same grounds. The hook in use for black-fish, varies in size, with many anglers, some preferring quite a small size for taking the largest size fish, say about No. 10; and others, ranging from No. 3 to No. 5, the most proper sizes for general fishing. These hooks, it will be noticed, by referring to plate 2. of hooks, are made of much stronger wire, and are known amongst anglers and dealers in tackle, as the black-fish hook. The hook should be attached to a strong piece of flax line about ten to fifteen inches in length; and if you angle with two hooks, they should be from four to six inches apart; your sinker should vary according to the tide, and be fixed above your hooks about twelve or fifteen inches. Some anglers prefer twisted gut lengths* to their hooks instead of flax; but as the tautog lies chiefly on rocky ground and on sharp stony bottoms, and are not very shy, it is hardly necessary to run the risk of losing gut tackle when plain line will answer.

The black fish being a bottom fish altogether, does not admit of such variety of modes of capture as others of the briny element. The most common mode of taking him is

* Others use short lengths of gimp. An old and experienced angler, who is very fond of taking the tautog, says that to fish pleasantly and with expedition, he always attaches his hooks to twisted snells composed of three strands of strong gut. In this manner he avoids the delay and perplexity occasioned by the frequent entangling of the ordinary flax line snells, and can take more fish than by any other method

with a common drop line made of flax, and from ten to thirty yards in length, according to the depth of water.

When the black fish favors you with a bite, give particular attention and pull quickly, for he has a hard, tough mouth, and if your hook and tackle are strong, you need not be fearful of any damage to your tools, and with proper precaution, you can call him in.

Give him no quarter, when using the hand-line, (until you quarter him for dinner;) keep your line tight, and draw him straight up until he snuff the pure air of heaven, much to his chagrin, and greatly to your satisfaction: and remember, should you be unwatchful, and he take you unawares and go to the bottom, your chance is very small; for although he may roam occasionally, in search of his favorite food, still he loves his rocky home, and down he will go with your bottom tackle, unless you are on the alert. Remember, then, that "Eternal vigilance is the price of"—a black fish.

How to Cook the Black-Fish—Not seemingly by a professor of the rod and line, yet certainly by one who well understands how to bring out the gastronomic properties of the subject under discussion, the following, from the pages of the Knickerbocker magazine, although containing much that is extraneous, will, we think, suit the *taste* of our reader:

"And now, fair ruler of the destinies of dinner! (for if thou beest a man, I have no sympathies toward thee,) smoke-compelling Betty, or Mary, or whatever else may be the happy appelative in which not only thou but all of us rejoice, thou hast lying extended before thee one of the most delicately absorbent substances in nature, imbibing flavor from everything which surrounds it, whether of adverse or of propitious tendency; subject, as Warren Hastings said of the tenure of the British possessions in India, alike 'to the touch of chance, or the breath of opinion.'

"Thou hast it, my choice Mary! The small, deep stew-pan—with its thin cullender or strainer, on which the fish is to be lowered to the bottom, that it may, when stewed into soft delight, be gently raised again, without injuring its integrity of form—glows with brightness in front of thee! Thy vigorous arm of mottled red, thy round wrist, and small compact fingers grasp the sharp pointed knife with which to satisfy thyself that not one scale remains around the head, the fins, the tail.

"Now tail and fins are nicely shortened in their termination, not hacked off. A little salt is thrown over the fish, merely to *harden* and *not salt* it, and it lies two hours for this purpose. It is then scored, that it may not break when it swells, and browned well upon the gridiron: from which it is carefully taken up, and laid to repose upon a bed of nicely peeled and very fresh mushrooms, daintily spread over the strainer.

"While the fish was hardening, Mary has had a communication from up stairs. An extra bottle of the Chateau of twenty-five had been unavailingly opened the day before, to tempt a total temperance friend who had arrived from the country. Good part of it remains, and at this moment it is decanted into the stew-pan; the freighted strainer descends into the wine; and the fish, entirely immersed in the amethystine element, regrets no more its loss of life, of liberty, and youth. A white onion or two is sliced into rings, that fall as decorations over him; a few berries of pepper thrown in; six cloves; two blades of mace; an echalot, if you think proper; and cayenne or not, according to your taste. The stew-pan is then covered, and a careful, slow, epicurean simmer completes the work."

CHAPTER XIV.

OF THE DRUM.

This is a large, uncouth, ugly-looking fish, not often sought after as an object of sport, but sometimes, and when least expected, the subject of the angler's toil. If, however, he should be lightly rigged, and not on the alert, this elephant looking animal often has the *pleasure* of chewing the bottom tackle at his leisure, and the astonished sportsman unfortunately has to rig himself anew, (after twisting his segar in his mouth, or rolling his quid on t'other side, if he has either,) or *chew* the cud of discontent at not having supplied himself with extra tackle, or not being more strongly accoutred.

Mitchill has the following remarks on this fish:

"*Black Drum*—(Sciæna fusca)—Length when full grown, thirty-eight or forty inches; depth, fourteen or sixteen. Spreads from the back wedgewise towards the belly, which is rather flattish and broad, rendering it easy to turn the dead fish upon the belly for examination.

"The black drum often equals fifteen, twenty, and even thirty pounds. The individual now before me comes to thirty-four. I once weighed a drum that was as heavy as

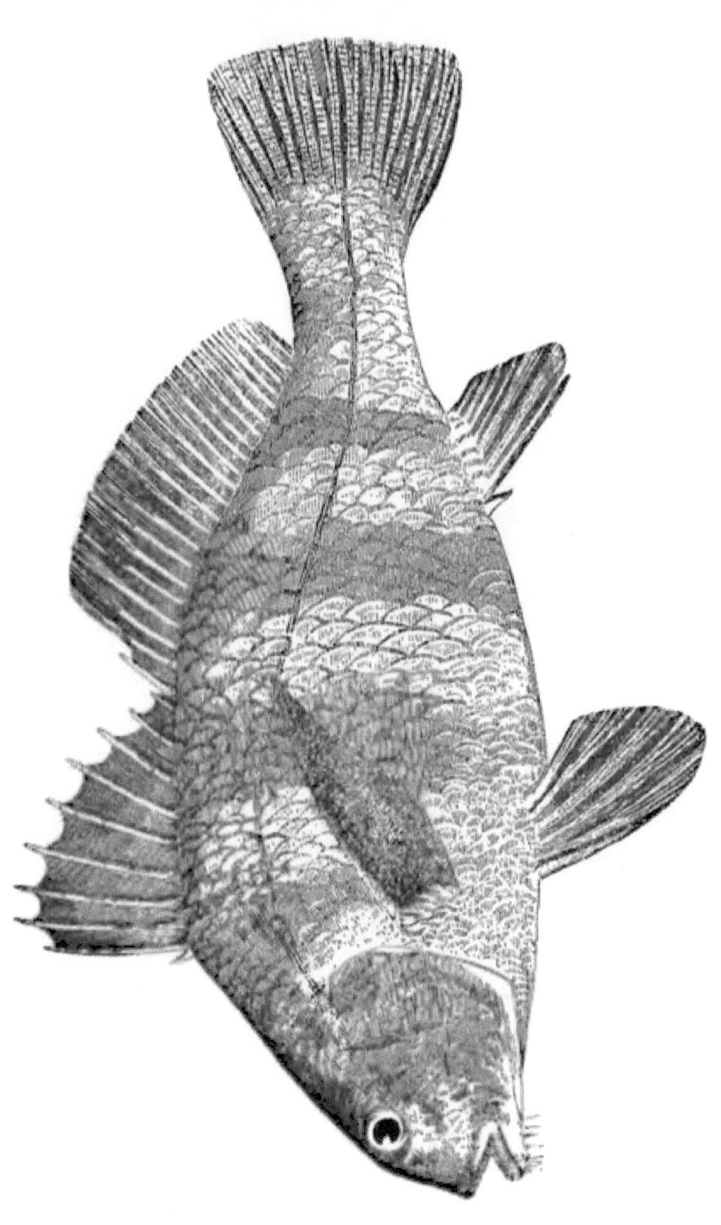

eighty pounds. I have been credibly informed of one that weighed a hundred and one pounds. He is taken abundantly during the summer, both with line and net.

"Color of the drum, a dull silvery, like the dross of melted lead, with a faint, brassy tinge of ruddy, though between the scales the skin is inclined to blackish on the back and sides, and thereby gives its denomination to the fish. Scales of the body exceedingly large, stiff, horny, and marked by radiated and concentric lines. Their form receding somewhat from square, and approaching the figure of the letter D. They are so planted in the skin, that it is difficult to remove them. Lateral line, broad, rather indistinct, and running scaly to the end of the tail. Under the scales the silvery hue is most considerable. A black patch on the other side of the older individuals, behind the pectoral fin. All the fins inclined to reddish, more especially the caudal, pectoral, and dorsal. Sometimes the space covered or shaded by the pectoral fin is pale or white. Tail even, eyes silvery yellow.

"His name of *drum* has been given on account of the drumming noise he makes, immediately after being out of water.

"He swims in numerous shoals in the shallow bays on the south side of Long Island, where fishermen, during the warm season, can find them, almost like a flock of sheep. Is a dull fish."

In addition to his whereabouts, stated by Mitchill, he is found in large company in the Kills and off Communipaw, where he is often taken by the weak-fish and basse angler. He sometimes takes a stroll up the stream, solus, and has been taken in Harlem river; and although a dull fish, it would seem, by the following extract from the New-York Herald, sometimes requires skill, experience, and activity, in taking him:

"*A great Haul.*—A gentleman of this city, who delight

in the rare sport of angling, and has spent a good part of the summer at Shantz's Hotel, Macomb's Dam, fishing with varied success for basse and blue-fish, day before yesterday,* (Thursday,) struck one of the monsters of the deep that sometimes visit that vicinity. On the first pull he thought that he had struck bottom, but his reel soon began to whiz, and his line to run with great rapidity. Finding nearly all his line, 300 feet, run out, he took up his anchor-stone, and away went the boat down the river about a mile; he then managed so as to make a tack, and up the river they went again, and down and up again for two hours and a half, until finally his majesty was got into shallow water, and a seizure made under the gills, but he slipped grasp and made a sudden lurch. taking rod and line, and floored himself on the grass about twenty yards from the boat. The gentleman, who is a muscular man, succeeded with some difficulty in getting him into the boat, when he proved to be a drum of the largest size, and on weighing at the hotel weighed a little over seventy pounds. This is believed to be the largest fish ever taken with rod and reel. The hooks were ordinary basse hooks, with a yard leader on double silk-worm gut. purchased at Brown's, a few days since, in Fulton street, near our office. A fish of the same kind was taken last summer in the Kills, by Mr. Michaels, weighing over forty pounds, and one by Mr. Keese, a few years ago, weighing over fifty pounds; but this caps the climax, and Mr. R. deserves a great deal of credit for his perseverance in this extraordinary feat."

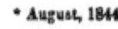

* August, 1844.

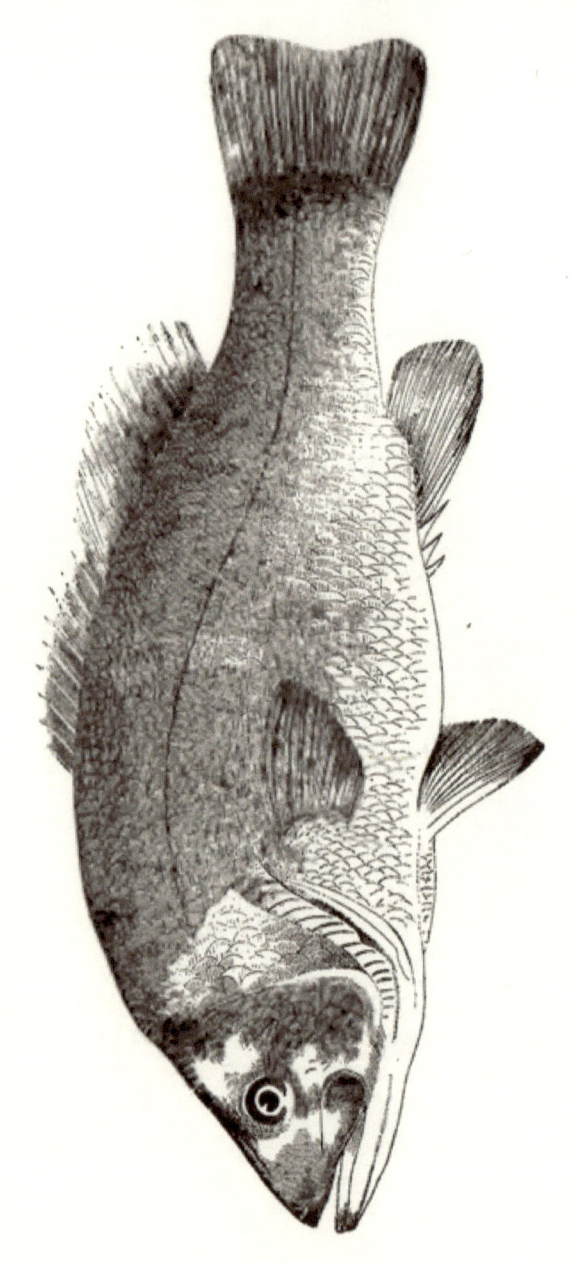

CHAPTER XV.

OF THE BLACK, OR OSWEGO BASSE.

This is the favorite game fish of the northern and western parts of our country, and is found in abundance in most of the northern lakes and western rivers. To our piscatorial friends in New-York, Ohio, Michigan and Kentucky, they afford unceasing delight, and no fish receives more encomiums as to the pleasure derived, either from the rod or fork.

His usual size is about twelve to fifteen inches in length by two inches in thickness and five inches broad. The color is deep black along the back and sides, growing lighter towards the belly, and becoming yellowish, in the female. It has a thick oval head; large mouth, with rows of small teeth; a wide dorsal fin near the centre of the body; another towards the tail, with corresponding pectoral and anal fins. The body is quite thick near the head, and tapers regularly, terminating in a swallow tail. It feeds principally on small fish, which betray its proximity by rising to the surface to elude pursuit. It is best taken with minnows and other kinds of small fish, but bites freely at lobsters and muscles.

The Buffalo correspondent appears to think that the black

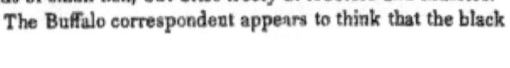

basse and Oswego basse are of different species. Hear him:

"*The Oswego and Black Basse.*—The Oswego basse and black basse bear so strong a resemblance to each other that not one fisherman in ten knows them as distinct entities. In form, color, weight, and habits, the two are almost perfectly identical; and yet their differences, though minute, are striking and essential. An Oswego basse, when placed by a black basse of the same size, is readily distinguished by his more forked tail, his greater thickness of shoulder, his coarser scales, and, above all, by his mouth, which, when open, is nearly twice as large as that of the black basse. In Lake Ontario the Oswego basse is abundant, and the black basse comparatively rare. In Lake Erie, the black basse greatly predominates, and it may be doubted whether the Oswegonian—like certain citizens of the Ontario shore—is not an interloper in our waters, who has found his way to us from below through some canal. However this may be, he is certainly right welcome!

"The black basse is our chief object of pursuit—his capture is our dearest triumph—his captive form our proudest trophy. When word first comes, in June, that the black basse bites in our river, what a stir there is among our anglers! —what questioning as to the when, and the where, and by whom, and with what bait, and the number, and size!—what an anxious inquiry after big minnows!—what a raking and scraping of pond-holes for soft lobsters!—what a watching of the skies!—and, if there be no wind, or a zephyr from the south or west, what bright and hopeful faces!—but if the storm rage, or an easterly wind, however gentle, fan our sleeping bay, what rueful countenances!—what half-suppressed repinings!—what a woful, spiritless attempting to be busy about our ordinary avocations! And why this commotion? Because this is the very prince of our game-fishes.

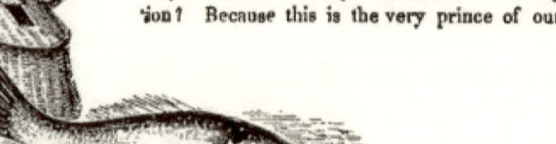

His capture is a less easy task, and involves, or is supposed to involve, more science, and to be a truer proof of merit as an angler, than any other tenant of our crystal waters. But (let me whisper it in thy ear, my friend!) there is much of fancy in all this. He is a noble fish, and struggles vigorously and most pertinaciously for liberty; but no art nor skill, unattainable by thee, or any one, is requisite to hook or draw him from his element.

"This fish beds in our streams and rivers, and probably, too, on the bars and shoals of our bay. Numbers run up the larger streams in May, and bite freely at the worm, in the middle and latter part of that month, in the Tonawanda. His appearance is too familiar to need description. His color varies, though it generally approaches black. I think only the smaller basse run up the creeks. Those taken in Tonawanda seldom overweigh two or two and a half pounds, and have a greenish hue. In the river they attain a weight of four and four and a half, and even five pounds; and occasionally heavier ones have been taken, weighing even eight pounds. The river fish, when fresh from the water, is frequently banded, like the perch, with broad bars of a darker hue, which disappear, however, and fade into the general color of the fish as he becomes dry. He seldom takes the hook, in the Niagara, until June. He is always fine eating, but is fattest and best in autumn."

He is angled for in the usual way, and with the same arrangement of tackle as the striped basse or salmon; and with some enthusiastic western sportsmen, is thought to give more amusement than either. But the most active and exciting mode of pursuit is with the trolling rod and boat. We are indebted to a friend who has frequented Lake George, for the following interesting communication:

"This is a game fish, affording the angler the very highest enjoyment. These fish are taken in various ways. When

13

collected on their feeding grounds, in August and the subsequent fall months, they are sometimes taken in considerable numbers. The usual mode of angling for them at this time, is either with or without a float, and with live bait—a small fish taken for the purpose, along the lake shores or in brooks. They are exceedingly strong and active—qualities which delight the angler. When first hooked, they run very wild, and almost invariably rise to the surface, and leap one, two, and even three feet in the air, shaking the head violently, evidently with a view to dislodge the fatal hook. Frequently, while making their runs, they will suddenly turn and come with all their power directly towards their enemy, and by thus slacking the line, will succeed in shaking the hook loose: this often happens with unexperienced fishermen, but more rarely with the angler who holds a good reel and winds rapidly. The most beautiful mode of angling for them known, is trolling either with live bait or an artificial fly of large size and gay appearance. The writer has succeeded remarkably well with a fly made on a large-sized Limerick hook, such as are used for striped basse when fishing with crab bait. The fly is made as follows:—Body of a peacock feather, wings of bright scarlet kerseymere and white pigeon feathers; or, the feather stripped from a white goose-quill, and wound round like the hackle, and surmounted with thin stripe of scarlet forwings. For trolling pleasantly and comfortably, the angler should provide a moveable seat, which he can place across the gunwale of his boat, in order that he may sit with his back to the oarsman, and facing the stern. Thus he will have full command of his rod and line, and not be sitting in the cramping attitude which the lowness of the seats would cause. He should reel off fifty to sixty, or even one hundred or more feet of line, and on going over shallow reefs of seven or eight feet depth, two hundred feet, as the fish feeding on the reefs usually dart aside as the boat passes, and do not return immediately to their harboring spot, which is one reason why those who do not use the reel are not as successful as those who employ it. After a few moments they glide back to their favorite spot, and as the fly comes along, dart at and seize it. A strong tug is felt by the angler, who has only to draw gently, and his prey is fastened. The oarsman rests on his oars, to give the angler full command of his line. The noble fish, after one or two runs to right and left, suddenly rises and makes his splendid leap, and plunging, again seeks the bottom, again rises, and then tries his last experiment of dashing right towards the boat. He struggles long and vigorously, but his strength is at last exhausted, and you trail your unresisting captive to the landing net. I have taken them of various weights, the largest weighing five pounds nine ounces: this was done last summer (1844) in Lake George. I believe they are sometimes taken much larger in the St. Lawrence river, and upper lakes, but my acquaintance with them is limited to the beautiful lake just mentioned.

"At Sherrill's capital hotel at Caldwell, every facility for enjoying this delightful sport can be had, though the best fishing grounds are down the lake.

"An excellent house is kept by Mr. Garfield, twenty-two miles down the lake, where the best fishing stations for the salmon trout are situated. There is a great deal of fine ground for the basse in the neighborhood.

"About ten miles from Caldwell, there is a place called the Narrows, where there are numerous small islands with shelving rocky shores, and fine trolling ground.

"Anglers will find good plain accommodation at a house kept by Mr. Lyman, who is very kind and attentive to his guests, and furnishes baits, guides, &c.

"In trolling for the black basse in Lake George, you will frequently strike those of one-half to three-fourths pound weight, even with the very large fly which I have described.

There is so great a difference, both in shape and color, between the fish of this size and those of two or more pound weight, that a stranger would never take them to be of the same species. These small fish are very similar in shape to the blue-fish of the salt water, while those of the larger size spread in width as they increase in size, so that a fish of two and a half to three pounds, is of a shape between a black-fish, or tautog, and the famous sheepshead. In color they differ also greatly: the small basse being of a light dull greenish color, while the larger grow darker as they increase in size, the largest being nearly black on the back, and of a very dark brownish green on the sides. The younger gentry, above described, are not to be despised on account of their size for when taken with a light trout rod, they will be found to be a fine vigorous fish, and when in their temerity they seize the large fly, on feeling the hook, they will, true to their nature, make the leap, in imitation of their sires, thus showing themselves to be game fish. I have known them to leap three times while reeling in the long trolling line, whereas the larger gentry rarely leap more than once."

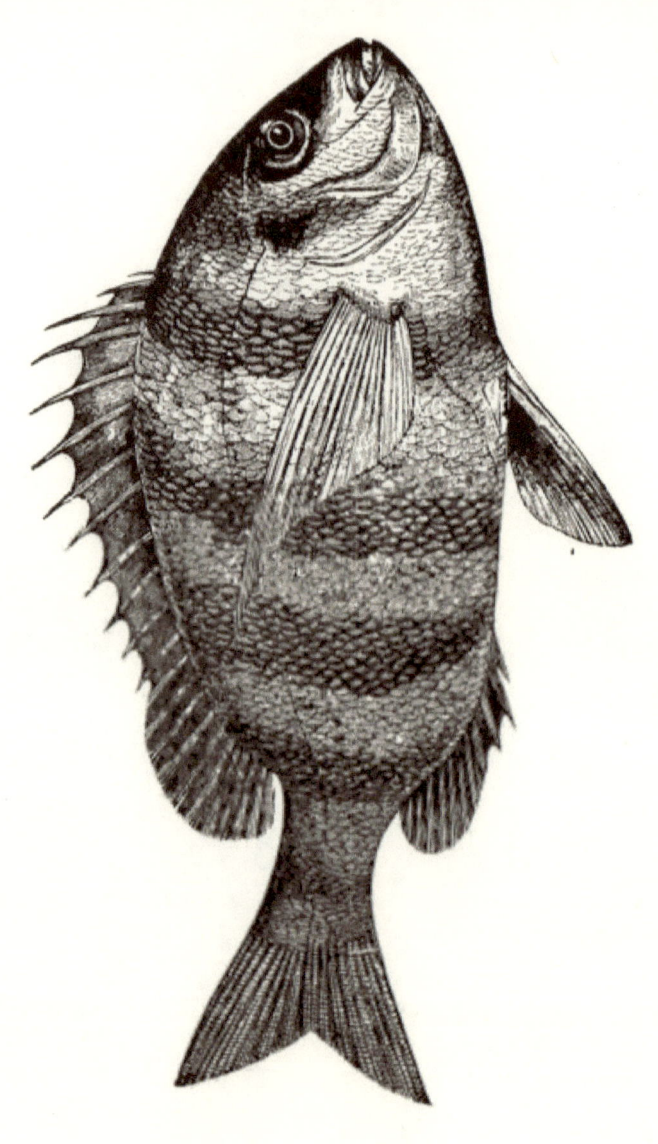

CHAPTER XVI.

OF THE SHEEPSHEAD.

This is another fish taken by the black-fish and basse sportsmen in the vicinity of New-York. He affords considerable excitement in capture, and much pleasure as a table fish.*
Of late years he has been considered very scarce, and does not seem willing, as usual, to tickle the palates of the inhabitants of Manhattan Island.

Sheep's Head—(sparus ovis.—Mitchill.)—" With smutty face, banded sides, pale complexion, prominent eyebrows, and grooved dorsal fin. The form of the mouth, and a certain smuttiness of face, have a distant resemblance to the physiognomy of the sheep. Thence comes the name by which he is usually distinguished.

" Grows big enough to weigh 14 or 15 pounds. One that weighed four pounds and a half, measured twenty inches in length, eight in depth, and three in thickness. Sheepshead is the most esteemed of New-York fishes, and fetches a higher

---

* It is said that the old adage, that "two heads are better than one if one is a *sheep's head*," will not apply to this fish.

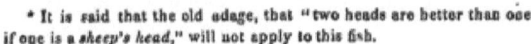

price than any, excepting, perhaps, fresh salmon and trout. The price varies from a dollar to one hundred and fifty cents, for a fish of middle size; that is, from four to seven pounds. Nothing, in the opinion of a New-Yorker, can exceed boiled sheepshead, served up at a sumptuous dinner.

" General color of the sheepshead a white or obscure silvery, with a smutty daubing over the face and chin, and a greenish tinge above the brow, and six or seven dark bands or zones of an inch or more in breadth, regularly slanting from back to belly: the latter a dull white, approaching, in some places and individuals, to cream color. Scales large, horny, distinguished by radiated and concentric lines, and somewhat like a square rounded at the corners. They are deeply inserted into the skin; adhere with remarkable firmness; and when they are separated, there is discoverable, on the edges of the skin that enclosed them, a sort of tarnished argentine or brightish leaden hue. Rays of all the fins coarse.

" This noble fish visits the neighborhood of Long Island annually. Emerging from the depths of the ocean, he finds in the recesses and inlets there, a plenty of the crabs, muscles, and clams, on which he loves to feed. He confines himself strictly to the salt water, never having been seen in the fresh rivers. His term of continuance is only during the warmest season; that is, from the beginning of June to the middle of September. He then departs to the unknown depths of the Atlantic, and is seen no more until the ensuing summer. I have, however, known him to stay later; for one of the most numerous collections of sheepshead I ever saw in New-York market, was on the 4th of October, 1814. I have seen him as late as the 17th.

" The sheepshead swims in shoals, and is sometimes surrounded in great numbers by the seine. Several hundred have often been taken at a single haul, with the long sweeping nets in use near Raynortown, Babylon, and Fire Island.

They even tell of thousands being brought to land at a draught.

"He also bites at the hook, and is not unfrequently caught in succession. The outfitting of a sheepsheading party, is always an occasion of considerable parade and high expectation, as I have often experienced. Whenever a sheepshead is brought on board the boat, more joy is manifested than by the possession of any other kind of fish. The sportsmen view the exercise so much above common fishing, that the capture of the sheepshead is the most desirable combination of luck with skill; and the feats of hooking and pulling him in, furnish materials for the most hyperbolical stories. The sheepshead is a very stout fish, and the hooks and lines are strong in proportion. Yet he frequently breaks them, and makes his escape. Sheepshead have been caught with such fish tackle fastened to their jaws. When the line and hook gives way, the accident makes a serious impression on the company. As the possession of the sheepshead is a grand prize, so his escape is felt a distressing loss. I knew an ancient fisherman, who used to record in a book the time, place, and circumstance, of every sheepshead he had caught."

"This fish is sometimes speared, by torch-light, in the wide and shallow bays of Queens and Suffolk counties, Long Island.

"The places where he is found in the greatest abundance, are about 40 miles from the city. He soon dies after being removed from his element, and in such sultry weather soon spoils after death."

The proper tackle for taking this fish is precisely the same as that used for the largest black-fish, to wit: a stout dropline, of hemp or cotton, from fifty to one hundred and fifty feet in length, and about one-fourth of an inch in thickness, and heavy sinker, according to tide and depth of water, and a stout black-fish hook of the largest size, each of which

should be thoroughly tried before they are cast into the water With such an outfit, the accidents spoken of by Mitchill may be avoided.

An amateur friend, who has had great success in taking this fish, furnishes the following:

"This noble fish has become quite scarce in our harbor. The writer has taken them repeatedly on a small reef near Governor's Island, opposite the Battery, but this was in days long since gone by. They are taken still occasionally at Caving Point, and opposite the signal poles at the Narrows; also at Pelham Bridge, and in Little Hellgate.

"Strong tackle is essential for taking them, as they are a very vigorous and powerful fish. They are usually found on reefs or in the neighborhood of large rocks, whither they resort for their favorite food, which is the small rock crab and the soft-shell clam—a very common bait is the latter. The clam is put on the hook whole, by inserting the point of the hook through the stem, and burying the whole of the curve in the body of the clam. This fish is furnished with a fine set of front teeth, very nearly resembling the teeth of the sheep—whence the name; the roof of the mouth is literally paved with round teeth, placed closely together, like the paving stones in the carriage track of our city, enabling them to crack the shell of the clams with perfect ease. Some anglers, after placing the clam on the hook, slightly crack the shell on one side; but this sometimes causes the flesh of the clam to be exposed to those enemies of the angler for sheepshead—the bergalls. The sheepshead will take the whole clam when he finds it, and crack it in his paved mouth, without the previous aid of the fisherman. Where the small fish are not plenty—which is the case on the feeding grounds in the south bays—I much prefer a bait of the opened soft or hard clam of large size—as large at least as a pullet's egg—and have been far more successful with it than with the

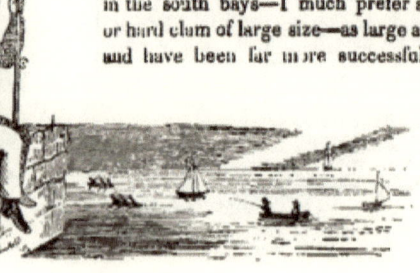

whole clam. The shedder crab is also a very fine, attractive bait for them, on grounds where small fish are not numerous.

"Great care and skill are requisite in playing a sheepshead. His runs are very vigorous, and his struggles to get rid of the hook very powerful. He will dash head-foremost against a rock, or the bottom of the boat, in the most violent manner, evidently striving to rid himself of the fatal hook, and has often been known to succeed in breaking the hook and escaping. I once saw a very fine one, which a companion was playing, dash violently against the large rock, (one of the famous stepping stones in Long Island Sound,) and in his next run, rushing against the bottom of the boat, with a loud thump; and when finally subdued and taken, the shank of the hook was found to be broken, and he was only held by the strong guaging of the line. The experienced fishermen along the Long Island shore of the Sound, often succeed in taking sheepshead, by selecting a rock not usually visited by fishermen, and baiting it by throwing in daily, for a week or two, in the proper season, a half-peck of soft clams, whole, depositing them on the eddy side of the rock, caused by the flood-tide. They are thus taken, sometimes, in very shallow water. These cunning fellows carefully conceal the operation of baiting, and when questioned by their competitors, often give evasive answers. I knew one, a fine old fellow, of Great Neck, who, when asked—'Uncle Jim, where did you catch your sheepshead?' very gravely replied—'In the mouth.'

"The general mode of fishing for them is with the hand line, and as before observed, with strong tackle; but they are also taken, by amateur fishermen, with the rod, and lighter tackle, affording great amusement by their powerful endeavors to escape. When angling for them with the rod, a large landing net should always be at hand. A friend of mine, now deceased, was playing a sheepshead with his rod

in Flatlands bay, some years since, and when he had fairly exhausted his strength by long and careful skill, and was reeling him towards the boat, on the surface of the water, lost his noble prize by the rapacity of a villanous shark, who seized the fish, and broke away with part of the line. In the evening of the same day, some net fishermen were hauling the seine on a neighboring beach, and captured the piratical monster; and on opening him, the sheepshead was found in his stomach, partly digested, with my friend's hook in his jaw."

The Buffalo correspondent remarks, of the fresh and salt water sheepshead—

"This is a villain in general estimation—the pest of the fisher for basse—a fish that putteth the cook, who would render him acceptable at table, in a quandary—from which, I am sorry to say, I cannot relieve her, though she be at her wit's end.

"He is generally brown, gray or reddish above, and of a dead, impure white below. His head is large, and his body is flattened latterly, though the frying-pan rejecteth him. His ordinary weight is two or three pounds, though he sometimes weighs five, and even six. His food, his haunts, his habits, are similar to those of the black basse, whom he ever accompanieth—as though he were intended by nature as a foil to set off the merits of that jewel of the flood. He is despised, yea detested by the choleric angler—who pulls him out, and then dasheth him upon the stones.

"The sheepshead of the sea is a lusty, crafty fish, bepraised alike by the fisherman and the epicure. At the turn of the tide, he takes the whole soft clam on your hook at a mouthful, and chews it shell and all, and pulls like a salmon as you draw him in; and his radiant, deep, and broad-barred sides, as he flaps about on the sand of that low islet in the Great South bay of Long Island, to which you have just hauled

him—how brilliantly they show, and make you think of the dying dolphin, and of old Arion! and when he reposes at the head of the table—fit place for him—beautiful, though boiled, how heartfelt is the homage he receives from all around! Truly, it is libel on him, to call by the same name this Paria of the lakes.

"And yet our fish is vigorous, and not altogether destitute of beauty, to the eye at least of those who know him not. Is it not chronicled, that at Black-Rock, a strange angler once bartered away two noble basse for two large sheepsheads, which, for the nonce, were called white basse? 'The freckled toad, ugly and venomous, wears yet a precious jewel in his head'—and our fish, in his clumsy cranium wears two small loose bones, serrate, and white and polished, which must have some use to him, some wondrous adaptation to his mode of life, which, when unfolded, will prove that he is not unregarded by Him who made the great whales and the fishes of the sea.

"His mouth is paved with large, flat, rough bones, or teeth, like those of the sea fishes that root up and devour the hardest testaceæ: and, I have little doubt but that the naturalist who watches him narrowly, will one of these days detect him crushing and consuming the Uni and Anadontas—the fresh clams of our muddy flats and sandy bars.

"He bites at the worm, the minnow, the chub, the lobster, and makes good play with the line, though he gives in more quickly than the basse. An experienced angler can generally distinguish his bite and his resistance—but the most knowing ones are sometimes taken in, and think him basse until he is fairly brought to view.

"When you have caught him, let any one who will accept him, have him; and take to thyself no merit for the gift. His meat is more like leather than fish or flesh. It is a common saying, that the more you cook him the tougher he becomes;

and I am not aware that he is ever eaten raw. But, some people do eat him, and profess to like him: they must have stupendous powers of mastication and digestion. I have been told, that, roasted whole in the ashes, just as he comes from the water, he is savory and tender—*sed credat Judæus!* I once did eat him, prepared as follows: He was split through the back, put upon the gridiron, there grilled enough to cook a side of pork: his flesh was removed from the skin, boned, chopped up into dice, (probably with a cleaver,) and stewed with milk, butter, pepper and salt. I must say, that, though it was meat of great tenacity, and might well be likened unto India-rubber, it had much sweetness "

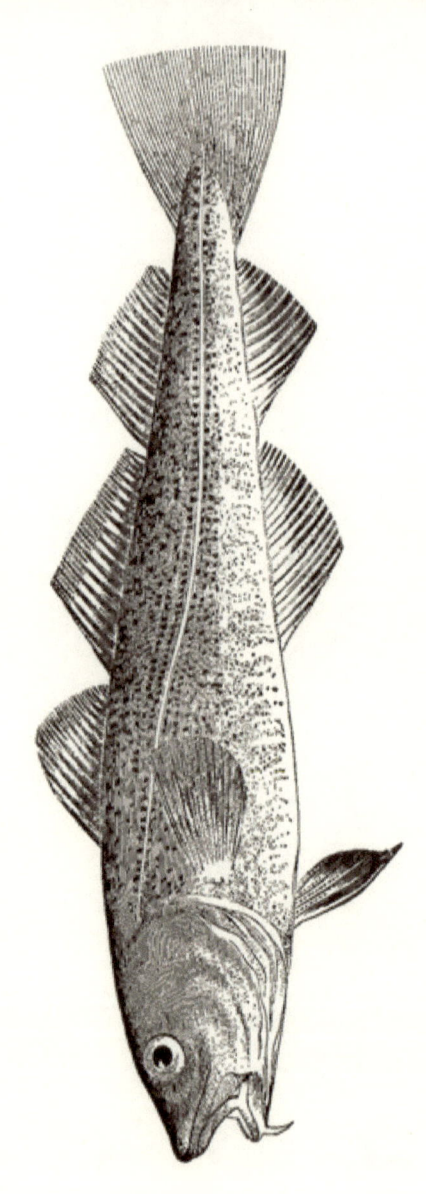

CHAPTER XVII.

OF THE COD AND TOM-COD.

The cod is another salt-water fish of the world, or, more properly, the more northern coasts of the civilized world, as far as known. They are taken in abundance on the coasts of England, France and Germany, and are found in immense numbers on the northern shores of our own continent. They are a fine, edible fish; and although not much of a game fish, afford considerable sport to many of our eastern anglers in the vicinity of Boston.

Smith remarks on this fish—"We consider it unnecessary to enter into a minute description. Known as the most valuable production of the sea to man, the cod abounds on the whole coast of Massachusetts, but flourishes in the greatest vigor and abundance still further north.

The cod is gregarious, going in immense armies from place to place, but remaining certain parts of the season at particular localities, which afford its appropriate food in the greatest abundance: sea-worms, small muscles, and marine plants, are common on clear, sandy or rocky bottoms—and there the cod is caught.

"The in-shore cod, as on the Great Banks, are caught with a line in two to six and eight fathoms of water, where the tide ebbs and flows with considerable force over rocky soundings. Pleasure boats are often successful in hauling one or two hundred in a day, weighing from one to fifteen pounds. Those large specimens seen occasionally in the stalls, are procured further out at sea.

"In the spring, the cod seems uncommonly voracious; for however unsuccessful it may have been in snatching the bait from the hook, and notwithstanding the mouth may have been lacerated, it seizes with avidity the very next it discovers. Wounds heal in a few days, so that however badly the skin is torn, the gelative of the blood is poured in so copiously as to close the breach much sooner than the healing process is completed in warm-blooded animals.

"Two or three years since, the keeper of Rainsford Island caught a cod which had suspended to about a yard of line, a lead weight of several pounds, the other end being secured to a hook which was deeply imbedded in the bones and integuments of the upper jaw. How long the fish had been dragging about the inconvenient burden, it was difficult to decide."

One of the most important features in this fish, is its astonishing fecundity. Leuwenhock has had the patience to count nine millions of eggs in a single cod; and although hundreds of millions of these eggs are hourly destroyed by the fishermen, who take them at all seasons, and their more voracious brethren of the ocean, who feed upon them—still, says a French writer, on the subject of their prolific powers, we have assurance of an inexhaustible supply of wholesome food, secured to all succeeding generations.

The best bait for a pleasure party cod-fishing, is the common mud clam; by some, however, the menhaden* is

* This fish also goes under the name of marsbanker, or mosbonker.

thought preferable. Many kinds of fish may be successfully caught by the flesh of their own species; but this is not the case with the cod. That the odor of some kinds of bait is particularly agreeable is well established; but the smell of putrid matter, to this fish, is so offensive, that instead of playing about the hook, they generally go beyond its influence.

They are made an object of much sport and pleasure by the angling inhabitants of Boston and vicinity. The usual mode of taking them is with a stout cotton or hemp line, from fifty to one hundred and fifty feet in length, and about one-fourth of an inch thick, according to the depth of the water, with the largest size black-fish hook, or a small size fisherman's cod hook, and a sinker weighing from one to four pounds. Parties on such excursions seldom return without a boat-load of cod, and a well-satisfied but very tired set of anglers.

As an instance of what can be done with this fish, with a light tackle, it was stated in the papers of the day, about a year since, that Daniel Webster caught, at Marshfield, a cod weighing nine pounds, with a common trout line and trout hook.

The cod is most delicious as a table fish, and is cooked in various ways: when fresh, he is usually fried or boiled; when dried, he is an object of export to all parts of the country: at the east, when in this state, he is prepared and mashed up into cakes with potatoes, and is a favorite dish. Of late years, the frequenters of New-York dining saloons have been rather amused by the often reiterated cry of the waiters—'*Hurry up them fish-balls.*' This is no more nor less than the potatoe fish-cakes of the east, prepared for the palates of the Gothamites by Sweeney, and Welsh, and other caterers for the appetites of the New-Yorkers.

they are found in vast quantities on the coast of Long Island, and in the bays and inlets of Massachusetts, where they are used for manuring the land.

The Tom-Cod or Frost-Fish.—This is a small species of the cod, that runs up the rivers in the vicinity of the ocean, and is found both in this country and many parts of Europe. Although not much of an angle fish, he affords, with the flounder, a *pan mess* for the angler in the vicinity of Boston and New-York, in the pleasant days of April and November, when the basse fishing season is over.

Smith says—"The tom-cod may be recognized by three dorsal fins, two anal, three abdominal, two pectoral. The abdominal are small and slender, being before the pectoral, as it respects the head; under the tip of the under lip is one short, stump-like cirrus. The caudal fin is broad, and rounded at the extremity. Teeth fine, both in the throat and jaws; white, small and plump tongue; the lateral line bearing upwards. Its color varies at different seasons of the year, from a rich orange to a light greenish yellow, shaded by a dark brown on the back, and gradually becoming light or yellow between the vent and the gills. It varies in length, from six to fifteen inches, and weighs from a quarter to nearly two pounds, depending, of course, on the age, sex and season. In the north of Europe—admitting this to be the fish, which at present cannot be doubted—they have been occasionally known to exceed eight pounds. The spawning season appears to be in February; in this climate, about the first of May, they begin to take the hook."

They are usually taken by the basse and tautog angler, with the ordinary tackle, with the exception of the hook, which should be a No. 9 black-fish, or No. 6 Kirby. When pursuing this sport exclusively, a small flax line about fifty feet in length, attached to a stiff rod, or in boat fishing, a medium sized hand black-fish line, with small hooks attached to flax or gut snell, will answer every purpose.

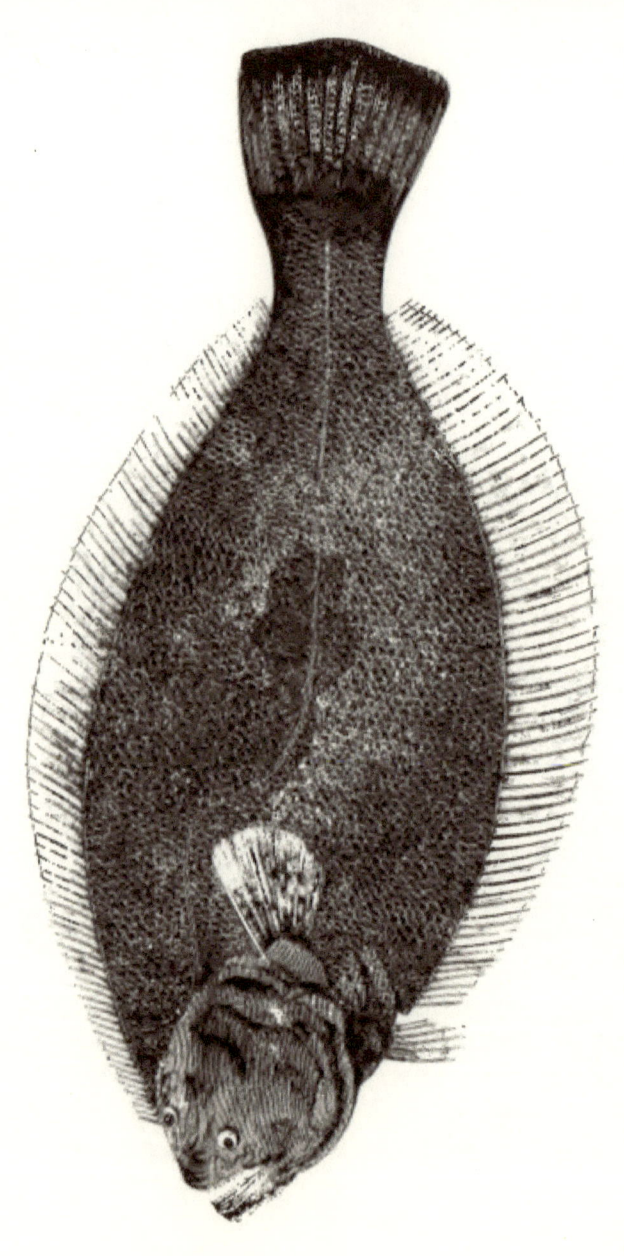

CHAPTER XVIII.

OF THE FLOUNDER.

This is one of the most singular and odd-looking productions of the deep, and were it not that they are the common salt water fish of the world, would be viewed with wonder and astonishment. One would suppose, from the flat appearance and formation of their bodies, that nature had been rather scarce of materials when making up this division of the salt water tribe. Besides many places of their abode, too numerous to mention, in the old world, they are found in most of salt water stations of the new. They are taken in goodly quantities, and in good condition, in certain seasons, according to Smith and Mitchill, in the vicinity of New-York and Massachusetts, and also to the south and north of these places. The former remarks—" No family of aquatic beings is characterized by so many strong circumstances. The eyes are both on one side, but so arranged as to look upward at an angle of about eighty degrees. The side on which the eyes are fixed is always colored, but the opposite one is quite light or whitish. In fact, their anatomy demonstrates the greatest want of symmetry. Writers remark, among other things

14

that the two sides are unequal, and it is very rare to find the pectoral fins resembling one another. In the branchial membrane are five rays; the body seems compressed, as though pressed between two stones; the dorsal fin encircles the fish like a ribbon, so that the *back* is on one side! The venter, or inside cavity, is quite small, but prolonged into a canal in the side of the tail. There is no air-bladder; and the skull is the oddest of all crania, in consequence of the arrangement for accommodating both eyes on one side.

"Notwithstanding the confused manner in which the skeleton is put together, distorted, and twisted in the queerest form, there is only about the ordinary number of bones, entering into the composition of other fishes.

"*Flounder.*—(Platessa Vulgaris.)—Being without the swimming-bladder, they naturally keep near the bottom. Indeed, organized, as they obviously are, for looking upward, rather than downward, for their food, as well as the objects they are to avoid. It is quite rapid in its movements, but prefers to remain on the surface of the mud, into which it nestles for concealment, in case of fright."

Mitchill has the following: "*Flounder of New-York.*—(Pleuronectes dentatus.)—With wide, toothed, oblique mouth, and pale brown uniform back. Grows to the size of twenty-four inches long, and twelve broad, in the south bays of Long Island, and weighs five pounds. I have seen him even larger than that. There is considerable variety in his color and spots. Color of the back and fins commonly a pale brown, without lines or spots; and yet varieties occur, where the spotted appearance is very plain."

The size of the usual run of this fish, at New-York and Boston, is from five to fifteen inches in length by three to ten in breadth. Like the eel, they lie in the soft mud at the bottom of rivers, near to the docks, lumber piles, bridge spiles, &c., living on muscles, insects, and the spawn of fishes.

They are in the best condition in the spring and fall, the heat of the summer not being favorable to their perfection, at which time their flesh is soft and not as palatable. They are a favorite angle fish at all the bridges near Boston, where fishermen can be seen at almost any time in mild weather, hauling them up or waiting for a bite. They are taken in Harlem river, New-York, in the vicinity of the bridges, and at the numerous black-fish and rock grounds. They do not appear to keep any particular kind of company, but give the more finished basse angler some trouble when seeking a ten-pound rock at the bottom, by nibbling the bait with his small mouth, and sometimes insisting on being hooked.

The usual mode of taking him is with a small flax dropline, and small black-fish tackle: to insure success, quite a small hook must be used, say about No. 8 hook. The basse angler often provides himself with small hooks, and when his favorite fish is not on the feed, is content to take, if he can get them, a mess of flounders. They are, when fresh caught, good pan fish, and by some, when in season and perfection, considered an epicurean dish.

CHAPTER XIX.

OF THE BLUE-FISH.

This fish is a species of the mackerel, and sometimes passes under that name. He has his peculiar grounds in Long Island Sound, where he schools from the ocean in the months of June, July and August, after which he returns to the sea to spend his vacation. They are taken only by trolling with the artificial squid—a mode of amusement calling into action the physical as well as scientific powers of the angler. They are a good table fish, when prepared and cooked immediately after being caught, but grow strong and rancid after being any length of time out of the water.

The Art of Trolling, of late years, has become a favorite mode of piscatorial amusement, and the blue-fish affords to the inhabitants of Connecticut, New-York and Long Island, a large amount of satisfaction in its pursuit. It is usually performed in a good sized sail-boat, with a guide who knows the ground, or by casting from the shore, and drawing in alternately. The former method is most practiced, and being highly approved of by the fair sex, who often compose the best part of a fishing party, of course stamps it at once with

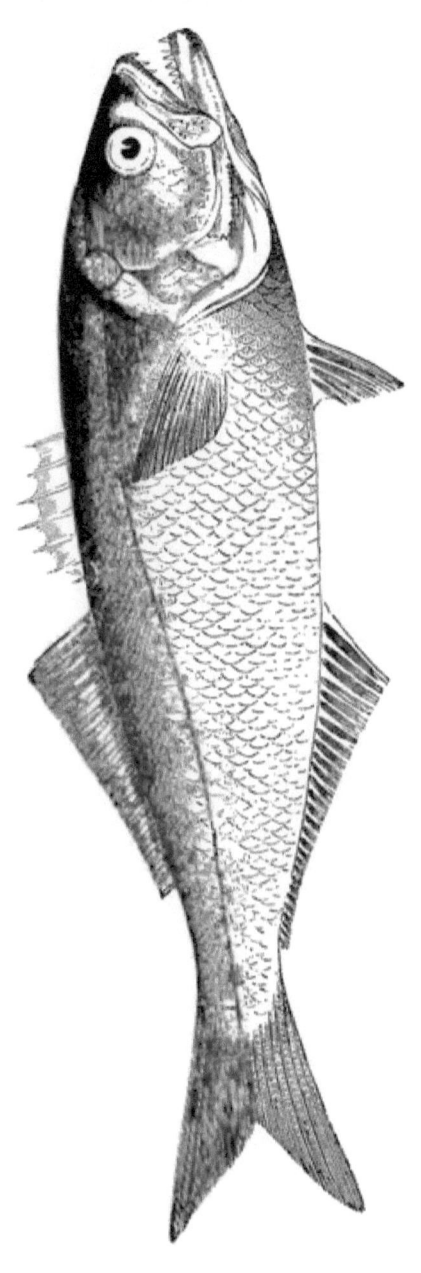

perfection. To those ladies who unfortunately have to be placed on the list of invalids, and can endure the delightful and bracing summer breeze and gentle south wind, a few days' sport in the Sound, with a blue-fishing party, will amply repay them for their exertion.

The tackle is simple, cheap, and easily arranged: it is composed of a squid made of bone, ivory, tin or pearl, with a stout line, of from 100 to 150 feet in length, attached: and when the boat is in full sail, the squid is thrown out, the fish hooked, drawn in and shaken off, and thrown out, alternately. We give an extract from a letter written by a gentleman on an excursion on the south side of Long Island:

"Who that has been a frequenter of our bays and inlets, can ever forget the intense excitement attending the sport of blue-fishing? Those who desire to be successful in this delightful sport, should provide themselves with a proper outfit, (which can be procured at a trifling expense at any of the shops where fishing tackle is sold,) as an omission in this may result in disappointment.

"The tackle in most general use, is a squid made of block-tin, lead, mother-of-pearl, or white bone, of a flat, narrow-oval shape, say four inches long, armed on one end with a good sized hook, (No. 0000 Kirby,) laid so that the point of the hook be perpendicular to the flat side of the squid. I would recommend a short length of stout gimp to be put through a hole in the other end, to attach it to the line. I have repeatedly witnessed, in excursions on the south side of Long Island, the loss of a squid at a time when a lover of this sport could least afford to lose time in making the necessary repairs to his damaged tackle. The line should be of cotton, large sized, and *well laid*, of, say from forty to sixty yards long. A thin, light line will not answer, as, in case a large fish is hooked, there is more than an even chance that the line part before the fish is secured; and should the fish be got in,

the fisher's lacerated hands will remind him that there is more comfort in trolling with the regular squidding tackle than with a light hemp line, such as we sometimes see used by the uninitiated.

"Being thus provided with the tackle suitable for this sport, you should get a good stout boat, with an experienced bay-man, who is *au fait* in its management, and intimately acquainted with the habits and localities of the fish; for upon this, in a great measure, depends your chance of a good day's sport. With a fine breeze, that will propel your boat some four or five miles an hour, you may embark, and having reached the whereabouts of the fish, cast over your squid, with from fifty to one hundred feet of line, which should be tied securely to the boat. The fish sometimes strike with great force, and neglect in fastening the line frequently results in its loss, with everything appertaining thereto.

"There is a great variety of opinion regarding the length of line most proper to use in this kind of fishing; but I have found that when the fish are inclined to take the squid, they are not over particular in the quantity of line out, as I have seen fish taken, not only with a very long line, but have hooked and secured some fine ones, myself, almost under the stern of the boat, with certainly not over twenty feet of line.

"When a school of fish is found, the boatman should be particular in crossing and re-crossing the spot where the school is, as in a very contracted space it frequently happens that the greatest sport is to be found. As an example of this, I was enjoying a day's sport at Shrewsberry Inlet, some two years since, and the only place where I took any fish, was some three hundred yards below the inlet, in the river; and instead of sailing up some half mile, and down again, over the same ground, I confined my operations to a space of about two hundred yards, and was very successful, returning with a full fare. When a fish is struck, the line should be hauled in with a steady pull—not jerked. If the line is allowed to slack, the fish is apt to throw itself off.

"To disengage the fish from the hook, take the squid in the right hand, and by giving it a slight shake, with the hook uppermost, the fish will drop off into the boat.

"When the boat is in stays, (*tacking*,) care should be taken to haul in the line; an omission in this will cause your squid to sink and foul in the bottom grass.

"Blue-fish are sometimes taken from the shore, by casting the squid as far as possible into the water, and hauling it in with sufficient rapidity to prevent its sinking far below the surface. This mode of fishing is attended with a large outlay of labor, but in reward, some fine fish are taken. The places best known and most resorted to for blue-fishing, are Babylon, Islip, and Quogue, L. I. The two former have the great South Bay, with Fire Island Inlet, for its ground; the latter the East Bay, and Pine Neck Inlet. Babylon and Islip are nigh at hand, and easy of access; Quogue lies some ninety miles east of New-York, but has become comparatively near by means of the Long Island railway, which places it within five hours of the city.

"In visiting the latter spot, the disciple of the rod and gun will find a good house, and a kind, hospitable, obliging man in its proprietor. Shrewsberry Inlet is another resort, near which, at Port Washington, a fine house has been opened."

CHAPTER XX.

OF THE SEA-BASSE, PORGEE, &c.

These are both sea fish, and abound in immense quantities in the ocean outside of Sandy Hook, New-York, on what are called the Sea-Basse and Porgee Banks. In the summer months, to the pent-up citizen who is obliged to stay in the city during the sweltering heat of July and August—the stranger who would view the beauties of one of the finest harbors in the world—and to the more scientific angler, who, after a season's fishing at the gently gliding stream, or the romantic mountain lake, would like to try the more bracing atmosphere of the ocean—this mode of angling will often afford a day of amusement and gratification.

During the above-mentioned months, steamboats are prepared and fitted up for this species of fishing, and make their trips sometimes daily, returning, often, with well-satisfied amateur ocean anglers, each with their string of fish.* In order to enliven the scene on these occasions, a band of music

* In the summer of 1843, immense quantities were taken—the steamboat often returning with from six to ten thousand porgees, and a porpoise weighing five or six hundred pounds.

is taken, and cotillion parties are made up on the upper deck. A skilful harpooner sometimes makes one of the party, and gives excitement to the scene by striking and taking a porpoise. The boat touches at Coney Island, giving the passengers an opportunity of a sea bathe and a clam bake; and also at Fort Hamilton, allowing an opportunity to view the fortifications of the harbor.

In addition to this mode, schooners and sloops are chartered by private pleasure parties, who spend two or three days on an excursion down the bay and sound, affording opportunity for ocean and inland fishing, and often return with an assortment of the finny tribe, consisting of perch, trout, rock, tautog, blue-fish, flounders, cod-fish, sea-basse, and porgees, enough to stock a small-sized fish market.

The proprietors of the steamboats endeavor to accommodate the passengers with bait and tackle, and sometimes succeed; but to insure success and satisfaction, the seeker of this description of sport should procure his own. The line should be of stout flax or hemp, from ten to twenty fathoms in length, (generally for sale, ready furnished, at the fishing tackle stores,) with two or three hooks attached, about a foot apart: those for porgees should be the round bent blackfish No. 3, described on plate 2. For sea-basse, the hook should be a stout Kirby No. 1. The assortment should always consist of both kinds, and plenty of them, as they are sometimes taken off by shark and blue-fish, or are broken against the side of the boat in hauling up. The sinker should be of common lead, and weigh from one-half to one pound (the latter size, if only one is taken, is the best.) Clam bait is the only kind used, and necessary: these can be purchased at the markets, ready opened. To render them tough and hard, add a little salt, which will make them cling to the hook much better. When luck favors these excursions, two, three, and even four fish are taken at a haul. It is necessary to be on the alert, and jerk strongly at each bite, or your bait will be taken off. The fish average from one to four pounds which, together with your pound sinker, makes a considerable weight to take in, in from ten to fifteen fathoms water. The finger and hand will often become chafed and blistered, where much luck is experienced; to prevent which, the knowing ones provide themselves with a pair of old gloves. With this additional equipment, you can fully enjoy a hardy and active day's sport, tempered with the benefits arising from the bracing ocean air, and the contemplation of the works of the Creator on the great deep, so beautifully described by the poet Dana, in the following beautiful lines:

> Type of the Infinite! I look away
> Over the billows, and I cannot stay
> My thoughts upon a resting-place, or make
> A shore beyond my vision, where they break;
> But on my spirit stretches, till it's pain
> To think; then rests, and then puts forth again.
> Thou holdst me by a spell; and on thy beach
> I feel all soul; and thoughts unmeasured reach
> Far back beyond all date. * * * * * *

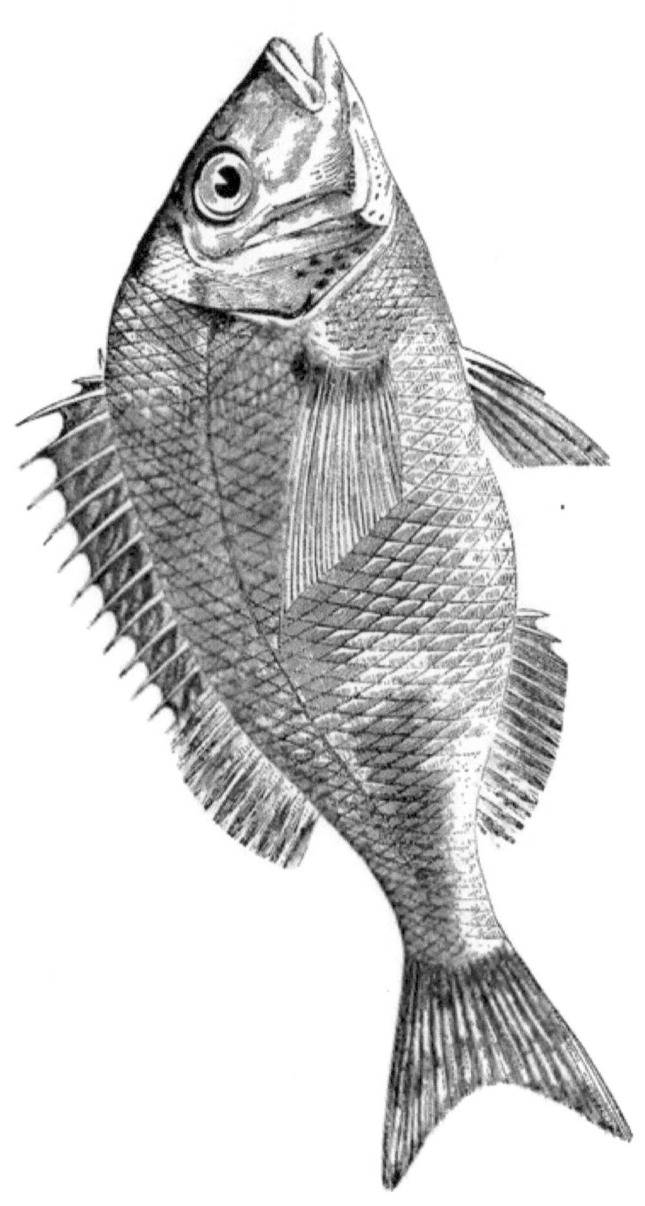

CHAPTER XXI.

OF SOME OF THE OTHER INHABITANTS OF THE WATERS.

In the foregoing articles on the different fishes, it has been the object, as far as possible, to give necessary information of all angle fishes, and the modes of taking them. In furtherance of this design, many more pages have been occupied than was originally intended; but such a variety of fishes is offered by the nature and extent of our country, that it has seemed almost impossible, without wading thus far, to do justice to our subject. For the further benefit of the reader, we will venture briefly to refer to some others of the finny tribe.

THE EEL.

This serpentine looking animal has its friends and foes, and is found in almost all fresh and salt water streams that circumvent the globe. In ancient times, it was highly valued; and at the present, although looked upon as belonging to the snake tribe, is considered, by the majority of fish eaters, as forming a very savory dish. Those that inhabit the salt water, are sometimes taken of a very large size. The largest taken, on record, was caught in one of the bays in Long Island, and weighed sixteen and a half pounds. They also, in some instances, grow very large in fresh water streams, and have been taken from seven to ten pounds weight. They are not game, but occasion the angler much trouble wherever he drops his line, by sucking off his bait or insisting upon being hooked; when, with all care, the most experienced sportsman seldom escapes without great derangement of tackle. When sought after, he is taken (we say taken, because no difficulty is ever experienced where he is) with any kind of tackle and any bait. The most common mode, however, with those who make a practice of taking him, is with a common drop-line, and a small black-fish or eel hook, No. 8 or 9.

A singular and beautiful description of the eel, if any beauty can be attached to the tribe, is found in some of our fresh water streams, called the lamprey or seven-eyed eel.

OF THE CHUB.

This beautiful fish is found, according to Smith, in some of the western sections of Massachusetts. "It is taken with a hook baited with an *angle-worm*. In winter it may be caught through the ice by baiting with cheese and Venice turpentine.

"The head is large, the back of a dusky green, the sides silvery, the abdomen white, the pectoral fins yellowish, and the ventral and anal fins tinged with red. This fish seems to be very timid, and the angler therefore, in fixing himself in a good position, over some deep hole, where the chub conceals himself under projecting long roots of trees, is obliged to move very cautiously, or he will frighten it away."

He is also taken in the Passaic river, N. J., Otsego lake, Fishkill creek, and many other parts of New-York and Penn-

THE PERCH.

THE CHUB.

THE EEL.

sylvania. Their length is not usually over ten inches, and the common size about six. In England and Germany they are sometimes taken weighing eight pounds. They may be taken with the same degree of caution, and with the same kind of tools as those used for trout. They are attracted also by similar bait: in the spring they will take the worm, and later in the season, the grasshopper, and the natural and artificial fly, of every description. In the fall they are again taken at the bottom, in the deep holes, with the worm, cheese, or bread-paste, salmon roe, &c. They yield considerable sport, and are worth the angler's toil, often being taken and placed as an edible on the table—they are not bad to take with the knife and fork.

OF THE BULL-HEAD AND SUCKER.

These are fish usually found in the same ponds and streams with perch and pickerel. They are sought after more as an object of sport, among the boys, than as forming an article of food, although they are sometimes cooked for the table. The sucker is also speared in large quantities by torch light.

OF THE BREAM, ROACH, DACE, BLEAK, AND GUDGEON.

These are all described by Smith as natives of the waters of the Eastern States. They are quite small in size, are all good and nutritious food. They are taken, with ordinary caution, with trout and perch tackle; but from their size, do not afford much sport. They grow much larger in England and Scotand, and find favor as a game fish, in English works and among English anglers.

OF THE HERRING.

A species of fish called herring, is taken by the angler, in

some of the fresh water streams of New-Jersey and Delaware In the latter state, they are very shy, take the fly, and require long rods and fine tackle, similar to that used for trout. In the vicinity of Baltimore they fish fine and far off, and with rods from 20 to 25 feet long, the sportsman experiencing as much pleasure in the capture, as in the taking basse, trout or salmon. In this vicinity they are called fall-fish.

A fish similar in appearance to the herring, and called by the same name, is taken in the bay of New-York, off Fort Lafayette. They jump readily at a white, red, or fancy-colored fly, and afford capital sport.

OF THE WHITE-FISH.

This denomination of the finny tribe is taken generally in nets, and sometimes by the basse and salmon angler, in many of the lakes in the western part of the state of New-York, and affords good sport. As a table fish, it has the highest encomiums from all sorts of people: it is spoken of as the *church-steeple top of perfection*, superior to the salmon or trout, or any other fish that breathes and swims. Those who have enjoyed a dish of white-fish, will allow him to be second to none.

OF THE CAT-FISH.

This is the common fish of the western waters, and is taken by western sportsmen, by squid and fly trolling, and affords capital amusement. They take their name from the noise they make, similar to the purring of a cat, very familiar to those who have frequented the west. They are also angled for with a stout drop-line, and tackle similar to that described for the sheepshead. They are fine table fish.

We might go on *ad infinitum* in our list of the fishes of America, but we trust that we have described those which generally give most delight to the angler, and must here fasten our *line*.

CHAPTER XXII.

CONCLUDING REMARKS.

We cannot omit inserting the following elegant and appropriate defence of our art, from the aspersions cast upon it by a great man, by a mild and enthusiastic amateur, who occasionally seeks enjoyment, from the cares and vexations of business, in more pleasant pursuits.

"The great and learned Dr. Johnson satirically described angling thus: 'A stick and a string, with a worm at one end and a fool at the other.' Dr. Johnson never sat in a boat, surrounded by a beautiful landscape, playing a basse of three, four, or five pounds; nor stood on the green bank, contending with a trout of like weight; nor struck an Oswego basse, one hundred feet astern of his trolling boat, in Lake George, or he would never have penned such a severe though stupid satire. There is no recreation so admirably adapted to recruit the body and mind of the toiling citizen, as angling. Breaking away from his confining and exhausting toil in the counting-house, office, or workshop, leaving all care behind,

the angler sallies forth to the river, the bay, or some more distant water; and there, amid the most beautiful scenery of nature, plies his art. The absence from the scene of toil and care, for a short season; the breathing the fresh and healthful air of the country; the transit to and from the place of amusement, and the exciting and delightful exercise of the art; all combine to give this recreation a high place in my estimation—and as a christian, I certainly say, that in some of my solitary rambles, or boat excursions, with my rod, I have been favored with most devout and grateful emotions of the heart, in contemplating the beauties of creation; and looking up from the works of my Maker around me, to Him who made them all, my meditations on the Divine goodness and grace have been most sweet. In these sentiments I fully accord with the pious old angler, Isaac Walton, who expresses them also in his ancient and noble work on angling."

Finally, and to conclude, although our art has been lightly spoken of by a few learned and well meaning men, who certainly never could have experienced any of its pleasures, it has the sanction of the great and learned of all ages and of all countries, where the mild and effulgent rays of the sun admit of the growth to perfection and beauty, of the inhabitants of the chrystal waters; and although we respect the learning and talent of those who we know never had the least idea of the science necessary to some of the modes adopted; yet when we examine the Book of Books, and find in the Book of Job, and in parts of the New Testament, references directly made to drawing out fish with a hook;* when we look at it as inducing to the contemplation of the works of the Creator, and leading man from nature up to nature's God; when we see, and hear, and read of the minister of religion, the philosopher,

* "Canst thou draw out the Leviathan with a hook, or his tongue with a cord which thou *lettest down!* Canst thou put a hook into his nose!"

the statesman, and the poet, however officially engaged, delighting in a few hours' daily recreation in the art, and speaking and writing enthusiastically in its favor, finding

> "Tongues in trees, books in the running brooks,
> Sermons in stones;

we think the objectors might as well have tried to hold a whale with the thread of a spider's web as to have caused any human being to abandon a recreation at once so delightful, amusing, and beneficial, by their aspersions; and where the light and airy nothingness of ridicule has caused a doubt in the mind of one of its followers, the *silken line* of praise has caused thousands to pursue and defend it.

Let all, then, who belong to the fraternity, having the great, the learned and the good for their example, follow in the footsteps of their illustrious predecessors; and that they may enjoy many a day of delightful pleasure and happiness, coupled with holy and contemplative feeling, binding them by the *cord* of friendship to their fellow men; and that

> "Their *lines* may always fall in lucky places,"

is the sincere wish of an ardent admirer of the art.

As the peruser of the foregoing pages might possibly become *too ardent* in his admiration of the science of angling, we close by inserting one more effusion of the objectors to angling, which, from the dangers seemingly attending the practice, will no doubt deter him from pursuing the sport

TO A FISH OF THE BROOKE.

Why flyest thou away with fear?
Trust me, there's nought of danger near
I have no wicked hooke,

15

All covered with a smarting baite,
Alas! to tempt thee to thy fate,
  And dragge thee from the brooke.

O harmless tenant of the flood,
I do not wish to spill thy blood;
  For Nature unto thee
Perchance has given a tender wife,
And children dear, to charm thy life,
  As she hath done to me.

Enjoy thy streams, O harmless fish,
And when an Angler, for his dish,
  Through Gluttoney's vile sin
Attempts—a wretch—to pull thee *out*,
God give thee strength, O gentle Trout,
  To pull the rascall *in!*   Dr. Wolcott.

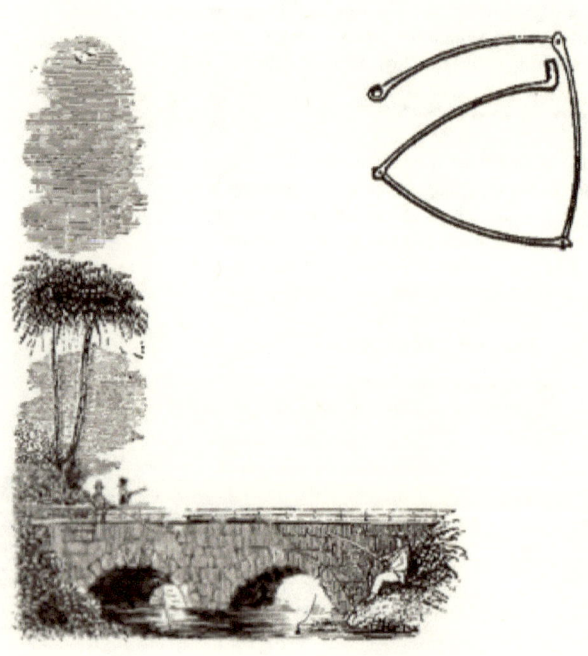

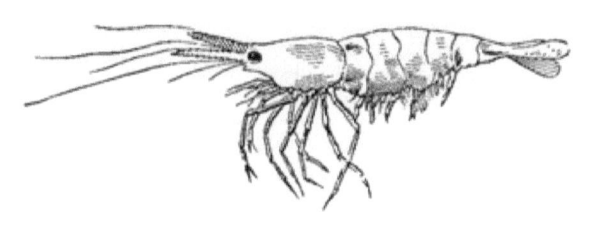

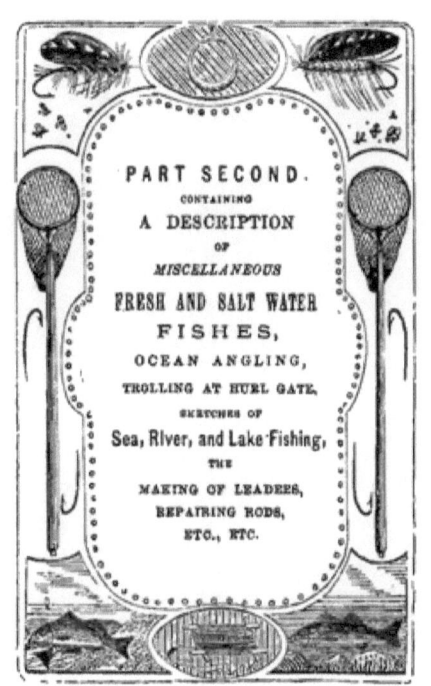

PART SECOND.
CONTAINING
A DESCRIPTION
OF
MISCELLANEOUS
FRESH AND SALT WATER
FISHES,
OCEAN ANGLING,
TROLLING AT HURL GATE,
SKETCHES OF
Sea, River, and Lake Fishing,
THE
MAKING OF LEADERS,
REPAIRING RODS,
ETC., ETC.

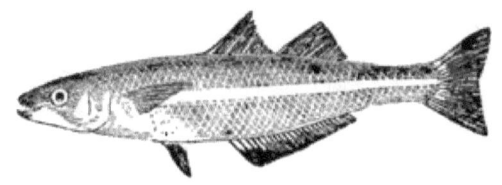

CONTENTS OF PART II.

	PAGE
PREFACE	227
FISH AND FISHING OF THE UNITED STATES	229
OF THE RED FISH OR SPOTTED BASSE	235
TROLLING FOR STRIPED BASSE	237
THE MACKINAW TROUT	240
BASSE FISHING ON THE SHORES OF LONG ISLAND	245
THE SMELT	247
SPOON BAIT	250
BERGALL, CHOCKSETT, NIBBLER, BLUE PERCH, OR CUNNER	252
BLACK FISH ANGLING IN SUFFOLK COUNTY, L. I.	254
THE WHITE LAKE BASSE	257
SILKWORM GUT, KNOTS, LOOPS, &c.	258
GRISWOLD SPRING SNAP HOOKS	262
FISH PONDS AND TRANSPORTATION OF FISH	264
GUTTA PERCHA AND INDIA RUBBER FLOATS	270
WEAK FISH OR BARB ANGLING IN LONG ISLAND SOUND	272
THE EEL	274
THE HAKE	281
WHITE PERCH AND CAT FISH ANGLING IN THE VICINITY OF NEW YORK	284
OCEAN ANGLING	288
INHABITANTS OF THE OREGON AND CALIFORNIA WATERS	292

	PAGE
OF THE WHITE PERCH	294
THE YELLOW PIKE PERCH	296
BLACK BASSE ANGLING IN MICHIGAN	298
THE MUSKELLUNGE, OR LAKE PIKE	303
THE CAT FISH	306
THE BLACK TROUT	309
MACKEREL	311
THE BUFFALO	313
FLUKE, PLAICE, TURBOT, &C.	315
THE SUCKER	319
TYING HOOKS, REPAIRING RODS, &C.	324
INTERESTING ITEMS OF INFORMATION	326

PREFACE TO THE SECOND PART.

The same want of complete and precise information in regard to a perfect knowledge of the fishes of the United States that existed at the time of the issue of the first edition, exists, with hardly an exception, at the present moment. The completion of the "Natural History of the State of New York" has added one link to the chain of information on the subject of natural science, which will one day extend around and bind together a mass of useful information, of vast importance to future generations. Professor Holbrook, of Charleston, is now engaged on a work on the Ichthyology of South Carolina, Georgia, and Florida, which promises to be one of the most complete and beautiful works of the kind ever issued. Would that other states, or scientific individuals, might follow in the footsteps of their illustrious predecessors! and that the tenants of the waters, as well as those of the air, had their Wilson or Audubon.

The remarks of the celebrated and learned Dewitt Clinton are as applicable to the subject now as at the time they were written: "The energies of the country have been more directed to the accumulation of wealth than to the acquisition of knowledge. But let us fervently hope, that after this passion, so energetic, is satiated in its present pursuit, it may seek more sublime sources of gratification."

"To either India see the merchant fly,
Scared at the spectre of pale poverty!
See him, with pains of body, pangs of soul,
Burn through the tropic, freeze beneath the pole!
Wilt thou do nothing for a noble end,
Nothing to make philosophy thy friend?"

But the temple of fame is yet open, and the name of the first ichthyologist of America is yet to be inscribed.* As was to be expected of a first attempt, the former editions contained many errors, but none of particular importance to the angler. It has been the object of the present edition to revise and correct, and also to add such further information as would be found useful, instructive, and interesting. The author returns his sincere thanks to his numerous friends who, with the true liberality of gentlemen and sportsmen, have kindly aided him in this undertaking. The writer considers that his situation, in the midst of the piscatorial world, is one that affords the best possible opportunity for collecting practical intelligence of interest to the angling sportsman; and since he has become known to some extent among his Waltonian friends throughout the country, concludes to subscribe his name, and solicit from those interested, such information as will be of value " to all true men who love quiet, and go an angling."

In conclusion. Gratefully appreciating the proof of approbation given him by the success attending the first two editions of this work, and asking further indulgence for imperfections and omissions (for to authorship he makes no pretensions), this volume is respectfully submitted to the anglers of the United States, by their fellow angler,

JOHN J. BROWN.

New York, 1849.

* Professor Agassiz, a celebrated German naturalist, is now engaged in this country on the subject.

THE FISH AND FISHING

OF THE

UNITED STATES.

CHAPTER I.

"I love the babbling brook, the placid lake,
Where spotted trout and pike their pastime take;
I love the rocky shore, the rushing stream,
Where lordly salmon leap, in sunlight gleam;
The stately river, the expansive bay,
Where striped basse and silver squeteague play;
The ocean's distant roar, the bounding wave,
Where monsters daily bask and dolphins lave;
These! these! I love, and oft away from home
Truant I stray, tempted by them to roam;
These! these! I love, and never can forsake,
For all the gold that trade or toil can make."

ANGLERS of the western world, you, as the lamented Power would have said, are "born to good luck." Your lot is cast in a land of many waters and many fishes. Loud should be your pæans of praise, profound your gratitude to the giver of all good, when you consider the many advantages you enjoy as anglers of the United States. Were you to traverse the circle of the globe for pleasure with the rod, you would return with an anxious step and a loving heart to the

"Land of the free and the home of the brave,"

satisfied that no country you had visited possessed half the

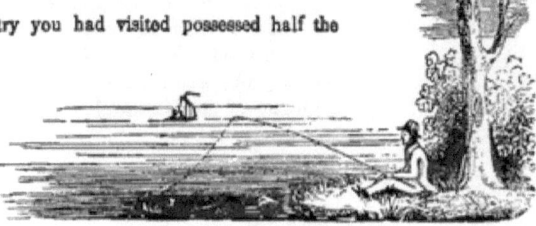

sporting advantages of your own; for it would occupy an ordinary lifetime, were a man, with angling implements, merely to explore the waters and make acquaintance with every variety of fish that has " a local habitation and a name" within its extended boundaries.

As the state of natural science in regard to the history and habits of our fishes is in its infancy, so also are the contrivances and arts employed in taking them, yet rude and undeveloped. But we are rapidly increasing our knowledge and refining our methods; as we *must* do when pleasure, and not profit, is the object of our pursuit, and the fish, constantly sought, become wary, and yield only to the utmost address of the angler.

Much certainly might here be said of the ordinary and extraordinary game fish inhabiting the waters of both hemispheres, which have long furnished themes to cultivated anglers and practical studies of the art. But much especially deserves to be said of the finny inhabitants of our own bright streams, which are unhappily unknown to our brotherhood in the old world. Who that ever took a striped basse or squeteague of five or ten pounds' weight can ever forget the pleasurable excitement and ecstasy of the moment; or what man, worthy the name, whose fortune has been cast among the northern lakes, can fail, even in his dreams, to remember the intense enjoyment that thrilled his soul and senses as he triumphantly drew from its pellucid waters, after a long skirmish and a doubtful struggle, a three foot trout or a large black basse? Who, too, that has made one of a party in the briny bay, and captured a mess of lively barb, or the noble sheepshead, after a vigorous contest and a beautiful play with rod and reel, wonders at the enthusiasm of the American angler, surrounded by such opportunities of enjoyment? The salmon, the trout, and the pike are almost the only game fish of Europe. It is true,

> "Their plenteous streams a various race supply:
> The bright eyed perch, with fins of Tyrian dye,
> The silver eel, in shining volumes rolled,
> The yellow carp, in scales bedropped with gold,
> Swift trouts, diversified with crimson stains,
> And pikes, the tyrants of the watery plains,"

but we have, in addition, almost innumerable objects of sport. For the lover of the breezy ocean there is the invigorating pastime of trolling for blue fish, or of drawing from its populous depths the valued sea basse, porgie, and tautog. In our larger rivers and lakes abound the mighty muskellunge, or ponderous cat-fish, and buffalo; and last, though not least, is the never-to-be-forgotten red-fish, which tenants the bays and mouths of our southern rivers. Happy and grateful then should our angler be that his lot is cast in such a land!

Surrounded by such abundance and variety of "finny attractions," is it wonderful that the angler falls into ecstasies, expatiating on his favorite subject? But we would moderate any pride of superiority we indulge in over our transatlantic brethren in respect to the quantity and quality of our game, by reasoning with ourselves and inquiring, Are our advantages to last, can they always be? You who have trod the mossy bank in pursuit of trout, and warred against the swift current when the striped basse was the object of your sport, will answer emphatically *no*. You are painfully assured that the well known haunts wherein in happy boyhood you took many a "silver side," are deserted, and the overarching banks of your favorite streams conceal your spotted friends no longer. You know that at your basse grounds you take few and still fewer fish, and that some of your former places are now never visited by the sought for game. It is the commonest complaint of the old anglers that fishing nowadays is uncertain; that it is much more difficult to take a mess of fish; there are too many after them; in short, that "times are not as they used to be," and so also says the gunner of his favorite sort of game. Now, what are the causes of this scarcity and disappearance; what the preventives and the remedy therefor?

The causes are easily seen, and almost as easily remedied, if those interested in the preservation of our game would unite their efforts to do so. The haunts of our favorite fish are *netted* by mercenary fishermen, who, in season or out of season, take large and small (for all is fish that comes to their net) to the nearest city, where they get extravagant prices for their unhallowed spoil. And this resurrectionism, for it is little better, is practised nightly* in our midst. Another reason is the indiscriminate taking of fish at spawning time by boys and (what is worse) ignorant men, and also by market fishermen, who take them in great numbers from their icy retreat and spawning grounds in tide waters. Add to this the wanton waste of fish by many who call themselves anglers, who (angling not for the pleasure of fishing, but to see how many they can take) leave them to gasp and die by the stream side, and you have reasons enough for the depopulation of all the waters in creation. Trout has almost become extinct in those parts of New York, New Jersey, Pennsylvania, and many of the eastern states, that are adjacent to the principal cities and towns, and are abundant only in the less populated and accessible portions, and even there are fast decreasing, owing to the same causes.

Now what are the remedies? The rod sportsman has several advantages over the gunner. Birds fly high, are as free as air, and so are those that pursue them; "they can be seen." Every boy in the country that has arrived at the age

* Very few streams where anglers much frequent are cared for in the day time by the *netters;* night is the time to cover their dark deeds.

of twelve years is a good shot, and can bag his game, in season or out, by getting out of hear-shot distance; and no obstacles can be interposed to this general and indiscriminate slaughter, except the enforcement of rigid laws, and the severe discountenance of public opinion.

But the lover of the finny race can protect his game with more certainty. Although the inhabitant of the crystal water can often be seen, there is no certainty of taking him, except it be with net or spear, and this can be prevented. A gentleman who had a fine pond, stocked with golden carp, was asked by a dealer in fish for the privilege of taking some fish from his pond. The gentleman, having been in a former instance imposed upon by the inquirer, answered, that he might come and take as many as he pleased; but immediately he set his men to work, and planted stakes throughout the pond. Much time was spent in the purchase and preparation of nets, at considerable expense; the netters went, but returned with torn nets and no fish, and a flea in their ear. A word to the wise is sufficient.

Were a few anglers in the vicinity of water netted by poachers to club together to protect it, and see that the ground was properly staked, the ponds and streams could in a measure be preserved from the depredations of such barbarians. Drawnets and seines are the most injurious; gill-nets and fykes cannot be used with much effect without being visible, and can be watched by the vigilant angler.

In regard, then, to the protection of game, we have the same interest with the fowler; and as there are many who pursue fish and fowl, and many epicures also

<blockquote>
Who love a dish
Of birds or fish,
</blockquote>

concert of action among them could not fail to be effectual.

Strong laws against taking or vending game out of season, strictly enforced by the rigorous prosecution of all offenders, would check, if not stop the growing evil.

To this end sporting clubs should be formed in the different cities, towns, and districts of country, which might be benefited by such laws; and vigilance committees formed to correspond with and visit the sporting grounds, and see that every violation of the statutes is thoroughly dealt with. By such a course of procedure our game grounds could be preserved, our pleasures greatly increased, and a stock of nature's "best gift, our ever new delight," preserved to future generations. We can do more. Where ponds and streams have ceased to be tenanted by the favorite trout, transportation and propagation can be carried on privately, at little expense, and the fish left to remain many years with safety and success. Then the streams we once loved may be made lively and joyous as in the days of our youth. There appears to be only one description of fish that we are destined to lose, and that is the king of the tribe, the salmon. The majority of our rivers being large enough to admit of all kinds of navigation, including that enemy of fish and fishing, the steamboat, we shall eventually have to bid farewell to this royal visitor. He cannot be domesticated, but roams as his instinct leads him. Other descriptions of game are ours, and in our keeping; and it behoves us, as true men and *faithful anglers*, to propagate and preserve them.

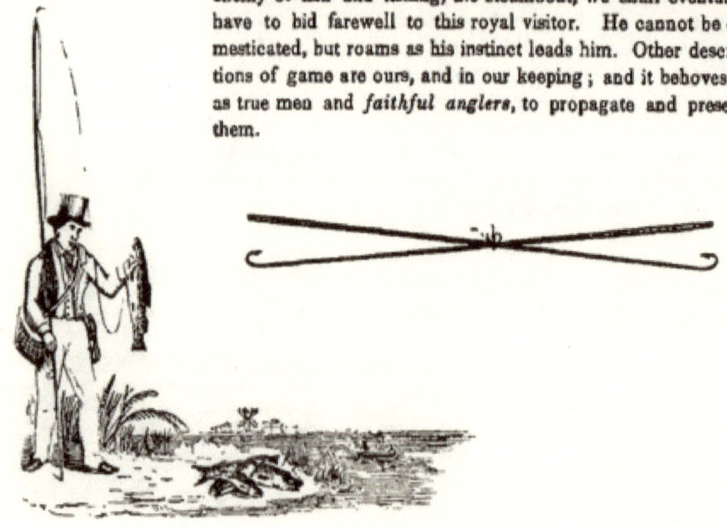

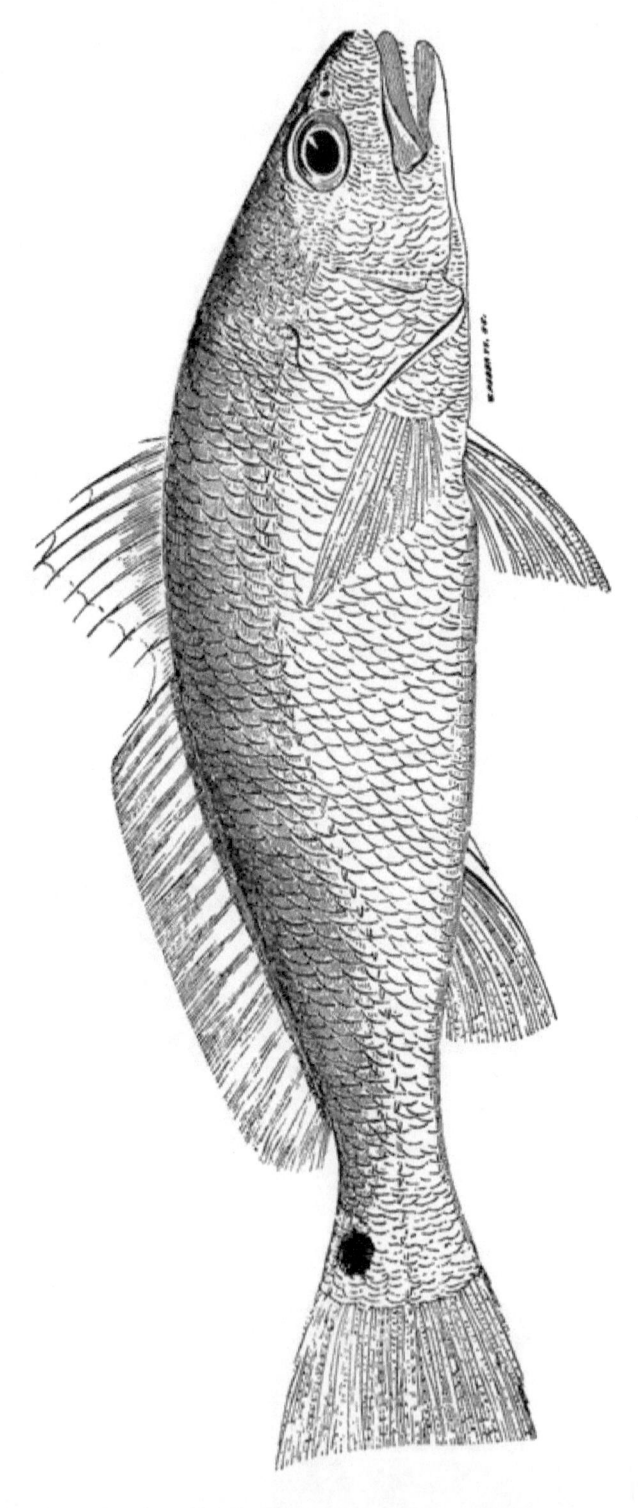

CHAPTER II.

OF THE RED FISH, OR SPOTTED BASSE.

Corvina Ocellata.—DeKay.

This fish is an inhabitant of our more southern waters, being found in great abundance on the Atlantic coast, in most of the bays that set in south of Cape Hatteras, although he occasionally, in limited numbers, roves as far north as New York. He is, however, more of an object of sport in the southern bays, and is taken in the northern part of the Gulf of Mexico, in Lake Borgne, at Pascagoula, Pass Christian, Bay of Biloxi, Mobile, Pensacola, and Apalachicola bays. At the south he is called the Red Fish (*Poisson Rouge*), and further north, at Charleston, the Basse, or Spotted Basse. He varies in size from one to four feet. When first taken from the water he is of a beautiful silver color, but after a little exposure becomes dark and clouded along the back, like many others of his species. In death he changes his color to rainbow hues. Beyond the caudal fin and near the tail he has a very singular and peculiar black or brown spot, bordered with white. A single spot looks, at first sight, rather unnatural, and one would be apt to suppose it the work of art or accident. The late Dr. Mitchell says, "it resembles the mark left by a heated iron, which has given rise to the name of branded drum." They are often taken having two, three, or even four of these strange looking spots clustered together in the same situation.

In the vicinity of Charleston he commences taking the hook in the early part of March, and is caught all through the season, until mid winter, at which time he is taken of larger size than at his early coming. Along the more southern coast,

at New Orleans and Mobile, he seems to be always on hand, and furnishes food for the table all the year round. He runs in shallow water, similar to the striped basse, and is taken mostly with the hand line with a small sized cod hook, baited with shrimps or pieces of mullet. He is a strong, powerful, and bold biting fish, and, with the rod and reel, affords as much pleasure in his capture as any of the tribe.

A friend relates that whilst fishing near the South Pass, Mississippi River, being tired and inclined to snooze, he wound his line around his wrist, and resigned himself to the arms of Morpheus; but before his nap was half out was suddenly awakened by a tug at his line, and before he could recover himself was pulled overboard by the extreme strength and vigor of this game fish.

He is held in high estimation as an article of food, and is well worth the angler's toil and patience. The rod and reel angler may fish for him in the same manner as directed for striped basse or weak fish, using *always*, to insure success, twisted gut leaders, and No. 00 Limerick, or Kirby hooks.

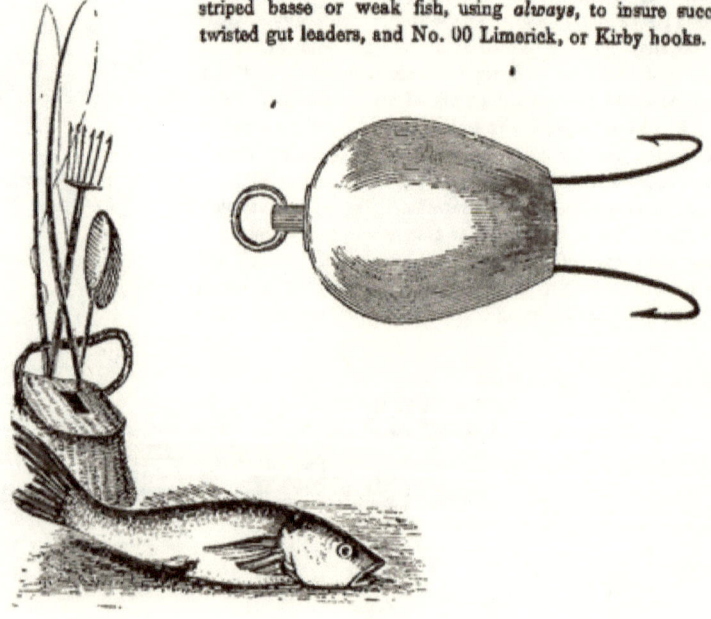

CHAPTER III.

TROLLING FOR STRIPED BASSE.

THOSE who prefer the more active and invigorating practice of our much admired art, will find trolling for this beautiful game fish as exciting a recreation as any that comes within the angler's reach. It has two advantages over the ordinary bridge and boat fishing (always allowing that the angler knows his ground well); one is, that, as in the scientific pursuit of trout, his scene is more changeful and varied, being relieved from the sometimes tedious and monotonous stillness; and the other is, that the game is more likely to be attracted by his bait, from the more continual change of position, than it could be by the usual mode of casting and drawing from the boat's side, bridge's height, or projecting bank.

At Harlem river and Hurlgate, near New York, they are taken

---

* Perhaps it were better to give this place its original and more appropriate appellation of Hellgate. No angler should attempt to fish there unless with an experienced hand who knows the ground; for unruffled and inviting as this favorite spot appears at slack water, less than an hour may change it from the gentleness of the lamb to the raging of the lion, and before he be aware of it he may be hurled into the Pot, among the Hen and Chickens, on the Hog's Back, Frying-pan, or Gridiron. Washington Irving, in his celebrated History of New York, says:—

"This is a narrow strait in the Sound, at the distance of six miles above New York. It is dangerous to shipping, unless under the care of skilful pilots, by reason of numerous rocks, shelves, and whirlpools. These have received sundry appellations, such as the Gridiron, Frying-pan, Hog's Back, Pot, &c. Certain mealy-mouthed men, of squeamish consciences, who are loath to give the devil his due, have softened the above characteristic name into Hurlgate, forsooth! Let those take care how they venture into the Gate, or they may be hurled into the Pot before they are aware of it."

of from three to fifty pounds' weight, with a natural squid or eel for bait. The line most proper to be used is a stout flax or cotton line, twenty-eight fathoms long and about one-eighth of an inch thick, the size of an ordinary cod line. The angler, to troll properly, should have a portable seat (which should be placed across the stern of the boat), and sit with his back to the person propelling him along. The boat should be rowed gently, and with the least possible noise, with muffled row-locks.

The size of the hook is about the same as that used in taking the ordinary cod. But how to put on the squid—by the way, brother angler, did you ever see a squid? If you have not, you will find a pretty good portrait of him at the bottom of page 239; but should you see him in his living person, you will never forget him. He is the most singular, odd-looking customer that has its residence beneath tide water. His size varies from four to ten inches in length.

"Gudgeons in rivers, dragonet in weeds,
Squid 'midst the rocks, in open water feeds."

He is not known to bite at anything, but is as good a morsel for a hungry basse as a roast turkey for us of the fraternity at a Thanksgiving dinner; and is as hard to be passed by the nimble basse as would be a gin palace by a regular toper.

To attach him to the hook, procure a stout needle and a good length of linen thread. This tie to the end of your hook's length, which indispensable to your success, should have been fastened with a strong winding of waxed thread to a piece of cord of the same thickness as your line, and twelve inches in length. Take off that calico spotted uniform that he wears, and leave him pure and white as the mountain snow. Divest him of that singular-looking transparent article called his back bone; now take your needle, with thread and hook attached, enter the needle at the opening of the neck from which you took his pellucid spine; draw the hook so far through, that the point of the hook will pass through near his eye; enter it there, cut off your thread, and commence at the tail by sewing him firmly around the projecting part of the hook, and continue to stitch him nicely and firmly all the way down to his neck, where you may, after a few turns firmly secured, clip off your thread and consider him fixed for his fate.

There are very few persons that attempt this mode of fishing Lewis Rogers and John Hilliker, who keep public-houses near the places mentioned, have taken some very large fish of late years, weighing in some instances as high as sixty pounds. The best time for taking them is in the months of October and November.

Another method of trolling practised is, with the usual basse tackle, with rod and reel, and with spearing, killy, or minnow for bait. The latter method is adopted in trolling in the various creeks that run into the Hudson River. In these places they are taken from one to ten pounds weight both in the spring and autumn; but the best time is in the month of October.

CHAPTER IV.

THE MACKINAW TROUT, OR MACKINAW SALMON.

Salmo Amethystus.—MITCHILL.

This appears to be a different species from that known as the common Lake Trout, *Salmo Confinis, Dekay.* It is described in the New York Fauna as follows:

"*Color.*—Dark or dusky grey above; chin, throat, and belly light ash grey or cream color; the back and sides sprinkled with numerous irregular lighter grey or brown, or soiled white spots, which do not, however, as in the preceding species (Lake Trout), rise upon the fins; ventrals and pectorals slightly yellowish; irides yellow; the teeth, gums, and roof of the mouth with a bright purple tinge; length, two to five feet."

"This magnificent trout, which is the largest hitherto known of Salmonidæ, exists in all the great lakes lying between the United States and the Arctic Ocean, is exceedingly voracious, feeding upon every fish within its reach, and, according to Dr. Mitchill, is sometimes of the weight of 120 pounds. It is a favorite article of food with the Canadian voyageurs, who frequently eat it raw. Its flesh is reddish. Like the *Salmo Confinis*, it resorts habitually to the deepest parts of the lake, and only comes near the shores in October to spawn, when the natives spear it by torchlight. Lake Huron appears to be its most southerly range in any considerable number, although a few are taken occasionally in Lake Erie, along the shores of Ohio, Pennsylvania, and New York." This kind is much superior to the common lake trout (with which it is often confounded), as an article of food; and by good judges of good things is considered equal in flavor to any fish that swims.

They are mostly taken with gill nets and set lines in deep water. The lines used are as large as the largest sized cod lines, and the hooks, which are generally made by the blacksmiths in the vicinity of the lakes, are equal in size to the biggest cod hooks. The bait is, pieces of the lake herring, or of the white fish. When the lines are taken up, if the fish are large, they are lifted into the boat with a large strong gaff. The most pleasant and exciting mode of capture for the angler is that of trolling with stout line and hooks, as before described,* and a piece of pork attached, or the spoon bait, or brass revolving hook. The best places for this kind of sport are in Lakes Huron, Superior, and the Straits of Mackinaw. He affords amusement and exciting exercise to the inhabitants near the lakes, and bites equally as sharp at the baited hook as Jack Frost does at the exposed features of the fisherman.

A friend at Detroit says:—

"During the winter, trout are taken in great numbers through the ice, in Green Bay; and the markets of Chicago, Galena, and many of the interior towns of Wisconsin are thus supplied. The bait (herring) are caught with small gill nets sunk through the ice. A hole is then cut over twenty-five or thirty fathom water, and the line, which is kept in motion, prevents the hole from freezing. When a fisherman has a bite, and strikes the fish, he throws the line over his shoulder and runs off, drawing the fish rapidly up to the hole and out upon the ice, where it is left to freeze. In this manner trout are taken in large quantities, and transported in a frozen state to the towns above named. Hundreds of barrels of them are salted and sold in the spring."

At Peseco Lake, Lake Louis, and Lake Pleasant, in Hamilton County, N. Y., and other northern lakes, much sport is had by boat trolling with the rod and reel, and parties are

* See Lake Trout, page 64.

made up from the cities of New York, Albany, Troy, Rochester, and places in the vicinity of the lakes, for a two-weeks' tour in that beautiful wilderness of exuberant nature. A visit to that lonely sporting region will richly repay the money and time spent 'in sweet communion with nature' by a store of health and contentment exchanged for the worn frame and haggard countenance caused by excessive city confinement.

The rod proper for this description of trolling is the same as that used for striped basse, only it should have a hollow butt and extra top, so that should you be so unfortunate as to break a top, you can easily replace it with another. Some use two rods at one time; but it requires a skilful and experienced troller to manage two, as the lines are apt to become entangled. To succeed well, you must have an experienced oarsman, who has been in the habit of trolling, and can row you gently and quietly about the lake. They have a mode of rigging hooks to the shiner or minnow a little different from the usual Waltonian method, and that recommended by Hofland, at page 87; it is called a train of hooks. These trains of hooks are made on a stout strand of single gut in the following manner. Take the largest and roundest piece of gut that you can procure; tie two No. 5 Limerick salmon (or No. 1 trout, or smaller, according to the size of the bait you expect to use) hooks to the end of it for tail hooks; about an inch further up place two others of the same size for back fin hooks; and about one and a half inches further up one more, for a lip hook; apply these hooks to your shiner in their regular order, fastening them through the toughest part of your bait, and attach them to your leader, and you are ready for your game. The lip hook can be attached with a small loop so as to slide and accommodate itself to various sized baits. Some prefer more hooks to their train, and put three at the tail and two at the mouth, making seven hooks in all; others prefer to use one large Limerick hook, say No. 1 or

0, salmon, after the Waltonian method, described on page 88; this latter method is more simple in construction, but not considered as sure as the train of hooks. Your leader should be of the best double or twisted gut, from three to four feet in length, and should you wish to use the fly (which is often done), it should be from two to three yards in length. For fly fishing use one or two large gaudy salmon flies, made on No. 3 or 4 salmon hooks, at a sufficient distance apart, to prevent their interfering with each other or the shiner. With your minnow and fly train you may take a speckled brook trout and a lake trout at the same time, of such proportions as will require your utmost skill in bringing them to your boat. A necessary article on such an excursion is a good sized gaff for securing your lake trout; your brook trout may be handled more carefully. When you feel a bite, lower the point of your rod so as to give your fish a chance to take the bait further in his mouth, and to place yourself and rod in such a position as to give your game play in case he needs it. Should the fish you seek run in deep water, place a light swivel sinker on your line before your leader. In all cases of trolling, use one or two swivels to allow free spinning of your minnow and prevent your tackle from entangling.

A curious way of taking lake trout, practised by the inhabitants living near the lakes, is to sink in some part of the lake a large piece of bark attached to a pole, some twenty-five or thirty feet in length, to which heavy weights are fastened; this is called an anchor, and is regularly baited two or three times a week, with small fish. A number of anchors may be set in this manner in different parts of the lake. These are kept baited for several weeks, until it is thought that the trout have fairly got into the habit of resorting to them. A fisherman will then tie his skiff to the end of the pole, and commence fishing with a common drop line, using a very large, straight, and pointed

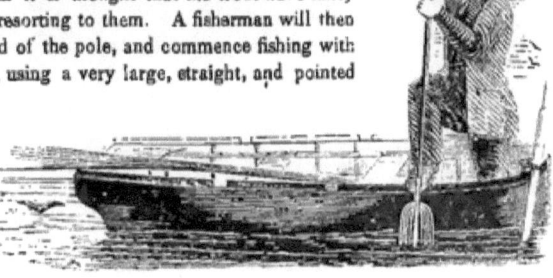

hook, called the lake hook. This method is called fishing at anchor.

New Yorkers who would visit the sporting lakes of Hamilton County, will reach them most speedily and economically by leaving the city by the Monday night's boat for Albany, and taking the cars for the west at 7 o'clock next morning. At about 10 you reach Amsterdam, where you take the stage for Northville. Here stay till morning, when the regular mail conveyance, which leaves but once a week, carries you to Lake Pleasant, the first of the series.

Salmon trout are there taken as the ice breaks up, and even in winter through the ice. But if you value comfort, and have no fancy for the keen air of those elevated regions (where the season is two months later than on Long Island), the four weeks from and after the middle of May are infinitely preferable, even if you regard the quantity and quality of the fish. The speckled brook trout do not bite until the end of May.

CHAPTER V.

BASSE FISHING ON THE SHORES OF LONG ISLAND.

Kindly furnished for this edition by T. D. Lowther, Esq.

Off the south-east shore of Long Island, during the fall months, Basse are taken in considerable numbers. About the middle of August, fish of from four to ten pounds begin to make along the coast between Montauk Point and Fire Island, and enter the Inlets, where they are generally taken upon the bar, or just beyond the surf, either by trolling, or by "heaving and hawling" from the shore. The latter is a favorite mode of fishing, but rather laborious, requiring both physical strength and practical skill. The squid for this purpose should be of block tin, full six ounces weight, with large hook (no kirb), size, number one Cod. This attached to a *cotton* line, full twenty fathoms long, light and close twisted, is made to gyrate around the head until it acquires sufficient velocity and momentum, when it is cast, with the full swing of the arm, into the breakers, carrying after it the line that is held loosely coiled in the left hand. The moment the squid strikes the water, it is hauled swiftly to shore that it may not sink, but play on the surface, and imitate the motion of the natural fish. At Montauk, they wind around a long squid-lead a strip of fresh skin from the belly of the basse, or draw and tie up over the lead the tail-skin of an eel. But hungry fish will snap at any moving thing. I have seen taken a basse of twenty-five pounds that bit at a rag.

As you will need a number of squids (for some will get broken and lost in the rocks), take various kinds if you please: —Fishermen have their fancies and so perhaps have fish; but

your success will depend much more on the reach of your cast, than on the sort of squid you employ.

In the like manner and place, but earlier in the season, Blue fish are sometimes taken in large numbers, and afford to the "lucky ones," for a few brief minutes, an exciting sport of the tallest kind. The capture of "Mackerel"* from the shore presents to even the most passive observer, a most animating spectacle. When Blue fish are announced as in sight, all who can, hurry to the beach and take stands upon some elevation of rock or platform, with coats off and lines ready, eager to receive them. Hovering over the approaching school career clouds of Gulls, screaming, diving, and eddying around the wounded Menhaden and fragments of fish that escape from the jaws of their pursuers. Nearer they come, their green backs darkening the broken water, and the still water within begins to ripple and sparkle and foam, till the sea is alive with fish, crowding upon the shore. A leap, a splash—again another— and a hundred silver sides are glancing in the sun. A dozen lines whiz glistening through the air, cleaving the waters in the midst of the school, and a dozen fish are instantly struck, and drawn hand over hand, swiftly and steadily to shore. Vigorously the fishers ply their lines with various chances of fortune, and so the battle rages until the mackerel, in diminished numbers, retire beyond the reach of their cunning enemies.

* The name for the Blue fish in Suffolk County.

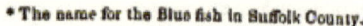

CHAPTER VI.

THE SMELT.

Osmerus Viridescens.

This beautiful, almost transparent, and prolific little fish, as an angle fish may be said to belong almost exclusively to the Bostonians, in whose vicinity it is found and caught in large quantities. It is supposed to derive its name from its peculiar smell when taken out of the water, being similar in scent to the cucumber. It is called the dainty of Boston, is taken in large quantities by hook and net, and makes quite a desirable article for the palate by the addition of a frying-pan operation.

"*Color.*—Pale olive green above the lateral line; opercles and sides silvery; obscure traces just below the lateral line, of a broad satin-like band, extending the whole length of the body; the place of the ribs indicates unusually lustrous stripes, which disappear shortly after death; upper part of the opercles, near the nape, dark green; caudal dark at the base, and with an obscure marginal band; dorsal caudal fins light green; pectorals, ventrals, and anal light colored, tinged faintly with bluish; irides silvery; bones of the head sub-diaphanous."—*DeKay.*

In habits they are similar to the salmon, and are classed by naturalists among that species. Their average size is from six to nine inches in length, and are occasionally taken as long as twelve or thirteen inches.* They run up from the sea into

---

* Narborough, a celebrated voyager, says.—"The smelts at Monte Video are four and-twenty inches in length; they are semi-transparent, and are most delicious eating; they are very abundant, and may be caught with the hook. They are also to be taken in the Straits of Magellan, twenty-nine inches in length and eight in circumference."

fresh water to spawn, in the months of March and April, and return home in the month of May. They pay their return visit for the benefit of the angler and epicure, and bite about the same time with Jack Frost, in the month of October or November. In the vicinity of Boston they are caught all through the winter in immense quantities, and sent to the markets. As many as one hundred dozen of them are known to have been taken by one man with two lines in one day.

The usual mode of fishing for them through the ice, is with a fixing consisting of a piece of brass wire, of ten or fifteen inches in length, passed through a small piece of lead which answers for a sinker; to each end of this is attached a Limerick trout hook, about No. 2 or 3, tied to the ordinary length of gut, baited with shrimps, or small pieces of minnow or frog. This is attached to a sufficient length of cotton or flax line, and finally fastened to a short stick of live oak, ash, or some other elastic wood, which is stuck into the ice through a hole about eighteen to twenty-four inches in diameter. An expert hand at this business can attend to two or three lines of this description, amuse himself by skating, and take home a sufficient quantity of smelts to satisfy a craving appetite sharpened by exercise, excitement, and a pure, healthy atmosphere.

At other places, and in other seasons, they are taken with the usual trout tackle, with the exception of the sinker, which should vary in size according to the strength of the tide.

This fish is very tenacious of life, has been known to exist a long time after being taken out of water, and is for this reason admirably adapted for transportation. They have been transferred successfully into fresh-water ponds, both in this country and England. Yarrell, in his "British Fishes," says:

"Smelts were kept for four years in a fresh-water pond, having no communication with the sea; they continued to thrive, and propagated abundantly. They were not affected by freez-

ing; as the whole pond, which covered about three acres, was so frozen over as to admit of skating. When the pond was drawn, the fishermen considered they had never seen so fine a lot of smelts."

Several years since the same experiment was tried with almost equal success at Jamaica Pond, on Long Island, with this exception, that although equal in flavor and quantity, they do not grow so large in size.

They are taken in considerable quantities in the rivers and bays that run up from the eastern coast, and also in the Passaic, Hackensack, and other small rivers of New Jersey, from which latter place the New York market is supplied during winter.

CHAPTER VII.

SPOON BAIT.

Dear brother of the rod, unless thou wast born, brought up, or been fishing in the northern part of the State of New York, you must certainly wonder at the above caption as a name for an article to bait fish withal. Shade of departed Walton! could you but imagine a silver plated table-spoon attached to a hook to lure the finny tribe with! thou wouldst shrink with utter dismay from the sight. But there were no Yankees in Walton's days, and the telegraph and spoon bait were alike unknown. This, dear reader, is a good trolling bait for Black Basse, Lake Trout, Pike, and Muskellunge.

It was first invented and used by a gentleman in the vicinity of Saratoga Lake for Black Basse. The idea occurred to him that the Lake basse would bite at anything bright if kept in motion; he procured the bowl of an old silver plated spoon, scraped off the silver from one side, cut off the point, flatted the shape, soldered two good sized hooks in the small end, and attached a swivel to the other. It worked like a charm, and he took more fish in the same space of time than was ever done before by any individual in the neighborhood. It has since been made up in various styles, with one, two, and three hooks, and is made with silver plate or brass on the convex side, and painted red (decidedly the best color) on the concave. They are for sale at the fishing tackle shops in the city of New York, and can generally be had in the vicinity of the lakes. It is used in the ordinary manner of boat trolling, or can be employed in hand trolling from the bank.

It would be well to try it for other descriptions of either fresh or salt water fish. If made small it would answer very

well for the usual size pickerel,* and perch, and, much larger and stronger, it would answer remarkably well for blue fish, or any of the more ravenous of the finny tribe.

It is difficult to tell what in earth, air, or water the spoon bait with its hooks and swivel looks like to the angler, much less what the deluded and ravenous animal thinks of it, when making after it with such extreme impetuosity. It would seem in its gyrations through the water to resemble the shape and motions of the frog more than anything else it could be likened to, and certainly goes to prove that a moving bait is more likely to take fish than a still one. The practise of boat trolling is by far the most pleasant mode of lake fishing, and the spoon bait has added much to the convenience and economy of this branch of the angler's delight.

This form would no doubt have equally as "taking a way" (if made larger and stronger) for the Blue Fish, Bonita, or the other inhabitants of the ocean's depths. It should be tried.

* A gentleman informs me that he has succeeded in taking a number of Pickerel with it from a pond in the northern part of the State of New York

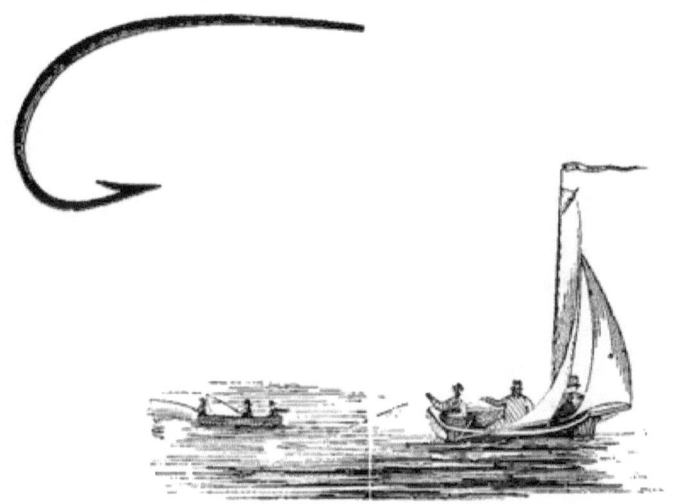

CHAPTER VIII.

BERGALL, CHOCKSETT, NIBBLER, BLUE PERCH, OR CUNNER.

Ctenolabrus Ceruleus.

THIS fish, although usually a pest to the Black fish angler, is by some of the fraternity at Boston and New York considered a worthy object of sport. It is usually so small and of such little capability of mouth, as to be a continual vexation when fishing for black fish with a hook of the usual size. Its weight averages from 4 to 16 ounces; but a 3-4 lb. Bergall is considered a large fish. Its flavor by epicures, and those who angle for the pleasures of the table, is considered inferior to no fish that swims; and there are a few, who really love angling in its perfection, that will occasionally, in anticipation of a rich repast, spend a day in the capture of these little fish with as much zest as they would when bagging as many woodcock, snipe, or quail. Its range is from the Delaware to the banks of Newfoundland. Of its color, De Kay says: There is scarcely any fish whose colors are so variable as this species. In the smaller individuals, the general color is blue, more or less mixed with brown; and faint, dusky, transverse bars may be frequently seen. In the larger specimens, as in the one now before me, which is twelve inches long, the colors are bright and showy, a light orange colored tint pervading the whole body. In these also, the head and opercles are of a beautiful chocolate, mixed with bright blue; the fins of a blue more or less brilliant."

Smith in his history of the fishes of Massachusetts says: "To all appearance, the Perch, or Cunner, is the Tautog in miniature, and if it were black, it would be supposed the young of that fish." But anglers who have often taken both descriptions of the same size and weight, could not be deceived in this respect.

> For a Tautog's a black fish the universe round,
> And a Cunner's a cunner though he weigh a full pound.

No difference of any consequence can be seen between a small black fish and a large one, but a wide difference between a Bergall and a black fish; and to us of the fraternity, why the two should be classed as relations of the same family is rather mysterious.

The most successful mode of taking this fish is with the usual black fish or hand line tackle, with the exception of the hook, which should be a Limerick trout, of either number 2 or 3, attached to single gut. The eye and hand of the angler should be active. A moderate but steady jerk is necessary to get him out of his element. Those who know how he tastes after being well cooked, recommend the following method.

Take this despised little animal and handle him as though he were a friend; take out from his interior the parts not designed for food, and cut off his head, tail, and fins; then (Eel skinning fashion), with a sharp pointed knife commence at the head and strip his skin entirely off: sprinkle a little salt over to *harden*, not salt his flesh, and let him lie a sufficient time for that purpose. You may then broil him on the gridiron and dish him; season him slightly with a little Cayenne pepper, and pour some spiced claret or port wine over him; or put him in the pan and "*do him brown*," with butter and flour, adding the seasoning and wine. A little celery well dressed with the dish adds to the perfection of the meal. Some prefer him stewed; but if properly cooked either way, one trial of the palate will give him his proper rank with the most finished epicurean.

17

CHAPTER IX.

BLACK FISH ANGLING IN SUFFOLK CO. L. I.

By T. D. L.

EITHER shore of the Sound affords fine fishing, but the reefs and boulders of the north side of Long Island, especially, are favorite feeding grounds of the Black Fish. Off Montauk on a calm day, after the clearing up of a southwest storm, may be seen a hundred to a hundred and fifty sail of smacks, busily employed fishing, and they generally succeed in filling their wells in a tide or two, at most. But the beautiful and picturesque north shore, anywhere between Port Jefferson and Oyster Pond Point, affords the true angler the best sport, because thereabouts fish are neither too provokingly scarce nor disgustingly abundant.

Greenport, the eastern terminus of the L. I. Railroad, is most deservedly a favorite resort of anglers in pursuit of health and pleasure. Having the Peconic Bay on one side, and the Sound within two miles on the other, it is a convenient point of departure for bay or sea fishing, as you incline, or wind and weather may determine. The Sound is the preferable fishing ground, for it always affords sport, though very unequal. A party in a boat, with hand lines, and bait of soft clams, or "Fiddler" (as the soldier crab is called), will always take fish at any time, because able to follow them unto water too deep or too swift for successful rod fishing. But there pleasure ends and labor begins. *One* skilful angler, who, with rod and reel, fishes from a good rock, between half tide and high water, where it never exceeds three fathoms, will not only have more sport, but get larger and better *game* than any ordinary party who, unrefined and unbelieving, fish in the common inglorious way. For taking Black Fish, as, perhaps, for all others, the morning, irrespective of tide, is generally best. But in fine weather, when high water happens just after sundown, of a warm summer afternoon, the last hour of flood is worth all the rest of the day. Then the large "tide runners" leave the cool deep water, and come in shore to feed on barnacles that grow against the rocks; and then often may be seen, around some insulated point of rock, the "flukes" of large Black Fish feeding.

The average size of the fish in good localities may be from twenty ounces to two pounds. Five pounds is large, and such are not numerous, though I have caught several the same day. Very rarely one of ten, even twelve honest pounds, is taken. A steel-yard, which I always carry, is a wonderful corrector of the judgment; it is a weighty sinker to the buoyant fancy, and often ungraciously translates the poetic quantities of the enthusiast into flat and *scaly* prose.

As in these waters the angler may chance to strike a huge Dog Fish, Fluke, or other ugly "varmint," he should be provided against accidents with an extra basse rod—the best kind for this fishing, and a dozen hollow sinkers. Hooks* from Nos. 5 to 8 (much smaller than those usually sold with hand lines), should be strongly bound with a well-waxed arming to a flax line, double and twisted; for stiffness, as well as strength, is most desirable in a snell, to avoid entanglement. For clear, warm days, when the fish are shy, and "off their feed," twisted gut is preferable. Then noiselessly approach a rock, gently drop your line, and let it slowly float into the eddy, drawing it along the leeward side, a foot above the bottom weeds, and if in five minutes a fish does not bite, or quietly *draw* the bait into his hole, be sure there is no fish there. You can often change your ground with advantage. The white-nosed variety

feeds everywhere, comes and goes with the tide. But the common Black Fish—the true darkies—seem to have "local habitations." The rock that is "fished out," though sometimes visited, will not soon have other finny tenants, unless you invite them by throwing overboard your spare bait, which often secures you next day an hour's good fishing.

In baiting with "Fiddler," pass the hook through the belly, and out at the back (careful not to divide the shell), and take off the large claw. If Bergalls (or "Cunners," as they are called) trouble you, leave the claw on, and the crab, in self-defence, will nip their noses. Whenever Bergalls suddenly stop biting, be sure a Black fish or sea basse is near. They respect their superiors, and keep their distance.

* A small, flat, stout, sharp hook, with short shank, and flat head, fastened by a double hitch to a flax line, armed for two inches above the hook, by the loose end being twisted around it and knotted—smack man's fashion—makes so superior a snell that none other should be used or sold for hand fishing. At the Angler's Depot, N. Y., they can be had, from one who is an old salt in these matters. Verbum sap. Hooks made of light wire are worthless. The Bottle, or Swell Fish, literally chew them up. A landing net, file, knife, and thin cotton gloves, are indispensable.

CHAPTER X.

THE WHITE LAKE BASSE

Labrax Albidus.

THIS is another species of the universal perch family, and is found in many of the lakes in the northern part of the State of New York. At Buffalo they are called the white basse. They do not partake of all the vigorous qualities of the black basse, neither do they attain to so great a size, but are, nevertheless, a very active game fish, and well worth the angler's patience and perseverance. A northern friend says:

" The white basse of the western lakes is a very fine fish, and gives good sport in the taking. They resemble in shape the white perch of the Hudson River, but are much larger, weighing from one to three and a half pounds. In color they are a blackish white on the back, and white on the sides and belly, with a few dark, parallel, narrow streaks along the sides. The live minnow is an excellent bait for them, but should be of smaller size than for their black brethren, as they are not so well provided for, in the way of gape. They are a shy fish, and very lively on the hook. Their season corresponds with that for taking the black basse. They run in schools, and you may sometimes take a dozen in half an hour."

CHAPTER XI.

SILKWORM GUT, KNOTS, LOOPS, &c.

We now come to a *knotty* question in our *line* of discourse. Those who are blest for the first time in their lives with an opportunity of viewing and handling the beautiful article called silkworm gut (and there be many, even anglers, who to this day have never seen it), are struck with perfect astonishment when they are told that this beautiful semi-transparent substance is the product of the silkworm.* It is not actually the gut of the worm, but what he would spin out into silk were he allowed to take the due course of nature. A few days before he begins to spin, the worm is immersed in a weak acid and left to soak about twelve or eighteen hours, after which he is opened and two pieces of the substance taken from him. These are drawn out with great care and stretched to their full length to dry. They are at first opake, but after becoming dry they assume their transparent appearance. They are put together in bunches of 100 strands, and the useless ends wrapped around with red twine, and exported to all parts of the world.

Those who first form an acquaintance with it for the purpose of making their own tackle, are apt to use it in its hard dry state, and condemn it at once as brittle and useless. But to work well and handsomely, it should be soaked in moderately warm water for about half an hour, or in cold water about two hours before using. It can then be tied or twisted into any shape to suit the capricious angler's will.

There are many kinds of knots used by the fraternity in

* See Part i., p. 31.

tying and looping, all of which have their advocates and contemners, but it will be well to remember that in all modes of tying, the simplest in construction, and freest from angles and abrupt turns, is the best; all turns should be made round and not short and quick so that one strand cuts the other. This doctrine holds good not only in regard to our subject matter, but also to the tying or putting together of any stiff substance. The best knots in use amongst anglers are sailors' knots, which afford the simplest and surest modes of rigging any line.

One of the simplest, and most secure is the double knot, made by passing the ends around each other after the manner of the common knot, but twice instead of once. For leaders or loops gut can be tied together at the ends, as in the drawings. The ends need not be whipped down, but can be cut close off, as they are perfectly secure, and not liable to break.

The double and single water knots for tying lengths of gut together are approved by some, and are made after the following manner:

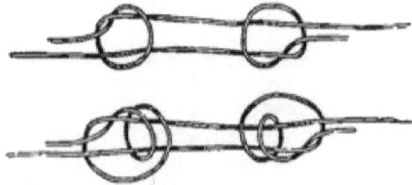

the single is found to be sufficiently secure, and being smaller and simpler, is more used than the double.

The loop knot is a very easy way of tying a line or piece of gut to a loop, and is made thus.

A facile mode of fastening gut together, is the loop hitch, but observe that the ends must be whipped down with silk. The gut in this case is not knotted, and when close together and properly fastened, it forms one of the smallest and most simple ties ever invented. The celebrated Theophilus South in his fly-fisher's text book, recommends it above all others.

Leaders or Bottom Lengths.—These useful articles of tackle need a more precise explanation than that given in former pages. They are made of lengths of silkworm gut, tied together as before described in lengths single, double, or twisted, of from one to four yards. When employed for trout they are invariably used singly; their position on the tackle is after your swivel or sinker, or if in fly-fishing, tied immediately to your line. The usual way of making them is with a loop at each end.

To fasten your leader to your other tackle pass the loop of your leader through the loop of your line, sinker, or swivel, whichever you be using, so that it will draw down as in the last mentioned cut above, and it will be firmly secured. When through your sport back out your leader and separate it from your line, and dispose of it in your tackle book. When fishing for salmon, basse, or other large fish, use your leader long or short according to your depth of water, single, double, or

twisted, according to the shyness, strength, or vigor of your game. The most experienced basse anglers fish with only one hook; but where the game is small, many fish with two; this is done by attaching two leaders, one of one yard in length, and the other of two, so that one hook will hang about one yard from the other; or use one leader of one or two yards in length, doubling it at about one third the length, and passing it through the sinker in the form of a loop, drawing it down as before described. Your leaders being rigged, pass the looped end of your hook through your leader and draw your hook through. Put your bait on your hook, and you are rigged for a bite.

Should the foregoing be not found sufficiently explicit for the tyro, he will find at the fishing tackle store these articles all ready arranged, which will give him more practical ideas than he can possibly get on paper, by which to arrange his tackle as he chooses.

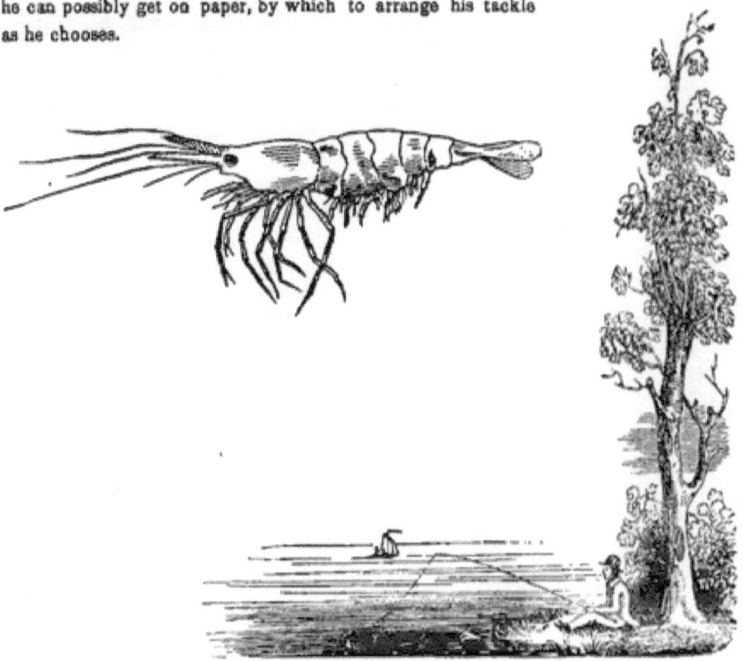

CHAPTER XII.

SPRING SNAP HOOKS.

"A WEAK invention of the enemy." Why the humble and gentle piscator should be called the enemy of the finny race, or why anglers, in speaking of their exploits, should call their finny friends their enemies, is a mystery yet to be explained. Such cannot certainly pursue their sport with a true Waltonian spirit; for the father of anglers never used the word enemy, and always spoke in the most mild and pleasant manner of the finny race. "Handle him as though you loved him," says he, when speaking of preparing a line bait for the hook. The piscatorial world was for generations without any invention for taking their game other than the ordinary kerbed steel until about fifty years ago, when the spring snap hook was invented. This was in general use until a few years since, when a boy by the name of Griswold, about sixteen years of age, living in the vicinity of Schroon Lake, conceived the idea of inventing a spring snap that would hold the fish after he was hooked. He succeeded in making the hook which is called the Griswold—see plate 1. It is arranged with a spring, lever, and striking hook. The striking hook is so adjusted that when set it lies alongside of the main hook, and is retained by a slide at the top; when the fish nibbles the striking hook descends and takes him on the outside of the head—see plate 2. By an improvement patented by Mr. Ellis, of Naugatuck, Conn., the striking hook is relieved from the lever instead of the upper part of the hook.

It was much approved of at the time, and considered an aid to the angler. Immediately the mechanical genius of the country was put in motion, and, *presto!* at least a dozen inventions of striking hooks of various descriptions were made to facilitate the taking of our scaly friends. They all have their merits or demerits, a diversity of opinion existing among the fraternity. Some consider them "a weak invention of the enemy," very cruel, and those unworthy of a sportsman's name who use them; others highly approve of them. They are not well adapted for salt-water fishing where there is a strong tide, as they are apt to spring before the fish bites. They are better suited to lake fishing for pike, black basse, and lake trout. They are preferred and recommended by some for that purpose, and for fish, such as often slip the hook, will always be used to a certain extent. Many improvements and suggestions have been made, but none to alter materially the character of the device.

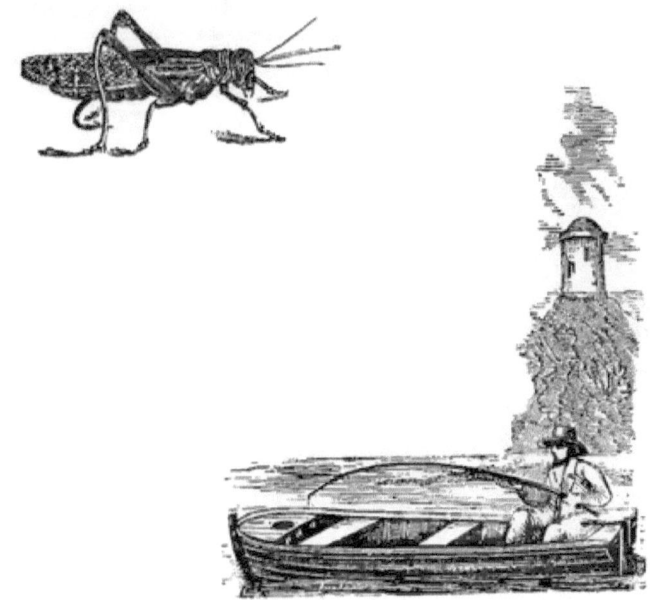

CHAPTER XIII.

FISH POND AND TRANSPORTATION OF FISH.

This is a subject of great importance, not only to the angler, but to those who own farms or property in the country. In Germany and France, the renting of fish ponds is a source of large income to the owners of land, and an acre of water is considered of equal value to an acre of soil. In our own country, a small sheet of water is considered of no particular advantage, except it be to keep a few geese or ducks, to amuse the children, to arouse the family in the morning by their incessant quack, or perhaps remind them of those in the city whose performance is the same, only one quacks through his natural instrument, and the other through the public press. Few lovers of the beautiful in nature ever think of improving, enlarging, or adorning a natural water spot, and making it joyous and lively with the finny brood. Fewer still may think of damming a natural spring, widening a valley, making an outlet, and modifying nature sufficient to allow depth of water capable of sustaining and nourishing an animal that will conduce not only to their pleasure and pastime, but also to their bodily comfort. Every piece of ground of a springy or marshy description is immediately drained, to make room for a crop of corn or potatoes, as though it were intended that " man should live by bread alone."

Many reasons might be urged in favor of artificial fish ponds, but as those who love the rod are largely on the increase throughout the land, the necessity of these additions to comfort, economy, and picturesque beauty as well as recreation, will soon be seen. The rearing and breeding of various kinds of cattle and feathered creatures for food, is an object of interest and study with the farmer, but the propagation, naturali-

zation, or transportation of the scaly tribe, seems to be with most tenants or owners of land beneath or beyond their notice.

As an article of food, the fish is given to us, without doubt, to gratify our varied tastes; and in some seasons, particularly in the early spring and summer, when other meats are out of season and without relish, is more tasteful, healthful, and desirable than any other palate delicacy. Include then the pleasure, excitement, and vigor embraced in his piscatorial capture, and we have a means of happiness which should be improved by all who study the pleasures of mind and body.

Most of the varieties of our subject can be transported or propagated with very little trouble, and some are so tenacious of life that they require no care whatever.

Perch, Carp, and Pike can be transported a long distance, say fifty or sixty miles, with ordinary carriage conveyance, and by the present railroad and steamboat conveyance, hundreds of miles. Capt. Henry Robinson, of Newburgh, N. Y., in the year 1832, brought some six or seven dozen Carp from France, and put them into a pond, supplied by springs of clear and pure water, on his farm, where they increased to a surprising degree. He has supplied many friends with them, who have distributed them about in various parts of the country. This public-spirited gentleman has also for a number of years put a few dozens in the Hudson river. They grow much larger in the river, and have increased so much that they are often taken by the fishermen in their nets.

The Black Basse can be made to change his residence by one or two changes of water for the same distance. This latter fish is growing in favor for large ponds, and will in the course of a few years become very generally distributed throughout the country. He is well worth the trouble of removing, and where a few gentlemen, or those of the craft join together in the expense, the amount would be small in comparison with the benefits which would accrue.

The Trout is the most delicate and difficult fish to convey any considerable distance, and should be narrowly watched during the progress, and the water kept clear and as cool as possible.

Salt-water fish can be easily transported by sea in cars, or the well-holes of fishing-smacks adapted for keeping them alive. The tautog, many years since unknown in the harbor of Boston, is now found there in great abundance, having been taken in cars from Newport, R. I. There are many fish that swim the southern waters that would thrive equally well in more northern latitudes, and *vice versa*.

Several years since, Mr. Pell, of Pelham, N. Y., had some shad in pairs conveyed from the Hudson river to a pond on his farm. A few years after he was much surprised to find, contrary to his expectation, that they had bred, and had grown to the size of six inches. There is hardly a doubt that our elegant striped bass of the salt water which goes up into the fresh-water streams to spawn, could be domesticated, and made a tenant of fresh-water ponds that are supplied with fresh-water springs. There are many other descriptions worthy a trial.

The celebrated Dr. McCulloch, of Edinburgh, succeeded in naturalizing eight different kinds of fish from salt water into fresh, with an improvement in their flavor; and the philosopher Bacon says, "that fish used to the salt water do nevertheless delight much more in the fresh." Speaking of the salmon and smelt, he says, "I doubt there hath been sufficient experiment made of putting sea-fish into fresh-water ponds and pools; it is a thing of great use, for so you have them new at a great distance; besides, fish will eat the pleasanter, and may fall to breed."

"Mr. Arnold, of Guernsey," says Pickering, in his "Remi-

niscences," " has in his lake, of about ten acres, chiefly supplied with fresh water, many sea-fish ; all have improved in quality and propagated. The lake, which before was worthless, producing a few eels, now yields a large rent. The bottom of the lake is various—muddy, rocky, and gravelly, and since the introduction of sea-fish, the eels have multiplied a thousand-fold." A mode of culture of carp, spoken of by Daniel, in his " Rural Sports," may be found useful to those wishing to breed that description of fish.

" It is supposed that ninety brace of full-sized carp, and forty of tench, are a good stock for an acre of water. In some parts of Germany, where the domestication of fish is practised, a suite of ponds are so constructed, that they can empty the water and fish of one pond into another. The empty one is then ploughed, and sown with barley. When the grain is in the ear, the water and its inhabitants are again admitted ; and by feeding on the corn are more expeditiously fatted than by any other management."

All ponds should have a brook or rivulet running through them, or fresh springs. It increases the feed and comfort of the fish during the heat of summer, and counteracts the effects of frost during the winter. All kinds of refuse grain, as beans, peas, &c., thrown into carp ponds, or sown in the mud along the edges when the water is low, will serve to fatten and improve the fish very much.

The following method of making artificial fish-ponds, from Best's " Art of Angling," will be found useful.

" It is agreed that those grounds are best that are full of springs, and apt to be moorish : the one breeds them well, and the other preserves them from being stolen.

" The situation of the pond is also to be considered, and the nature of the currents that fall into it ; likewise that it be refreshed with a little brook, or with rain-water that falls from

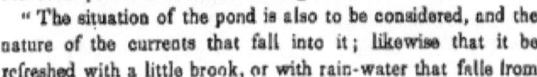

the adjacent hilly ground. And that those ponds which receive the stale and dung of horses, breed the largest and fattest fishes.

"In making the pond, observe that the head be at the lowest part of the ground, and the trench of the flood-gate, or sluice, has a good swift fall, that it may not be long in emptying.

"If the pond carries six feet of water it is enough; but it must be eight feet deep, to receive the freshes and rains that should fall into it.

"It would be also advantageous to have shoals on the sides, for the fishes to sun themselves in, and lay their spawn on; besides in other places certain holes, hollow banks, shelves, roots of trees, islands, &c., to serve as their retiring places.

"Reserve some great waters for the head-quarters of the fishes, whence you may take, or wherein you may put, any quantity thereof. And be sure to have stews and other auxiliary waters, so as you may convey any part of the stock from one to the other, so to lose no time in the growth of the fishes, but employ your water as you do your land, to the best advantage. View the grounds, and find out some fall between the hills, as near a flat as may be, so as to leave a proper current for the water. If there be any difficulty of judging of such, take an opportunity, after some sudden rain, or breaking up of a great snow in winter, and you will plainly see which way the ground casts, for the water will take the true fall, and run accordingly.

"The condition of the place must determine the quantity of the ground to be covered with water. For example, I may propose in all fifteen acres in three ponds, or eight acres in two, and not less; and these ponds should be placed one above another, so as the point of the lower may almost reach the head or bank of the upper which contrivance is no less beautiful than advantageous.

"The head, or bank, which, by stopping the current, is to raise the water, and so make a pond, must be built with the clay

or earth taken out of the pan or hollow dug in the lowest ground above the bank; the shape of the pan to be a half oval, whereof the flat to come to the bank, and the longer diameter to run square from it.

"For two large ponds, of three or four acres apiece, it is advisable to have four stews, each two rods wide and three long. The stews are usually in gardens, or near the house, to be more handy and better looked to. The method of making them, is to carry the bottom in a continual decline from one end, with a mouth to favor the drawing them with a net.

"It is proper to cast in bavins in some places not far from the sides, in the most sandy spots, for the fishes to spawn upon, and to defend the young fry, especially the spawn of Carp and Tench."

18

CHAPTER XIV.

FLOATS.

This buoyant article of our fancy has been of late much improved. Patience and perseverance, it is said, will work miracles; but the two invaluable substances, Gutta Percha and India rubber, having been successfully used in the manufacture of floats, will prove to be of great importance and utility to the angler, and will work wonders, as to the durability and convenience of this essential article of his equipment.

The great objection to the cork float was, that much difficulty was experienced in keeping it in order, either the quill or the stem becoming, with very little wear, loose and unfit for use.

The turned hollow float, almost as light as air, being glued or cemented together in the centre, by the constant action of the sun and water, was apt to part in the centre, or by its extreme thinness, liable to be broken almost as soon as a soft boiled egg, particularly if the gentle Piscator, in his boat movements, happened to tread too hard upon it.

In the manufacture of the new descriptions, all these difficulties are obviated, and the angler can now be furnished with an article almost as light as air, and durable as time.

Gutta Percha is admirably adapted for the formation of this implement of tackle, being, from its nature, very tenacious, and easily worked into the desired shape. Those made of this substance are lighter than wood, and cannot come apart in the centre, nor break at the ends, except by extreme hard usage and carelessness; and even where this happens, they can be repaired by the angler himself, with but little trouble. The caoutchouc float is made in the usual form of the sheet rubber,

with a screw valve at the top, and can be put in the vest pocket, or even the pocket-book, and inflated for use at the pleasure of the possessor. The float has been considered the most inconvenient article for use on a long tour, and is often left behind on occasions of distant excursions. But all difficulties of this kind vanish in the convenience of the rubber float. Those of the fraternity who find it difficult to keep their temper, when not in the usual luck, will therefore please *blow up their floats* instead of the fish, the weather, or some less harmless object of their displeasure.

CHAPTER XV.

WEAK FISH OR BARB ANGLING ON LONG ISLAND SOUND.

By T. D. L.

INTO the Peconic Bay—that most noble and beautiful harbor—flow a number of small streams, brooks deep at the mouth, but short, shoaling into a grassy bottom, full of crabs and other food for fish. Up into these, for food or shelter, run at night, tide permitting, Weak Fish (or *Cheecout*), and Barb or King Fish (*Tom Cod* they are there called). Across these creeks nets are sometimes set, which yield in a tide perhaps a hundred weight of " yellow fins," from two to five pounds each.

The south shore of the Great Peconic is famous ground, and parties often take boat at James Port or Canoe Place, for a day's fishing there. Let the angler anchor off any of the larger inlets to the Shinnecock Hills, and amuse himself, if he please, catching pound Porgies, until the tide is well up. Then draw in towards the mouth of the creek, and he will probably have lively sport for an hour, catching King or Weak Fish, enough to astonish the natives, as your thorough-bred angler generally contrives to do. When the Toad Fish begins to attack you, the game is up, and the fish gone. For Barb use a Kirb hook, about No. 5 Salmon, *short in the shank*. More good fish of all kinds have been lost by using a *long* shanked hook (which has become the fashion), than by any want of skill in the angler. The wire outside the mouth often acts as a lever, and enables the fish to throw himself off in the struggle. For Weak Fish crab is undoubtedly the best bait, but I have caught more Barb with shrimp—so despised in those parts—than with any other bait. King Fish average over a pound, fight hard, and die nobly—" die like demi-gods." No one who takes the Weak Fish of these crystal waters and clean gravelly shores, can fail to see the propriety of its nome d'honneur, " the salt water Trout." The brilliant tints that spot its silver sides render it indescribably beautiful.

CHAPTER XVI.

THE EEL.

Anguilla Vulgaris.

"Saw you that snake, sir?"
"No; 'twas an eel."

THIS crooked subject of our discourse is a pest to the regular angler. As an object of sport he is far beneath the contempt of a regular game fisherman, and is only "taken" when he cannot be "shaken" from the hook by all the arts of his unfortunate possessor. They are not particular as to their meal. The finest worm thrown for a trout will often bring his snakeship out. The best shrimp or crab bait in salt water is good enough for him, and he seizes it with avidity as a creature of taste. The truly patient Waltonian angler dispatches him without complaint; and if he happen to be of a goodly size, is invited to partake of the hospitalities of his table. There are seven or eight different descriptions, some of which grow to quite a large size. (See page 217.) The eel belongs to no particular place or clime. He is a cosmopolite, and is always where water flows and mud grows. He is a warm-blooded animal, and has been known to climb up trees and poles, but not to get very near the north pole, the only exception to their general distribution being in the more intensely cold latitudes. Says Yarrell, one of the best English writers on the subject, "Eels are in reality a valuable description of fish; their flesh is excellent for food; the various species are hardy, tenacious of life, and very easily preserved. They are in great esteem for the table, and the consumption in our large cities is very considerable. The London market is principally supplied from Holland, by Dutch fishermen There are two companies in

Holland having five vessels each; these vessels are built with a capacious well, in which large quantities of eels are preserved alive until wanted. One or more of these vessels may be constantly seen lying off Billingsgate; the others go to Holland for fresh supplies, each bringing a cargo of 15,000 to 20,000 pounds' weight of live eels, for which the Dutch merchant pays a duty of £13 per cargo for permission to sell."

Their serpentine form has rendered them objects of dislike in this country among some people. The fair sex, in particular, have a great aversion to them from their resemblance to the snake. But all objections are removed when they are brought upon the table as an article of food. The New York market is abundantly supplied by the fishermen from Long Island and adjacent places. Being easily taken, and found in great abundance, they furnish a cheap and healthy food for the poorer class of people. In some parts of the country where they are taken in fresh water, they are held in high estimation, and are made the object of sport by the young fishermen, by night and day, with bobs, eel pots, and spears.

A singular practice was in vogue at Catherine Market, foot of Catherine Street, New York, some years ago. The fish markets, as usual in large cities, were open on Sunday morning, in the summer season, for a few hours after sunrise. At the above-mentioned market the negroes used to gather from all parts of the city to the skinning, immense quantities being brought in for that purpose. After the operation was performed and the fish were tied into bundles, certain lots were purchased by the lovers of fun, to be danced for by the negroes. The ceremony of dancing for eels was performed with great skill and dexterity by the sons of Afric's soil upon an ordinary shingle, brought by each competitor for that purpose. The spectacle was witnessed by hundreds of lookers-on, composed of all classes of people, who expressed their satisfaction and approbation or dissent by cheers, claps, or groans. There were certain rules for the regulation of the dance, one of which was that the individual who shuffled off the shingle lost the prize, and was considered beaten. On some occasions, to produce more excitement and stimulate them to greater effort, larger bunches were put up for the dance. The grotesque appearance of the crowd, with the negro in the centre, attired in a white or check shirt, little the worse for absence from the wash-tub, an old straw hat, and pantaloons rolled up to the knees,

> "Intense emotion glitter'd in their eyes,
> Each eager watching for the slimy prize,"

surrounded by the fishermen with their red shirts and tarpaulin hats, the various dark-skinned polished face and white-teeth competitors with shingle in hand, watching anxiously their turn, surrounding the inside of the ring, and the motley laughing, joking, and betting crowd without, furnished a scene which we believe has been undeservedly neglected by the artist, and belongs to the history of *New York as it was.*

The discussions of naturalists respecting Eels, have been as crooked as their line of locomotion. Ichthyologists are generally of opinion that Eels make two migrations in each year, one in the autumn to the sea, and one, returning up the rivers in the spring. Yarrell says, "I am, however, of opinion that the passage of adult Eels to the sea, or rather to the brackish water of the estuary, is an exercise of choice, and not a matter of necessity; and that the parent Eels return up the river as well as the fry."

There are several different kinds of these fish found in both fresh and salt water; a singular description, called the Syren Mud Pup, or Rain Eel, is taken in one of the rivers near Charleston, S. C. Their shape is similar to the ordinary Eel,

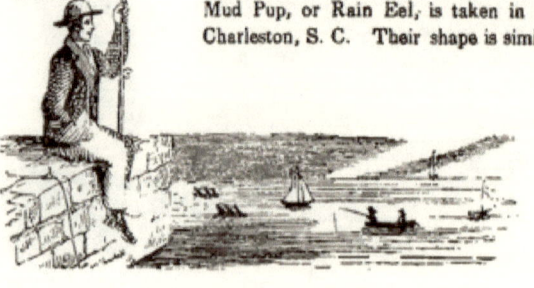

with the exception of two paws similar to a dog's, that they carry in front, to scratch their way in the mud, to avoid their enemies.

A friend who lives in the northern part of the state of New York, says he has observed two descriptions of fresh water Eels. "One having a small sharp head, tapering out very narrow towards the mouth, being larger according to their weight, and thicker through the middle than the common Eel. They generally inhabit clearer water, and are more frequently found above waterfalls. Their flesh is a lighter color, having more the appearance of fat pork. They are also much better, and when boiled or fried are a great relish." The other description has a larger head, wider mouth, the lower jaw projecting beyond the upper; they are largest through the gills, and taper to the tail; their flesh of a bluish color, and not as palatable as the former description. "All Eels are spawned in the ocean; the young ones commence running up rivers and smaller streams the latter part of April or beginning of May. They are then about the size of large needles; they go up along the shores and the edges of streams, and also up wet rocks near waterfalls, and over mill-dams, by exhausting the atmosphere under their bodies, then by raising their flat tail over, with or above their head, exhaust the atmosphere under that, and raise their head again; in this way they ascend the swifter streams, and reach the remotest lakes, except those above Niagara Falls, which they are never known to ascend. They select deep still water with soft bottom, and hibernate where old deep channels are filling up; at this time they are taken through the ice, or in boats with spears. They are in much better condition at this time than in summer, and offer more inducement to the angler with the spear, than when taken in that season with pot or line. They never spawn in lakes or rivers. Take them there as

large as you will, and you cannot find the least appearance of spawn; on the contrary, take a sea Eel in the latter part of winter, and you will find it full of spawn.*

Since, then, they are an object of sport, and the truly scientific angler, when in want of excitement, is sometimes seen by torch light, with spear in hand, striking for him in the depths below, it will be well to remark on some of the methods pursued in his capture.

In England they have a mode of taking the eel called *sniggling*, which, says Blaine, is a practice so ingenious and full of artifice, that it might reconcile the sportsman to Eel fishing. For the benefit of country friends, who are fond of Eel fishing, the following description of the tackle, and mode of operating is here given. A stick two yards long, with a cleft at each end, a strong needle whipped to a small whip-cord line, from the eye to the middle, which, with a lob-worm stuck on the needle, leaving the point to be inserted in the cleft of the stick, constitutes the simple apparatus. The art consists in putting the worm, needle, and line softly into the mouth of the Eel holes, which are suffered to remain until taken by the Eel, when the line and hook are again reclaimed, but accompanied by the Eel also. The most common modes of angling for them in this country are with the hook, bob, pot, and spear. For hook fishing, take an ordinary line, such as used for pickerel, in fresh water, or black fish in salt water, attach by a short length of line, gimp, or twisted gut, a size Black fish or Eel hook, suited to the size of fish expected, and a sinker ac-

* Dr. Mitchill says the roes or ovaria of Eels may be seen by those who will look for them in the proper season, like other fishes. Yarrell also remarks, Eels that have lived in brackish water all the winter, under the constant influence of the high temperature of that locality, probably deposit their spawn earlier in the spring, than those who have passed the winter in places from which there existed no probable egress

cording to the tide or current; see that all your tackle be strong, and you are rigged. If in fresh water, bait with worms, pieces of fish, frogs, entrails of chicken; for salt water, pieces of clams, fish, shrimp, or anything else you think they will fancy. The largest and oldest of the family snake along the muddy bottom at night, and perhaps accommodating you with a bite, will allow you to draw them up, of a size such as may trouble your dreams. Some salt water anglers take them with shedder crab and shad roe, after the following manner; they procure some white horse hairs, and work them into the shape of a bag, and within place their bait, or wind them thoroughly around a good size bait. They attach this to a hand line, with a sinker of sufficient weight to sink it to the bottom. The Eel takes hold, and soon entangles his teeth in the mesh of the bag, and is brought up without difficulty.

The bob is made by stringing on to a strong piece of worsted yarn or linen thread, a large number of worms, wound up into a ball, and by attaching your line, and letting it down with an appropriate sinker, to the bottom; when you feel any bites, give a little time, that they may get well hold; pull up moderately until at the top of the water, then give a jerk, sudden but steady, and you will, if successful, have several that will clear themselves without your help.

Pot fishing is still more of the wholesale kind, and is much practised in the country streams. The pot is made much after the fashion of an Irish potatoe hamper, but of the commonest basket materials, and the end like the entrance to a mouse trap, forming an inverted cone, with an elastic hole, large enough for the animals to squeeze their way through. These ends are constructed so that they can be taken off to bait, or to remove the fish. They are usually from 3 to 4 feet in length, and 6 to 8 inches in diameter. The bait, consisting of pieces of meat, fish, or garbage of any description, is placed in the inside, with a weight to sink it. To the centre is attached a strong cord or rope. When ready, it is let down to the bottom of the stream, and it is hauled up at turn of tide, or when its weight indicates a sufficient quantity of the desired fish.

Last, though not least, and probably the best mode, is spearing. This is done with a steel spear, made with five or six flat or square prongs, attached by a socket to a strong ash handle. They can be had at the fishing tackle stores, or made to order by the nearest blacksmith. These are forced into the mud from a boat, or used in wading, accompanied by an assistant, with a basket, to receive the result of the operator's skill.

They make a capital dish for eating, by either stewing, frying, *pyeing*, or better, according to Walton, as follows: " First, wash him in water and salt; then pull off his skin below his newt or navel, and not much further; having done that, take out his guts, as clean as you can, but wash him not; then give him three or four scotches with a knife, and then put into his belly and those scotches sweet herbs, an anchovy, and a little nutmeg, grated or cut very small; and your herbs and anchovies must also be cut very small, and mixed with good batter and salt; having done this, then pull his skin over him all but his head, which you are to cut off, to the end that you may tie his skin about that part where the head grew; and it must be so tied as to keep all moisture within his skin, and having done this, tie him with tape or packthread, to a spit, and roast him leisurely, and baste him with water and salt until his skin breaks, and then with butter, and having roasted him enough, let what was put into his belly, and what he drips, be his sauce." Thus endeth the chapter on Eels.

CHAPTER XVII.

THE HAKE.

Merlucius albidus.—DEKAY.

This fish is similar in appearance to the Tom-Cod, for which it is often mistaken by those who have never examined the two together. They, however, belong to the cod family, and are classed among ichthyologists as being related, although somewhat distant, to that species.

They are found in great abundance in England and France, where they are caught and sold in immense quantities. They are also caught of very large size, measuring three to five feet in length. Mr. Yarrell says, that they are "so abundant in the Bay of Galway that it was formerly called the Bay of Hakes. On that part of the Nymph off the coast of Waterford, the Hake is also so plentiful, that one thousand have been taken by six men with lines in one night. It is a voracious fish, as its systematic name of *Merlucius*, sea-pike, implies. They feed upon a description of fish called Pilchards, on which they glut themselves to their heart's desire. I have seen seventeen Pilchards taken from the stomach of a Hake of ordinary size. Their digestion, however, is quick, so that they speedily get rid of their load, and fishermen observe that upon being hooked, the Hake presently evacuates the contents of his stomach to facilitate its escape; so that when hundreds are taken with a line, in the midst of prey, not one will have anything in its stomach. When near the surface, however, this rejection does not take place until after they are dragged on board."

They do not appear to be so generally distributed in this country, as they are in others, neither do they grow to so large a size, and although not a game fish they are easily taken with the hook, and are considered very palatable. They are exceedingly common, says Dr. J. V. C. Smith, though not taken in any quantity in Massachusetts. The largest caught here seldom exceeds two feet. They are denominated *Poor Johns.* The best hake are taken off Cape Cod and sold under the name of *stock fish.*

When very hungry, the hake exhibits considerable voracity, and does not hesitate to seize a crab, which, in self-defence, sometimes fixes its shears in the retractile lips of the enemy, who whirls it through the water with surprising velocity, till it is finally obliged to let go its hold.

DESCRIPTION.—*Dekay.*

Characteristics.—Reddish brown above; long, acute, palatine teeth; lower jaw largest; length one to two feet.

Color.—Reddish brown, with golden tints towards the shoulders; sides of the opercle silvery, with a pinkish lustre; summits of the head dark brown; lower part of the body soiled white; lateral hue brownish black; tongue, surface of the bronchial arches, fauces, and interior of the opercles, deep bluish black; irides golden, mottled with brown; dorsals light brown, the rays lighter; caudal dark brown; remaining fins whitish, minutely punctate with brown.

They were formerly little known at New York, but of late years have become quite abundant, where they are taken at the docks generally at night by boys, and those of the craft that cannot spare time during the day. The Hake, like the Tom-Cod, is a bottom fish, and is taken generally with hand lines, and the usual black fish tackle. Being of the voracious order, he seems to love the eddies and currents, and is better taken when the tide is running strong, where he delights to feed upon what is forced in its way. On such grounds the line should be

rigged with a heavy sinker, and a hollow one if it can be procured, as the bite is much easier felt. Some prefer instead of a black fish hook a Limerick, about No. 4 salmon. He is fond of shrimps, crabs, and clams. Economical anglers universally use the latter bait, considering it good' enough to take him or any of his family.

CHAPTER XVIII.

WHITE PERCH AND CAT-FISH ANGLING IN THE VICINITY OF NEW YORK.

By T. D. L.

LAKE fishing lacks one element of interest possessed by the salt water, namely, the condition of hopeful uncertainty respecting the sort and size of your game. Between the humble Flounder and the noble Sheepshead are many kinds of game fish, and greater disparities of weight and value than exist between the fish of fresh ponds, which are less various and more equal. Moreover, the salt water tribe come and go with seasons and tides, and cannot, like their inland brethren, always be followed and found. There is therefore an excitement in the doubtful chances of sea-fishing wanting in that of the lakes which presents greater uniformity of character and certainty of success.

But though still water fishing, as compared with the flowing salt, is inferior in interest, perhaps it has superiority in the general satisfaction it affords. In the numerous lakelets of New York, fish, of some sort, can at any time be taken. Not, however, always with equal ease. When the water is warm and the fish well fed, the angler will find occasion for all his art;—in the successful exercise of which, and not in the magnitude of his fishing, lies, after all, the chief satisfaction. Perch, large and lively, both yellow and white: Sunfish, sometimes of considerable size; Pickerel, which are shy, and employ all your cunning and skill; Cat-fish, whether you would or no; are taken in our hundred little lakes; and the angler, with light rod and fine tackle (which are indispensable to enjoyment), will find fishing in them anything but a dull and tame affair.

WHITE PERCH AND CAT-FISH ANGLING.

The baits used are various: live bait, as worm or fish, is generally best. But whatever you take

"To bait fish withal,"

if it will feed nothing else, 'twill feed Cat-fish, which are omnivorous. They are the fresh water Toad-fish, and, like others of the family, seem to subserve the purpose of purification, by the reconversion into life of corruptible organic matter. Though esteemed delicate eating* when well cooked, they are not pleasant to *take* raw;—their ugly mouths, slimy skins, and dangerous horns, causing the dainty angler to avoid their neighborhood. This he can do only by fishing some feet above bottom. But drop below that discreet distance, and he will surely damage his tackle in the jaws of some bull-headed Mandarin, to be disengaged only with infinite difficulty and disgust. Fishing for them, when rightly prepared, is, like fishing for Eels, well enough and quite another thing. You will then use gimp, and a kirb about No. 3 Salmon, upon bottom. The best time is sundown, and after. Then they bite boldly, and are a sure fish. Glove your left hand and seize them fearlessly but firmly behind the horns when you disgorge the hook. Boys with stick and string, a rusty hook and piece of pork, take "Bullheads" (as the small Cat-fish are called) in almost every pond and fresh stream in the Northern States.

But angling for the White or Silver Perch—the graceful bright-eyed Perch—with pliant rod and gossamer thread of gut —this is no boy's play, but a true exhilarating sport. A nimble, strong, *clean* fish, that springs voraciously at the bait, struggles hard, and dies game, is a respectable adversary, and occasions you to

"Know the fierce joy that anglers feel,
In fishes worthy of their steel."

* From Philadelphia, pleasure parties very commonly visit the falls of the Schuylkill, to despatch them with knife and fork.

Seen at daybreak or sundown, playing in sparkling schools on the sunny side of some lakelet, he is an object of attractive beauty to the poetic angler. Perch bite best in early morning and evening about the shallows near shore; but at mid-day, when they retire to bars that run out into deeper water, they become dainty, yet may, however, be there taken. Worm, upon a Limerick hook (1 to 3 trout), is a common bait. But the "killy," and small brook shiner, or gold fish, are better. Prepared with these, I generally contrive to drift with the wind, if there be any, outside the shadow of the woods and beyond the weeds, trailing a light float, with swivel just weighty enough to dip it and balance the live bait swimming at half depth. This is the ground and mode of fishing, good alike for Perch and Pickerel. Be therefore prepared for the latter, and if one bite give him no quarter, but bring him in steadily, and *quickly*, if you would save your tackle. His bite may be distinguished from that of the Perch. His is a long pull, holding the float under; whereas the Perch bite is comparatively quick and short.

Slowly drifting, then, fishing between the boat and shore, and drawing or casting my line into every likely nook, I generally strike upon a school of Perch, when I quietly drop anchor. When they cease biting I row above, float down again, and commonly take more in the same place, or if not, continue to drift as before. Large fish, as Perch over half a pound may be called, are more solitary in their habits; the smaller the more gregarious, as though instinctively associating for mutual protection. I choose the sunny side, because I think the Silver Perch (other circumstances equal) prefer the strong lights to the dark waters of the pond; and this may be one reason why they swim nearer the surface in the twilight of morning and evening. If then the fish don't bite freely, examine the crop of one, and suit your bait to its apparent food.

The White Perch, though less common than the Yellow, is

yet widely distributed in our waters. It is found in the Hudson and tributary streams. The Passaic river abounds with a small size. Very fine fish are taken in most of the lakes of Putnam county (accessible by the Harlem railroad), and in many ponds of that paradise of sportsmen, Long Island, especially in Suffolk County. There, a short ride through the pines from almost any point, will bring you to some quiet spot, where you can find fair sport angling, "under the shade of overhanging boughs," yet within sound of the ocean surf. The pine woods, interlaced with their bright sandy avenues, have a peculiar beauty, and to fish in their still depths, of a serene day, in a light skiff, gently gliding over some mirrored lake,

"Fair as the bosom of the swan,'

is a luxury they can best appreciate who are *ennuied* by fashion, or distempered by the wear and tear of an intense business life. To minds of any sensibility, the mere repose of these suburban solitudes is "a feeling" of beauty, and awakens the consciousness of an infinite *presence*, replete with religious emotions.

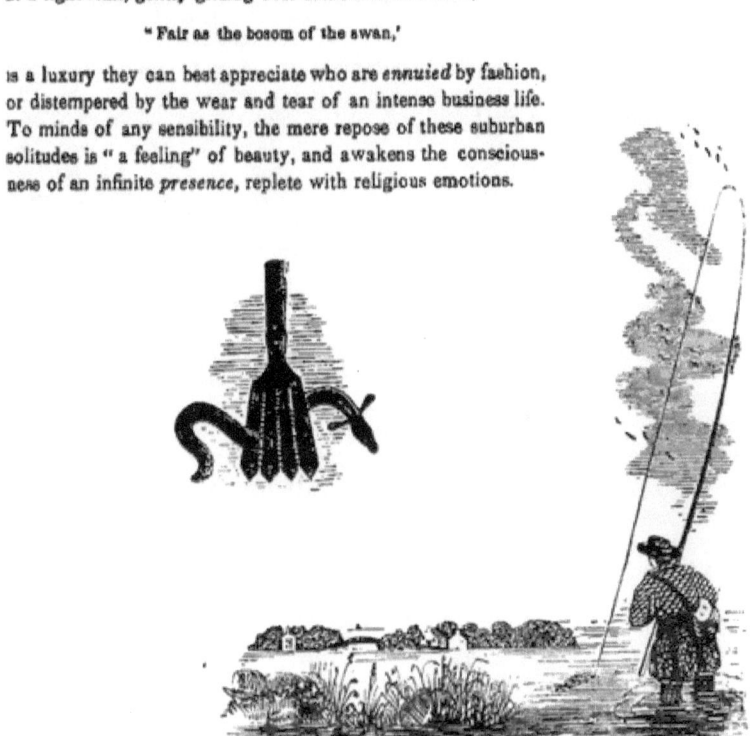

CHAPTER XIX.

OCEAN ANGLING.

> Likeness of Heaven!
>   Agent of Power!
> Man is thy victim,
>   Shipwreck's thy dower
> Spices and jewels
>   From valley and sea,
> Armies and banners
>   Are buried in thee!

THE art we love being admirably adapted to recruit the broken-down or enervated constitution; and the pure breath of heaven, as it comes from off the dark blue sea and the white capped wave, being a more potent medicine than that prescribed by the physician, or compounded by the apothecary, no excuse need here be offered for a few remarks on a subject of interest to those who may cast their first line from the side of a ship. Those who have never been to sea are apt to think that such a large pond was only made for the leviathan whale, the ponderous shark, or the Nahant Sea Serpent, but a little reflection would convince the most sceptical that they labor under a delusion.

The depths of the trackless ocean, wherein the monsters bask in broad noon-day, as well as the reefs and shallows nearer land, are teeming with shoals of the living brood of smaller size, which are designed not only to feed and fatten the larger majesties of their own species, but to minister to the appetite, comfort, amusement, and support of the man in whose power they are placed. The poor sailor, who is obliged to make a voyage of many months, is ever on the alert for a change of diet, and the sight of a school

of fish is a subject of gratification to the whole of a ship's company, and more particularly to those who have never before tempted their precious souls and bodies on the ocean wave.

> "And now approaching near the lofty stern,
> A shoal of sportive dolphins they discern.
> From burnish'd scales they beam refulgent rays,
> Till all the glowing ocean seems to blaze
> Soon to the sport of death the crew repair,
> Dart the long lance, or spread the baited snare."

The ocean is supposed to have as many tenants as the earth or the air. But few of the descriptions are much known by any particular names, and very few described by naturalists. The Dolphin, whose fame has been said and sung by poet and philosopher, is worth a sea voyage for the pleasure of his capture, and the satisfaction of " being in at his death." Their usual size is from 2 to 5 ft. in length. The variableness and beauty of his rainbow colorings, as he shuffles off his mortal coil, is a subject indescribable by pen or pencil. He is not a handsome fish as he is lifted up and exposed to the view of those who make his acquaintance for the first time; on the contrary, his proportions and appearance as to beauty are rather ordinary, and not until a change comes o'er the spirit of his dream, and he flaps his tail upon the white deck of the vessel, and, gasping, dies, is his beauty acknowledged.

> "What radiant changes strike the astonish'd sight!
> What glowing hues of mingled shade and light!
> Not equal beauty gilds the glowing west,
> With parting beams all o'er profusely drest;
> Nor lovelier colors paint the vernal dawn,
> When orient dews impearl th' enamell'd lawn,
> Than from his sides in bright suffusion flow,
> That now with gold imperial seem to glow;

> Now in pellucid sapphires meet the view,
> And imitate the soft, celestial hue;
> Now beam a flaming crimson on the eye,
> And now assume the purple's deeper dye.
> But here description clouds each shining ray;
> What terms of art can nature's power display?"

He that would prepare himself for the pleasure and excitement of his capture, should provide himself with a stout hawser-laid cotton or hemp line of 28 or 30 fathoms length, and in thickness about one-eighth of an inch; to this should be attached one of the largest size Cod hooks, seized on to the line with the stoutest kind of white, black, or colored No. 12 thread, or small fish line, well waxed with shoemaker's wax; for bait, use a large piece of salt pork, about six inches in length by 2 or 3 wide, made well fast. Fasten your line, cast your baited hook overboard, and troll till you get a bite; pull him in with a steady line, stout heart, and strong nerve, and he will soon repay the trouble of his capture, both by the excitement of the occasion, and the table exercise with the instruments of appetite. You will not find his meat as pleasant to the taste as some others of the tribe, but rather preferable to the salt pork upon which he expected to dine himself. The sailors take him with a large piece of bone, tin, or lead attached to a good sized hook; but you will find a much better article called an artificial squid, of handsome shape, from 4 to 8 inches in length, and composed of tin, after a similar manner, at the general fishing tackle stores. This article is used without bait in its simple form, being made something in the shape of a fish.

There are other fish captured in the same way, on sea voyages; among them the Bonita, Barracouta, and Skip Jack. Smaller squids are employed, similar to those in trolling for blue fish, say from 3 to 5 inches in length, of tin or bone, the former to be used in rough water, and the latter in smooth; those who contemplate going to sea, to be sure of success, should take both kinds. The Bonita and Skip Jack vary in size from 1 to 2 feet, and can be taken with lighter tackle; but to be on the safe side, and insure success, employ your Dolphin line; and should you use beef or pork instead of the artificial squid, attach to your line stout Kirby sea hooks, the size of 1-0 or 2-0 Limerick. In purchasing and rigging your sea tackle, see that it is well made, and perfectly strong. Let not parsimony deter you from preparing it of the best quality, and you will never regret your angling enjoyments on the ocean.

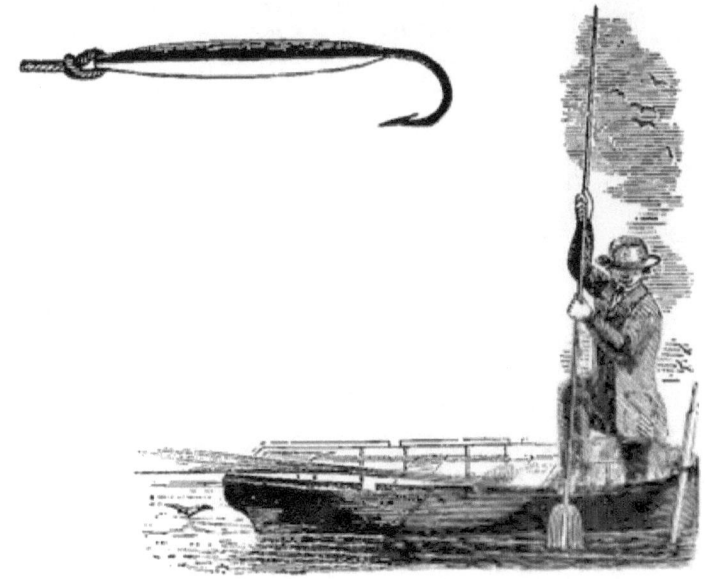

CHAPTER XX.

INHABITANTS OF THE OREGON AND CALIFORNIA WATERS.

The waters of California are alive with a great variety of the finny race, equal in value to the angler as are its golden sands* to the adventurer. In the bay and harbor of San Francisco are found the Haddock, the Black Fish or Tautog, the Flounder, the Mackerel, the Weak Fish or salt water Trout of the south, the Mullet, and the Red Fish, or Spotted Basse. These different descriptions, which are taken with rod or hand-tackle in the usual manner, are of unusually large size and of very fine flavor. The Red Fish is said by those who have tried it with the knife and fork to be superior in gastronomic qualities to the celebrated fish of the same name at New Orleans and Charleston, being also much finer in outward appearance, having more delicate skin, smaller scales, and its superficial surface more beautiful. They bite at the hook baited with pieces of mullet, beef, or pork, very freely, are very vigorous, and give good play with the rod and reel. The beautiful Mullet is also found here in all its glory, and grows to quite a large size, being taken from 6 or 8 inches to 2 or 4 feet in length in seines or nets. A singular description of fish is also taken in the bay called the Trigger Fish. This member of the family has a singular projection on the back, similar in appearance to the trigger of a gun, from which much amusement is had by the inhabitants by its singular motions,

* In the time of Cortes gold was reported to be so plenty in Mexico, that the fishermen used gold weights to their nets. *Our Salmon anglers of the Sacramento will of course use golden Rods and Reels.*

when pulled by the knowing ones. The fresh water fish swarm the streams and lakes in abundance. The Salmon here lord their way through the Sacramento and Columbia rivers, and their branches, in such large numbers, that they can be seen in immense shoals when entering the rivers in the month of April, and are speared, or captured by the Indians with a wicker basket, with much ease. The natives, also, set fences across the streams where they go up, and confine and secure them in large quantities. They take the fly finely, and afford good sport with the rod and reel.

The lakes and inland rivers, also, teem with an abundance of Catfish, and Salmon Trout of the finest quality and flavor. Capt. Fremont, in his narrative of his exploring expedition to California, says, in speaking of those of the Salmon Trout River: "Their flavor is excellent—superior, in fact, to any fish that I have ever known." In the mountain streams, the Spotted Trout is found in large quantities, as are the Yellow Perch and many other smaller descriptions of fish. The River Gila, which empties into the northern extremity of the Gulf of California, contains fish similar in shape, general appearance, and color to the Trout. "At a little distance," says Lieut. Emory, "they seem covered with scales, but a closer examination detects nothing of the kind, but small marks of a scaly appearance, making them look entirely different from what they seem. Their meat, although very palatable, is rather soft, and not equal to the Spotted Trout. On the coast are to be found the Green Turtle, Oysters, Mussels, Clams, and other kinds of shell-fish of the largest size, and of the finest flavorable qualities. Altogether California and Oregon offer great inducements to the angler and epicurean."

CHAPTER XXI.

OF THE WHITE PERCH.

This fine fish, although a general inhabitant of most of our fresh water ponds, is often found in many of our large rivers, where he partakes more of the active nature of the striped, or Black Basse (to which family he belongs), than of that of his more sluggish but less active and nearer relative, the Yellow Perch.

At the High Bridge, Harlem River, they are taken in large quantities, and sometimes of large size, all through the summer season; they also abound in many parts of the Hudson, Delaware, and Schuylkill rivers, and are the objects of much sport in many parts of Connecticut, the large ponds of Long Island, and the streams of various other parts of the United States.

They are generally caught with the usual Trout, or Perch tackle, except when found in the more rapid rivers, when the angler delights to master him with his Basse rod, stronger bottom lengths, and hooks in proportion. It is also well to prepare in this manner, in order to be in readiness for larger fish, which in the rivers and often in the large ponds, give considerable trouble. A Connecticut friend, who was once almost mastered by a large pike, whilst angling for white perch, gives the following graphic account of his success.

"I had been fishing nearly the whole afternoon; the sun had almost set, and I was drifting along with the declining wind, not far from the shore of a lake, near the southern part of the state, when I felt a most violent jerk at my line, which immediately began to run out with great rapidity. Supposing my fugitive to be only a remarkably vigorous perch, I attempted to check him, but found the strain so great as to convince me that I had encountered a more powerful opponent. I had only a slight trouting-rod, with a very slender silk and hair line, and a very fine gut bottom with a number 6 trout hook, and I saw at once that skill and patience and not force, must win the day. I accordingly gave out plenty of line, keeping it tight, however, and very soon my antagonist rose to the surface, while I reeled in again with my utmost celerity. He then leaped with extended jaws a full yard from the water and immediately plunged again towards the bottom, where he *dug* along until he very nearly carried out 40 yards of line, when luckily he turned once more and came directly towards the boat. After a contest of about 25 minutes, sustained with great strength and perseverance on the part of the fish, and the utmost skill I could muster on my own part, and the most intense excitement on both sides, I fairly overcame my scaly friend, and led him, gasping at length and unresisting, with his broad green sides gleaming in the sunset, to the side of my boat, placed my landing net under him, and in an instant he was at my feet; he proved to be one of the largest pike I had ever taken in that water, and weighed 7 1-2 pounds." The same gentleman fishes for Perch in the following manner. "My common method of taking white Perch, is with a small minnow or shiner, placed upon two Limerick hooks, tied about an inch apart, on a bottom length of five or six feet of fine single gut, furnished with a couple of swivels. The lower hook is about No. 3, and the other No. 6, according to the arrangement of hooks in the Angler's Guide. I row my boat out nearly to the middle of the pond and then allow it to drift before the wind, with my line run off the reel to just about such a length as that the motion of the boat will keep the bait near the surface of the water. The white Perch play about in schools, constantly leaping above the water in a fine breezy day, and often in seizing the bait, they will spring entirely from the surface, as a trout does in taking a fly. In this way, with two rods, I have frequently captured from 80 to 100 in a few hours."

CHAPTER XXII.

THE YELLOW PIKE PERCH.

Lucioperca Americana.

THIS is a very fine fish, both for table and rod exercise, and seems to partake of the nature of both the pike and perch family; like the trout he loves the more bold and rapid parts of rivers and lakes, and also the deep holes, and under weeds and grass, and with some of the fraternity is considered equal in vigor and activity to the favorite trout. A friend who sent two from Albany this winter (1849), as specimens, says they are taken in Lake Ontario, and also in the Mohawk, where they are called Mohawk Pike. It has also been ascertained that they abound in the Susquehanna and its tributary streams, where the true pickerel also are found. They grow in the above mentioned places to the weight of ten or twelve pounds, are fearless in attack, roaming the streams a terror to the finny race, often endeavoring to gorge more than they can swallow.

Color.—" Yellowish olive above the lateral line; lighter on the sides, silvery beneath; head and gill covers mottled with green, brownish and white; chin pale flesh color; pupil dark and vitreous; sides mottled with black and yellowish; membrane of the spinous dorsal transparent, with a few dark dashes; the upper part of the membrane tipped with black; the posterior part of the membrane, including the two last rays, black; the soft dorsal fin light yellowish, spotted with brown in such a manner as to form irregular longitudinal dusky bars; pectoral fins yellowish olive, with maculated brownish bars; ventral fins transparent yellowish; anal fin of the same color, with a broad whitish margin; caudal fin with irregular dusky bars."
—*Dekay.*

"This is the common Pike, Pickerel, Glass Eye, and Yellow Pike of the great lakes and most of the inland lakes of the western part of the State. In Ohio it has received the name of Salmon. The ordinary name gives no correct idea of its character. It is a true perch, although its form and habits suggest very naturally the idea of pike. I have, therefore, applied to it a name which indicates its true position, and is a translation of its classical appellation."

"The Pike-perch is exceedingly voracious, and is highly prized for food. It is caught readily with the hook, and appears to prefer as bait the common fresh water cray-fish (Astacus Bartoni). According to Dr. Rutland it is one of the most valuable fish for the table found in the western waters, and sells readily at a high price. It is found in such quantities about the Maumee River, as to induce the fishermen to make it an article of commerce. At Lake Huron it spawns in April or May. In Chatauque Lake I was informed of one which was thirty inches long. It had swallowed a duck, which had thrust its head through the gill openings of the fish, and having thus destroyed it, both were found dead upon the shores."

The best arrangement for his successful capture is a good size basse rod, and the regular basse tackle, with the exception of the hook, which should be about the size of that used for the king fish, say about No. 4 salmon. The bait most generally used is the minnow or shiner.

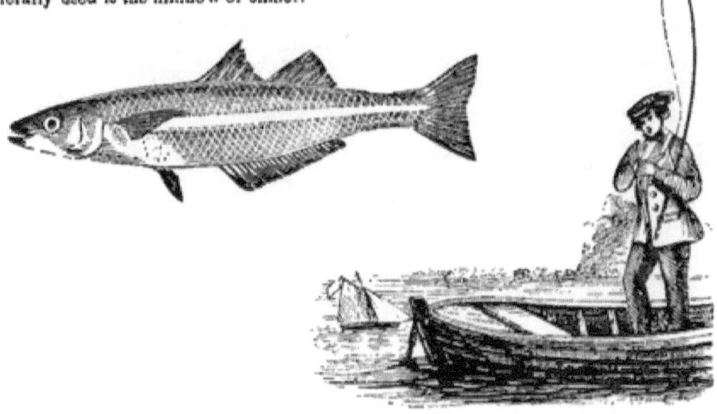

CHAPTER XXIII.

BLACK BASSE ANGLING IN MICHIGAN.

Kindly furnished for this work by a friend at Detroit.

BLACK BASSE are found in all the great Western lakes, and in all the rivers connecting them or tributary to them. They abound also in the picturesque and beautiful lakelets with which the peninsula of Michigan is studded. There are several species of fish which pass by the general name of Black Basse, but two or three of which appear to be described by naturalists— The Black Basse (*Huro Nigricans*) of Lake Huron, the Black Basse (*Centrarchus Fasciatus*) of Lake Erie and the Ohio River, and *Labrax Nigricans*, or Small Black Basse. They differ in different localities in form as well as in color. They all belong to the great Perch family, and are a game fish, affording fine sport to the angler. They, with the White Basse, Pickerel, Pike, Yellow Perch, and Catfish, comprise the list out of which the Detroit River angler is to find his sport; but the one which will most reward him for his toil, is the Black Basse. He is shy and capricious, yet when feeding bold and voracious. In size and shape he strongly resembles the Blackfish (*Tautog*) of salt water, and like him is found among rocks and reefs, and stones, and rapids, and eddies.* In weight they range from one to five pounds.

On the eastern coast of Lake Michigan, and in Green Bay,

---

* Another variety of this species does not appear to have been described by naturalists. It is never black. The back of the fish is a dark color, shading gradually into green on the sides, and from that into a whitish cream color on the belly. The characteristic mark of this variety is two broad longitudinal parallel lines running the whole length of the body. They are commonly called the Green Basse, and are found where there is grassy bottom. Their weight ranges from one to five pounds.

they are somewhat larger. In color, too, at times, the Black Basse is like the Tautog; but his color changes with the season, or from some other cause, from a dingy black to a dark green. Perhaps these varieties of color are the result of age or sex, though it is said that the same fish, kept in a vessel of water, will change its color repeatedly in a short space of time. The Black Basse makes his appearance in the Detroit River about the latter part of May or first days of June, as the season is early or late. He is then in fine condition, and at his feeding time, which is from sunrise till half-past seven or eight o'clock A. M., and from four P. M. to sunset, will give good sport till the last of July. In August they are spawning; and though the bait be cast in the midst of "a crowd," as it sometimes may on a gravelly bank over which the water, two or three feet deep, runs rapidly into an eddy or pool, they will nose it about in turn as disdainfully as though they were innocent of ever masticating a minnow. If you do succeed by artifice, as you flatter yourself, in enticing one to take the hook, he gives but little play, and comes out with scarcely a struggle. You will find him hollow over the eyes, sharp on the back, thin and shrunk and so woe-begone of look, suggestive of fishy fever and ague, that his taking the hook, you are convinced, is mere desperation, in fact a piscatory suicide. You throw him back into his native element, and he swims languidly off with an air which plainly says his destiny is a matter of indifference to him. You may succeed during the month of August, even at mid-day, in taking a few stout, frisky young fellows of a pound or a pound and a half in weight, which the accomplished fishing correspondent of the "Buffalo Commercial" calls "yearlings;" but there your sport will end. Reel up then, friend, and hie thee to the edge of the sedge, to inveigle Yellow Perch or a stray Pickerel, and leave the "yearlings" to grow, and their emaciated progenitors to recover their plumpness and vigor.

It is said that at this time they will greedily take the grasshopper and artificial fly, but the fish are not generally good; in this season you will rarely succeed in inducing them to rise to the simulated insect. The proper months, then, for black basse fishing, are June and July, and from the beginning of September to the middle and last of October. Basse seldom take the bait during the prevalence of a north-east or east wind. In the latter part of September or during the month of October, basse may be taken at almost any time of day, but they bite better mornings and afternoons, even in that season.

The modes of taking this delicious fish, are by trolling, and still fishing with the rod and reel.

In trolling, the spoon may be used with success, or a few white feathers fastened around the shank of the hook with a bit of red woollen yarn or red flannel. White deer hair adorned with bright red, is said to be a killing trolling bait; a tuft of hair, two and a half inches in length, and nearly the thickness of one's finger, is laid along the shank of the hook and securely fastened in the middle by binding on sewing silk, which is covered by red yarn or flannel. As it is drawn through the water, the ends of the hairs above the yarn spread out and turn back; this bait is showy and said to be very effective. It is used in the rapids of rivers, and for trolling in the small inland lakes. The baits used with the rod and reel are minnows, small frogs, and the common craw fish, or little fresh water lobster. The live minnow is the best, though there are times when their voracity will prompt them to take almost any bait. The bait, whatever it may be, except the angle worm, should be kept in motion, by drawing it through the water a yard or two at a time; this seems to act as a provocation, and they will dart at it, when, if the bait be dead and stationary, they will not touch it. A strong, live minnow of three inches in length is a very killing bait. Use a gut leader of four or five feet in length. Pass your hook through the eyes of the minnow, taking care not to wound the brain, and he will live and swim about, the full length of his tether, in the most natural manner possible. With this description of bait, and this mode of adjusting it, you cannot fail to take basse, if they are in the mood to bite at all; whilst others, fishing near you with portions of minnow or dead bait, will meet no encouragement to continue their sport.

Basse invariably swallow the bait head first. The manner pursued by the boys living near the small lakes in Michigan, will illustrate the superiority of live bait in taking Basse. They take a small live sunfish, and after running a hook through the extreme end of his nose, conceal its point with an angle worm; then, when it is cast overboard, a number of sunfish gather about it attracted by the worm; the collection draws the attention of a basse, who straightway darts among them—the little fellows "all immajiately swim away" to shallow water, leaving the decoy to the mercy of the hungry basse, who in his turn becomes the prisoner of the ingenious young piscator. But Basse, like others of the finny tribe, are not always caught when hooked. In the season when in full strength, they make most violent efforts to release themselves from the "barbed steel," and will frequently, after making a burst or two, throw themselves two or three feet out of the water with a flutter, shaking their heads most intelligently to throw out the hook. This is a ticklish time for the angler, and unless he keeps his strain upon the fish, and drops the end of his rod, he will lose his prize. This manœuvre, a strong basse will repeat several times. The angler who wishes to have a day's sport for Black Basse, should catch his minnows the afternoon before, keeping them in a vessel perforated with small holes and sunk in the water. At early dawn he must be off for the ground. If he has selected an eddy, above which the water ripples over a rocky ledge or gravelly

20

bank, he should not go straight to the place, splashing the water with his oars, but make a circuit above, and drop down with the current, keeping his anchor overboard till he reaches the proper spot, then let it go with as little noise as possible. Cast the bait well out into the stream, and let it swing round into the eddy, keeping it in motion by drawing it towards him a yard or two at a time, and letting it run out again with the stream. My word for it, if he is on Basse ground, he'll soon have a lusty pull. Now care is necessary. Cool now! Don't strike too quick, for the scaly rascals like to mouthe the tempting, struggling morsel a bit (and they have to swallow it head first, you know). So wait, my friend, till he gives another strong decided pull, then "have at him." Now caution and steadiness are required—if he make a burst, keep your drag upon him, but not too strongly, or he'll spring from the water and shake the hook out if it has merely gone through the membrane which lines the tough cartilage of the nose, but steadily, and he'll give you fine play, for he is full of vigor. Reel him in gently, but be careful he don't run under your boat, and foul your line or leader; there he is, within reach! Now the landing net—and voila! the stout rogue, flapping in the bottom of your boat, with his capacious jaws wide spread, and the morning sun gilding his emerald side.

The sportsman on a western angling tour will find Basse ground in the Niagara river, at and near Black Rock, a few miles from Buffalo; at the islands near the head of Lake Erie; at many points in the Detroit river; on the St. Clair flats, or western "overslaugh," at the upper end of Lake St. Clair; and at Fort Gratiot near the entrance to Lake Huron.

CHAPTER XXIV.

THE MUSKELLUNGE, MUSCALINGA, OR LAKE PIKE.

Essex Ester.

This capital fish, from his size, if for no better reason, deserves more attention than we have given him in former pages. By some naturalists he is classed as a distinct species, and different from the ordinary pike or pickerel of the ponds and rivers, but ichthyologists generally consider him nothing more than a monstrous fresh water pike,[*] or "Jack" as he is called in England. While on this subject, it may be well to remark that there are in some ponds and small creeks, a species of stunted pickerel that grow to about the size of from three to six inches, and never attain to a greater length; they seem not to have the same rapacious habits as the true pickerel which grows to pikehood, and are often found in trout streams, where they are said to be harmless, as would naturally be the case, for from his limited dimensions he could not do much harm. The appearance, especially when large, of the various inhabitants of the waters, they being more coarse, ill-shaped, and less symmetrical, leads many inexperienced persons to call them by different names, and consider them different species, though, in fact, often the same. This fish, also, in his variety of size and age, has been a subject of much discussion among the knowing ones. The writer recollects the many remarks made upon a portrait of a very large trout, hung in a place of resort for the fraternity. With some his head was too large and his tail too small, others his head too small and his tail too large; some would have his tail more square, and others more forked; some said his eyes were too small, and others the

[*] In Ireland and Scotland they have been taken weighing eighty and ninety pounds.

reverse; and so from head to tail not excepting his fins, which were too long or too short, too wide or too narrow, or too far apart or too close together. Some would have him a salmon trout, and others would not let him be a trout at all, and still others said he was a salmon, and nothing else. And in this manner was this correct subject of the painter's study criticized, because he happened, like the Belgian Giant or Daddy Lambert, to grow higher or broader, grosser or coarser than the rest of his species. If a pike in his youthful days must be called a pickerel, in manhood a pike, and when in larger waters he enlarges in size, or increases in age, a muskellunge; why should not the trout or bass be called by some other name when he comes to manhood or full size? The same in regard to the salmon; when young, he has some half dozen names, such as parr, grilse, smalt, smolt, pink, &c. With equal propriety we might call our own species by different names in different stages of growth and forms of development. Brother anglers, let us simplify instead of mystify, and avoid the multiplication of names that only serve to mislead those who would otherwise arrive at just conclusions. But to our subject.

The following description of the muskellunge is taken from the New York Fauna. Body cylindrical, elongate, somewhat quadrate; scales thin, small, orbicular, ascending on the cheeks; the upper part of the head smooth; snout broad, rounded, and depressed; head covered with numerous pores on the summit and sides; an oblong cavity between the orbits; mouth very large, a single row of small recurved teeth in the anterior part of the upper and lower jaw; sides of the lower jaw with long acute distant teeth; bonds of small teeth on the vomer and palatines; a series of minute teeth on the bronchial arches; tongue truncate, with asperities on its base; bronchial rays eighteen; the dorsal fin with twenty rays, of which the

first five are applied closely to the base of the sixth; anal similar in shape, with its first four rays similarly applied to the fifth; pectorals small; ventral on the middle of the body, and small; caudal large, lamellated with rounded lobes.

Color.—Deep greenish brown; darker on the back; pale on the sides, with numerous rounded, distinct, pale yellow or greyish spots on the sides. These spots vary in size from two to three-tenths of an inch in diameter; they become occasionally confluent. Each scale has a bright quadrate spot, which reflects brilliant metallic tints of various colors. Length one to three feet.

Like the smaller denominations of his tribe his propensities are shark-like; he feeds, fattens on, and makes prey of everything that comes in his way; he is in no respect an epicurean, but seems ready to dine, breakfast, or lunch, whenever invited out. A slice of pork, a bundle of worms, the entrails of a fowl, a frog, the part of a fish, or a whole one, he is not particular, if his capacious jaws can be extended wide enough. A piece of beef, an artificial tin squid, or a spoon bait, is sufficient to tempt him to bite. You may fish for him as for a smaller pike, only be sure that your tackle is strong in proportion to the size of your game. In the larger lakes a good size cod line is not too large, nor the largest cod hook too small to attach a bait of sufficient size to suit his extended jaw and fill his capacious maw. In smaller lakes your tackle should be proportionally light. His successful capture requires the utmost vigilance, and sometimes the most extreme exertion of the physical power of the angler. With a stiff breeze upon a large lake, with the waves running high, one can readily imagine himself fishing upon the ocean, and as far as the exercise and excitement is concerned, be really as much benefited. He is considered one of the best fish for the table that inhabits the western waters.

CHAPTER XXV.

THE CAT FISH.

Pimelodus Catus.

This aquatic family is as large as any that comes under the notice of the naturalist or the pleasure or displeasure of the regular angler. There are eleven different species described in the Natural History of the State of New York. They are a bottom fish, and like the eel, are tenants alike of the smallest pond, the largest river, and the mighty ocean. They occur in most of the fresh water streams and ponds from Maine to Florida, and vary in size from six inches in length to the untold length and weight of the ponderous inhabitant of the mighty Mississippi, or the "Almighty Ocean."

In some parts of the country they are found of superior flavor, and highly prized as an article of food, and in other places they are not respected either by the hook or the cook, and are only used as bait to catch their more highly prized brethren.

Dr. Dekay says of the brown cat fish (Pimelodus Pullus), "This is very common in Lake Pleasant, Lake Janet, and many of the other lakes in the northern districts of the State of New York. There are many varieties in its markings, and it occasionally exceeds a foot in length. Its principal use in these regions appears to be to serve as a bait for lake trout."

COMMON CAT FISH.

Color.—Dusky, with a deeper shade on the back and summit of the head; sides of the head with a greenish tint; cupreous on the sides; abdomen pearl grey; fins dusky. After death from infiltration, some of the fins become tinged with red; irides white.—*Dekay.*

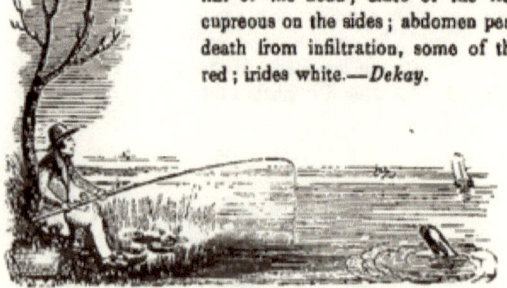

This is one of the most common species, and makes its appearance in market in the first days of April. A peculiarity connected with this species, and perhaps with others of the same family, is that it occasionally appears without any ventral fins. I have seen two thus deprived of these fins, and thus furnished a naturalist with an opportunity of forming a new genus—*Pimapterus*. The specimen thus defective agreed in every respect to the minutest particular with the species above described, so that I am induced to conclude that it was entirely accidental.

THE GREAT LAKE CAT FISH.—*Pimelodus Nigricans.*

Characteristics.—Large; deep olive brown; caudal forked; anal fin with twenty-five or twenty-six rays; length two to four feet.

Color.—General hue olive brown; the upper part of the head and cheeks bluish; the sides of the body towards the tail, ash white, with occasional large confluent black spots; a few irregular distant round spots on the upper part of the body; upper lip maculated with black; all beneath bluish white, varied with darker; base of the ventrals and pectorals whitish; pupil black; irides varied with blackish and golden.

I have seen them weighing from twenty-five to thirty pounds, and have heard of others that reached the weight of eighty pounds.

Those who wish to capture the cat fish, whether in pond, river, or lake, need not be particular as to the size or appearance of their tackle, provided it be strong enough to bring the fish to land. Of course the hooks and lines (which should be hand lines, although some prefer the rod) should be in proportion to the size of fish expected. Worms, minnows, insects, or pieces of fish, if cast within his reach, are certain to bring out the common cat fish from his slimy bed.

An esteemed friend who would infinitely prefer the capture of a single trout or black basse, to the taking of a cart-load of cat fish, thus discourseth of his first and last lake cat fish.

"I have taken the cat fish but once, and on that occasion used a long, strong hand line, heavy sinker, and No. 1 Limerick salmon hook. I baited, as one would a mouse trap, with a bit of toasted cheese. I fished at night, and the result of this scientific procedure was a cat fish weighing seventeen and a half pounds. My ambition was satisfied. I have never repeated the experiment. A great many are taken by the dock fishers at night in this manner from the wharves (Detroit). The baits are toasted cheese, chicken guts, and raw liver, or beef. The latter, impregnated with asafœtida, is said by the knowing ones to be the best of the lot. These fish suck the bait in, rather than bite, giving a tremulous motion or series of little jerks to the line, much in the way an eel takes the bait. They are vigorous, exceedingly tenacious of life, and when 'laid to the land' denote their satisfaction by frequent groans and grunts. A year or two since whilst basse fishing (from the government wharf at Springwell's, three miles below the city of Detroit) with a friend, he took a cat fish weighing twenty-two pounds, with a live minnow, on a single gut; subsequently the same gentleman caught several others of as great weight with the minnow, by casting in very deep water and suffering the bait to lie on the bottom.

"In the hands of an experienced cook the lake cat fish makes a dish fit for the gods! It should be parboiled to extract the oil, then stuffed and roasted 'à la dindon.'"

CHAPTER XXVI.

THE BLACK TROUT.

This fish, found in most of the Southern states, is a trout by name, and perhaps by nature, but not in appearance, being very unlike the beautiful, bright sided, red spotted, lovely creature of the North. He is not noticed by any of our ichthyologists, but is classed by experienced anglers with the perch family, where he no doubt properly belongs. In appearance, nature, and habits, he is similar to the black bass of the Northern streams and lakes, and by some amateurs in the art is believed to be the same. Like other species of which we discourse, he varies considerably in the different latitudes in which he is found, and in some parts is called by different names. His general color is dark on the back running into white on the belly; the fins are of the same shape, and disposed similar to those of the black bass. He has a large head and capacious mouth, and like many others of our game fish has a projecting under jaw. When boiled (decidedly the best way of cooking him), the color of his flesh (although coarse) is as white as that of the halibut. If put into the pot soon after being brought from his element he makes a dish worthy of the angler's toil.

The black trout commence taking the hook in the month of April, and continue biting until June. In the months of July and August they are hard to take, being on their spawning beds. But in September and October they are again on hand for a bite (at which they are pretty good), when they are much sought after. They delight to sun themselves near the surface, about logs and lily pads, and are there caught (fishing two feet deep) with the minnow, killy, or what is better, the roach; " a dainty dish for this lively fish," is the small " horny head,"

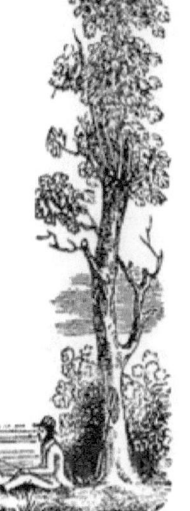

a small species of fish, which, when well secured to the hook, is a killing bait. They bite only when the water is clear; at all other times, whether from defect of vision, or from fear, they cannot be persuaded to bite, but remain

"In *muddy* meditation, fancy free."

A small size basse rod, with light basse tackle, is a good outfit, and will enable the angler to capture him provided he also take with him the usual skill and patience required in the game fish of the same name at the north.

There is another mode of taking this fish. A fly made upon a good sized salmon hook dressed with red and white flannel or feathers, is attached to a short line and southern reed pole, with which it is cast and whipped to and fro upon the water. A good rod, and reel with 50 to 100 yards of line, although not much used, should always accompany the angler, and indeed is not only a convenient, but a necessary appendage in the full enjoyment of a refined sport. The black trout is well flavored, but like most other fish, his character is in the hands and at the mercy of the cooks.

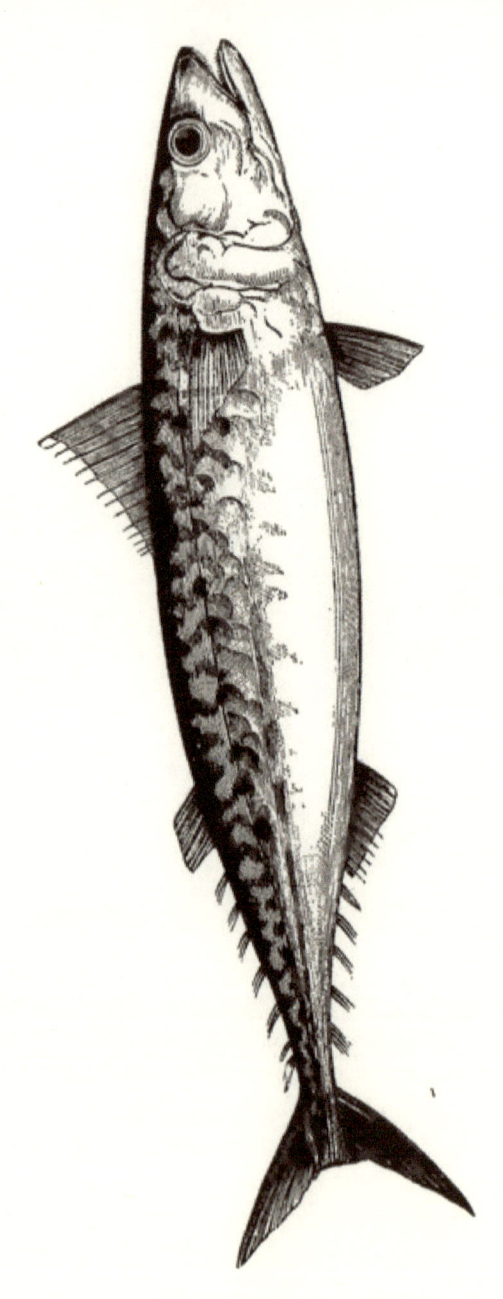

CHAPTER XXVII.

MACKEREL.

Scomber.

THIS world-renowned fish, although not much sought after by sportsmen, deserves a higher place in the catalogue of *hooked* fishes, than he has usually received. He is in all respects a game fish, and the only reason why he does not receive more attention from anglers than others of his race is because he prefers to remain outside on the coast, instead of running up the bays and rivers. The fishermen who make it their business to take him for a living, and the means of a living, delight to tell of his activity and beauty, and he is certainly worthy of all praise in these respects, but more particularly for his beauty. He is undoubtedly the handsomest sea fish that swims, and is worthy of the title he sometimes receives, of the Adonis of the sea.

Great preparations are made by the fishermen for the coming of the mackerel, which happens about the 1st of May, when those who are fond of sea fishing should leave their relations, take a *smack* and go to the "deep deep sea" with some old salt who knows the whereabouts of the fish. They are found in most abundance along the coast of Massachusetts, and near Sandy Hook, New York. At the former place they are taken in immense quantities, salted, packed, and sent to the four quarters of the globe. In the year 1837, says Dr. Storer, 234,039 barrels were taken, equal to $1,639,042. They vary in size from fifteen to twenty inches, and are taken with a line about ¼ of an inch thick attached to a stout pole about twelve feet long.

The hook generally used is called the mackerel hook, and is

about the same size as No. 0 Limerick salmon, but of the kirby pattern, quite stout, much smaller, and narrow in the bend. Others prefer a straight short bend, black fish hook. They love the bright and beautiful, and all the bait necessary for their speedy and certain capture is a small piece of red cloth or flannel, firmly tied to the hook. Like the blue fish they can also be easily taken with a tin squid, or, as fishermen call it, a jig; this is made by running a small piece of block-tin of an oblong form on a long shanked hook and skittering or trolling it about in the water. The sport is preferable to that of cod fishing, and is highly relished by those who have once tried it.

CHAPTER XXVIII.

THE BUFFALO.

Catostomus Babulus.

Is a singular looking fish with an odd name, having his abiding place in the waters of the Mississippi, Ohio, and many other of our western rivers.

In appearance he somewhat resembles the porgy of salt water, except that he is much thicker through the body. The formation of his mouth is similar to that of the common fresh water sucker. In color we would liken him to the salt water sheepshead, being of dull silvery and smutty hue. He varies in size from one to four feet in length, although he is sometimes taken of much larger dimensions.

Mr. Flint, in his History of the Mississippi Valley, describes the several different species as follows:

"Catostomus Niger, Black Buffalo fish, found in the lower waters of the Ohio, and in the waters of the Mississippi. Sometimes weighs fifty pounds."

"*Catostomus Babulus*, brown Buffalo Fish.—One of the best fishes in the western waters, and found in all of them. Length from two to three feet, and weighing from ten to thirty pounds."

"Buffalo Carp Sucker. Found on the lower waters of the Ohio; vulgar name, Buffalo Perch: one foot in length. One of the best fishes for the table."

The Buffalo is not a game fish, and consequently is not often an object of sport with the scientific angler. Nevertheless, he is much sought after with the hook and line, and forms a staple commodity in the markets of many of the southern and western cities and towns.

The requirements for taking him are not very extravagant as

to quality. A line about the size of an ordinary Black fish (Tautog) line is sufficiently strong to land him. To this should be attached a stout kirby or round bent hook of about the size of No. 1, salmon, with a sinker of sufficient weight to suit the current of the water and take your bait to the bottom, and you are rigged. *Except with your bait;* and what shall that be? Nothing that is used or heard of in the capture of others of the finny tribe. To attract him then, you are to take some soft cheese and raw cotton, and work them thoroughly together. Bait with a piece of such a size as you think will suit his fancy and cast into the water, and you will hardly fail to hook a Buffalo. He is prepared in various ways for table use, and makes a fair dish for a hungry man, but not such an one as would suit the fastidious epicure.

CHAPTER XXIX.

FLUKE, PLAICE, TURBOT, &c.

THESE flat friends of ours are to the scientific sportsman "stale and unprofitable" as regards their game qualities, but make about as good a dish as the angler could wish, after a few hours' exercise with squid and line, or rod and reel, on the ocean's breezy shore. This class of fish belong to the universal flounder family, and to the untutored eye appear precisely the same, except being of larger size.

The fish called in some parts of the country the Plaice, is taken mostly along the white shelving shores of the ocean, from Maine to Florida. The species known by the same name to the inhabitants along the coast near Shrewsbury, N. J., is, according to Dr. De Kay, related to the general tribe of Flounder, and is called the *Oblong Flounder—Platessa Oblonga.*

Characteristics.—" Oblong, smooth, nearly uniform brown; occasionally with spots. Caudal fin angulated. Length fifteen to twenty inches.

" *Color*, dark olive-green, with somewhat lighter spots on the head and body; these spots are occasionally distinct, but oftener with no vestige of them. Dorsal, anal, and caudal, dusky, tinged with sanguineous. The pectoral, anal, and ventral of the under side reddish; above, dark olive, with dusky bars. Bronchial membrane bright olive. The lower parts white, with a faint blush of pink. Interior of the mouth rosaceous. Pupils black; irides yellow."

The Ichthyological description is here given, in order to set many of our friends aright, and enable them to call the objects of their pleasure by their right names.

It is during the summer season, when Basse and Blue Fish

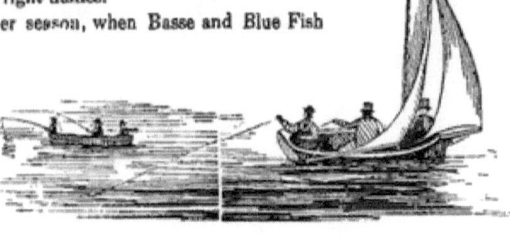

are plenty, and anglers seek the cool retreat of the sea-shore at Shrewsbury and other places, that these fish are mostly taken. There the sportsman, standing with his rod in hand or his line and squid thrown over his arm, occasionally casting and drawing, and when he hopes to take a ten pound Basse, he is obliged often to be satisfied with the more humble flounder.

> Hope reigns for ever in the angler's breast,
> He never is, but always to be blest.
> His largest fish lies hidden in the deep,
> Often he takes him in his dreamy sleep;
> But wakes, and opes his ever eager eyes,
> And finds the game is yet to be his prize.
> The liveliest fish that weighs a pound or two,
> Is small to that within his fancy's view;
> Ten pounds, at least, he always hopes to reach.
> And land his scaly friend upon the beach.

Those who wish to fish for him, may take him with the above description of tackle, with crab and killy bait, on good sized kirby or Limerick hook, say about No. 1, or 2, salmon, is necessary. Bait with a good sized piece of crab or a killy, and when the tide is coming in you will not fail to catch many of them, and may be a mess of Blue Fish, and perhaps, if good luck favor you, a ten pound Basse. When you fish for him by casting from the shore, after feeling a bite, you should run straight back on the shore and draw your prize out as quickly as possible. Should you be using the rod, after striking your game, you must take a backward march, keeping the point of your rod down; otherwise, if your fish be a heavy one, your top will stand a poor chance.

The fish taken in our bays and rivers, called by our friends the Fluke, is not described by naturalists as a species distinct from the flounder. Where the cognomen Fluke originated, is not known. Dr. Dekay speaks of a kind denominated the

Rusty Dab—Platessa Ferruginea, which comes very near to that known as the fluke.

"*Characteristics* —With numerous minute rusty spots over the body; Dextral. A series of four white distinct rounded spots along the dorsal and abdominal outline: length twelve to twenty inches."

"*Color*.—Head and body greenish, with numerous irregular, crowded, chocolate or rust-colored spots, giving a rusty hue to the animal. These spots appear to be confined to the body alone, not extending over the fins. A series of four or five distant obscure rounded spots appear along the dorsal, and a similar series along the abdominal outline. When held up to the light, these spots are deep black, and the whole body pellucid. Beneath, white, except the lower margins."

The angler will often, when fishing in deep water for basse, be favored instead with a bite from one of these, which will weigh three or four pounds. When fishing with a rod, if you chance to hook a Dab, you should, after reeling him well up (if he be of good size), take hold of your line and lift him into your boat, otherwise he may give a flap of his broad white belly and break the top of your rod, as often happens to the inexperienced. Very often in reeling in or drawing up the line, you will hook one of these fellows in the belly or near the tail. In this case, having the advantage, he will give you some play, and cause you to mistake him for something of more grit. Should you get on ground where you can catch nothing else, take off your light basse tackle and put on good sized black fish hooks, on twisted gut.

Another description called the *Turbot, Pleuronectes Maculatus*, from twelve to eighteen inches in length, is rather rare.

It is called also the *Spotted* or Watery Turbot, and on the coast of Massachusetts, says Dr. Dekay, it is called the English Turbot, from which, however, it is readily distinguished by the absence of the numerous tubercles on the colored side, which characterize that species.

"*Color.*—Dark olive brown above, with rounded deep chocolate brown spots on the body, becoming larger behind, and oblong on the fins; are rather of a lighter color than the body. When held up to the light, the whole animal is diaphanous, showing the position of the viscera in the abdominal cavity. The under side of the usual bluish white." It has been known to weigh twenty pounds. It is sometimes called the *Watery Flounder*, and more frequently the *Sand Flounder*.

All of this singular looking flat family are delicious in quality for the table, and worthy the angler's toil. They are best when fried in flour and butter, and give entire satisfaction to the lovers of pan-fish.

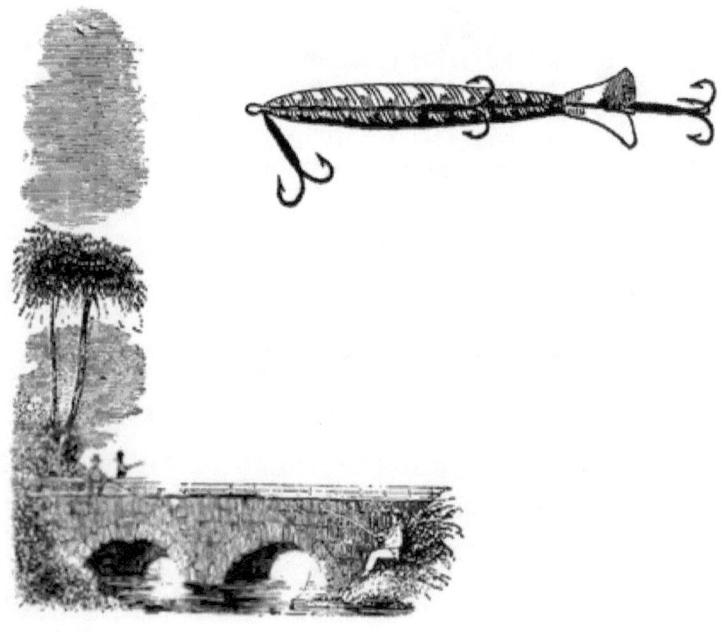

CHAPTER XXX.

THE SUCKER.

(*Catostomus.*)

THE generality of the tribe are not of much importance to the angler, as they do not often bite at the baited hook. There are, however, some descriptions that will take the hook readily. Dr. Dekay mentions fifteen different species belonging to this family. Those which will not bite, are either taken in nets, speared, or noosed with a wire. They inhabit all our fresh water places, from the smallest brook to the largest lake. They are called in different parts of the country by the various names of Mullet, Barbel, Dace, &c. A particular reason for giving them a place here is, that they may get a proper classification by the angler as well as ichthyologist.

" *Common Sucker. Catostomus Communis.* Characteristics—body long, rounded, and tapering; caudal fin lunate, almost furcate: length 12 to 14 inches.

" *Color.*—Head dark green above, verging to black. Cheeks bronze and golden. Body above dark purplish, with pink and metallic tints on the body, frequently of a resplendent golden hue, extending over the abdomen; beneath white. Pectoral, ventral, and anal, orange-colored; dorsal, light brown; caudal, deep brownish or blackish; irides varied with brown and white."

No attempts of the fisher with any description of bait have succeeded in getting him to bite. His ingenious and never-tiring pursuer, however, contrives to get him on the table, where he finds much favor, by the means of a wire slip-noose, or by a small spear made from a large size Cod-hook, straightened for the purpose, and secured into an ash pole. A friend uses the snare after the following manner: To the end of a very stiff

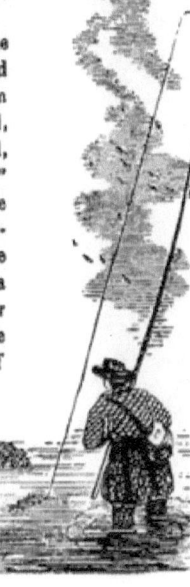

rod fasten a short line, to be kept straight by a heavy sinker, heavier or lighter according to the force of the stream; make the noose or snare of fine wire, and about 6 inches diameter when open or set, which should be a circle, and attach to the lower end of the sinker; thus equipped, lower the snare into the water, a few feet above the fish to be caught, and slowly move it down the stream, passing it over the head, and jerk quickly as soon as it passes the gills. I have frequently caught suckers by the above method, weighing from ½ lb. to 1½, in the various small streams running into the Hudson river, particularly in Dutchess county. N. B. Annealed iron wire should be used for the snare, as those made of brass are apt to startle the fish.

The Oneida Sucker, *Catostomus Oneida*, is somewhat similar in description, and taken by those who like him in a similar manner.

"*Characteristics.*—Back gibbous, with two short sub-spinous rays to the dorsal fin, head smooth, with numerous mucous pores. Length 12 inches.

"*Color.*—Dark, bluish-brown above; lighter on the sides, whitish beneath. Common in lake Oneida, where it is called *Mullet* and *Sucker*."—*Dekay.*

The Horned Sucker—*Catostomus Tuberculatus.*—This little fish abounds in many of the streams throughout the country, and has about as many names as he has relations. He does not live by suction alone but will bite at a baited hook, and consequently receives many appellations more properly belonging to other denominations of the tribe.

"*Characteristics.*—Body short and thick, caudal lunate; three to five tubercles on each side of the snout. Length seven to nine inches.

"*Color.*—Head, dark olive green. Back and sides of the body green, with purple and golden reflections; sides tinged with yellow: abdomen yellowish, with a faint flesh color. Anal

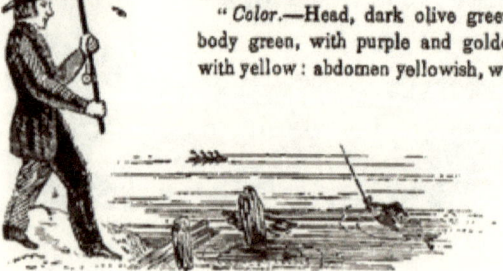

in dark blackish-brown, the caudal rather lighter; the remaining fins light olivaceous. Base of the pectorals flesh-colored."

"The Horned Sucker is common in most of the fresh-water streams of the state of New York, and is also found in New Hampshire, Massachusetts, Connecticut, New Jersey, and Pennsylvania. It is known under the various popular names of *Barbe, Dace*, and *Horned Dace*. It is considered by many as well tasted, and begins to bite about the middle of April. Dr. Storer has described a specimen fourteen inches long, which is unusually large."

The tackle required is the same as that used for trout or perch. The bait mostly used is worms.

Another larger and more beautiful species described by Dr. Dekay is called the Mullet Sucker, *Catostomus Aureolus*.

"*Characteristics.*—With four or five longitudinal stripes. Anal extending beyond the base of the caudal fin, which is furcate. Length twelve to eighteen inches.

"*Color.*—Greenish above, with metallic greenish reflection when viewed in certain lights, sides lighter, with the same metallic reflections; beneath white. About five dusky obsolete longitudinal lines on each side above; the superior pair arising from the dorsal fin, diverging and then uniting beyond the neck; gill-covers with metallic brassy reflections. Upper part of the head and snout bluish brown; pectorals, ventrals, and anals, tinged with reddish; dorsal and caudal bluish brown; irides golden, varied with white."

"The specimen described above was one of the largest dimensions. It is very indifferent food. It is very common in Lake Erie, and at Buffalo passes under the various names of *Mullet, Golden Mullet*, and *Red Horse*. In August and September I observed them to be full of worms. The dusky longitudinal lines, which are distinctly visible in the newly captured

fish, disappear almost immediately after death. It is a very beautiful and distinct species."

This fellow may not live altogether by suction, as he is known to contain worms. A hook baited with worm would then be a sufficient inducement to make him bite. Should you wish to take him, use a Limerick salmon hook, No. 5, attached to stout trout tackle, or spear him or noose, which you will.

A description called the Black Sucker, length about 13 inches, is taken in Lake Erie, and at Walpole, Mass., where, says Dekay, it is frequently called by the whimsical name of *Shoemaker*, probably in allusion to its being something of the color of shoemaker's pitch. In the western rivers also, there is a variety of the Sucker family, some of which bite readily at the hook, and are also of superior quality for the table.

The Kentucky sucker, *Catostomus Fluxuosus*, is a fine fish, varying in size from 6 to 12 inches in length, and bites readily at the worm baited hook.

The Pittsburgh sucker, *Catostomus Duquesni*, grows much larger, and is found in the Ohio river near Pittsburgh; length from fifteen to twenty-four inches.

A very pretty fish called the red tail sucker, *Catostomus Erytarus*, is taken in some of the western rivers. In some places he is called the Red horse. He is a lively fish, takes the hook freely, and is by some sportsmen considered game. Length about 12 inches.

There are two other descriptions of this family taken in the Ohio River. The Long Sucker, *Catostomus Elongatus*, a fine fish, of from fifteen to twenty inches in length, and the Ohio Carp sucker, length from one to three feet. The Carp sucker bites freely at the baited hook, and affords some sport. In the shallow, clear parts of the streams, at certain seasons, he is

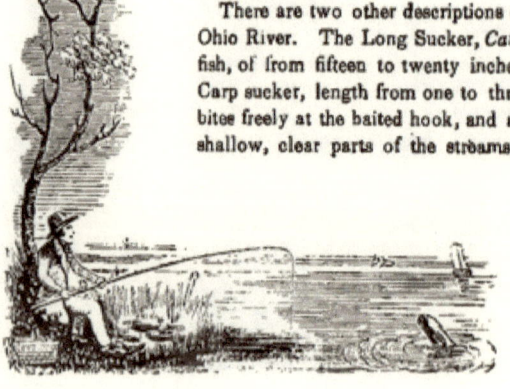

taken in large quantities by spearing. They are both highly prized for the table, when properly boiled or fried.

In the Delaware river is found a kind known by the name of the Large Scaled Sucker. He is similar in appearance to others of the species, except that he has larger scales. Some of the members of this large family are highly esteemed as food, and others might be, if properly cooked. They are undoubtedly placed in the fresh water streams, where the monsters rove not, for the use and benefit of man, and not made, as some others of the tribe are, to fatten on their own species. The most sport is had by spearing them, both in lakes, ponds, and rivers.

CHAPTER XXXI.

TYING HOOKS, REPAIRING RODS, &c.

"A little learning is a dangerous thing"

But what is here set down, although it may not seem of much importance to those unaccustomed to rig their own tackle, may at some future time, and when they least expect it, be made available. "Accidents will happen in the best regulated families," and so will they to the angler, be he ever so careful. When the tackle maker is not near by to assist, how to help oneself may be a secret worth knowing.

To tie or whip a hook to Gut or Line.—Prepare, by waxing with shoemaker's wax, a piece of strong silk or thread: take your hook in your left hand between your thumb and forefinger, about as high up as the point of the barb or a little higher, as you may fancy; place the end of your silk under your thumb, take three or four random but *firm* turns around the shank of the hook until you reach the end (for the purpose of preventing the gut being cut by the hook, and moreover that your gut may stick firmly without the possibility of coming off); now lay your gut or line (the inside of the hook, up) on to this winding, holding it with the end of the thumb, and commence whipping it around firmly and closely, occasionally pressing the turns to keep them even; continue this operation until you get within three or four turns of the finishing point; *in order to fasten firmly*—give three loose turns, then insert the end of your silk under them, and drawing it through, you have a secure fastening, called the hidden knot. Another method of finishing when you have arrived at the fastening point, is to make two or three *half hitch knots:* this is done by passing

the end under one turn of the silk, making a loop, and drawing it down. The hidden knot is the better and most secure mode.

To repair a broken joint.—Should you be so unfortunate as to break a top or joint, which misfortune, brother angler, has happened to many a more careful and scientific sportsman before you—proceed in this manner. Take your two broken parts, and with your knife, or a plane if you can get one, smooth down each part in an oblique direction, fitting them closely together, and rubbing some shoemaker's wax on to the parts to make them stick; now take a long length of waxed thread or silk and wind it around, similar to the commencement of hook-tying, merely to keep the parts together, continuing it a little beyond the extreme end of the fracture; then carefully and firmly whip it evenly around until you pass the other end of the fracture: here halt, and wind the three last turns on the forefinger of the left hand, extended for that purpose; now pass the end of the silk or thread under the windings, carefully drawing out your finger, and pull it through, and you have the hidden or inverted knot, as before described. Be careful in finishing, see that your thread does not get loose, and your whippings are firm and even. In all cases of winding, see that your silk is well waxed. Some take a small piece of wax and rub it evenly over their hook or rod windings, which adds somewhat to its security.

To splice a rod properly at home, when you can have everything you desire, the parts should be sawed with a fine saw, and afterwards filed down evenly with a fine file; they should then be well glued, and left to dry before winding; to finish neatly after winding, take a round, smooth piece of wood or bone and rub down the surface of the thread; then give it a coat or two of thin varnish.

CHAPTER XXXII.

MISCELLANEOUS ITEMS OF SOME INTEREST TO THE ANGLER.

The fin of a trout or other small fish is successfully used in some parts of Pennsylvania, for taking the trout. It is used by casting and drawing, similar to roving with a minnow, or in the manner of throwing the fly.

The fleshy part of the shell-fish called the Horsefoot is much used in some parts of Long Island, and considered an excellent bait for Black fish.

Night fly-fishing is much practised in the northern part of the state of New York. The fly used is of light color if the night be dark, but if moonlight, any of the ordinary colors answers the purpose. Those who follow this method say that they bring out the older and larger members of the family, who are not so imprudent as to venture out when anglers with rods are seen walking about.

The Horse Mackerel, or small blue fish, is for all salt-water fish a most excellent bait. In swift water use the tail, leaving the fin *on*.

A simple but ingenious way of *taking* pickerel, when they won't bite, as practised in some parts of the country, is with a running noose of fine brass wire. This, fastened to the end of a stick, is slily slipped under and around the body of the fish, when, with a jerk, he is snared and secured, and brought struggling to land, fairly *lassoed*. This may not be called taking them with a hook, but is certainly an ingenious mode of *hooking fish*.

Frogs, as bait for Pike, are much used in some parts of the country. They are generally employed as live bait, by passing the hook through the skin of the back or belly. Some use the double Limerick Pickerel hook, attached to brass wire, making a hole through the skin of the back or belly with a baiting needle, and fastening it with thread to prevent its getting out of place; others pass the hook through the lip of the frog, and some again through the back muscle of the hind legs, and then tie up the limbs to conceal the hooks. They are mostly used on the top of the water (still-fishing, or trolling). When employed in mid water, or near bottom with a float, it will be necessary to use a good size sinker, or a few large shot, to keep them down. In all cases, in live bait angling, they should be allowed to come to the top occasionally for air; but not quite as long as the Virginia abstractionist, as related in the N. Y. Spirit of the Times, who, using an insufficient weight, or giving his line too much freedom, found, after fishing all the morning without a bite (whilst taking a *bite* at his 12 o'clock lunch), his veritable bait sitting on a stump opposite, looking at him. Frogs are very tenacious of life, the piercing of the skin in baiting doing them very little injury. The hind legs are very successfully used in trolling, and make a bait, when skinned and placed on the double or single hook, perhaps the most taking in the whole list of pike baits.

The gentler sex in this country as well as in the Old World are becoming captivated with, and enthusiastic on the subject of angling. In some parts of our trouting districts there are many ladies that can throw the fly with as much dexterity and grace as those that are made of sterner stuff.

An artificial bait called the Kill-devil, which has been in use a number of years in England, has proved very successful with some of our sportsmen, in trolling for trout or pike. In appear-

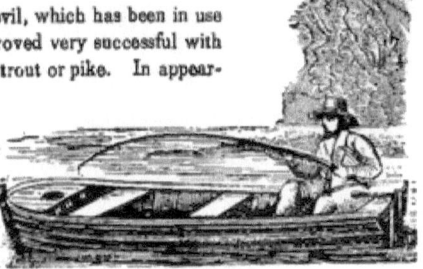

ance it is similar to a caterpillar; the body is composed of coarse thread windings, finished over with the most gaudy silk colors, and wound with silver tinsel; the hooks, numbering seven, are arranged according to the usual minnow rigging; the tail is composed of tin or bright metal, split up or bent at an angle, to insure swift spinning. They are made strong and durable, and their cost is trifling: they are worth a trial.

An odd looking hook, and to make a *home*-ly expression, odd as the angler's notion, is used at Baltimore, Md., and vicinity, called by some the Capt. Jack Thomas hook, but more generally known as the Chestertown pattern. The artist has endeavored to give a proper representation, see page 308, which, by a careful examination, may, to an experienced eye, appear sufficiently explicit. It is considered a very sure hook, the advantages being its singular shape, narrow bend, and low point. It is highly approved of by some of the fraternity at New York for black fish angling.

Care of Rods.—When the fishing season is over, this essential implement of equipment should not be thrown carelessly by, but be cleaned, nicely oiled, and put away in a cool place, in readiness for the next campaign. The best of wood that a rod can be composed of, even though it be kiln-dried, if exposed a length of time in a dry atmosphere will shrink some, causing the ferules and guides to become loose. A moist atmosphere is preferable to a dry one. When rods that have not the ends covered where the joints are put together, become by a day's service swelled and difficult to separate, hold the ferule over a candle or lighted paper until it become sufficiently hot to dry out the moisture, and the parts can be easily separated. To prevent this annoyance, occasionally oil the wooden part that is let in to the socket.

Preservation and care of Lines.—Many adepts in the art are careless and neglectful of their lines, often leaving them (when soaked with water) on their reels, in which wet state, if they long continue, they are apt to mildew and rot. Every line, immediately after being used, should be run off from the reel and laid out freely, or stretched on pegs to dry. Should they have been lying by for any length of time, they should be thoroughly examined and tried in every part before used. Lines will chafe and fray out by constant wear, and many large fish are often lost by carelessness in these small but important matters.

The scientific and graceful art of throwing the artificial fly is a beautiful accomplishment, but not so difficult as is generally imagined. In the months of May and June, the raft and lumbermen from the Delaware and rivers of Pennsylvania, are seen in the fishing-tackle stores of New York, selecting with the eyes of professors and connoisseurs the red, black, and grey hackle flies, which they use with astonishing dexterity on the wooded streams of their mountain homes. Those, therefore, who have never tried this method of fishing, with such untutored examples before them, should make a little effort towards the successful practice of this branch of the art.

A feeling Angler.—A New Hampshire fisherman occasionally when in need of amusement for an evening, and in want of fresh fish for breakfast, takes a blazing torch of twisted birch bark in his left hand, and goes down to the bank of the stream at the time when the fishes dream, and cautiously takes out his quantity of Trout and Perch, with his right hand, assisted in his feeling propensities by his lighted torch, and retires to his home with his stolen property.

A Mr. Oliver, an experienced fly-fisher of England, contrary to the opinion of many of his brethren, does no' believe in examining the stomach of a Trout to find the successful fly: he says—" I have often known a red hackle or a dun fly take trout when they would not look at either the artificial or natural May-fly, though hundreds of the latter were at the time skimming the surface of the water. No directions for fly-fishing are better than the following rhyme:—

> "A brown red fly at morning grey,
> A darker dun in clearer day;
> When summer rains have swelled the flood
> The hackle red and worm are good;
> At eve when twilight shades prevail,
> Try the hackle white and snail;
> Be mindful aye your fly to throw,
> Light as falls the flaky snow."

In some parts of Pennsylvania, a fly called the Professor is used with good success. It is made on a number 4 Trout hook, and is dressed with a bright yellow worsted or silk body, and a light grey mottled wing.

On Long Island and in the northern part of the state of New York, a bright red fly is often in favor. Red body, red wing, and red tail. A fly called the grey drake, with grey wings, and a transparent body similar to the appearance of a worm, is also used at the above mentioned places.

Trout are certainly very capricious in their tastes, and there is no accounting for their desires or fancies, any more than for the changeable notions of the angler who pursues them. The best way is to be well prepared, and if *plain bread* (*red Hackle*) won't suit them, try them with *plum* pudding, a fly composed of a variety of bright colors.

MISCELLANEOUS ITEMS.

In the St. John's river, Florida, a fine game fish called the Trout, but belonging to the Perch family, is taken by trolling, or heaving and hauling, with a piece of deer's tail. Like the common trout of the south they give great play, and afford the highest perfection of sport with the rod and reel. The striped Basse or Rock fish are also found along the coast, and in most of the streams running up therefrom. They are taken of large size, and are as active when hooked as those of the more northern latitudes.

The most daring and exciting sport in the world that is called fishing, is the capture of the inhabitants of the " deep, deep sea." Of this description are Shark and Devil fishing. Parties are made up in the hot summer months from the cities of the Atlantic coast, to take a shark or catch the devil. For shark fishing the nearest ship-chandler's store furnishes the *line*, which should be a rope large and strong enough to *hold him*, and the nearest blacksmith's shop will get ready to order a large hook and chain with swivel attached, sufficient *sometimes* to hold him. The hook is baited with a large piece of beef or pork, and thrown overboard from a good sized row boat. The line is fastened to the stern of the boat, which is propelled rapidly along by good oarsmen, until you get a bite. Any lover of ocean sport may imagine that when such an event happens, if the monster be well hooked, how many knots he will go an hour, what will be the course pursued, and what the amount of excitement.

Catching the devil is practised by the sturdy, athletic sons of the south along the sea coast, but principally in Port Royal Sound, near Beaufort, S. C. Great preparations are made when the devil fish, or "Vampire of the Ocean," begins to school around the sound: large parties of strong men, in large and strong boats, with from four to eight oars, big ropes of great length, long and strong harpoons, hatchets, muskets, rifles, &c.,

make up the party, and its equipments. These monsters of the deep are captured of immense size, measuring often from sixteen to thirty feet across the back. They will tow a party about for many miles, and often succeed in breaking away, after two or three hours' play.

Our *line* of discourse on the different modes of taking the variety of the finny inhabitants might be extended *ad infinitum*, but the *length* already exceeds the design; we shall, therefore, brother anglers, make a *half-hitch* here, to be extended perhaps more profitably and pleasantly on some other occasion.

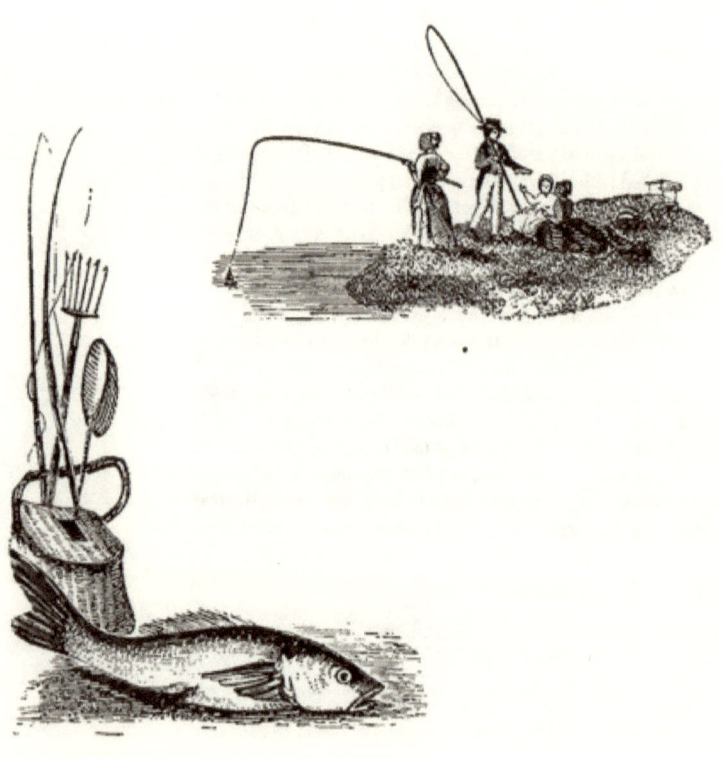

THE PLEASURES OF ANGLING.

" 'Tis sweet to view the limpid waters dance,
　　As o'er their pebbly bed they eager rush;
　　Or in the sun's effulgence brightly glance,
　　As through the mead meandering they gush;
　　Now ringing forth rich music, now all hush,
　　While song-birds chant the ever varied lay,
　　From out the willow and o'erhanging bush:
　　O, sweet it is to thread the blithsome way,
Clad in an angling guise, to spend a happy day

" O, ever healthful is the mountain air,
　　And ever pleasant is the verdant glade;
　　'Tis sweet to wander through the greenwood, where
　　The sparkling current hath its passage made.
　　I love, at times, the cooling stream to wade,
　　Where brushwood dense a way will not allow;
　　I love the arching bowers, and sylvan shade,
　　And blossoms sweet that wave from many a bough.
As cautiously adown the rippling path I go.

" How meagre seems the world of business strife,
　　Compared with pleasures which the angler knows;
　　A scene of toil with disappointment rife,
　　And scarce an hour of calm and sweet repose,
　　This lovely world is made a world of woes,
　　To him whose soul is wrapped in selfish gains:
　　From manhood's prime, till life at length may close,
　　His feelings all are bound in Mammon's chains,
And wealth at most he hoards for all his pains. "

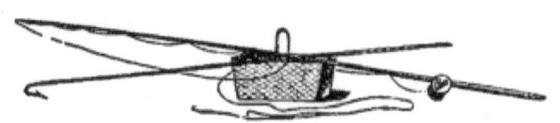

PART THIRD.

CONTAINING A

MORE PARTICULAR

DESCRIPTION OF

SOUTHERN

AND

WESTERN FISHES,

TOGETHER

WITH OTHER MATTER OF
MUCH INTEREST

TO

THE ANGLER.

CONTENTS OF PART III.

CHAPTER		PAGE
I.	In Memoriam	339
II.	Southern Fishes	343
	The Sea-Trout, or Spotted Squeteague	344
	The Red Snapper	344
	The Black Snapper	345
	The Kingfish	345
	The Grouper	346
	The Cavallo	347
	The Pompano	348
	The Mullet	349
	The Silver Mullet	349
	The Black Mullet	350
	The Golden Mullet	350
	The Crocus	351
	The Chub, or Trout	351
	The Lafayette, or Spot	351
	The Growler	353
	The Blue Cat	353
	The Virginia Hog-Fish	354
	The Common Hog-Fish	355
	The Robin	355
	The White Perch	356
	The Bream	356
	The Jew	357

CHAPTER		PAGE
III.	The White-Fish	358
	The Cisco of Geneva Lake	361
	The Siscowet	364
	The Cisco of Lake Ontario	364
	The Herring	365
	The Rock Basse of the Lakes	366
IV.	The Michigan Grayling	368
	Crawfish and Prawns	374
V.	The Spanish Mackerel	376
	The Sting-Ray	378
VI.	The Menhaden	382
	How to keep Shrimp	384
VII.	The Bonito, or Bonetta	385
	Spawning-Time of Fishes	386
VIII.	The Sturgeon	388
	How to keep, stain, and preserve Gut, etc.	391
IX.	Amusement for the Ladies	394
X.	Ichthyology for the Angler	396
XI.	Pisciculture	400
XII.	A Fish-Chowder	407
	American Method of cooking Eels	408
	Recipe for dressing Salad	409
XIII.	Where are they?	410

CHAPTER I.

IN MEMORIAM.

"Bright visions filled with faces of old friends
Long since departed to the silent land."

ANY years have elapsed since the first issue of the "GUIDE." Many of its early friends, and those who took pleasure in contributing to its pages, and counselled with the writer,

"Have crossed the shining river."

Among them none was more revered, respected, or beloved as a divine, a Christian, a gentleman, a scholar, or follower of the art we love, than the American editor of "Walton's Complete Angler," the Rev. George W. Bethune, D. D., of whom his personal friend, the Rev. Dr. Willets, says: "How many rare and royal qualities united in that single man! The learned scholar, the eloquent reader, the impassioned orator, the graceful poet, the polished wit, the charming conversationalist, the humble and devout Christian, and the able and eloquent preacher of the gospel—he was in each of these qualities eminent, and with all combined one of the choicest and rarest of men."

How beautifully he speaks, and how reverentially, of the time he spent in the pursuit of the "gentle art" in his "Wal-

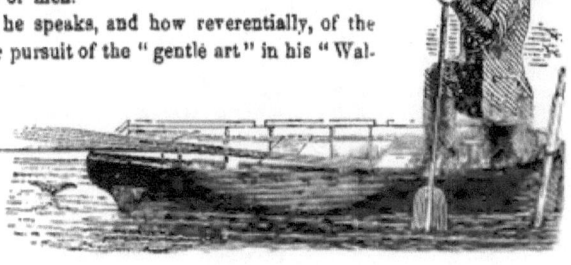

tonian Notes:" "The stream-side is ever dear to me, and I love to think of the times when I have trudged merrily along it, finding again in the fresh air and moderate exercise, and devout looks of Nature, the strength of nerve, the buoyancy of heart and health of mind, which I had lost in my pent library and town duties; I trust that I have drunk enough of the old angler's spirit[1] not to let such pastime break in upon better things; but, on the other hand, I have worked the harder from thankfulness to Him who taught the brook to wind with musical gurglings as it rolls on to the great sea."

And, again, who does not remember the kind, amiable, modest, and retired business-man and Christian angler, John D. Keese, Esq., who enjoyed the pastime at Lake George, and who described in these pages the noble black basse.[2] He it was that penned the first lines ever written on taking that delicious fish with a red-and-white fly; and of the crafty salt-water sheepshead,[3] and of the active and elegant king-fish.[4] One cannot but admire his rebuke to the learned Dr. Johnson,[5] with which he concludes: "And as a Christian I certainly say that, in some of my solitary rambles, or boat-excursions, with my rod, I have been favored with the most devout and grateful emotions of the heart in contemplating the beauties of creation; and, looking up from the works of my Maker around me to Him who made them all, my meditations on the divine goodness have been most sweet."

Gone, also, is Henry Inman, the renowned landscape-painter, and one of the most graceful and accomplished fly-fishers of this century; again, from the higher walks of legislation have departed the Hon. Daniel Webster and ex-Presi-

[1] Izaak Walton.   [2] Page 191.   [3] Page 173.
[4] Page 221.   [5] Page 198.

dent Martin Van Buren, whom we have noticed in former pages as enjoying themselves with the rod along our mountain-streams, or within the boundary of our beautiful lakes.

Many other companions of our enticing pleasures have gone—not "out into the night, but have been translated from the beautiful rivers of earth to the golden rivers of heaven." Let us emulate their good deeds and follow their good examples, that we also may be worthy of a place in the abodes of the blest.

Our first love in the domain of magazine literature was for the *Knickerbocker Magazine;* we were delighted with the easy and pleasant flowing style of Lewis and Willis Gaylord Clarke; the Editor's Table and the many gems of prose and poetry that its ever-welcome pages contained—of Lake George, of the Thousand Islands, the Adirondacks, etc. Among the contributors was the refined, calm, contemplative, and eloquent divine, the Rev. Gurdon Huntington, brother of the celebrated artist, Daniel Huntington. The *New York Evening Post*, speaking of his life and death, which occurred November 29, 1875, says: "His various fugitive pieces contain passages of rare beauty, show a passion for Nature, and breathe a contemplative spirit. He was a disciple of Izaak Walton, and in the spring and summer often sauntered, with angling-rod in hand, by the sparkling brooks which abound among the wooded hills of Delaware County."

The following lines, a portion of a little poem contributed to the *Knickerbocker Magazine* of October, 1852, by Mr. Huntington, had a charm for us at that day that we have not forgotten, nor will they ever be by any contemplative angler who reads them:

"THE WHITE LAKE CREEK."

A SKETCH, BY REV. G. HUNTINGTON.

"How lone and beautiful this place! Here flow
  The White Lake's waters, forcing 'midst the rocks
  Their foamy pathway. High o'erhead the trees
  Of this wild forest-track branch wide around,
  Forming vast, vaulted chambers, wrapped in shade
  Cool and delicious. Down the varying stream
  Tempting the trout from his cold haunts,
  We pass; but not with eye unmindful now,
  Nature, of thy wild beauty, we renew
  Our wanderings along this lonely creek.
  The laurels tangled on the banks forbid
  The sportsman's steps upon the shore; nor, now
  That June's rejoicing sun is reigning high,
  Need he regret his steps must be along
  The pebbly channels of the cooling stream.
  Or if we rest upon some open bank,
  Still cooling visions shall delight us; rocks
  Dripping with foam, and beautiful with moss;
  The shadowy haunt, above, of orioles,
  The glassy cove of yon old trout, who scorns
  Our fly and squirming bait, but darts like thought
  At every luckless miller fluttering by,
  With startling and exciting splash—
  These shall our thoughts beguile."

CHAPTER II.

SOUTHERN FISHES.

WAY down South in Old Virginia, at Charleston, along the coast of Florida, around and through the Gulf of Mexico, and in all the ponds, lakes, and beautiful rivers, in addition to the spotted basse and black trout, before mentioned, are found a large variety of fishes, most of them entirely distinct from those of the North; and many of them, with the exception of the salmon, giving quite as much sport and pleasure to the angler. Florida and many parts of the Southern coast having become a winter resort for many of our Northern invalids—

> Who, having fished for trout and basse,
> Now angle near the Christian Pass—

is visited by hundreds and thousands who fly to a more congenial clime during the cold season, a description of the inhabitants of the waters of the "balmy South," together with their mode of capture, has become a necessity in a work on the Fish and Fishing of the United States.

Among the coast-fishes that are found North and South, and that vary but little, if any, are the sheepshead, the red drum, the bonita, and the Lafayette-fish, or spot. The cavallo, one of the finest of Southern fishes, has occasionally made his appearance as far north as the New Jersey coast, and has been sold in the markets of New York City, but his acclimation North seems to be a matter of uncertainty. In many of the lakes are found the black basse of the North; in the brooks running from the mountains of Georgia, the speckled trout; and in the ponds, a species of white perch, nearly allied to the same description of fish at the North.

THE SEA-TROUT—SPOTTED SQUETEAGUE—
Lab. Sq. maculatis

Is taken all along the coast, from Delaware Bay to Florida, and occasionally as far north as New York Bay (see p. 272). They are caught also along the Southern coast in much larger quantities than the weak-fish or squeteague of the North, and by many are considered a better table-fish. Although the fish of the North is one of the most beautiful of salt-water game-fishes, his neighbor of the South must be awarded the championship on account of its beautiful black spots and bright, silver-white sides, from which metallic splendor it has the additional name of "Spotted Silver-Sides."

They grow to a much larger size in Southern waters, varying from one to fifteen pounds, and are taken with the usual basse or weak-fish tackle. The usual bait is crab, clam, or shrimp. Ordinary basse-tackle is used in their capture.

THE RED SNAPPER,
Lutjanus Aya,

Called red from its color, and the latter appellation from its habit of snapping at the bait, is an exclusively Southern aquatic inhabitant. The form of the fish and the disposition of the fins are very similar to those of the black trout. In color they are unlike any Northern fish, being a beautiful bright red on the back, blending into a lighter or softer color on the belly; color of the eye red, with a dark orb. Their feeding-grounds are in the Gulf of Mexico and along the coast of Florida, in the channels of the islands in the viciuity, and as far south as Cuba. They are taken with the rod and stout bottom tackle of twisted gut or gimp, by still-fishing, with mullet, crab, or prawn for bait. Hand-line trolling with a light metal, bone, or pearl squid, is sometimes practised with success. They are an active fish and give much sport, seldom weighing less than ten pounds, and often turning the scales at forty and fifty pounds. The meat of this fish is quite white, hard, and moist, and of fine flavor. It is highly relished as a table-fish.

THE BLACK SNAPPER

Resembles the red in many respects, the color being black on the back, graduating to white on the belly. It inhabits the inlets and rivers, bites at mullet, crabs, shrimp, and clams, and weighs from three to fifteen pounds. It is quite as good on the platter as its aforementioned namesake.

THE KINGFISH

Is an exclusively Southern sea-fish, seldom frequenting the rivers, but appearing on the coasts and bays; obtaining often to a great size, but generally weighing from ten to thirty pounds. In habit they are similar to the bluefish, bonito, and Spanish mackerel. In color they are of a deep blue on the back, moderating to nearly white on the belly. In shape they resemble the above-mentioned fishes, the tail being large and of the half-moon shape.

The usual mode of capturing them is with heavy bone or tin squids, although they will often jump at a red or white rag. Enthusiastic anglers have been known to take them with the rod and reel and gimp snells, but they are much too powerful a fish, often jumping five or six feet out of the water, and should not be trusted with any but the strongest of tackle. They are an excellent table-fish.

THE GROUPER

Is another exclusive sea-fish, and is caught in the Gulf of Mexico, on the Florida reefs, at the Bahama Islands, and on the South American coast, mostly for the market, by deep-water fishermen, with clams, mullet, and crab for bait, although they are sought after and often taken by the angler by trolling deep with heavy metal squids armed with large-size cod-hooks. In form they resemble an immense sheepshead. In color they are a dark gray on the back, blending into nearly a white on the belly. By the Southern people they are ranked quite equal in flavor to many of their most esteemed fishes. They are certainly a rich-meated and much-favored fish; weight from ten to upward of one hundred pounds.

> " All hail to the grouper, the pride of our coast,
>   To boil or to bake, to fry or to roast,
>   'Tis the prince, 'tis the king, yea, even the boss,
>   Served with butter, with shrimp, or pure lobster sauce!"

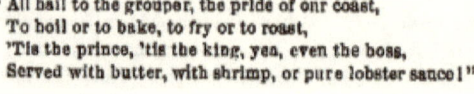

THE CAVALLO, CAVALLEY,

Carangus.

The cavallo is known from Charleston to the Florida coast, and is one of the most esteemed of Southern table-fish, although of late years he has been caught as far north as Delaware Bay, and even on the Jersey shore, and is occasionally to be had in the New York market at as high a price as the Kennebec salmon.

Like the drum, sheepshead, and bonito, it is of a migratory character, and often changes its place of abode, or extends its range of travel. They are very abundant in the Southern rivers that run directly into the sea, and are especially taken in large quantities in the rivers of Florida.

The cavallo in shape and disposition of fins is similar to his friend the pompano, although he grows to a much larger size. The dorsal and ventral fins extend nearly to the tail, a barb or spike preceding the commencement of the anal fin in the cavallo, and three preceding the dorsal in the pompano.

The cavallo averages from three to fifteen pounds in weight, and differs from most fishes by being defended by a small line of spikes or bones extending from the pectoral fin to the tail, which is forked similar to that of the mackerel; but the color of the cavallo is almost transcendent in beauty, vying with the rainbow in its beautiful tints. The upper part of the head is quite dark, verging on to a black, the back a dark blue blending into a beautiful mixed brilliant light blue and rose color, and thence to a bright silver-white on the belly. Fins dorsal—a tinted red; pectoral, ventral, and anal, light gray.

A magnificent fish and a friend of the troller; takes the artificial squid adorned with red cloth or worsted with hand-

tackle, or rod and reel; is an active fish and affords good sport. When angled for with rod and reel the rigging should be as strong as in heavy basse-fishing.

THE POMPANO,

Trachynotus

Is the *crême de la crême* of Southern delicate-meated fishes, a regular palate-tickler.

> "Away in the night! away from the shore!
> They net him and eat him and still cry *encore!*
> No stream in the world, not the Rhine nor the Po,
> Produces a fish like the famed pompano."

Small and beautiful, of rainbow hue, weighing from half a pound to a pound, and sometimes a pound and a half; occasionally visits the Northern coast in small numbers; is sold in New York at almost fabulous prices. The *Forest and Stream*, a reliable New York sporting paper, of June 4, 1874, says: "Only one was caught off the capes of the Chesapeake last week, and was sold in market for three dollars. What did it weigh? Why, only three-quarters of a pound."

They are taken at night in set nets, and occasionally with perch or trout rod and tackle. This pearl of the Southern waters is considered superior in flavor to the salmon or trout; is broader in proportion than the cavallo, and has three barbs or spikes in front of the dorsal fin. The scales are quite small and delicate, and the beautiful colors shading into a pure white, when first brought from the pellucid waters into the bright sunlight, give a brilliancy exceeding that of any other fish. A remarkably prolific inhabitant of the sea, and worthy the attention of pisciculturists. Is generally broiled or fried in butter, although when large is stuffed and baked, and occasionally boiled.

THE MULLET,
Mullus.

The reputation of the mullet as a table-fish dates back to the time of the Romans, at which era a fish of four pounds' weight was said to have been sold for five thousand sesterces, and presented to the Emperor Tiberius—a sum equal to two hundred dollars in American gold ; and one was afterward sold for eight thousand sesterces, being three hundred and twenty dollars of our money. Juvenal remarks on this enormous outlay for these delicacies:

> " Six scanty pounds the mullet weighed,
> Six thousand sesterces the *wise men* paid."

At the South are found three descriptions of the mullet family, called by the names of the gray or silver mullet, the black mullet, and the golden mullet.

THE SILVER MULLET

Is well named, for nothing, not even the polished metal itself, can exceed the brilliant white of the sides of this dainty little fish, that is taken along the coast of the Carolinas, Virginia, and Maryland.

There is but one dorsal fin, situated in the centre of the back, of this beautiful little gem of the salt-water, and directly opposite on the belly are the ventral fins. The head is nearly black, and the tail forked. The back is dark as far as the lateral line, and shades down to the most beautiful white, and the delicate little scales shine with a brilliancy hardly approached by any other fish. Weighs from half a pound to a pound and a half, and sometimes two pounds.

It is a most delicious pan-fish, and is taken with small pieces of crab or clam on a trout-hook with basse-rod, and sometimes with lighter implements.

THE BLACK MULLET

Frequents the same waters as the gray mullet, and is considered a fine-flavored fish by those who take him with the hook or net. Color of a grayish-silver hue, becoming white on the abdomen, darker on the upper part of the head and back, with two dorsal fins, between which and near the centre of the body is a large black spot, giving it a singular appearance. Tail rather convex at the end, and mouth large. Taken with lighter tackle than the previous description, usually small trout-hooks with small pieces of fish, clam, crab, or shrimp. Caught in large quantities in nets for market; weighs from one-quarter to three-quarters of a pound.

THE GOLDEN MULLET

Is a pretty little fish, active and voracious as a biter, and weighs from one-quarter of a pound to a pound. In shape and disposition of fins is similar to the spotted squeteague. Has several small black spots near the tail. The color is nearly black, on the back shading into a brown, and from that into a golden yellow, blending into a white on the belly. Tail nearly straight, scales quite small. Bites quick and rapidly at shrimp and clam cut up in pieces. Has a small mouth. Use a basse-rod with light bottom-tackle and small hooks as described for his black namesake.

They swim the coast from Delaware Bay to Florida; are

quite a delicacy at the table, possessing a rich, fat, and moist flesh, and are fine eating from the pan or gridiron.

THE CROCUS

Is a delicate little fish running in Southern waters, and like the smelt of the North is the dainty of the South, seldom weighing as much as a half-pound, and generally measuring from four to six inches. They are taken with the usual perch-tackle with shrimp or pieces of clam for bait, and are caught from the capes of the Delaware, all along the coast, and in the salt-water streams as far south as Florida.

THE CHUB, OR TROUT,

As it is sometimes called, is similar in shape to the engraving of the chub on page 218, but otherwise finned like the perch, and is not classified by ichthyologists. He has, however, more of the characteristics of the perch family than the chub. Grows quite large, and sometimes attains to the weight of eight or ten pounds. Is reckoned among the finest fishes of the Southern waters. Is a free biter, and will jump readily at the red-and-white fly, the minnow or grasshopper; is active when hooked, and gives good sport with basse-tackle. They are taken in many of the Southern rivers, ponds, and lakes. Color is dark-blue on the back, fading into a clear white on the belly. Head dark, tail slightly forked. Has two dorsal fins, giving it somewhat the appearance of a perch, to which family it undoubtedly belongs.

THE LAFAYETTE-FISH,

Leostomus Obliquus,

Called at the south "The Spot," runs the coast from New York to Florida, but in greater abundance in the neigh-

borhood of Virginia and the Carolinas. Was first taken in New York harbor in 1824 during Lafayette's visit to America, hence its name. The Southern people call him "The Spot," from a singular round, black mark near the point of the gill-covers below the lateral line and above the pectoral-fin. They grow much larger at the South, attaining to the weight of one and a half pounds, while in the more northern latitude of New York their maximum weight is less than a half-pound.

They bite readily at shrimp, clam, or crab bait, from the latter part of May until November.

In shape they somewhat resemble the sheepshead. Their color is dark on the back, softening to a white on the belly, the fins varying in color from a subdued black to a yellow and white. The Lafayette is highly esteemed and considered an exquisite little pan-fish at the North; while at the South he is often, when of good size, baked or broiled. There is a richness and delicacy of flavor of the juicy white meat of this fish that anglers and epicures do not often forget.

At the North the best fishing-ground for the Lafayette is in Newark Bay. Basse rigging is necessary in taking this fish North and South; of equal importance North on account of the larger and more nimble fish that are apt to take the bait. Some anglers rig with a small blackfish or a Limerick trout hook on the end of a yard leader, and a basse-hook about two feet farther up, and sometimes are successful in taking both descriptions of fish, or, failing in one, they succeed in the other.

When a school of these little delicacies can be found and they bite freely, it is best to use small blackfish, or trout hooks baited with pieces of clam.

THE GROWLER, OR WHITE SALMON OF VIRGINIA,

Grystes salmoides,

Is similar in appearance to a large fresh-water basse. The color is lighter than the basse, beginning with a dark gray on the back and blending into a grayish white on the abdomen. Fins similar to the perch; tail dark and slightly forked, similar to the salmon, with a dark bar across the centre, and a similar one near the caudal. They are found in some of the rivers of Virginia, and in the Mequary River in New Holland, and no other place on the globe. The growler is a fine-flavored fish, and takes the hook baited with small fish, clams, or shrimp; weighs from a few pounds to fifteen pounds.

THE BLUE CAT, LADY CAT, OR CHANNEL CAT.

A friend, who has caught these fishes near the mouth of the Mississippi, says, "They are a very lively fish, and the beauty of the catfish tribe." They are taken in large quantities in the vicinity of New Orleans, where they are sometimes called the "croaker," and run up into many of the tributaries of the Father of Waters.

It is certainly a beautiful fish, and, were it not for the horns or feelers depending from its head, would be called by any other name than a catfish.

They are delicate and slender in form; head pointed and mouth small; tail forked; anal fin long, and running nearly down to the caudal. Color, dark-blue or grayish-blue on the back, and dissolving into a pure white below the lateral line, giving it a beautiful appearance, and making it worthy of the compliment of "Lady Cat." Found mostly in swift-

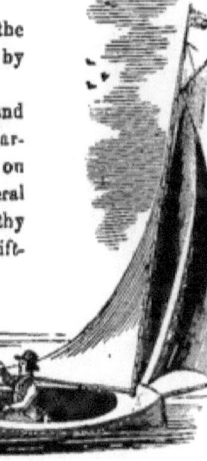

running and bold rivers; runs as far up as the Upper Missouri River; makes a croaking noise similar to the squeteague, hence its additional name of "Croaker." Length, from one to four feet; weight, from one pound up to fifteen or twenty pounds, and sometimes more.

Is an excellent table-fish when baked or broiled, and takes the hook freely when baited with a live minnow or fresh-water lobster, or crawfish. The regular basse-rod and strong tackle should be used in the capture of this description of the cat species, as they often, when in good condition, give as lively play as a basse or salmon, and, when of large size, give nearly as much sport. The meat of all catfish is of fine flavor, but the blue cat exceeds all, and when roasted or stuffed and baked, they make a splendid dinner-dish. A Missouri correspondent says they take them by attaching a line to a large jug, baited with a bit of raw meat, similar to the float or bladder fishing, and often take fish ten or fifteen pounds in weight. We have no objection, provided the jugs are empty.

THE HOG-FISH.

Why called so we know not. Is an exclusively Southern fish. There are two entirely distinct fishes called by this name, and look about as unlike each other as a shad and a flounder.

The Virginia hog-fish is found only in the salt-water rivers of that State, and weighs from half a pound to a pound and a half, is of quite dark color, being nearly black on the back, blending into a light gray on the abdomen, with occasional slanting and short, straight yellow lines on its sides. Fins on the back spinated and dark; tail, same color; lower fins dark yellow. Is a good table-fish, and is not to be de-

spised for rod-exercise. They bite at clam, crab, and pieces of mullet.

THE COMMON HOG-FISH

Of the coast ranges from Maryland to the West India Islands; is a large fish, weighing from a few pounds up to ten or fifteen pounds, and is very unlike his namesake in appearance. He has a large head, and a capacious mouth with which he demolishes crabs, mullet, and other small fish. In form it somewhat resembles a black basse. The color is dark on the back, fading into a pure white on the belly, with banded cross-bars of a reddish-brown color, similar to a perch.

The scales are as large as those of a shad, and as difficult to remove as those of a blackfish. Is considered a fine table-fish at the South, when stuffed and baked or broiled. In good condition is quite fat and needs but little butter in its cooking. He is generally angled for with hand-lines and stout tackle. Use heavy Virginia or large blackfish hooks, with crab or clam for bait.

THE ROBIN, OR CHUB ROBIN,

Is a fish taken at the South, nearly a duplicate of the same fish of the North. The belly below the lateral line is quite red and of a similar shade to the robin red-breast, from which feathered songster it is supposed its name originated. The back is dark, fading into yellow, as in the sunfish, and the fins are of a reddish tint.

The robin flourishes in many of the Southern ponds, lakes, and small rivers, and is taken from a pound to two pounds in weight, and growing much larger in the lakes. Makes fine sport for ladies and children, and is not neglected by the

regular angler. Bites freely at the minnow or worm, and will sometimes take the fly. A trout rod and tackle should be used for this pretty little robin. He is good for the table, fried or broiled.

THE WHITE PERCH,

Bodianus pallidus of the Southern waters.

A fine fish, caught in the Southern fresh-water rivers and spring-supplied ponds and lakes. At a first glance it would be taken even by a scientific angler as the white perch of the North; the general resemblance, with the dusky banded sides, being the same, but a closer examination detects a difference in the form and size of the fins. The two dorsals are united, the anal is longer and extends nearly down to the caudal. Tail slightly forked, similar to the common perch, and the belly is nearly white, making it an attractive fish. A good table-fish, and weighs from one to five pounds. Caught during the summer, but is in better condition in the fall months after spawning. Angle for him with trout or perch rod and light tackle; bait with minnows or any kind of small fish.

THE BREAM

Is taken of small size in many of our Western streams and as far north as Wisconsin, but they breed and mature much faster in Southern waters, and are taken of quite a good size in the inland waters of South Carolina. In England they are said to attain to the weight of ten pounds. They are quite as prolific in the ponds of the "sunny South" as in Europe, and have turned the scales at five and six pounds in weight.

Being possessed of a large amount of caution they require all the skill and patience of the angler, and the finest de-

scription of tackle. A trout-bait rod with a fine line, and every article attenuated down to a good-sized trout-hook, baited with a grub, red angle-worm, cricket, or grasshopper, if cautiously used, will generally tempt him from his element, and when caught he is in appearance much like a carp in form, and feature, and disposition of fins. Color, dark-grayish on the back, the back changing to a white on the belly. Dorsal and ventral fins directly opposite. Head and mouth small, latter lined with very fine teeth; scales quite large. Is good on the platter.

> "A capricious little fish,
>   That swims in pond and stream,
>   And a dainty on the dish,
> Is the cautious, cunning bream."

THE JEW

Is caught in the Gulf of Mexico from the coast of Florida to Texas; weighs from twenty pounds up among the hundreds. One taken near Galveston, in the summer of 1874, weighed over four hundred pounds. The French at New Orleans call him "*Un Grand Poisson.*" He is caught in deep water with extra strong lines and heavy hooks, and comes out of the water without resistance, as if *terra firma* was a matter of indifference to him; but when brought to land shows his dissatisfaction by groaning and flapping his tail. When of large size he is cut up into steaks after the manner of the halibut of the North. The Jew is an excellent chowder-fish, and whether boiled, baked, or fried, is considered second to none, not even the boasted pompano.

CHAPTER III.

WESTERN FISHES.

THE WHITE-FISH,

Coregonus albus (Poisson Blanc, Ad-dik-keem-maig,* or Ticameg†).

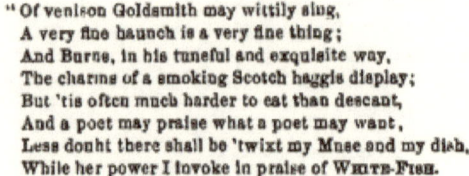

"Of venison Goldsmith may wittily sing,
A very fine haunch is a very fine thing;
And Burns, in his tuneful and exquisite way,
The charms of a smoking Scotch haggis display;
But 'tis often much harder to eat than descant,
And a poet may praise what a poet may want,
Less doubt there shall be 'twixt my Muse and my dish,
While her power I invoke in praise of WHITE-FISH.

"All friends to good living, by tureen or by dish,
Concur in exalting this prince of a fish ;
So fine in a platter, so tempting to fry,
So rich on a gridiron, so sweet in a pie,
That even before it the salmon must fail,
And that mighty *bonne-bouche* of the land—beaver's tail.
  *   *   *   *   *   *

"There are, in gastronomy, sages who think
'Tis not only the prime of good victuals but drink;
That all sauces spoil it—the richer the quicker—
And make it insipid, except its own liquor;

* Indian name.
† French orthography for the Indian name.

These roll in a mild, epigastric mirage,
Preferring the dish *à la mode de sauvage;*
By which it quells hunger and thirstiness both—
First eating the fish, and then drinking the broth;
We leave this unsettled for palates or pens,
Who glean out of hundreds their critical tens,
While drawn to the board, where full many a dish
Is slighted, to taste this American fish."

H. R. SCHOOLCRAFT.

SCHOOLCRAFT, who had an early acquaintance with this beautiful and palatable fish, praised him in rhyme; and any one who has ever tasted or written of this wonderful tenant of the lakes, including the Chippewa Indian, who is known to have lived on his flesh for six months at a time, and called him Ad-dik-keem-maig, or deer of the lakes; or the French-Canadian—

" Who sings, as he paddles his birchen canoe,
And thinks all the hardships that fall to his lot
Are richly made up at platter and pot;
To him there's a claim, neither feeble nor vague,
In the mighty repast of the grand Ticameg;"

or the great and learned De Witt Clinton, who, as early as the year 1815, said, "The white-fish may be placed at the head of the Western fishes, and is universally admitted to be the most delicious;" all, down to the humblest fisherman who hauls him by the thousand from his clear bed of the lake, speak in his praise. A more intimate acquaintance of the writer with this most excellent and esculent fish has not changed his opinion, and no discount is made from the former opinion given on page 220. He is really "at the top," and the king of the inland seas.

The length of the white-fish is from twelve to forty-eight

inches; body rather round than flat; weight, one and a half to ten pounds; color, entirely white, with the exception of a slight grayish tinge along the back; caudal, ventral, dorsal, anal, and pectoral fins, of a blended grayish and white; tail somewhat forked; scales large, and of a beautiful metallic lustre. On the whole, a superb-looking fish, with pure, white, and juicy flesh, and of a taste similar in sweetness and delicacy to the Connecticut River shad.

Taken in nearly all the Western lakes, but more abundant in Lakes Michigan and Superior. Of late years the amount drawn from Lake Michigan has been so great, that they have become comparatively scarce, and the fishermen have been obliged to reduce the size of mesh of their nets and haul in deeper water, in order to supply the demand; but, thanks to the science or art of pisciculture, the race of this most important commercial fish is to be perpetuated. The commissioners of the States bordering on the lake are making preparations at this date (the spring of 1876) to restock with immense quantities of fry. At the Detroit hatching-house eight million spawn are being hatched, and Wisconsin is making efforts to do its share toward repopulating Lake Michigan.

It is proposed to put the same amount of white-fish fry in Lake Erie. The acquaintance of this fish with the "barbed steel" is quite slight. He is sometimes taken with the trolling-spoon, and red-and-white fly. When he shall be placed in the smaller lakes and less extensive feeding-grounds, he may be more readily enticed by the allurements of the angler.

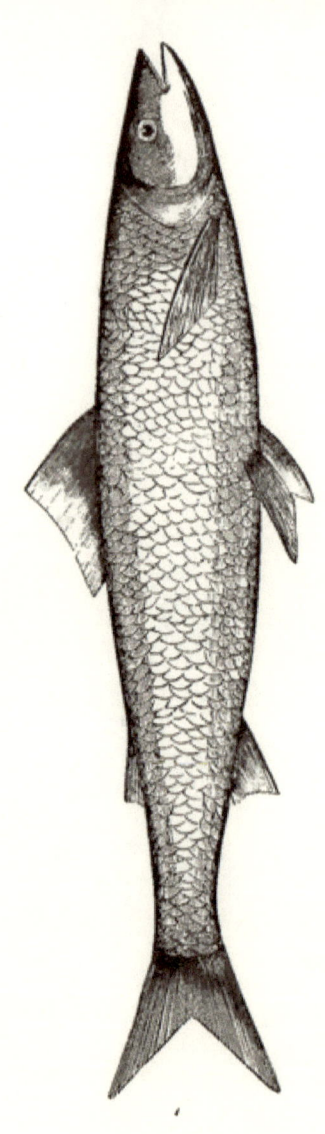

THE CISCO OF GENEVA LAKE, WISCONSIN.

> "A thing of beauty
> Is a joy forever."

A specialty for ten days only!

In a beautiful sheet of water, called Geneva Lake, situated on the Northwestern Railway, seventy miles from Chicago and forty-five miles from Milwaukee, swims this charming little game-fish—a specialty for ten days only! Appearing in June, when the May-fly first begins to glide o'er the surface of the lake, and disappearing like a shadow at the exodus of the fly, it is sought after for ten days with great pleasure and much excitement, and is *gone*.

When it is known that the cisco has come, every man, woman, and child that can swing a line in the neighborhood, besides sportsmen from Chicago, Milwaukee, and towns in the vicinity that can spare the time, hastens to the pure and placid sheet of water, prepared for its capture. This wonderful silver-sided dainty of the lake is a member of the universal herring family, averages about eight inches in length, and seldom weighs over three-quarters of a pound. When scaled for the pan, its flesh is quite transparent. Its meat is clear white, and said to be of a flavor unequalled by any other fish.

> "Beautiful fish of Geneva Lake,
> Strange cisco by name, what pleasure we take
> In thy capture by fly, or even with bait,
> Charming, indeed, when lured to thy fate!
> Bright gem of the deep, where'er thou art known,
> Thou shinest in resplendent beauty alone;
> Pearl of the water, so rich and so rare.
> No fish in the world can with thee compare."

A friend writes as follows: "The length of our lake is nine miles, average width three-quarters of a mile. There are no rocks, neither high banks, however, sufficiently elevated to prevent marshy grounds; the water, which is said to be the clearest in the State, is supplied wholly by springs, one of which, located at the head of the lake, furnishes water-power for a flouring-mill. We have, in addition to the cisco, pickerel, rock basse, black basse, and perch. The cisco averages about eight inches in length; in breadth, one and a quarter inch, and weighs from one-quarter to three-quarters of a pound. Its color, as near as I can describe it, is of a bluish tinge on the back and sides; the belly is silver-white; the scales are very small.

"The time for cisco-fishing is from about the 1st to the 20th of June, varying with the season. They are seldom or never caught more than ten rods from the shore; however, it has been the case in fishing through the ice that occasionally some have been caught; this being a very rare exception.

"Parties angling for the cisco station themselves on the shore in line, as the fish go in schools, and, starting from a point, usually follow the shore. The best time of day for taking them is about four or five o'clock in the morning, or at about sundown. They are caught on all parts of the lake, and, when hooked, extreme caution must be used, as their jaws are very tender. The fly, which is called the 'cisco-fly,' is first seen about the time the cisco begins to run, which indicates the time in which to prepare for fishing. The fly is not the only bait used; they will often bite at a red string attached to a hook."

After their term for fly-feeding is over they return to the deep parts of the lake, and are seen no more until the next year. This fish is entirely distinct from the cisco of Lake

THE CISCO OF GENEVA LAKE.

Superior,* and from extensive inquiry, it is not known to exist anywhere else but in Geneva Lake, Wisconsin. N. P. Fairbanks, Esq., of Chicago, a gentleman of wealth, who has a summer residence on this beautiful lake, has erected a hatching-house for the purpose of perpetuating this and other fish : 500,000 salmon-trout, white-fish, brook-trout, black and Oswego bass, and California salmon, have lately been placed in the lake, and 2,000,000 more are being prepared for another season, making this the greatest fishing-

---

* After being informed on good authority that the Cisco of Lake Superior was entirely distinct from those of Geneva Lake, I find in an article in *Scribner's Monthly* for April, 1876, from the pen of Martin A. Howell, the following paragraph tending to identify the two descriptions as one and the same species:

"It is a fact, well known to many who have visited Northern Wisconsin, that there are lakes near Superior whose waters rise and fall with those of Superior. At Lake Geneva, Wisconsin, it is well known that a fish known as the 'cisco' comes and departs at regular periods every year. It remains a few days and is gone. These same fish are found in Lake Superior only, and it is believed by many that there is a subterranean passage by which they come and return."

A writer in the *Milwaukee Sentinel*, of March 20th, commenting on the above, has the following: "In July, 1873, cisco were observed in the Troy Lakes, Walworth County, Wisconsin, and when the dam at the foot of the lakes broke away in March, 1874, great quantities of cisco were carried out of the smaller lake into the stream below. A small dark culvert was thrown over the stream at the foot of the lake, and under this the cisco crowded in such numbers that the boys of the neighborhood scooped them out by the bushel. As almost every one in the neighborhood had been to Geneva Lake in the cisco-season, there can be no doubt that these fish were the 'true cisco.' The fact that they were found here in March, coupled with the fact that they crowded under the culvert, into darkness, convinced me that the fish lived in deep water most of the year, and came to the surface in 'cisco-time.'"

place in the world. All this will be done through the energy and enterprise of Mr. Fairbanks. If every lake had a Fairbanks, there would be no scarcity of fish.

Those who use the imitation-fly in taking the cisco complain that after the fly gets wet, the fish ceases to rise at it. This is perfectly natural, the fly loses its form, and is very unlike the natural fly. It is very easily obviated by varnishing the fly with a coat or two of *pure white* gum-arabic, and keeping a number on hand for the occasion. The lake was originally called Big Foot Lake from its form being something like a boot.

THE SISCOWET,

Salmo-siscowet (Agassiz).

A commercial fish of the Salmo order. Inhabits Lakes Michigan and Superior. At Milwaukee they are considered a great delicacy as a broiler, and by some superior in richness of flavor to the renowned white-fish.

Their flesh is white and juicy and more adipose than the former, in which respect he more approaches the peculiar flavor of the shad of the salt-water.

It is said that this noble fish takes the fly and spoon. This is probably the case when roaming far from their accustomed depths into shallow water, or at the mouths of rivers in search of feed, as is sometimes the case with the *Coregonus albus*. Could these two fish be made to inhabit other than the deep water, they would afford fine sport for the angler.

THE CISCO,

Argyrosmus Cisco of Lake Ontario.

An esculent gridiron fish that is said to take the fly and spoon, but on which subject there is a variety of opinion, as

there is also in regard to his class, some writers classing him with the salmon, and others with the herring family.

Mr. John C. Hooper, of Winneconne, Wisconsin, says of the cisco and siscowet, which are often confounded together: "As to the 'cisco,' they are very distinct from the siscowet. The word is spelled '*cisco*.' In Northern New York vast numbers of them are and have been taken for the last fifty years around the shores of Lake Ontario, especially at the lower end of Chaumont Bay, and around the mouth of the St. Lawrence. They are herring. I never knew of the cisco of the East taking the hook." Many people think that the ciscoes and siscowet are hybrids or crosses between the salmon, salmon-trout, and herring, a subject that fish-culturists, ichthyologists, and naturalists, with the new system of water-farming, will have an opportunity to scientifically investigate.

The art of pisciculture, when thoroughly understood, may lead to the cross-breeding of many species, and the variety of the finny family may be greatly increased as to objects of sport and food.

THE HERRING,
Clupea marengus.

This fine little commercial fish, so much respected abroad, and so little thought of in its American home, is about receiving the attention it deserves, not only as an object of food, but also of sport.

They are found in great abundance in both fresh and salt water, in rivers as well as lakes, and with the uninitiated are called by a variety of names (see page 219). At certain seasons of the year, generally during the summer months, they appear in large schools, and are taken with a small minnow, or fly of red and white feathers, or any bright, attractive colors, and afford capital sport. A stout fly-rod, with a bright fly on a number one trout-hook, will be found sufficient for his capture.

The Commissioners of Fisheries of Wisconsin are having them hatched for stocking some of the ponds and lakes of that State. In their report for the year 1875 the commissioners say: "Mr. John Palmer, who has had charge of taking the spawn, in addition to the white-fish spawn, has taken 200,000 of the lake herring-spawn. This fish is known in Madison as white-fish, and Fourth Lake is very full of them, a few of them having been put in there by ex-Governor Farwell, who, no doubt, thought them to be white-fish, as many still do. While in flesh and size they are not quite the equal of the white-fish, they are better for lakes, where netting is not allowed, as they will take the hook (and being very prolific, a large one having about 20,000 eggs), and being superior to the fish native to our interior lakes, we think them well worth introducing." The report says that 350,000 white-fish spawn and 200,000 herring-spawn were taken in good condition. The hatching-house is situated at Pensankee, on Green Bay, and is under charge of the Fish Commissioners of the State.

THE ROCK BASSE OF THE LAKE,

Amplobites œnus

Found in most of the Western lakes. At Lake George, many years ago, it was familiarly known as the Democrat. They resemble, in some respects, the sunfish, although not so wide and chubby, and attain to about the same weight, and are found on the same grounds with the black basse, sometimes insisting upon being hooked, to the great inconvenience of the basse-fisher, on his best scarlet-ibis fly. Color dark on the back, softening into a yellow on the belly, with dark, clouded spots on the sides; jumps at the fly or any kind of fresh-water bait. When angled for alone, ordinary perch or trout tackle is used.

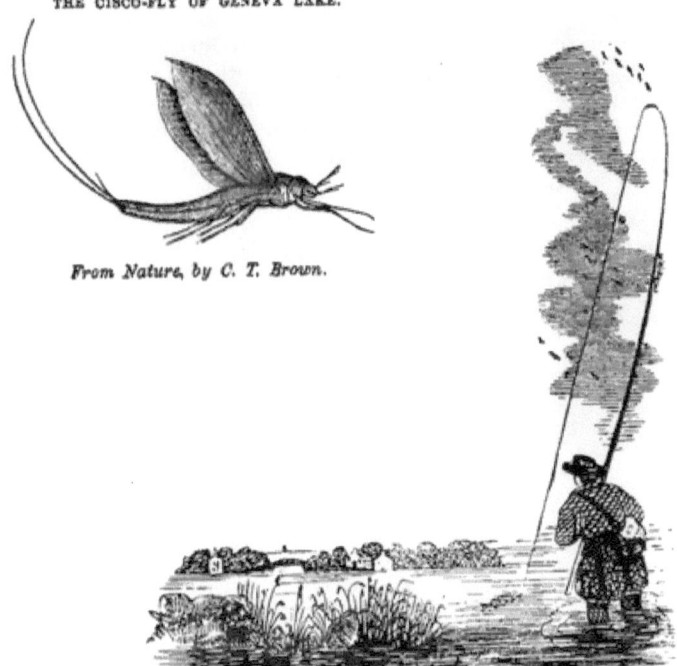

THE CISCO-FLY OF GENEVA LAKE.

From Nature, by C. T. Brown.

CHAPTER IV.

WESTERN FISHES.

THE GRAYLING,

Thymallus vulgaris (Cuvier), Thymallus vexillifer (Agassiz), Thymallus tricolor of Michigan.

"A bright particular star."

Hail! lively, spotted, silver-sided stranger!
For many years wast thou a ranger
O'er pebbly beds in Michigan's bright streams,
A subject only of the patient angler's dreams;
But now he fits his rod and casts his fly,
And among the brush and grass you lie,
A victim caught by treacherous steel,
Fit trophy for the sportman's creel.

ANOTHER star has been discovered in the angler's firmament. By firmament is meant the angler's heaven on earth. His paradise while in the flesh, apart from his Christian duties, is by the stream-side, the lake, amid the mountain's cliffs, or on the placid sea.

No event in our piscatorial world, except the discovery of artificial fish-breeding, has produced such excitement as the discovery of this beautiful little fish in the

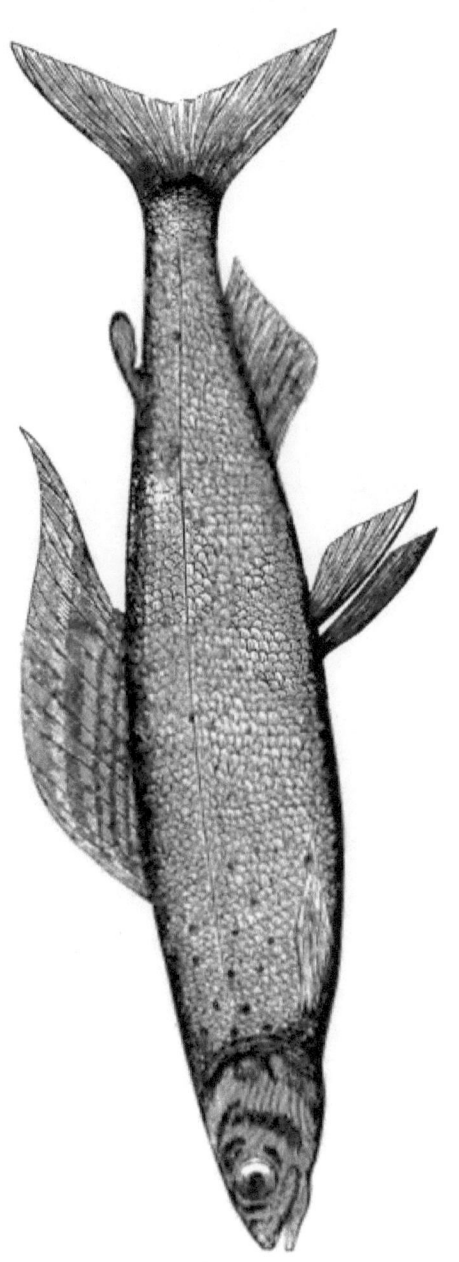

wilds of Michigan. Spawning in the month of April, and being in good condition from July to November, when the streams in our country shall have been made populous with this active tenant of the brook, the fly-rod will be in use from the beginning to the closing of the Northern fishing-season.

In the early history of this fish its limit in America was not designated any lower than the arctic regions, "where," says Richardson, "a splendid specimen was found, requiring as much dexterity to land as a trout six times its size." Its habitat in a lower region than the Mackenzie River is still denied by some, but, thanks to the ardent and enterprising fish-culturist, Frederick Mather, Esq., the ubiquitous Seth Green, and the persevering editor of *Forest and Stream*, the matter is set at rest in the minds of all reasonable men.

Although an old inhabitant, and often taken in Michigan and Montana, this fish has not been identified until the past two years as the true grayling.

Some years since it was found in the Au Sable River, in Michigan, and the attention of Frederick Mather, Esq., the well-known pisciculturist, was called to it, and he has since been breeding them at his hatching-house, at Honeoye Falls, New York.

Seth Green, who is an accomplished fly-fisher as well as an experienced fish-culturist, visited the Au Sable region in the spring of 1874, took eighty of these fishes and transported them to the Caledonian Trout-Ponds, New York. He ascertained that they existed also in the Muskegon, Manistere, Boardman, Sheboygan, Au Gris, Rifle, and Marquette Rivers. They have been since discovered in the Jordan and Bowen, and are said to exist in all the rivers of the Grand Traverse region. As they have been found in Montana, they will no

doubt be ascertained to exist in Northern Wisconsin and the range through to the Pacific.

The first engraving of this fish ever made was published in that excellent sporting journal, *Forest and Stream*, of July 9, 1874, from a fish donated by Mr. Mather. On comparison with engravings from English works, of which I have many, it is, no doubt, identical with the fish of the same name of European waters. The engraving in Yarrell's "British Fishes" gives that wavy appearance of the dorsal fin, and the form is similar, with the exception of the American fish being slimmer toward the tail and a less disposition to fork of the caudal fin. In some of the older and coarser engravings the black spots commencing near the gill-covers, and extending as far back as the dorsal fin, are not visible, probably the fault of the engraver. The same defect exists in an engraving in a work on fishing lately issued in this country.

The sportsman will never get a better, more accurate, nor livelier description than the following by Mr. Mather, taken from the columns of *Forest and Stream*, describing him in his own liquid element:

"The grayling has all the fins of a trout; his pectorals are olive-brown, with a bluish cast at the end (I am describing him in the water as I saw him in my ponds an hour ago); the ventrals are large and beautifully striped with alternate streaks of brown and pink, the anal is plain brown, the caudal is very forked and plain, while the crowning glory is its immense dorsal; this fin rises forward of the middle of its back, and in a fish a foot long it will be nearly three inches in length by two high, having a graceful curved outline, and from eighteen to twenty rays dotted with large red or bluish-purple spots, which in life are brilliant, and are surrounded with a splendid emerald green, which fades after death; it does not seem as if this green could be represented by the painter's art; it is that changeable shade seen in the tail of the peacock.

"In shape the fish is like a trout, a trifle slimmer, perhaps, and not so thick near the tail, but the fin on the back of a trout looks so small and square, so deficient in outline and color, after beholding the graceful curve of a grayling's dorsal! The scale is large, silvery, with sometimes a copper tinge; near the shoulders there are black spots, sometimes triangular, and at others V-shaped; in some fish these extend nearly to the tail near the back; they are in lines, which gradually shorten toward the belly; the mouth is small (nearly square when opened), and the teeth are merely a slight roughness on the lips, none on the tongue. But you want to see him come in on a line, with his fins all standing, and your eye will then give you a better idea than all the cold-blooded descriptions could ever do." And, again, he says: "I wish to add a little to the description given in my former article, as a little longer acquaintance has developed new beauties.

"The eye of the grayling is large and full, with a beautiful yellow iris, and when I wrote 'the tail is forked and plain,' I had not observed its pinkish edge, nor the changeable metallic green lustre that it shows in some lights, which is more like that seen in silk. A glint of the same is also observable on the second dorsal. Many letters have asked the question, 'Is this fish as handsome as the trout?' And in answer I will say, to some eyes, while to others it may not be. Seen from above it does not appear so, as the pink and white of the trout-fins are more showy. The form of the grayling is more graceful than the trout's, and the head is beautiful, while the side of the trout and its lower fins are more gorgeous than

the grayling's. The trout has not a handsome head to my eye; the lines are hard, and there is an expression of savageness in the jaws." The sides of the grayling are of a grayish steel color, the lines on the back and edge of the belly being darker and nearly a brown color.

Prof. Milner thus writes of him: "There is no species sought for by anglers that surpasses the grayling in beauty. They are more elegantly formed than the trout, and their great dorsal fin is a superb mark of beauty. When the welllids were lifted, and the sun-rays admitted, lighting up the delicate olive-brown tints of the back and sides, the bluishwhite of the abdomen, and the mingling tints of rose, pale blue, and purplish-pink on the fins, it displayed a combination of living colors that is equalled by no fish outside of the tropics."

My old and respected friend Dr. Rufus Brown, of Detroit, Michigan, who contributed the article on "Black Bass Fishing in Michigan," on page 288, writes, in February 18, 1876, of the grayling:

"A beautiful specimen is now swimming in the tank of the fountain of the Michigan Exchange Hotel, in this city. It is about twelve inches in length, gray on the back, whitish sides, large very dark eyes, and a large and peculiarly flexible dorsal fin, the lower and broad end of which is ornamented with sky-blue brilliant spots on a blackish ground, not unlike the end of a peacock's feather. This fin expands in swimming. The ventral fins are of a peculiar shape and variegated."

"The term *thymallus*," says Yarrell, "is said to have been bestowed upon this fish on account of the peculiar odor it emits when fresh from the water, which is said to resemble that of thyme; and from its agreeable color as well as smell. St. Ambrose is recorded to have called it the flower of fishes,

The name grayling is supposed to be a modification of the words gray lines, in reference to the dusky longitudinal bars along the body.

"The grayling thrives best in rivers with rocky or gravelly bottoms, and seems to require an alternation of stream and pool. It has been considered that the large dorsal fin of the grayling enabled it to rise and sink rapidly in deep pools; but this power would rather seem to be afforded by the large size of the swimming-bladder. The very large dorsal fin, compared to the small size of all the other fins, renders it unable to stem rapid currents; they are much more prone to go down stream than up, and are never seen leaping a fall like a trout." The largest grayling is recorded to have been caught near Shrewsbury, in England, and weighed five pounds.

Hofland says: "The same flies recommended for trout may be used for the grayling, with the difference that for the latter fish they must be smaller; and all that I have previously said of fishing fine for trout will most especially apply to the grayling—for, if you do not use a single hair, your gut bottom must be as fine as hair and the color of the water you wish to fish."

Satter says, "This fish is generally called a grayling until full grown, then it is entitled to the name of umbra." The appellation of umbra is derived from the swift motion of this fish, it often darting like a shadow—

"The umbra swift escapes the eye."

"If a worm is used which they are very fond of in the spring or the early part of a summer morning, if the water is somewhat colored, then angle within a foot of the bottom, and use a No. 9 hook to your line."

Seth Green says of their gastronomic qualities: "They are

a good eating-fish, but I would rather have a trout or some other kinds of fish. They have a peculiar flavor, such as I have never tasted before; the flesh is firm and coarse-grained, and is as free of bone as a trout."

"They rise at a fly as readily as a trout, and make a good fight before you land them."

"They take the same kind of flies that trout do; a No. 6 hook is about the right size, but I caught them on flies tied on No. 4 and up to No. 12."

"Their growth is very rapid," says an English writer. "The grayling hatched in June becomes in the same year, in October or November, nine or ten inches long, and weighs from half a pound to ten ounces; and the year after they are from twelve to fifteen inches long, and weigh from three-quarters of a pound to one pound; and these two sizes are the fish that most usually rise to the fly."

Undoubtedly the grayling is a great acquisition to the lover of fly-fishing. Being a tenant of the same stream as the trout, coming in season long after the pleasures of trouting are over, and jumping readily and perseveringly at the same description of flies, they will ever be a source of great enjoyment to those who love to ply the gentle art by the brook-side.

CRAWFISH AND PRAWNS,

Palæmon serratus.

"Get some prawns, cheese, and macaroni, and live," said a Southerner once to a Northerner. These little subjects of our discourse are not angle-fish, but, as the little darkey said, "They are mighty good for bait." The crawfish is nothing more nor less than a miniature lobster, and grows at the South as large as four and five inches, and is a good bait for most descriptions of salt-water fish. Used with a lettuce-salad or cooked macaroni and cheese, they are a fine relish. The little children take them with a stick and a string, to which is attached a small piece of meat.

They are found in nearly all the fresh-water rivers and lakes at the North, are used as a bait for black basse, and do not attain to over three inches in length. The prawn is merely a large-sized shrimp. They are both good boiled, and are taken in some parts of the Southern coast, and in the Gulf of Mexico, in great abundance.

A friend who has lived at the South many years says that he once took two bushels of prawns in half an hour in the bay west of the South Pass lighthouse, that averaged two and a half to three inches.

CHAPTER V.

MISCELLANEOUS FISHES.

THE SPANISH MACKEREL,

Scomber maculatis (Mitchill).

WITHOUT a doubt the most beautiful fish, both in form and color, that swims either in salt or fresh water. The dolphin when dying exhibits a greater variety of intensely beautiful colors, and therein its celebrity lies; but when first taken from its native element, this subject of our discourse is unsurpassed for its rich colors of blue, white, gold, and purple, transcends anything ever beheld in the animal kingdom, and reigns triumphant as the gem of the ocean.

"But here description clouds each shining ray;
What claims of art can Nature's power display?"

In form the *Scomber maculatis* resembles its congener the bonita, except that it is much narrower, longer, and more graceful in its proportions. It is a well-known Southern fish, and is described by Dr. Mitchill as coming on the coast of New York in the month of July. Color—back, a dark blue, blending into a magnificent purple, shading into a light dove-color, and thence into a beautiful satin-white; chin,

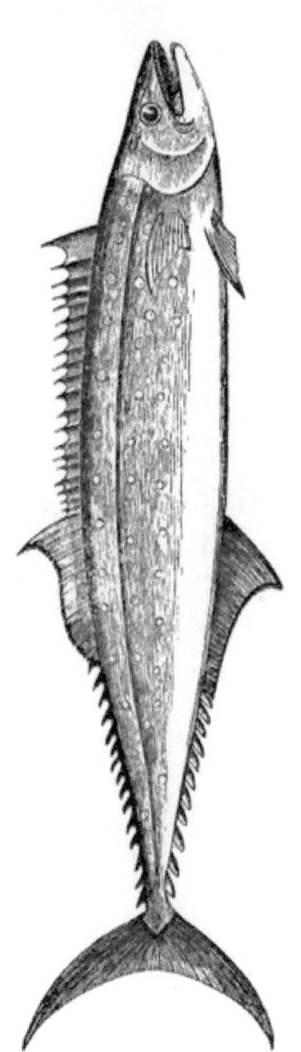

neck, gill-covers and belly, a resplendent white. Ventral, anal, and spurious lower fins exhibit a whiteness scarcely less brilliant. About twenty golden-yellow spots, some of them a quarter of an inch in diameter, decorate the sides and impart to them a gay appearance. The lateral line does not travel straight, but crooks and meanders toward the tail. Eight finlets above, and as many below. Two dorsal fins, with a small spine between them. Second dorsal fin and finlets and caudal brown. Tail widens almost into a crescent. Mouth large and armed with distinct and cuspidated teeth. The meat of this fish is the most delicate and high flavored of any of the ocean species, and is considered equal to the sheepshead, salmon, or white-fish of the lakes, and, as if to tickle the palates of the New-Yorkers, he has condescended for the past few years to make his visit to the bays and sound in greater numbers than at his first advent in 1815. He does not take the metal squid as readily as the bluefish or bonita, and the dealers in the implements of the art have contrived different devices for his capture, composed of bone, tin, ivory, and pearl, to which is attached scarlet ibis-feathers, red worsted or strips of red flannel, fastened to the usual bluefish line. No angler should rest satisfied until he has taken a *Scomber maculatis*. Go, then, when you hear of his coming in July, visit his sporting grounds, which are the same as the bluefish's, view him as he leaps from the emerald wave: careful, now, as you haul him in, lest you spoil your prospects for dinner, for he is tender-mouthed, and will not bear as rough usage as others that take the squid, and moreover he is apt to swim deeper after being hooked, and when your sport is over enjoy a feast from his delicate flesh fresh from the gridiron, the only true method of cooking him, and you will never regret

The exciting sport, the eventful day!
When on you dashed through foaming spray;
The tremulous pull of the flaxen cord,
The royal fish that you hauled on board.
With sides of white, and blue, and gold;
The elegant form, the splendid mould,
Of this king of the sea! this exquisite fish,
So regal when taken by hook or from dish.

THE STING-RAY,

Trygon pastinaca (Cuvier).

Not an object of sport, but sometimes by too intimate intrusion the cause of great excitement and skill by the professional angler. A fish with a tail! not a mere caudal fin, but a real tail like unto that of the cunning beaver, but a much more formidable one, with two serrated barbs or stings, which are to the uninitiated a great terror.

Form of the body rhomboidal, head inclosed laterally by the pectorals; posterior portion of the disk of the body somewhat rounded. Tail from two to five feet long, somewhat rounded and armed, near its origin, with a long and sharp flattened spine serrated on both edges. The rest of the tail slender and ending in a point; one or two serrated stings in the fleshy part of the tail. Upper surface of the body running from a muddy black into a dirty yellow; under surface nearly white; teeth small.

A strange-looking fish that has often set the angler into a fever-heat on account of the report that the sting he carries in his tail is venomous, which is a great error. Mr. Couch says: "This species keeps on sandy ground at no great distance from the land, and in summer wanders into shallower water. He feeds on clams, mussels, and oysters. The menner in which this fish defends itself shows its consciousness of the formidable weapon it carries in its tail. When seized or tempted its habit is to twist its long, slender, flexible tail around the object of attack, and with its serrated spine tear the surface, lacerating it in a manner calculated to produce violent inflammation." Other authors state that it is capable of striking its weapon with the swiftness of an arrow into its prey or enemy, when with its winding tail it secures its capture. These spines, as may be supposed, *possess no venomous quality;* when lacerated wounds happen to men of bad habits of body, the symptoms are frequently severe, but no more serious effects have ever followed from the sting of a ray.

They are occasionally encountered by the angler on sheepshead-grounds in the Lower Bay of New York, and in the waters of Long Island Sound, and afford considerable sport, although their rank and disagreeable flesh is of no use except as a fertilizer, but when captured their stings, of which there are often two, are preserved as a trophy.

The writer, while fishing in the Lower Bay with rod and reel for sheepshead many years ago, a style of angling practised before the year 1845, and of which a description is given on page 201 of this work, although Dr. Scott, in his "Estuary Fishing," claims to have inaugurated that method of capturing that vigorous fish—but to return to our story: Being rigged with stout Virginia hooks attached to twisted gut, and baited with a whole clam, the party, five of us in number, cast our bait upon the waters and down they went, with the heavy leads, to the bottom. A short period of time elapsed and the line was raised, and it appeared evident that my tackle had fouled on the bottom, but, on a second pull, the line, which was of linen and 200 yards long, began to run

with great rapidity and the reel to whiz like lightning. With a design to check the progress of this unknown monster, a pressure of the thumb on the line resulted in taking the skin from that digit in not the most scientific manner. About three-quarters of the line was run out, when lo! he stopped. "Reel him in! reel him in!" cried all on board. This was done with the utmost dexterity, the line passing through the jewelled tip and on to a stout German silver reel until the nondescript was within a few feet of the boat. The captain of our craft, a stout ship's yawl, stood ready with the gaff to haul him in, but, when within reaching-distance, he broke water and passed off like a rushing wind, taking out about the same amount of line, but, being held more firmly, he slacked up sooner, caused by feeling the pangs of the "barbed steel," and after a timid and wavering resistance was again reeled in, gaffed, and taken on board, amid the exultations of the angling crew. The old salt who managed our boat, and knew every inch of ground in the bay and in the sound, and probably every tenant of the deep, was left alone in his glory with this diamond-shaped, black-snake-whip, tailed inhabitant of the sea; the affrighted sportsmen occupying the extreme bow and stern of the boat, but the excitement was soon over. His Mighty Ugliness was easily dispatched, his tail cut off, and his trunk, weighing about forty pounds, cast to the boisterous waves. Two stings about three inches long by three-sixteenths of an inch wide, with a feathered edge and covered with a thin skin or slime, were taken from his tail and preserved as a memento of the event. After changing base several times and taking a lot of sea-basse, we concluded it was not our day for sheepshead, and adjourned to the city.

Such is the sting-ray. No fisherman need fear his stings,

for they are not poisonous; therefore, should he insist upon being hooked, the only recourse is to play him to the extent of the ability of your tackle, enjoy the sport of his capture, haul him on board for examination, deprive him of his stings, and cast him into the briny deep with a strong reprimand not to take food designed for more noble game.

CHAPTER VI.

MISCELLANEOUS FISHES.

MENHADEN, BONY-FISH (HARD-HEADS OR MOSS-BUNKERS),

Clupea Menhaden (Mitchill).

NECESSARY mention is made of this fish as a bait for the angler. He seems to have been created as food for other members of the aquatic family, or as a fertilizer of the barren sands of Long Island. No figures have ever been made large enough to estimate their immense numbers. This bony inhabitant of the sea is not counted, but measured, by the load or by the acre. Seines, miles in length, hauled by machinery, are used in his capture, and many tons of them are taken in each net that is hauled on old "Long Island's sea-girt shore." Dr. Mitchill, in his work on fishes, says: "I have seen acres of them; and the whalemen say that the great bone-whale (*Balæna mysticetus*) has been seen with his great mouth open gulping down some hogsheads of them at a single gulp! What a gulp! probably a trifling appetizer before dining on some of the larger species that sport in his *little pond!*"

The New York *Evening Post* some years since, in speaking of a haul of this fish, says: "This is no fish-story; we have seen an acre or two of these fish, a foot or two in length, and a constant procession of carts taking them back into the

country to enrich the sand-hills where the oak of Jerusalem will hardly vegetate."

The menhaden, in appearance, form, and feature, resembles the shad, and is in size between the herring and the latter dainty esculent, although they sometimes attain to the size of a small shad. Cut up into small pieces, they are used to bait the ground where basse and other sporting-fish congregate. On the shores of Long Island the small fish of this species are used for bait by cutting them in two in the middle, and again through the sides and fleshy part of the extremity of the fish to the tail, which is cut off and thrown away, or chopped up and used with the remaining part of the fish on the baiting-ground. The hook, which is generally a flatted end, Limerick or Kirby, in size about one 0 or two 0, is passed through and brought out, so as to be nearly or quite concealed between the divided parts. A strong piece of linen thread or twine is then wound around the shank, terminating with a few half-hitches to prevent the bait from pulling off. A good method is to have about a dozen large hooks with loops of strong line whipped on, and prepared ready-baited for the occasion to attach to your trolling-line, and use as described on page 246. When the rod is used in this description of sport, the excitement is much greater than heaving or hauling or casting, and the best and strongest implements are necessary. If you have a rod with separate tops, the shortest one should be used, leaving the full length not over eight or nine feet. The tip and guides should be large enough to let the largest-sized reel-line pass through freely, and all should be thoroughly jewelled with cornelian. The reel also should be furnished, if possible, with the same kind of gearing.

Reels, holding from two hundred to four hundred yards of

heavy linen line, are now manufactured, and also rods specially adapted for this hardy and nerve-bracing style of angling. Let every article used be of the best and strongest description, that no regrets disturb your slumbers after your day's sport is over.

> "Spare not on rod, reel, hook, or line,
> Let perfection, strength, and unity combine,
> Then shall your joy be full; nor sorrow
> For misfortune attend you on the morrow."

HOW TO KEEP SHRIMP.

Many plans and devices are in operation for keeping this delicate little bait. Some pack in sea-weed, some in sawdust, and others in sand; but more or less of them die within twenty-four hours. The best method is to put them clear and clean *en masse* in a basket, and place them on ice. They will keep in this way a week. Take sufficient ice with you, to keep them of the same temperature until you get to your fishing-ground. Then put them in your perforated shrimp-box and place them in the water, and you will hardly lose a bait. This has been demonstrated. All fish will live in extreme cold water. They will even freeze solid, and thaw out and swim away. Try the cold method, if you want clean, hard bait.

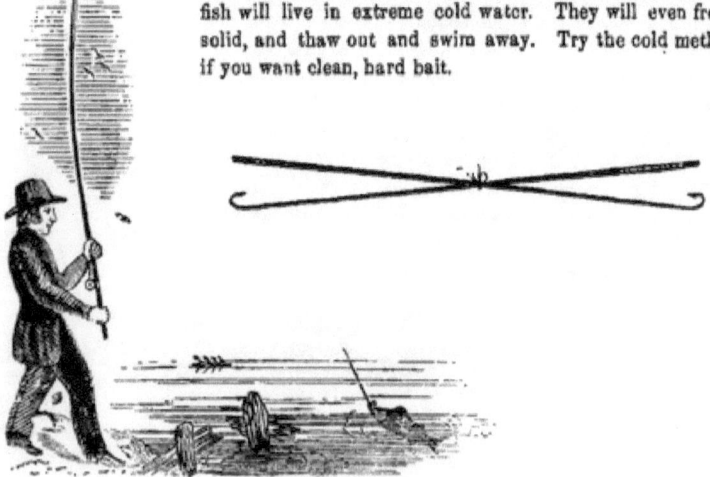

CHAPTER VII.

MISCELLANEOUS FISHES.

BONETTA, OR BONITO,
Scomber sarda (Mitchill).

This beautiful fish having of late years become more abundant along our coast, and an active and lively biter at the artificial squid, a place is given him among our game-fishes. He frequents the same waters as the bluefish and Spanish mackerel, and, if eaten broiled soon after taken, is a fine table-fish, and weighs from three to fifteen pounds. "The figure of this fish is cylindrically round, tapering toward the head and tail; the belly is nearly white; back blue, similar to the common mackerel. From the sides six or seven darker lines slope upward toward the back, and about ten or a dozen bands of a fainter line diversify the sides transversely from head to tail; the teeth are sharp and distinct. The skin generally smooth and silky, but patches of minute scales are found between the nape of the neck and the rear of the pectoral fins, and sometimes at the pectoral and caudal. There are eight spurious fins on the upper side toward the tail and seven below. There are two dorsal fins, the foremost of which has twenty rays and the hindmost fourteen. The eyes are large, and the irides yellowish; nostrils double, and the openings a quarter of an inch apart. The lateral line waves prettily along its course, pectoral fin rather short, and contains twenty-four rays; the ventral smaller, and has six, the anal fourteen; caudal twenty-four, with some imperfect ones. Tail forked and almost lunated; three longitudinal excrescences on each side."

Caught all along the coast from New York to Florida, and in the Gulf of Mexico; afford good sport with the trolling-line and metal squid, and are sometimes taken with the rod and reel and heavy implements, as in casting for the striped basse. Is a good broiler, and very highly esteemed at the South, where they sing his praises in rhyme in the following lines:

> "Bright bonetta! or bonito!
> It matters not to me
> What they call thee,
> Thou Adonis of the sea!
> Oh, what rapture
> In thy capture,
> Or, when served
> Upon the platter,
> For breakfast or for tea,
> It matters not to me,
> None is richer, none is fatter,
> Than the Adonis of the sea!"

FRESH-WATER FISHES.

TIME OF SPAWNING.

Salmon	November to March.
Brook Trout	October to February inclusive.
Grayling	March and April.
Pike, Pickerel	February to April.
Perch	March and April.
Pike, Perch, or Glass-Eye	February and April.
Sunfish	"
Carp	May to September.

Chub	May to September.
Black Basse	April and May.
White-fish of the lakes	September to November inclusive.
Catfish	July to October.
Redfish or Spotted Basse	February to March.
Bream	May.
Eels	April.
Southern Trout	July to September.
Red Snapper	March and April.

SALT-WATER FISHES.

TIME OF SPAWNING.

Bonito or Bonetta	May and June.
Bluefish	"
Drum	January and February.
Striped Basse or Rock Fish	March to July and Oct. and Nov.
Squeteague or Weak-fish	March to May.
Kingfish or Barb	"
Blackfish	March and April.
Sheepshead	April and May.
Cod and Tom Cod	"
Flounder	"
Sea Basse	May and June.
Porgy	"
Smelt	March and April.

The time stated in the above tables varies according to climate. The spawn or ova commence *making* in many fish months before, and do not fully develop until the times stated, when they are ready for hatching. Southern fishes vary much from the temperate, to their extreme limit or range, toward the torrid zone.

CHAPTER VIII.

MISCELLANEOUS FISHES.

THE STURGEON,

Acipenser (Mitchill).

EVERY boy living along the banks of our Western rivers that is old enough to handle a pole cut from the woods knows more about the sturgeon than he does of the State that he lives in. Of this leaping and diving fish there are several kinds that take the hook, and are an object of sport. The round-nose sturgeon, *Acipenser sturio*, is found in the Hudson River, and is taken as far up as Albany, often being seen leaping his whole length from the water. "He has a roundish and elongated snout, with four cirrhi. There are five rows of scales, making the body a sort of pentagon. Body elongated, mailed above by scaly tubercles. Two lateral fins. Dorsal fin behind the scales near the tail composed of thirty-eight rays. Anal fin nearer the tail than the dorsal. Caudal, anal, and lateral and pectoral fins often reddish. Tail unequally forked, and the larger division slanting upward. Mouth beneath the head ovate, toothless, retractile."

Sharp-nosed Sturgeon (*Acipenser oxyrhynchus*).—" Having a pentagonal form, with scabrous asperities between the scales and a sharp snout. Has the same general form, but in many respects different. The scales themselves are bony, rough,

THE STURGEON.

and serrated behind, and very distinct in their configuration. The number of scales in the sharp-nosed sturgeon are not so great as in the blunt-nose." The boys remark that the gristle taken from the sharp-nose is much less elastic than that from the blunt-nose.

The last-described fish, commonly called rock-sturgeon, inhabit most of the Western rivers, and, with the round-nose species, are very common in the Mississippi and its tributaries. They are taken in the Wisconsin River of from two to six feet in length, by the spear or the ordinary red-horse tackle, with a ringed Limerick hook attached to a stout flax or hemp line, with worms or small pieces of fish for bait.

The Winnebago Indians spear them in large quantities and dry and smoke them for food, using their entrails when taken as a choice morsel for their *delicate appetites*. Their flesh is coarse and of a reddish color, but as a food-fish they are not held in high estimation, although sold in most of the markets in the cities. The taste of the meat when cut into steaks and fried is not unlike that of coarse beef, whence it has been called Albany beef. In the towns on many of the Western rivers they are chiefly the sport of the boys, and often Young America is seen hauling a sturgeon through the streets that will measure a foot or two more than the length of his body.

Much of the meat of this fish is salted and packed for the winter season by the economical and working millions.

My friend John C. Hooper, who fishes in Winnebago Lake, Wis., says: "Sturgeon pass up by here in May. They are caught with a four-tined hook attached to a long pole, long enough for hooks to rest on the bottom of the river. The popular notion here is that they are inclined to 'rub' against any object on the water, like logs, stakes, etc. When the

fisher feels something touch his pole he hauls up quickly, and the sharp-barbed prongs are fastened into the fish, and if a large one the struggle to land him is a severe one. The sport is exciting, for our inhabitants will leave their work when the sturgeon comes! The merchant leaves his counting-room, and the mechanic his tools. There have been over one hundred caught thus in one day. A large quantity of eggs are saved for the manufacture of caviar."

The hooks are made by the blacksmith of three-eighths inch wire, steel-tipped and bearded, and as sharp as a needle. "We have both the rock and the round-nose sturgeon, the same that are on the Hudson and the great lakes."

In the olden time the sturgeon was regarded as a royal fish, the property of the crown. R. B. Roosevelt, Esq., President of the Fish Culturists' Association, at the fifth annual meeting of the society, in New York, in February, 1876, said of this fish: "Sturgeon was so abundant in old times that it was sold as low as one cent per pound, but its indiscriminate destruction promised to run up the price to one dollar per pound, like that of trout. Sturgeon is a most excellent and nutritious fish; so is the fresh herring, much valued in the old country, but here both are treated with contempt."

Mr. Seth Green has been directed to restock the Hudson with this fish, and in a few years they will exist in as great plenty as when the renowned Hendrick first sailed up this most grand and beautiful river, and isinglass and caviar, the great production of the sturgeon, will be as cheap and abundant as in the olden time.

HOW TO KEEP, STAIN, AND PRESERVE SILKWORM GUT, GIMP, AND LINES, AND THE CARE OF REELS, ETC.

It has become fashionable in this country to stain silkworm-gut; the father of anglers, old Izaak, and his follower Salter, gave directions for "dyeing hairs." The idea is prevalent with most anglers that silkworm-gut should be stained. It is possible that there may be some instances in the extreme shyness of the fish, and clearness of the water, that it may be necessary; but they are rare, and this beautiful and valuable adjunct to the angler's art should be kept in its natural state, or as nearly so as possible. Being nearly transparent, and barely perceptible in the water, it makes hardly as much show as the many fine roots and weeds and floating matter to which the fish's ever-watchful eyes are accustomed.* Theophilus South gives a number of receipts, in which copperas is a principal ingredient, and which with certain other substances gives a variety of shades, but the use of copperas, unless in a very mild state, is injurious to strands of gut, and should not be employed. When necessary to stain gut, prepare a portion of tea or coffee, as your taste for color inclines, and after boiling to get the full strength of your dye, then having previously trimmed your lengths, place them in your liquid while quite hot, not boiling hot, and allow them to remain a sufficient time to get the needed color, after which take out and rinse in moderately warm water, and when dry rub, by holding each strand separately between the teeth, with a clean piece of India-rubber kept for the purpose. The outer skin

* A late writer on fishes says: "The brain is very small, and the organs of sense calculated to receive only the simplest impressions of sight, smell, hearing, taste, and touch."

of a red, or Shaker, or Wethersfield onion gives different shades, and the bark of the walnut or butternut gives another color. The leaves of the tomato, when they can be had fresh, give a beautiful green, and a different shade from green tea.

To preserve Gut.—Always keep your stock on hand, or when not in use for a length of time or during the winter season, in stout parchment-paper, or parchment if you can get it, slightly saturated with *pure* olive-oil. Do not coil your gut, but let the strands be at full length. After placing your lengths in position, roll up your paper, tie up, and envelop with an outside wrapper. An old angler of thirty years' experience gave this as his method some years ago, and Rev. Dr. Bethune, in his "Waltonian Notes," approves of it. It can be relied upon as the best method.

Gimp is a thicker substance, and much more easily seen by the fish when fresh and bright. To discolor, rub over with a light coat of beeswax slightly softened.

To preserve Lines.—Always, after using your line, be you at your home or abroad, run your line off on the floor or dry boards, where exposed to the sun, or, if in the house, in a dry room, until the moisture is entirely evaporated. A reel, such as is used by the ladies for winding off yarn, worsted, or thread, is convenient, and should be a part of the angler's outfit. There are some that are made with narrow slats, and can be screwed to a table, and being designed so that they can be opened and closed like an umbrella, they are easily carried with the other fixtures of the sportsman. Some anglers use oil, spermaceti, or India-rubber preparations on their lines for their preservation, but, as a general rule, they are better for your boots or shoes than your line. When rubber is used, white is preferred, unless your line be dark: one part of rubber to two parts of turpentine, heated until the rubber dissolves; to

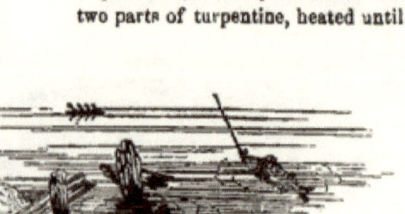

prevent burning, place the pan containing your preparation in a vessel of water. Boiled linseed-oil and tallow are recommended; if considered necessary, rub on to the line with a piece of soft cotton cloth or canton flannel, and use as little as possible—the lighter your line the better and the easier dried. The amount expended on lines is small in comparison to other articles of the angler's outfit, and they should be replenished often. After much use of your line, or even of short duration in severe contests with your fish, test them and throw them away rather than run the risk with a large fish.

Your *reel* also needs attention, and should be as often and as carefully examined as the watch you carry in your pocket. Procure from your watchmaker a vial of watch-oil, and use it as occasion requires.

Your hooks also, whether blued or japanned, should receive equally as much care. Keep them *always* in paper slightly moistened with olive or watch oil—small items are these, but immensely important to the truly scientific sportsman. "An ounce of prevention is worth a pound of cure."

  Never let it be said to your shame,
  That, by neglect of your tools, you lost your game.

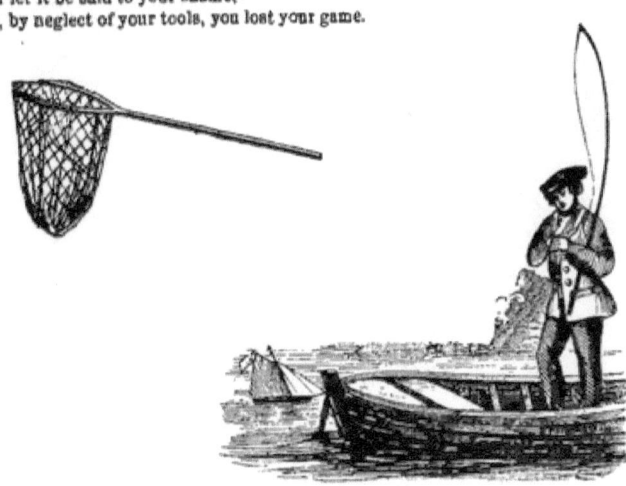

CHAPTER IX.

AMUSEMENT FOR THE LADIES.

BALLOON OR FLOAT FISHING.

GREAT sport is had by the ladies at the summer resort lakes and ponds, and many other waters of a similar description, by a species of amusement called float-fishing. This is performed as follows: A number of bladders, rubber balloons, or floats of wood, or cork, are procured, to which is attached to a stick passing through the float, or to the bladder or balloon, a line from six to eight feet long, on which is whipped a suitable hook baited with a minnow, as described in former pages, so that the bait will not be injured, but can swim near the surface of the water; a few split-shot or a small sinker, to keep it a little below the surface, being necessary.

These implements of the art, say from six to twelve, are then placed on the lake or pond where the fish are usually found. The ladies take their position on the veranda of the hotel, if near the fishing-ground, or otherwise in their boats in readiness to push off from shore. When the fish begin to bite, away go the floats, and away go the ladies with their boats after them. The resistance of the float generally hooks the fish, and a large one will sometimes cause the instrument of his capture to disappear for a time beneath the

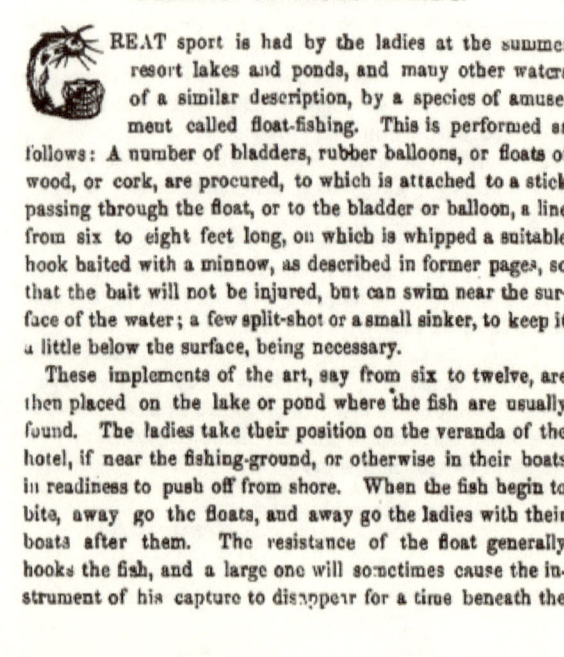

water, but, as the victim tires, it again rises to the top. The party with all possible dispatch row to their respective floats, seize their lines, haul in their fish, then bait, and repeat the process. This description of sport is practised at all times of day for perch, pickerel, and basse, but, in the warm summer months, from about five o'clock in the afternoon until sundown.

When pieces of wood (square blocks of wood two or three inches thick are better) are used, a hole is bored through and a stick inserted, projecting through three or four inches at the bottom, and about six inches at the top, to which can be attached various colored flags to distinguish the ownership of each.

Although this description of sport is mentioned as amusing to the ladies, it does not exclusively belong to them. Gentlemen often unite with them and assist them in taking their fish, and also are fond of hooking the finny family in this way themselves when more scientific modes of angling cannot be engaged in.

The simplest method of baiting with the minnow is to put the hook through the mouth, bring it out at the gills, and again through the hard fleshy part of the back, the shank of the hook being long enough to come nearly or quite out of the mouth.

When minnows cannot be had, small sunfish or frogs are substituted, the sunfish being hooked through the centre of the back, and the frog with a double hook through the belly, by an incision made with a small knife or baiting-needle. When the float of wood or cork is used, it should be *firmly* tied to the bottom projection of the stick, and, if the game be pike, a reasonable time should be allowed the fish to gorge the bait.

CHAPTER X.

ICHTHYOLOGY FOR THE ANGLER.

ANGLERS should have a sufficient knowledge of the science of Ichthyology to be able to describe the various members of the finny family; and, as many of our scientific sportsmen inconversation by the stream-side, or at the fishing clubs, are well posted in the science, a few remarks on this subject will not be considered out of place.

Those who have studied and written upon this subject, have different methods of classifying the large variety of fishes.

Dr. Mitchill described them, by the situation or arrangement of their fins, into five divisions. Agassiz classed them in four divisions, based on the character of their scales; but Baron Cuvier, a French naturalist, described them in three simple divisions, that are much easier understood than any of his predecessors. Says a late writer * on this subject: "The disposition to make new genera is carried to a puzzling extreme. In getting rid of the too great condensation of Linnæus, naturalists have fallen into the worse extreme of too extensive subdivision."

* Professor Kneeland, in Appletons' "American Cyclopædia."

Simple enough for our purpose, then, is the classification of Cuvier, which is as follows:

1. Spine-rayed bony fishes.
2. Soft-rayed bony fishes.
3. Cartilaginous fishes.

The fins are described as follows: First and second dorsal fins, where there are two fins on the back; the pectoral or breast fins, of which there are two, one on each side, near the gill-coverings; two abdominal or belly fins; two anal fins, and the caudal fin or tail. Spine-rayed are those that have sharp bony divisions in their fins. Soft-rayed are those that are destitute of the spinal feature; and the cartilaginous are those that have gristle or cartilage in their whole skeleton, instead of bone. The fins of the latter class, however, may be spinated or soft.

In the first class, spine-rayed bony fishes, are comprised fully three-quarters of the inhabitants of the fish kingdom, among which may be enumerated all of the perch and basse family, the blackfish, porgy, sheepshead, weak-fish, drum, kingfish or barb, chub, mackerel, bluefish, bonito, dolphin, Spanish mackerel, etc.

The second class, soft-rayed bony fishes, have soft and flexible rays. The rays in this class of fishes are formed of pieces of bone united by cartilage, rendering them more flexible than those composed with spines; comprised in this class are the salmon-trout, grayling, carp, sucker, herring, catfish, white-fish, shad, menhaden, cod, flounder, etc.

The third and last class, cartilaginous fishes, are those having gristle in place of bone in their whole framework. In this division are some of the largest and most powerful of the inhabitants of the great deep. Behold among them the ravenous shark, the dogfish, the sawfish, the sturgeon, the sting-ray, the sea-devil or ocean-vampire, etc.

In the last-named description of fish, and most of the ray family, the fins consist of broad and thinner extensions that project like wings from the body, and by which they adhere to the bottom, and with which they swim with great rapidity. The ventrals of some of the sucker family are also used in the same manner, they being able at times to secure themselves in a position in a swift current of water, giving them an opportunity to feed on the small prey that are driven by the force of the tide or current.

The three divisions are divided into subdivisions as follows:

Soft-rayed bony fishes with abdominal ventral fins, such as the salmon, trout, herring, shad, etc.

Soft-rayed bony fishes, with the ventral fins beneath the pectorals as in the cod, hake, flounder, etc.; and the

Soft-rayed bony fishes without ventral fins, called apodals, including the different species of the eel family.

A singular fish called the Fiji eel, caught in the waters surrounding the islands of that name in the South Pacific Ocean, are said to fight their captors. They are of a brownish mottled color, and will snap at the hands, feet, or legs, after being taken out of the water. One of these eels of four pounds' weight, after being pounded on the plank of a dock, and the hook released from his mouth, sprang at the unlucky angler's wrist, and made two frightful gashes, nearly severing some small arteries, and just missing the main one of the pulse.

In addition to the fins, their character and position, the size, form, and shape of the eyes, teeth, tongue, and gill-coverings, are means that will assist the angler in his de-

scription. Some fish have no teeth, or a mere semblance of them, as in the grayling; and others, like the sheepshead, have them in the back part of the mouth. Some have a soft lining around the mouth, which tears almost like paper, and are called tender-mouthed, while others have tough, bony, or grisly linings that give them the name of leather-mouthed.

By carefully noting the points enumerated, and a thorough examination of the subjects of his day's sport, the most inexperienced angler will soon learn to class the different species, talk ichthyologically, and discuss scientifically of the form, nature, and habits, of the objects of his pleasure by the brook-side, the tenants of the lake, or of the ocean's depths.

CHAPTER XI.

PISCICULTURE.

"And God said, Let the waters bring forth abundantly the moving creature that hath life" (Gen. i. 20).

COMMENCING back at the earliest period of recorded time, we find the All-wise Creator of the Universe commanding the waters to bring forth "abundantly of the moving creature that hath life," and they did. The early history of every country on the face of the globe reveals the fact of a once superabundance of the inhabitants of the waters. In England, many years ago, that "royal fish" the salmon was so plenty that they were fed to the hogs; and in Scotland they were so abundant that the farmer's servants stipulated to have them but twice a week for food! On the northwest coast of America they were found in such great numbers that they could be killed with an axe, and in the early history of Connecticut these numbers were so great that the fishermen would not dispose of their shad unless the purchaser would take a certain portion of salmon.

A few years ago nearly every stream within a reasonable distance from the great marts of civilization was more or less depopulated. Hundreds of miles had the angler to travel even for a moiety of his favorite game, while at the

market-stands the trout, salmon, and other fish, once so abundant, commanded an exorbitant rate.

> "The ox, the sheep, the swine, each feathered creature,
> Were reproduced of every kind, and form and feature;
> The finny race were nearly from the waters gone,
> The flocks had ne'er supplied the meat alone;
> When science, art, and labor, well combined,
> Re-peopled streams and depths with millions of each kind."

Indiscriminate fishing by net, spear, and even by hook, in spawning-time and out, and through the ice in breeding-time, were the causes of the rapid depreciation in numbers of the subject of the angler's toil, and of the poor man's food.

The *New York Sunday Times* of March 19, 1854, in commenting upon the wholesale and wanton destruction of fish, says of parts of Connecticut: "The unchecked lust for shillings has not left a fish or a bird in whole counties. So, too, on the south side of Long Island, once esteemed among the best trouting localities in this State, where mischievous boys and vulgar men have been allowed to destroy them until now, a trout can scarcely be found. Nor are these worse than some of our city 'sportsmen!' whose highest 'idea of sport is wanton destruction.' We heard one boast last summer of having killed twelve hundred trout in two days at Catskill! Of course, they were all young fish, probably three inches long. A very few brought home (putrid when they arrived), and the remainder left to perish on the bank of the stream. . . The man ought to be prohibited from all 'sport' but catching bull-frogs forever after."

But thanks to the energy and perseverance of two poor and humble fishermen, by the names of Rémy and Géhin, of the rivers flowing from the mountains of the Vosges in

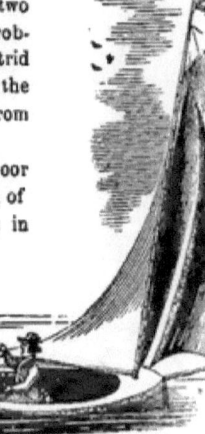

France, who seeing their occupation nearly gone by the rapid decrease of fish in their favorite streams, turned their attention, in the year 1841, to the close observation of the habits of their favorite fish, the trout. Closely attending to and watching the nature of the fish night and day during a full moon in November of the year mentioned, after many experiments they succeeded in devising a plan for the artificial fecundation of fish-spawn, which has made them famous from one end of the civilized world to the other. Although a work was written upon the subject and published by one Jacobi, a soldier in the Hanoverian army nearly a hundred years previous, the system was not put in practice for the benefit of mankind until re-discovered by the French fishermen. The discoverers were presented with a medal by the French Society of Emulation of the Vosges, but it was not until 1848 that the Academy of Sciences, through the report of M. Milne-Edwards, and on the proposition of M. Coste, a model establishment was founded near Huningen, under the auspices of the government; now the most noted hatching-establishment in the world. The poor fishermen were invited to Paris and loaded with the highest honors. The report of their success set the scientific world in motion, and all the governments of the Old World and the New have slowly and gradually put the system into practice. In England and Scotland many salmon-rivers were restocked, and immense excitement produced among the fraternity of anglers and the lovers of fish throughout the United Kingdom.

In the United States, the translation of the treatise of M. Coste, on "Artificial Fish-Breeding," by W. H. Fry, Esq., and its publication by Appleton & Co., in 1854, had an equal effect on those interested in this country, and private hatching-houses were erected on rivers adapted to the purpose-

In 1853, Dr. Garlick, and Prof. Ackley, of Cleveland, Ohio, are mentioned as the first who successfully hatched the eggs of the brook-trout; they were followed in 1859 by Stephen H. Ainsworth, of West Bloomfield, New York, and afterward by Seth Green, of Mumford, New York, and Livingston Stone, of Charlestown, New Hampshire, and subsequently by many others in all parts of the country.

> "Soon the bright streams
> That once were scant of fish,
> Will swarm with myriads
> For the poor man's dish."

Under the superintendence of Mr. Green, a large hatching-house was erected near Mumford, New York, by the authority of the State government, which is now producing immense amounts of the eggs and fry of nearly all descriptions of game and food fishes. In the year 1871 Congress established a Commissioner of Fish and Fisheries, whose duty it was to investigate the matter; and Prof. Baird, of the Smithsonian Institution, was appointed commissioner. His exertions were crowned with success, and the United States, in proportion to the time occupied, is not behind other nations in the great work.

Commissioners have been appointed by most of the States in the Union, and the breeding of fish has become almost as common as the raising of stock for food. Mr. Green, who, with Mr. Ainsworth, is the pioneer of fish-culture, says that "an acre of water can be made to produce as much as two acres of land;" and R. B. Roosevelt, Fish Commissioner of New York, asserts that 500,000,000 shad ought to be hatched in the Connecticut River every year. Already millions of the last-named fish have been deposited in the Hudson, Connecticut, and other rivers, and shad have been

transported from the Hudson to the Sacramento in California. The ova and fry of different varieties of fish are forwarded from this country to Europe; and England has successfully transplanted the ova of salmon into the rivers of Australia.

Thaddeus Norris, of Philadelphia, the accomplished writer and angler, has interested himself in the art of water-farming, and has published a work on American fish-culture, as has also Seth Green, and the knowledge of pisciculture is increasing in every civilized country on the face of the globe.

For thousands of years have the people of heathen China propagated fish from *naturally* fecundated spawn, and fed their starving millions. The liquid containing the ova is sold in China-jars or vases, and the fry that are taken by divers, who gather them in nets from the bottom of the rivers, who preserve them in copper vessels, feeding them on the pulverized yolks of hard-boiled eggs, changing the water often until placed in the needed streams or ponds of the "Flowery Kingdom," thus increasing the food for that over-populated nation.

It is impossible at this early period in the cultivation of the art in this country to estimate the immense advantages that will accrue to the unborn millions of this Western Hemisphere. The nineteenth century has not developed an invention of as great magnitude, neither do ancient or modern times record a discovery of so great importance to the human race.

A subject that has engaged the time, the talents, and the ingenuity of the philanthropists of all ages, "the providing of food for the poor and toiling masses," has been solved by two humble fishermen of La Bresse, in France, and their

names will go down to posterity as the greatest benefactors of humanity since the creation.

And thus has the great problem of ages been solved. Why the riots and disturbances in this country and Europe? Why so many strikes among the mechanics and laboring-men? Why so many revolts against existing governments? Trace them to their source, and you will find in most cases the first and prime cause is an insufficiency of food for the support of life in large and growing families. "Hunger knows no law." Residents of crowded cities, who are importuned from early dawn to almost midnight for aid in the shape of money or food, realize the vast amount of suffering from the need of the necessaries of life. Many will remember the sacking of a flour-store in the city of New York some years ago, caused by the high price of that ingredient of the "staff of life;" and even during this, the mildest winter (1876) known in years, have destitution and famine stalked abroad.

A Montreal paper says: "A very serious state of destitution at present prevails among the lower classes at Montreal. On Friday last about 1,000 persons assembled at the City Hall determined to have bread or blood!"

"Let the work, then, go bravely on," brother-philanthropists, fish-culturists, and anglers; "let the waters bring forth abundantly," as designed by the All-wise Creator. Place fish-food within the reach of the toiling and destitute millions, and misery and crime will decrease in proportion.

In former pages we have advocated the making of fish-ponds and the transportation of fish. How simple the method, and how certain is the success of water-farming as at present conducted! See to it, brother anglers—see to it, brain-workers of the nineteenth century—use every endeavor

to have every water-course, pond, and lake stocked to its utmost capacity with the finny race, and your angling pleasures shall never fail.

" In mountain-stream, by pebbly shore,
He takes his game as heretofore—
Not by the few, but by the score,
As oft he did in days of yore."

CHAPTER XII.

CULINARY.

A FISH-CHOWDER.

A FISH-CHOWDER is a simple thing to make. For a family or party of twelve or fifteeen persons, all you have to do is this: In the first place catch your fish, as Mrs. Glass would say; a codfish of ten or twelve pounds, or the same quantity of any firm-meated fish. Clean it well and cut it into slices of an inch and a half in thickness, preserving the head, which is the best part for a chowder. Take a pound and a half of clear or fat salt pork and cut it into thin slices; do the same with ten or twelve middling-sized potatoes, then make your chowder thus: Take the largest pot you have in the house if it be not as "large as all out-doors;" try out the pork first, and then take it out of the pot, leaving in the drippings. Put three pints of water with the drippings, then a layer of fish so as to cover as

much of the surface of the pot as possible; next a layer of potatoes, then put in two tablespoonfuls of salt and a teaspoonful of black pepper, then a layer of fish and potatoes alternately until all are used; then put in a sufficient quantity of water to cover the whole. Put the pot over a good fire and *let the chowder boil* twenty-five minutes. When this is done, put in a quart of sweet milk and a dozen of hard crackers split. Let the whole boil five minutes longer and your chowder is then ready for the table, and an excellent one it will be. Let these directions be strictly followed, and every man and woman can make their own chowders. Long experience enables me to say this without pretending to be a cook's oracle. A few onions sliced up and added to this chowder much improve it to the taste of those who are fond of that vegetable; and a few dozen oysters, when they can be had, make it still better.

AMERICAN METHOD OF COOKING EELS.

The eel is a much-abused and despised fish by some, and by others considered a great delicacy, and as sweet as any fish that swims, if cooked after the following method: They should always be parboiled. First cut up your fish and put them into a pan of scalding hot water and let them remain at least five minutes to take away the rank and disagreeable taste common to the tribe, then pour off the water and let them remain at least twenty minutes. Have your frying-pan ready with a sufficient quantity of boiling hot lard, and having rolled your fish in flour, cast them in and let them cook until done brown. Prepared by parboiling in the same way they make with a little butter an excellent pie, or a delicious chowder.

RECIPE FOR DRESSING SALAD.

"Two large potatoes, passed through kitchen sieve,
Smoothness and softness to the salad give;
Of *mordant* mustard add a single spoon,
Distrust the condiment that bites too soon;
But deem it not, O man of herbs, a fault
To add a double quantity of salt;
Four times the spoon with oil of Lucca crown,
And twice with vinegar procured from town;
True flavor needs it, and your poet begs
The pounded yellow of two boiled eggs;
Let onion-atoms lurk within the bowl,
And scarce suspected animate the whole;
And lastly, in the favored compound toss
A magic spoonful of anchovy * sauce;
Oh, great and glorious! oh, herbaceous treat!
'Twould tempt the anchorite to eat;
Back to the world he'd turn his weary soul,
And plunge his fingers in the salad-bowl."

                                            SYDNEY SMITH.

* Smelts and shrimps or prawns are often used as a substitute for the anchovy.

CHAPTER XIII.

WHERE ARE THEY?

RESPECTING the whereabouts of the finny family, we had almost said they are everywhere; but we recall to mind the fact that water-farming is not universally practised. When the raising of fish shall have become as common as the propagation of other stock, the above reply may be made, and the wild and mountainous regions with their black flies, oils, camphor, ammonia, veils, tobacco, and smudge-smoke, will be unknown except to the daring tourist or enthusiastic artist. That is contemplating the time which is not far distant, when the rivers and brooks that dash and foam nearer to civilization shall again teem with the spotted beauties and the silver-sided salmon.

Without the intention of guiding the angler to all the places of resort, a few of the most prominent will be given, leaving the particulars to books adapted to the purpose, such as the "Tourist's Guide,"* which should be altered from time to time as the routes, rates of fare, guides, and proprietors of places of resort change. To begin, then:

JACKSONVILLE, ST. AUGUSTINE, AND TALLAHASSEE,

are the principal Southern points, while the whole range of towns and cities situated on the Gulf of Mexico, including

* See "Hallock's Fishing Tourist."

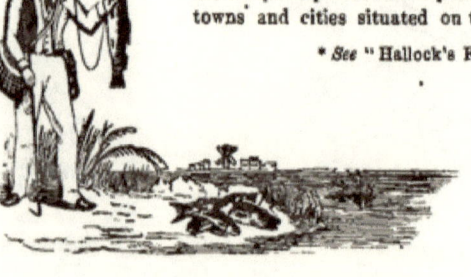

New Orleans and the coast of Texas, afford fine sport for the angler in the taking of the redfish or spotted basse, the sheepshead, the bonito, Spanish mackerel, etc.

Charleston, and most of the cities on the Atlantic, from Delaware Bay along the entire extent of the coast, and the beautiful rivers that flow to the sea, afford an equal variety of game for the angler, while the inland lakes and fresh-water rivers are populated with the perch and the black basse. In Virginia and in the mountain-streams of Georgia, the speckled trout are found in abundance. From

NEW YORK CITY

excursions are made to that paradise of trout-anglers, Long Island, which, with its numerous brooks and ponds, furnish the best fly-fishing in the world; and along the coasts, and in the inlets on both sides of this beautiful island, are found the striped basse, bluefish, bonito, Spanish mackerel, and other salt-water inhabitants in great abundance. The coast and beaches of

CONNECTICUT,

Massachusetts, and Rhode Island, throng with a multitude of the same description of fishes, including the "sly and treacherous tautog;" while the tributaries of the Connecticut River, extending away up into the northern parts of Vermont, New Hampshire, and Maine, together with the beautiful lakes, amid the most wild and enchanting scenery, swarm with trout. Moosehead, Schoodic, Profile, Echo, and other lakes, the Belgrade Ponds, the Pemigewasset River, and the numerous liquid courses that run down from the Franconia and other mountains, where the almost virgin streams produce brook-trout that will turn the scales at eight and nine pounds. In

NEW YORK BAY

and Hudson River, the favorite ground of the vigorous and enticing striped basse, that ranges from Chesapeake Bay far up the Eastern coast, entering the Potomac, the Delaware, the Passaic, the Hackensack, the Raritan, Newark, and other bays and rivers, frequenting Harlem River, and furnishing sport at Hell Gate, Pelham, and King's Bridge; also the beautiful squeteague, the highly-prized sheepshead, the tautog, and others of the finny family. In the wild and elevated regions of

PENNSYLVANIA,

the tributaries of the Delaware, Susquehanna, and brooks that run into the main river, furnish "speckled beauties" in sufficient numbers to satisfy the most ardent sportsman. Passing into

THE STATE OF NEW YORK,

we find the well-known White Lake, where trout have been taken of seven and three-quarters pounds' weight; and the wild, romantic White Lake Creek, the resort of the late Rev. Gurdon Huntington, who thus apostrophizes on the beauties of this charming brook:

> "O lonely, wild, romantic stream! with thee
> And with the regions where thy waters gleam,
> There are blithe memories woven—of fair youths,
> Sunny and glad and winning—as with rocks
> And lonely cliffs upon the ocean-shore,
> Majestic and rude, on Memory's glass
> Are blent the images of lovely vines,
> And soft, young blossoms of the tinted moss."

They also are found in the Beaver Kill, the Mongaup, the Willewemock, and many other kindred streams. Toward the northwest we strike the lesser lakes, where the black basse, pickerel, and perch are found in abundance. Then turning again to the northeast, we find the summer resorts of Saratoga and other lakes celebrated for the delicious quality and activity on the hook of the same description of the finny race; and next is that attractive and world-renowned spot—

LAKE GEORGE.

"Holy depths of stainless crystal,
Sown with islands out of dream-land."

"Divinest of waters! fairest of lakes! And thou art beautiful, greatly beautiful, in thy length and breadth, in thine islands and meadow-shores and mountains, and in the calmness and isolation of thy dwelling. Fairest of lakes!" I said; "Clarens is not so fair, nor Constance, nor Grassmere, nor Lomond. Not so fair in water, in islands, in shores, in skies, or in mountains. It is, in modest speech, the most delightful summer resort for those who love the beauty in Nature, or the sports of hunting and fishing, in this or any other country!"

A correspondent says that 50,000 salmon-trout have lately been put into the lake, and many new hotels have been erected at Bolton and other parts of this charming sheet of water. To the west and north, in Hamilton, Essex, and Franklin Counties, are Schroon Lake, Paradox, Raquette, Peseco, Saranac, Tupper and Osgood, Ausable Ponds, and rivers Saranac, Chateaugay, Raquette, and other ponds, lakes, and tributaries too numerous to mention in the Adirondack region, made noted by the Rev. W. H. H. Murray and other ardent and persevering followers of the "gentle craft;" and again—

THE THOUSAND ISLANDS

of the river St. Lawrence, that enchanted spot that the lover of the beautiful revels in as in a dream—

"Sailed through all its bends and windings,
Sailed through all its deeps and shallows:"

"This is the region that the angler of the present day contemplates with unmixed satisfaction. * * * Our skiff is continually threading its way among these *land aquatics*, affording the most agreeable employment for the hands, engagement for the mind, and variety for the eye. Now we are stemming the rapid current of some narrow 'gut,' with a black basse on every fly, and now quietly gliding back into a deep and tranquil basin to relieve our rod of the life that bends it almost to breaking; now we push out into a wider expanse of water, where the tempting 'shoals' successively appear swarming with myriads of the finny tribe, and inviting employment for all our equipment and skill, fortunate if both fail not in reciprocating as they ought the multiplying and affectionate attentions of this gamesome fish."

The black basse of the St. Lawrence equal, if they do not surpass, those of any other water, often giving several of their beautiful leaps before reaching the boat, when taken with the rod and reel. The troller will take basse, pickerel, and perch at the same time, if rigged for the purpose. We once took over seventy basse, pickerel, and perch at the end of a two hundred feet line, to which was attached a two-yard gut-leader with an artificial minnow at the end, and a red-and-white fly at intervals of three feet, in a few hours' trolling

around the islands, occasionally taking an assorted two or three at a time.

Passing westward to Lakes Huron, Erie, Ontario, and the Niagara, Tonawanda, and Detroit Rivers, we meet the same species, together with the white basse, catfish, and other varieties that are subjects of the sportsman's pastimes; thence northward, to the Grand Traverse region, and we encounter the speckled trout and the beautiful and newly-discovered "grayling" in the same stream, a district that will receive a large share of the angler's attention; and again westward into Wisconsin, at Green Bay and Winnebago Lake, the Wolfe River, where the black and white basse, pickerel, glass-eyed pike, perch, catfish, sturgeon, and muskellonge, are objects of sport. "The white basse," says my correspondent, Mr. J. C. Hooper, "come up the river in great quantities in June; they swim near the surface; they take the fly readily, and furnish as much sport as any fish of twice the size that I know of. The average weight is one and a half pound. They will also take the spoon freely, but it must be a small one. I think they are the handsomest fish in our waters."

The black basse average four and a half to five pounds, and have been taken as large as eight pounds. In regard to the quantity of fish in the lake and river, he says: "I have been a practical fisherman for thirty-five years, and am convinced that there are as many fish in these waters as can find food to live on. It is impossible to sensibly diminish the quantity of fish in the waters in question. Their wonderful powers of fecundity are such that, should one in five thousand, more or less, come to maturity, the stock will be kept good."

Still farther west, in Marquette County, on the northern

division of the Chicago, Milwaukee & St. Paul Railway, is the celebrated summer resort called

GREEN LAKE,

a beautiful sheet of water of great depth and clearness, peopled with black and other descriptions of basse, pickerel, etc., and visited by people from New York, St. Louis, Chicago, and Milwaukee. A friend, who writes me of the game in this lake, says: "It is noted for its fine fishing and still finer fish. The *boss* game-fish, however, are the black basse, the yellow or white basse, and what is called here the 'green basse'—all celebrated for their fine qualities at the table and gameness in the water. The black basse, taken in the lake, average four and a half to five pounds in weight, and run as high as eight pounds each. Ten thousand California salmon, now six inches long (winter of 1876), are in the lake, and several thousand land-locked salmon from Maine are to be added, making it a lively place to fish. The lake contains, besides, pickerel, perch, rock basse, and whitefish."

GENEVA LAKE,

forty-five miles from Milwaukee, the home of the celebrated little "cisco," is an attractive and much-admired place of pleasure for visitors from Chicago, Milwaukee, and the Southern States. In addition to the usual stock of pickerel, perch, and basse, a half-million of black and Oswego basse, salmon-trout, and California salmon, have been put in the lake, to which assortment two millions more are to be added from a hatching-house on the banks of the lake.

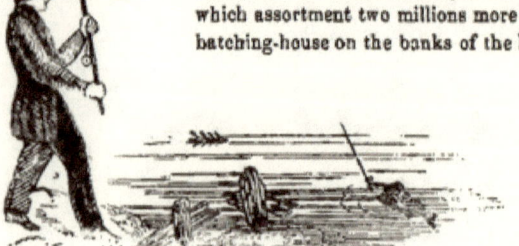

MADISON,

the capital of the State, is beautifully located, and is also a great place of resort for pleasure-seekers, tourists, artists, and sportsmen. It is surrounded by four beautiful lakes, in which swim nearly all the varieties that we have named, including the fresh-water herring, which has lately been put into one of the bodies of water called "Fourth Lake," affording additional sport to the angler. The *Oconomowoc Times* says of Madison: "Its surroundings, while entrancing in beauty, are perfectly captivating in their nature; and the custom of falling in love with Madison is common to all who journey there. The place is vastly popular and greatly frequented."

OCONOMOWOC,

thirty miles from Milwaukee, on the Chicago, Milwaukee & St. Paul Railway, is another noted summer resort, called by some the "Saratoga of the West." "It affords the most delightful scenery, and is noted for its numerous lakes and streams, and superb fishing-grounds and magnificent drives. Taking this as a centre, we have, within a radius of eight miles, twenty-four lakes whose waters are literally alive with fish."

ELKHART LAKE,

on the Wisconsin Central Railway, fifty-seven miles from Milwaukee, is another popular resort for anglers and pleasure-people. A large amount of salmon-fry and other descriptions of fish have lately been placed in this lake, and also

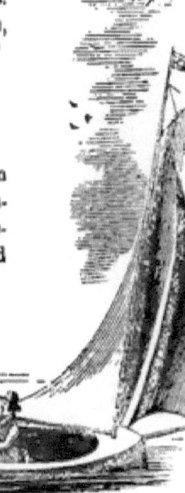

DEVIL'S LAKE,

politely termed "Spirit Lake," a charming and romantic little gem of water, composed of pure crystal springs, having no visible inlet or outlet, nestled in among the Baraboo Bluffs, in Sauk County, one hundred and seventy miles from Chicago, on the Chicago & Northwestern Railway, where the delighted pleasure-seekers and friends of the finny family can drop a line to a variety of the species.

THE "DELLS OF THE WISCONSIN,"

at Kilbourn City, in Columbia County, is another wild, romantic, and enchanting place of resort frequented by people from all parts of the country. A late writer says: "It is only after repeated visits that one can say he has *seen the 'Dells ;'* indeed, after passing through them again and again, the tourist is charmed at some new revelation. The following members of the family that are the objects of sport inhabit this beautiful river: black basse, pickerel, pike-perch, or glass-eyed pike, sheepshead, herring; the whole family of suckers, including the red horse and buffalo; the catfish, sturgeon, the gar or bill-fish; and the broad-bill or shovel-nose sturgeon, called by the Indians the hopossun-chunker. The glass-eyed perch have been taken weighing fifty-two pounds, and the pickerel of seventeen pounds' weight."

About eight miles from this place, at Big Springs, is the trout-hatching house of Freeman Richardson, and fourteen miles northeast is the Jordan Lake, well known in that region for the pleasurable trolling for black basse, pickerel, and pike-perch. In the Baraboo River, trout are again found, and westward and northward in all the minor streams as far as the Mississippi. From

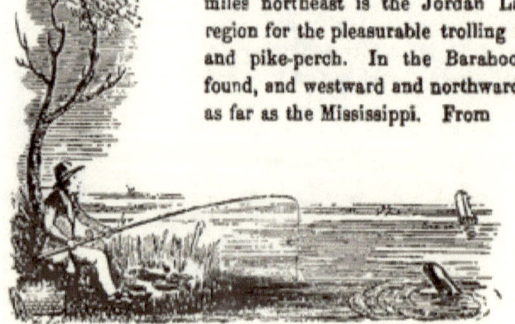

SPARTA,

a watering-place celebrated for its mineral well-waters, from Artesian Wells northward, the angler for "speckled beauties" finds abundant reward and a full pannier from the pebbly brooks that are tributary to the bolder streams that run from the more elevated northern regions. Southern people have taken a great fancy to this healthy point, and populate the hotels and enjoy the angling. From

HUDSON CITY,

in nearly all directions, are numerous trout-streams that are literally alive with fish. Wilson's, Bolle's, and Sand Creeks are favorite resorts, while the Kinnikinick and its branches, extending twenty-five miles north, furnish trout from a quarter of a pound to four pounds' weight. The branches of the Eau Claire, Chippewa, St. Croix, and Black Rivers, teem with equally large and fine game. Willow River, near Hudson, abounds in pickerel, basse, and muskellonge, as well as many others to the north, even unto Lake Superior, where, it is said, trout are found that will turn the scales at from five to eight pounds. This comparatively unknown region undoubtedly equals the celebrated tract of Northern Maine and the Adirondacks, in regard to its wildness and beauty, and its quantity and quality of game, both for the rod and gun; and still farther west, in

MINNESOTA,

from about the forty-third parallel northward to St. Paul, St. Anthony, and westward, the rivers and lakes abound in multitudes of trout and others of the finny race.

MONTANA AND COLORADO

also produce from their nearly ice-cold streams magnificent trout and beautiful grayling, that will keep in the dry and pure atmosphere of Colorado for many days without taint; and thence to the Idaho, Washington, and Oregon regions on the Pacific—

> "Where rod and gun but seldom fails,
> And dry, pure air each lung inhales."

We have attempted to describe a few of the principal places of resort as proposed at the commencement of this article. To describe all in the limits of an ordinary book would be simply impossible. It is supposed that about one-half of the almost innumerable points have been mentioned, and for further information we refer the reader to guide-books that more particularly describe places of resort and the way to reach them.

Then there was heard a most celestiall sound
Of dainty musicke, which did next ensue
Before, *That was Arion crowned:*
Who, playing on his harp, unto him drew
The eares and hearts of all the goodly crew;
That even yet the dolphin, which him bore
Through the Ægean seas from pirates' view,
Stood still by him astonished at his lore;
And all the raging seas for joy forgot to roar."

GENERAL INDEX.

Advertisement to 5th edition, 3.
A feeling angler, 329.
A great haul, 187, 188.
A perch eats its own eye, 144.
Aberdeen hooks, 28.
Abundance of trout, 66.
Abstinence of the pike, 120.
Abundance of salmon in Scotland and America, 52.
Adonis of the sea, 311, 386.
American flies, 62, 99; hooks, 29; how to make them, 109-114; reels, 24, 85; rods, 22, 23.
Angling and temperance, 14.
Anglers' dress, 50; health, 51; souvenir, playing the salmon, 59, 60.
Angling like mathematics, 46.
Ancient instructions for taking pike, 115.
Angling for sunfish, 160.
Anecdote on angling, 49; of the redfish, 336; where to catch sheepshead, 199.
Appeal to anglers, 229-234.
Apostles, fishermen, 18.
Artificial flies for trout, 47, 99-106, 330; for salmon, 61; for minnows, 88.
Aristotle and Ausonius on the perch, 149.
A bright particular star, 368.
Abundance of fish, 403, 415.
Accomplished angler, 369.
Advantages of fish-culture, 404.
A fish with a tail! 379, 380.
A new idea about the cisco, 303, note.
A fish-chowder, 407.
Affrighted sportsmen, 380.
A great acquisition. 374.
Albany beef, 389.
Ainsworth, W. H., on fish-culture, 403.
A great problem solved, 404.
American method of cooking eels, 408.
Amusement for the ladies, 394, 395.
Appetizer for a whale, 382.

Bacon and Byron's objections, 47.
Bait-net, 33.
Baits used in angling, 34, 35.
Bait, salmon-roe, 40; spoon, 250.
Baits made with pastes, 41.
Bait for trout, 73, 90, 231; lake-trout, 65; pickerel, 122; striped basse, 167-169, 238; salmon, 57, 58, 61; sea basse, 215; black basse; 190, 192; bluefish, 211; blackfish, 179, 180; Buffalo, 314; squeteague, 172; perch, 145, 147, 148; sunfish, 160; kingfish, 176, 272; carp, 166; sheepshead, 198, 211; cod and tom-cod, 204, 205; flounders, 208; chub, 219; eels, 278, 218; catfish, 285, 307, 308; redfish, 236; dolphin, 290; smelt, 248; bergall, etc., 215; hake, 282; pike-perch, 297; mackerel, 312; Mackinaw salmon, 241; black trout, 309; suckers, 320, 321; porgy, 215; muskellonge, 304.
Bank-trolling for pike, 135.
Barker, methods of cooking trout, 96, 97; poetical description of trout-flies, 98, 99.
Berners's, Juliana, first book on angling, 13; how to take pike, 115.
Best silkworm gut, 31, 258.
Basse, striped, trolling, 237.
Best time for angling, 48, 49.
Basse, black, 190-194; sea, 214; striped, 159, 245; green, 298.
Blackfish or tautog, 176.
Black-basse angling in the Niagara, 190; in Michigan, 298-302; in Lake George, 193.
Black gnat, a good fly, 102.
Basse, a Dutch word, 160.
Blackfish angling in Suffolk County, 254, 255, 256.
Beware of his jaws, 137.
Black trout, 309.
Beauty of the trout, 73; of the salmon, 56.
Bush-fishing for trout, 81.
Baiting with the minnow, 87.
Bottom or worm-fishing, 89.
Bottling flies, 90.
Beware of poor hooks, 26.
Blue dun-fly, 101.
Best dish of stewed fish, 96.
Bait for pike, 122.
Beautiful colors of the pike, 120.
Bottom tackle for pike, 126.
Bluefish, tackle for, 211.
Blackfish, where to find him, 181.
Brown basse, 69.
Bob-fishing for eels, 279.
Brookes on angling, 19.
Blaine on worms, 34; on caution, 93; on the pike, 123-126; on snap-angling, 129; on taking carp, 152.
Black Tom for kingfish, 175.
Blaine's night-flies, 105, 106.
Bull-head, 219.
Bream-roach, etc., 219.
Black sucker, 322.

GENERAL INDEX.

Buffalo, 313, 314.
Black trout, 309, 310.
Brown catfish, 306.
Brown, Dr. Rufus, on the black basse, 269.
Balloon or float fishing, 394.
Beauty of the cavallo, 347; sea trout, 344; pompano, 346.
Benefactors of the human race, 405.
Best fishing-ground for Lafayette, 352.
Bethune, Rev. Dr., 339, 392.
Black basse of the St. Lawrence, 414.
Black snapper, 345.
Bream, Southern, 356.
Bread or blood, 405.
Bonetta, or bonito, 385.
Brains of fishes, 391.
Brown, Dr. Rufus, on the grayling, 372.

Catching the devil, 381.
Caution in angling, 49.
Calcutta rods, 22.
Casting for pike, 133.
Common trout of Massachusetts, 67.
Common mode of cooking trout, 97.
Common perch, 140.
Carp, tenacious of life, 153.
Carp, the, 151; 100 years old, 152; imported from England, 151; where found, 153.
Care of rods, 328.
Catfish, 285, 306.
Codfish, 203; codfish-balls, 205.
Contents of Part I., 9, 10; of Part II., 225, 226.
Cotton, rod for trout, 76; on dibbing, 80, 81; on angling with hair snells, 77; on casting the fly, 77; on the chub, 218; where taken, 219.
Cow-dung fly for trout, 101; where taken, 219.
Cleopatra fond of angling, 13.
Clearing ring, 33, 202.
Clinton, Hon. Geo. W., on the black and Oswego basse, 190; on the sheepshead, 195.
Clam for blackfish, 35.
Clear-weather fishing, 92.
Cheese and cotton for bait, 314.
Crab bait for basse, 35, 167.
Curved Limerick hooks, 27.
Curious mode of taking lake-trout, 243.
Care of reels and lines, 391, 392.
Catfish, the blue, 353.
Cavallo, 347.
Chub, the Southern, 351.
Chub-robin, the, 355.
Cisco, the, of Geneva Lake, Wisconsin, 361-364; color of, 362; fly for, 362; of Lake Ontario, 364; scooped up by the bushel, 363, note.
Classes of fishes, 396, 398.
Coast fishes, North and South, 343.
Contents of Part III., 334, 335.
Crawfish, the, 374.
Croaking of the blue cat, 354.
Crocus, the, of the South, 351.

Dana, poetry on the ocean, 214.
Davy, Sir Humphrey, on angling and health, 16; on cooking salmon, 68.

Davies, Joe, poetry on angling, 14, 15.
Dewey, Rev. Dr., on bad effects of incessant toil, 18.
Dancing for eels, 275, 276.
Dewitt Clinton on the striped basse, 159.
Dekay on the mackinaw trout, 240.
Decreased voracity of the pike, 120.
Dibbing or dabbing for trout, 81, 82.
Description of a basse rod and tackle, 164, 165.
Directions for making a snap-bait, 131.
Difference of opinion on cookery, 148; on the trout, 96.
Description of the kingfish, 174, 175.
Detroit angling, 299, 322.
Deer's tail for trolling, 331.
Double swivel trace, 126.
Dr. Johnson rebuked, 223.
Dolphin fishing, 289.
Dr. Donne's love-song, 15.
Dress of the angler, 50.
Doctors disagree, 163.
Drayton on the somersault of the salmon, 53.
Dromming of the squeteague, 172; of the drum-fish, 187.
Drum-fish, 186.
Dun-flies for trout, 100, 101.
Duck swallowed by a pike-perch, 297.
Dutch fishermen in the eel business, 275.
De Witt Clinton on the white-fish, 359.
Delicate appetites, 389.
Delicacy of the white-fish, 360.
Description of the white-fish, 360; grayling, by Mather, 370, 371; Spanish mackerel, 376; sturgeon, 358.
Dr. Scott on the sheepshead, 379.
Dorsal fin of the grayling, 370, 373.

Eel, the, 217, 274; variety of, 276, 277; a savory dish, 217; bobbing for, 279; a cosmopolite, 274; sniggling for, 278; the lamprey, 218; in Holland, 275; rain or mud pup, 276; dancing for, 275.
English fishing parties in the United States, 47.
Extraordinary length of time to gorge a bait, 136.
Exploded ideas on fly-fishing, 98.
Experienced angler on striped basse, 166.
Excitement in bluefishing, 211.
Exciting Connecticut fishing, 294, 295.
Evening Post on the menhaden, 382; eulogy on Rev. G. Huntington, 341.

Feathers for flies, 114; fish-hooks, 26.
Fecundity of the cod, 204; filing hooks, 29.
Float, description of, 29, 270, 271; for basse, pickerel, salmon, etc., 31; for trout, 30.
Fishing out of season, 51.
Flies, artificial, 100-106; how to make them, 109-114.
Fly-fishing for trout, 73, 74; for salmon, 60, 61; for lake-trout, 243; for black front, 210; for mackerel, 312.
Fishing at Hell Gate, 163.
Fiddlers for tautog, 254, 256.
Flounder, the, 207, 208.

Fish-ponds and transportation of fish, 264–269.
Fish and fishing of the United States, 229–234.
Fluke, plaice, turbot, etc., 315–318.
Frogs for bait, 35, 327.
Franks, playing trout, 93, 94.
Fresh-water sheepshead, 200.
Fly, green-drake, for June, 103.
Fairbanks, N. P., of Chicago, 363.
Farwell, Governor of Wisconsin, 366.
Fecundity of fish, 415.
Fighting eels, 398.
Figure of the bonito, 385.
Fish by the load and acre, 382.
Fish-Commissioners of Wisconsin, 366.
Fish-culturist association, 390.
First engraving of the grayling, 370.
Fishing at Charleston, etc., 411; in Florida, 410; Connecticut, 411; the Adirondacks, 413; Eastern States, 411; Elkhart Lake, 417; dells of the Wisconsin, 418; Devil's Lake, Wisconsin, 417; Geneva Lake, Wisconsin, 116; Green Bay, etc., 415; Michigan, 415; Madison, Wisconsin, 417; Lake George, 418; Minnesota, 419; Montana and Colorado, 420; Oconomowoc, 417; Oregon, 420; New York Bay, 412; New York City, etc., 411; Hudson City, Wisconsin, 419; Sparta, Wisconsin, 419; the Thousand Isles, 414; the State of New York, 412; Wisconsin, 416, 418; White Lake Creek, 412.
Flavor of the cisco, 361; siscowet, 364.
Flies for the grayling, 373; Seth Green's, 374.
Fins of the grayling, 370, 372.
Forest and Stream on the pompano, 348; on the grayling, 370.
Form of the grayling, 372; of the sting-ray, 378–380.
French Canadians on the white-fish, 359.
French, the, on the jew-fish, 357.
Fry, W. H., on fish-culture, 402.

Gastronomic properties of the perch, 149.
Gaff and hooks, 33.
Gamy fish, 174.
Gay's poetry on the trout, 95; poetry on fly-making, 108.
German mule and the pike, 116.
Glass-eyed pike a perch, 297; swallows a duck, 297.
Gold weights for nets, 292.
Gold and silver fish, 154.
Golden mullet, 321.
Gorging the bait, 136.
Great kingfishing, 177.
Great age of the pike, 117, 118.
Grub, method of baiting with, 39; worm, 34, 35.
Great caution necessary, 81.
Grasshoppers for bait, 35, 100.
Green-drake fly, 100, 103.
Gray drake, 320.
Gut of the silkworm, 31; for salmon and trout, 32; leaders or bottom lengths, 32.
Gastronomic qualities of the grayling, 373.

Geneva Lake, Wisconsin, 361, 363, 416.
Grayling coming in on a line, 371; the, of Michigan, 368; Montana, 369; at Detroit, 372; Prof. Milner on, 372; Dr. Rufus Brown on, 372; largest, 373; of Richardson, 369; where found, 369.
Great sport for the ladies, 394.
Grouper, the, 346.
Growler, the, 353.

Habits of the trout, 71; of the English pike, 120; of the American pike, 122; of the striped bass, 166, 167.
Hand-line fishing for tautog, 254.
Hake, the, 281–283; contained seventeen pilchards, 281; fond of crabs, 282; voracity of, 282.
Herring, the, 219; at Baltimore, 220.
Health of the angler, 51.
Hearing of fishes, 49.
Hiding-places of the trout, 84.
High estimation of angling, 17.
His first and last catfish, 308.
Hooks, importance of, 25; Aberdeen, 28; flattened end, 26; O'Shaughnessy, 27; Limerick, 27; American, 29; Sir Humphrey Davy's opinion of, 27; spring snap, 28; the kinsey, 45; sproat bend, 45.
Hofland's rod for trout fly-fishing, 75, 76; on angling with the minnow, 87; method of making flies, 109, 110; on baiting for the pike, 127, 128.
How to angle for pike, 122; by Juliana Berners, 115.
How to cook a salmon, 62, 63; a trout, 96, 97; a blackfish, 184; the carp, 153; a perch, 148; a bergall, 253; eels, 280; a catfish, 308.
How to bait and catch sheepshead, 197; to bait the squid, 238, 239; to catch the codfish, 205; to fish after a rain, 48; to skin a perch, 148; to unhook a pike, 137; to find the proper fly, 107.
Habit of the sting-ray, 379.
Habitat of the grayling, 369.
Hatching-house at Big Spring, Wisconsin, 418; Geneva Lake, Wisconsin, 363; Honeoye Falls, New York, 369; Mumford, New York, 403; Pensaukee, Wisconsin, 366.
Heathen Chinee as fish-culturists, 404.
Herring, the, 365; of Fourth Lake, Madison, Wisconsin, 366; flies for, 366.
Hibrids or cross-breeds, 365.
Hog-fish, common, 355; the Virginia, 354.
Hofland on the grayling, 373.
Hogsheads of menhaden at a gulp! 382.
Hooper, John C., on the cisco, 365; on the sturgeon, 389; on the white basse, 415.
How to keep shrimp, 384; to stain gut, gimp, etc., 391–393; to take the Spanish mackerel, 377.
Huntington, Rev. Gordon, 341; poetry by, 342, 412.
Huningen hatching-establishment, 402.

Increase in the size of pike, 119.
Improvement in angling implements, 44, 45.
Importance of health, 51.

Immense amount of eels sold in London, 217.
Introduction, 9-12.
Introductory remarks on angling, 13-19.
Introduction of pike into England, 115.
Instructions in taking the pike, 134.
Ichthyologists on eels, 276.
Inhabitants of the Oregon and California waters, 292, 293.
Inman, Henry, 17, 334.
Isinglass from squeteague, 172.
Ichthyology for the angler, 395-399.
Immense amount of fish in Geneva Lake, Wisconsin, 353; in Green Bay, 415.
Indiscriminate fishing, 401.
Indians spearing sturgeon, 389.
In memoriam, 339-342.
Invalids angling at the South, 343.

Jewsharp and violin, 123.
Jewels on his head, 201.
Joy on the capture of the sheepshead, 97.
Jew-fish of the South, 357.
Jug-fishing, 354.

Kendall, Capt., kills salmon with an axe, 53.
Kerns, experiment on the increase of salmon, 55.
Killyfish, bait for striped bass, 168.
Kingfish, 174; best bait for him, 176; large amount caught, 177; finest tablefish, 175.
Kirby hooks, origin of, 26.
Knots, loops, etc., 260.
Keese, John D., 340; on the black bass, 191; sheepshead, 195; kingfish, 175.
Kingfish of the South, 345.
Knickerbocker Magazine, 341.

Lake-trout, 64, 65.
Landing-nets, 32, 51.
Leaders of gut, etc., 32.
Lady-anglers, 150, 327.
Leaders or bottom lengths, 260, 261.
Leaping of the salmon, 52.
Large perch, 144.
Length of the striped bass, 245.
Large haul of striped bass, 163.
Legislation for protection of carp, 151.
Lively description of black bass, 190, 191.
Lines, description of, 25; for trout, pickerel, salmon, and bass, 25.
Large quantities of mackerel, 317.
Limerick hooks for trout, salmon, bass, etc., 28.
List of illustrations, Part I., 7; Part II., 8.
Locusts, bait for squeteague, 85.
Lowther on trolling for striped bass, 245; blackfish, 255; weak-fish, 272; white perch, 264.
Lady-cat, 353.
Lafayette-fish, 351.
Lake Ontario cisco, 364; Lake Geneva cisco, 361-363; Michigan and Superior siscowet, 364.
Lettuce-salad with prawns, 409.
Low price of sturgeon, 390.

Mackerel, 311, 312.
Mackinaw trout, 311, 312; trolling for, 241.
Materials used in angling, 20, 21.
Method of procuring worms, 34; of baiting with the minnow, 85; of trolling for striped bass, 238.
Mode of baiting worms, 88; of baiting grubs, 39; of fishing for perch, 145; of angling for the flounder, 209.
Montevideo and Magellan smelts, 247.
Monsters of the deep, 331, 332.
Minnows for bait, 85; imitated, 88; fishing for perch, 146, 296.
Miscellaneous items of interest to the angler, 326-332.
Mitchel's description of the trout, 67; white perch, 142; on the striped bass, 161, 162; blackfish, 179, 180; squeteague, 170, 172.
Muskallonge, 303-305; bait for, 305.
Mud-pup, 276.
Mather, Fred., on the grayling, 369, 370.
Menhaden or mossbunker, the, 382; for bait, 382; method of baiting with, 383.
Method of taking the sturgeon, 390.
Milwaukian's opinion of the siscowet, 364.

Natural squid, 238, 239.
Naturalization of carp, 116.
Nelson, Lord, passion for angling, 16.
Necessity of knowing how to make flies, 107; superior tackle for striped bass, 164.
Netting game-fish for market, 232.
Nets, haft, and landing, 32, 51.
Night flies for trout, 105, 106.
Night fly-fishing, 326.
No quarter for the blackfish, 134.
Nobbs's mode of cooking pike, 139.
North country angler on salmon, 54; on trout, 71; on baiting with the minnow, 85.
Nowell, Dr., an angler, 16.
No danger from the stings of the ray, 379, 390.
Northern and Southern coast fishes, 343.
Norris, Thaddeus, angler and fish-culturist, 404.

Obeying instruction, anecdote, 145.
Observations on angling, 45.
Ocean angling, 268-291.
Of the hooks in snap-fishing, 132.
Oliver on fly-fishing, 330.
O'Shaughnessy hooks, 27, 251.
Oswego bass, 190.
Odor of the grayling, 372.

Paley, Dr., a fly-fisher, 16.
Palmer flies for trout, 99; how to make them, 111.
Painters and poets, anglers, 17.
Patience necessary, 33; in pike fishing, 134.
Pastes for bait, 40, 41.
Perch, the yellow, white, and black, 141, 142; a good table fish, 143; white, angling for, 284, 285; in Niagara River and New York lakes, 147.

GENERAL INDEX. 427

Pike, the, 115-139; a universal fish, 115; sold for the price of two lambs, 115; eating pike, 118; trolling for, 135; time for poaching the bait, 136; of the Mississippi River, 138; Essex Vittatus, 138; how to cook, 139.
Piccausu, 138.
Pleasure parties' excursion for cod, 204, 205.
Poor Johns, 282; poor rich men, 18.
Poisson Rouge, 235, 236.
Poetry, love of angling, 229; on the trout, 66, 94, 108; on the salmon, 53; on the dolphin, 289; on angling, 14, 15; on the fly, 330; on the angler, 19; Dr. Wolcott's, 223; on the bonito, 386; on the cisco, 361; on the grayling, 368; on the grouper, 346; on the pompano, 348; on the Spanish mackerel, 378; on the white fish, 358, 359; on the White Lake Creek, 342, 412.
Porgy-fishing, 214, 215.
Porpoise harpooned, 214.
Places for taking squeteague, 172.
Physicians' prescriptions, 51.
Prolific perch, 143.
Proper rod for tautog-fishing, 183.
Protection of the finny race.
Preface to Part I., 11; to Part II., 227.
Preservation of lines, 329.
Professor, the, a good fly, 330.
Palate-tickler, 377, 378.
Palmer, John, on fish-culture, 366.
Pearl of the Southern waters, 348.
Perpetuation of the cisco, 363.
Pisciculture, 400-406.
Playing the sting-ray, 379, 380.
Pompano, the, 348.
Prawns of the South, 374.
Price of the mullet, 349; of the pompano, 349.
Prof. Milner on the grayling, 372.

Quality of rods, 22; lines, 25; hooks, 29, 27.
Quantity of smelts taken in one day, 248; of mackerel, 311; of basse, 163.

Rapacity of the pike, 118.
Rapid growth of the pike, 119.
Reels, described, 24; the click, for trout and perch, 75; basse, salmon, pike, etc, 67, 171; improvement in, 44.
Reddish or spotted basse, 235; anecdote of, 236.
Red-fly for trout, 380.
Red-horse, 322.
Renme's method of making the Palmer fly, 111.
Requisite tackle for taking the carp, 155.
Ring, the clearing, 33, 202.
Roe, salmon, for bait, 40.
Ronconkama pond, 141.
Rods, variety of, 21; for pike, basse, salmon, 22; for trout, 23; general, 23; for fly-fishing, 75; for pike, 124; for striped basse, 164; for salmon, 57.
Rusty Dab, the, 330.
Ray, the sting, 378; the family, 398.
Range of the striped basse, 412.
Rémy and Géhin, the fish-colturists, 401.
Recipe for dressing a salad, 409.

Restocking rivers in England and Scotland, 402.
Red snapper, the, 344.
Re-populating Lakes Erie and Michigan, 360.
Richardson's grayling, 369.
Robin, the, 355.
Rock basse of the lakes, 366.
Rod for surf-fishing for basse, 383.
Roosevelt, R. B., on hatching shad, 403; on the sturgeon, 390.

Salmon, the, 52-63; bait-fishing for, 57; fly-fishing for, 58; worm-fishing for, 58; flies for taking, 61, 62; spearing, 62; known to the early Romans, 52; on the Hudson and Connecticut, 53; on the Sacramento, 293; time of spawning, 54; size and weight of, 65; sport, Sir Walter Scott's opinion of, 55; spawn, how to preserve, 40.
Salmo Hucho, 70.
Salt-water fish transferred to fresh water, 266; sheepshead and fresh compared, 200, 201.
Salter on caution, 49; on drawing in the pike, 137; on the grayling, 373.
Sea-basse and porgy, 214.
Separate rods for each kind of fishing, 23.
Sinkers, description of, 29, 30; improved swivel, 30.
Shot, split, 30.
Shiner for bait, 286, 295.
Shrimp, bait for basse and squeteague, 35, 172.
Shad-roe a bait for basses, 166.
Shoemaker, the, 322.
Soft-shell clam for tautog, 35; for basse, 168.
Solitary habits of the pike, 119.
Silkworm gut, 31, 258.
Silver trout, 66; perch, 142.
Spearing eels, 280.
Spoon-bait, 250, 251, 236.
Spring snap hooks, 262.
Spearing striped basses, 169.
Splicing rods, 325.
Squid, the, 238, 239.
Squeteague, 170 to 173; where found, 172.
Slow growth of the perch, 143.
Smith's pike story, 117; on the abundance of salmon, 52; on Salmo Hucho, 70; on the hearing of fishes, 48; on sea-trout, 68, 69; on the striped basse, 160.
Snaring suckers, 320.
Sportsmanship in worm-fishing, 92.
Splendid leaps of the black basse, 193.
Smelt, the, 247-249; experiment at Jamaica Pond, 249.
Snap-bait, 131.
Sucker, the, 319-323; horned, 320; Oneida, 320; mullet, 321; red-horse, 321; black, 322; Kentucky, etc. 322.
Street, poetry on the trout, 66.
Striped-basse angling on Long Island Sound, 245.
Stone-fly in windy weather, 102.
Sheepshead, 195-202; fresh-water, 200; where found, 197, 198; anecdote, 199; his jewels, 201.

Sunfish, 140, 150.
Sunny side for trout-fishing, 82.
Swivels, advantage of, 126; for spinning-bait, 30.
Sea trout or spotted squeteague, 344.
Seth Green on the grayling, 369; on the fly for grayling, 374; on fish-culture, 408.
Scarcity of fish, 400, 401.
Schoolcraft, H. R., on the white-fish, 359.
Shad from the Hudson to California, 408.
Simple method of baiting with the minnow, 395.
Siscowet, the, of Lakes Michigan and Superior, 364.
Smith's, Sidney, receipt for a salad, 409.
Snapper, the red, 344; the black, 345.
Southern fishes, 343–357.
Spot, the, 351.
Spanish mackerel, the, 375–378.
Splendid specimen of the grayling, 369.
Spare not, 384.
Spawning-time of fishes, 386, 387.
Sting-ray, the, 378–381.
Sturgeon, the, 388–390; in the Wisconsin River, 389; in the Winnebago Lake, 389; in the olden time, 390.
Sunday Times on wanton destruction of fish, 401.
Superabundance of fish, 401.
Subterranean passage connecting the great lakes of Wisconsin, 363.

Tackle for sea-basse and porgy, 210; for sheepshead, 197, 198.
Tameness of the carp, 154.
Tallow-chandlers' scratchings for bait, 42.
Taylor on fly-fishing, 78, 79; on pike, 97; on taking perch, 146.
Testing hooks, 29.
Time for taking carp, 154; for taking perch, 147.
The prince of game-fishes, 190.
The mouth of the sheepshead, 198, 199.
The cod a delicious table-fish, 205.
Tools for angling, 42, 43.
Tom-cod or frost-fish, 205.
Toasted cheese, bait for catfish, 308.
Trajan, the Roman Emperor, an angler, 13.
Transportation of fish, 265, 266; perch, 141.
Trigger-fish, 292.
Trolling for black basse on Lake George, 192, 193; on Lake Michigan, 309, 301; for striped basse at Hell Gate, 168, 237; for Mackinaw trout, 242, 243; for pike, 135; lines, 25; for dolphin, 290; for bluefish, 211-213.
Trout-rods, 23, 76, 81, 89.
Trout, the common, 66-114; the lake, 64-66; Mackinaw, 240-244; black, 67; sea, 68; Salmo Hucho, 70; time of spawning, 70; twenty-eight years in a well, 73; fly-fishing for, 73-80; bush-fishing for, 80-84; fishing with the minnow, 84-88; with worms, 89-92; in clear weather, 92; how to cook, 96, 97; pie, 97; casting the line, 77.
Trout-basse, or brown basse, 69.
Trout-flies, 96-107; how to make them, 104-114; feathers for, 114.
Turbot, etc., 314, 318.

Tying hooks, repairing rods, etc., 324, 325.
Tender month of the Spanish mackerel, 377.
The blue cat, 353.
The boys' opinion on gristle, 399.
Tourist's guide, 410.
Transparency of the cisco, 361.
Transportation of salmon-ova from England to Australia, 408.
Trophy from the sting-ray, 379.
Two bushels of prawns, 357.

Up or down the stream, 80.
Uncle Jim's reply, 199.

Van Buren, Martin, 17.
Vaulting of the salmon, 63.
Velocity of the salmon, 54.
Voracity of the pike, 116–119; of the muskellonge, 305; of the pike-perch, 297.
Virginia hooks, 28.
Varnishing flies, 364.

Walton, Izaak, on angling materials, 20.
Walton on the carp, 156, 157; on baiting with the minnow, 88; on angling, 16; on poor rich men, 18; on procuring worms, 34.
Wesk-fish or squeteague, 170-173; Indian name, 171; a companion of the basse, 171, 173; a drummer, 172; spotted, 172; weight of, 173.
Weight of German pike, 118; of American pike, 119.
Webster, Daniel, an angler, 17; takes a cod, 215.
Washington Irving on Hell Gate, 237.
Water souchy, 149.
White-fish, 120.
White pickerel, 138; fish, 120.
White and scarlet fly for black basse, 192.
White hackle, or miller, for a cloudy day, 99.
White perch, 142, 284; perch and catfish angling, 284-287.
When to take trout, 70.
Who fish for trout, 73.
White Lake basse, 257.
Where to find large trout, 82; to find striped basse, 166.
Winter fishing at Green Bay, Wis., 241.
Winds, best for fishing, 48.
Wolcott's, Dr., advice to the trout, 294.
Worms for fresh-water fish, 34; how to preserve, 38; fishing for trout, 89, 90; Cotton's method, 91.
Wotton, Sir Henry, 14.
Winter resort for anglers, 343.
White basse of Green Bay, Wis., 415.
White perch of the South, 356.
White Lake brook, 342, 412.
White salmon of Virginia, 353.
Where are they? 410-420.
Where the bonita is taken, 386.

Yarrell on eels, 276; on the grayling, 372.
Yellow perch, 140; of New York lakes, 147; pike perch, 296, 297; pike-perch swallows a duck, 295.
Young America and the sturgeon, 389.

www.ingramcontent.com/pod-product-compliance
Lightning Source LLC
Chambersburg PA
CBHW051235300426
44114CB00011B/750